Divas on Screen

Mia Mask

divas on screen

**BLACK WOMEN IN
AMERICAN FILM**

UNIVERSITY OF ILLINOIS PRESS

Urbana and Chicago

Manufactured in the United States of America
1 2 3 4 5 C P 5 4 3 2 1
∞ This book is printed on acid-free paper.

Library of Congress Cataloging-in-Publication Data
Mask, Mia, 1969–
Divas on screen : Black women in American film /
Mia Mask.
p.   cm.
Includes bibliographical references and index.
ISBN 978-0-252-03422-0 (cloth : alk. paper)
ISBN 978-0-252-07619-0 (pbk. : alk. paper)
1. African American women in motion pictures.
2. African American motion picture actors and
actresses—Biography. 3. Actresses—United States
—Biography.
I. Title.
PN1995.9.N4M327   2009
791.43'6352996073—dc22   2008041246

Contents

Acknowledgments

So many people have contributed to the development of this proj-ect, which in many ways began long before the actual writing and research it entailed. I must acknowledge the fact that without encouragement (from family, friends, teachers, and mentors) to pursue film studies, I certainly would not have written the manuscript for this book. Instead, I would have pursued a career as a journalist and written film reviews, possibly publishing a collection of reviews rather than this book on African American women celebrities working in the film and television industries.

Chief among the colleagues and mentors to encourage me to pursue a doc-torate in cinema studies was Robert Stam. During my graduate training, he provided the tutelage, advising, and general guidance I needed to survive a competitive, overpopulated program at New York University's renowned Tisch School of the Arts. I was grateful that anyone—not to mention a prominent, prolific scholar—would take interest in and encourage me. Despite the atten-tion and concern Professor Stam and Professor Ella Shohat showed me, there was—for a short time—something missing from my experience at NYU.

The missing ingredient was that sense of community, camaraderie, and friendship that comes from spending time with one's peer group. For me, that peer group was a collective of young African, African American, and Afro-Caribbean graduate students with similar aspirations, goals, and life experiences. There were, of course, many other students of color and white students in our circle. However, as students of color, we were closer because we shared a sense of our "double consciousness." After all, graduate depart-ments in the aftermath of the Culture Wars attracted a cross-section of ambitious, intelligent, literate, and sometimes condescending folks from around the world. I sometimes felt these folks too quickly absorbed the dominant ideology of American race relations, questioning the legitimacy of black participation in higher education.

Fortunately, for many of us who were graduate students in programs and departments across New York University, Manthia Diawara took the helm of Africana studies and the Institute for African American Affairs. Like a benevolent pied piper, he demonstrated a unique ability to draw people to him and band them together under the program's auspices for the purpose of intellectual and artistic engagement. Over the years, I witnessed literati and luminaries alike cross the threshold of Diawara's office door. Manthia succeeded in making many of us feel *not* simply that we belonged, but that we were *entitled* to spaces, places, and locations on campus where ruminations on the African diaspora would be taken seriously. During our time, Andrew Ross accomplished the same for my peers in American studies. I am grateful for the kind of community that Manthia Diawara and Andrew Ross created for graduate students at NYU.

During this time Ed Guerrero also joined the cinema studies faculty. We appreciated his candor and accessibility when so many others were indirect and misleading. Even today, Ed is a friendly colleague and source of information. He reminds me that as film scholars and critics, we help create audiences for films through our scholarship and published criticism. Chris Straayer was, and still is, a strong feminist voice that emboldened many graduate students.

Beyond graduate school, I would like to thank Sarah Kozloff for recruiting me to Vassar College. She provided professional mentoring and personal support throughout my years as untenured faculty. Over the years, Sarah helped me wade through the dispiriting voices from colleagues seeking to discourage young African American faculty from believing they can succeed at predominantly white educational institutions. Dudley Andrew and Charlie Musser must be acknowledged for their generous offer. It is one I will not forget.

At the University of Illinois Press, I would like to acknowledge the support and guidance of veteran editor Joan Catapano. Thankfully, Joan was interested in *Divas on Screen* from the early stages. Her assistants Alison Goebel and Danielle Kinsey were instrumental in pulling together art design, imagery, and logistical details. Danielle was especially helpful during the final, and perhaps most important, phases of the book's publication. Assistant managing editor Angela Burton was also part of the team. I appreciate the access I was given to John Kisch's *Separate Cinema* archive in Hyde Park, New York. John offered film production stills, movie posters, and sound advice about illustrations for the text. Were it not for my colleague Judith Weisenfeld, I might not have met John Kisch when I did or sought his assistance with photography. Finally, I would like to acknowledge "the elders": the generations of African American cultural critics, scholars, and professionals who came before us and led the way. The elders in my own family to whom I owe eternal gratitude include (but are not limited to) my parents, George and Barbara Mask, Melissa and Marc James, Cheryl Odim, and Ruth Jeffries. It is my sincere hope that my generation can continue the tradition of providing increased access to opportunity for those who will follow.

Divas on Screen

Introduction

The charismatically dominated masses in turn become
tax-paying subjects, dues-paying members of a church,
sect, party or club (*Verein*), soldiers who are systematically
impressed, drilled and disciplined, or law-abiding "citizens."
—Max Weber

Rather, one needs to think in terms of the relationships
between stars and specific instabilities, ambiguities and
contradictions in the culture (which are reproduced in the
actual practice of making films and film stars).
—Richard Dyer

Ever since the silent era, African American women—like their Asian American, Hispanic American, and Native American sisters—have broken new ground, paved the road, and struggled alongside their more privileged white counterparts, seeking inclusion, access to acting opportunities, respectable roles, and professional treatment. Traveling this winding road, women of color have met with varying degrees of career success. *Divas on Screen* is an examination of the star personae of five African American women, all of whom have transcended—but also been shaped by—personal, professional, and sociopolitical obstacles to cross over into mainstream international celebrity. Dorothy Dandridge, Pam Grier, Whoopi Goldberg, Oprah Winfrey, and Halle Berry have deftly negotiated the uneven terrain of racial, gender, and class stereotypes, ultimately complicating the conventional discursive and industrial practices through which blackness, womanhood, and African American womanhood have been represented in commercial cinema, independent film, and network television. Arguably, these women—along with many others—have helped pave the way for succeeding generations of African American women in film and television (i.e., Sanna Lathan, Kimberly Elise, Thandie Newton, Persia White, Tracee Ellis Ross, Jill Marie Jones,

Golden Brooks, Essence Atkins, and Rachel True), who now have relatively more access to employment opportunities in mainstream entertainment.

Invariably, however, many of the trailblazing pioneers who came a generation or two earlier (e.g., Bessie Smith, Nina Mae McKinney, Fredi Washington, Louise Beavers, and Hattie McDaniel) and their successors (e.g., Ethel Waters, Lena Horne, Vivian Dandridge, Abby Lincoln, Cicely Tyson, Rosalind Cash, Carol Speed, Tamara Dobson, and Denise Nichols) possessed untapped talents they were never given opportunity to cultivate or regularly exhibit. Juanita Moore, for example, entered films in the early 1950s, a time in which very few African Americans were given an opportunity to act in major studio films. Fortunately, Moore's roles began improving as Hollywood developed a modicum of social consciousness toward the end of the decade. In 1959 she received an Academy Award nomination for her performance as Annie Johnson in Douglas Sirk's glossy rendition of *Imitation of Life* (1959), a stylistically baroque (and overanalyzed) melodramatic remake of John Stahl's 1934 adaptation of Fannie Hurst's controversial 1933 novel.

Moore's career trajectory exemplifies author James Baldwin's now well-known observation that black actors have been woefully misused (and that few have ever been challenged to deliver the best in them).[1] Baldwin's insightful remark (as well as his ruminations in the cathartic tome *The Devil Finds Work*) still holds true today despite the Academy Award wins of actors Denzel Washington, Cuba Gooding Jr., and Jamie Foxx and actresses Halle Berry and Jennifer Hudson. The vast majority of African American actors are still underutilized and underemployed. However, the roles in which many of these actors appeared are layered palimpsests upon which the contradictions and fictions of identity categories[2] have been written and rewritten. Precisely because these roles and personae are multilayered palimpsests, these performances and career trajectories warrant additional archival research, closer textual analysis, and thorough contextualization. *Divas on Screen* is indebted to the legacy of theoretically informed, politically motivated scholarship in African American film studies, as initiated by artist-intellectuals like James Baldwin, Lorraine Hansberry, Gordon Parks, Toni Morrison, Manthia Diawara, Isaac Julien, and Julie Dash.

One of the aims of this book is to depart from—while still acknowledging the existence of—vacuous star-struck interviews, tabloid journalism, and (un)authorized biographies, which sometimes encourage uncritical consumption of pop idols, star gazing, and celebrity prattle. *Divas on Screen* offers a contextualization of stars as intertextual, semiotic signs. The term *intertextuality* derives from the work of literary scholar Mikhail Bakhtin, anthropologist Claude Levi-Strauss, semiotician Roland Barthes, and feminist philosopher Julia Kristeva, for whom it referred to the multidimensional way a particular text is intelligible in terms of the other texts it cites, reiterates, revises, and transforms.[3] As intertextual signifiers, stars (much like their films) reveal the instabilities, ambiguities, and contradictions of their construction as well as the contradictions of the culture industry.[4] Not only is the culture industry laid bare, the changing configuration of American culture is revealed in an examination of celebrity and stardom as social phenomena. Scholars Christopher Lasch, David Riesman, and Erving Goffman have argued the existence of a rising cultural tide that has—since World War II—become more appearance-oriented, performative, and narcissistic than in past generations.

In *The Culture of Narcissism,* for instance, Christopher Lasch discussed the late twentieth-century American psyche. In a postindustrial, service-based economy, he argued, the managerial and professional classes have replaced landed aristocracy to emerge as the new elite. The new elite identifies itself not with the work ethic and responsibilities of wealth, but with an ethic of leisure, hedonism, and self-fulfillment.[5] Evidence for Lasch's assertion can be found in the highly mediated lives of Patricia Hearst, Amanda Hearst, Lydia Hearst-Shaw, Paris Hilton, Sean Stewart, Randy Spelling, and David Weintraub, among others. Echoing Thorstein Veblen,[6] Lasch's assertion regarding the decline of "bourgeois culture" and the rise of "the culture of narcissism" is debatable. Yet support for his suggestion abounds in popular (consumer) culture, which often reminds us of the limited alternatives to the socially stratified world in which we are involuntarily immersed. We can aspire to join the elite, the bourgeoisie. Or, we can watch them—however critically and analytically—on our televisions, in the cinemas, and on video screens. Nowhere was this more humorously articulated than in actor Peter Bergman's now classic 1980s Vicks cough syrup commercial in which he declared: "I'm not a doctor, but I play one on TV."[7]

Lasch's discussion of self-absorption was a reconfiguration of David Riesman's *The Lonely Crowd* (1950). America, Riesman asserted, was moving from a society governed by production to a society governed by consumption. The character of its upper middle classes was shifting from "'inner-directed" people, who formed goals that would guide them in life to "other-directed" people, sensitized to the expectations and preferences of others. In Riesman's view, the new American no longer cared much about adult authority but was hyperalert to peer groups and gripped by mass media. Similarly, Erving Goffman's *The Presentation of Self in Everyday Life* (1956) explored social interaction through the lens of theatrical performance. In Goffman's model, interaction is understood as a "performance" shaped by environment and audience, constructed to provide others with impressions consonant with the desired goals of the actor. Goffman's "performing actor" is analogous to David Riesman's "other-directed" persona and comparable to Christopher Lasch's "culture of narcissism."

All three aforementioned texts inform *Divas on Screen*. By examining the persona of five African American women celebrities, *Divas* seeks to push the discussion of African American celebrity beyond the "good, politically progressive role model" versus "bad, regressive black stereotype" binary that stifles dialogue and divides scholars. Instead, the ensuing chapters address how African American celebrity functions as a social phenomenon. This is not to minimize the prevalence of racial stereotypes in the twenty-first century. The Michael Richards diatribe at the Laugh Factory, the Don Imus invective "nappy-headed hos," and the recurring incidents of police brutality against young black men like Sean Bell remind us that the problem of the twenty-first century is still (to invoke W. E. B. Du Bois) the color line. But the focus of *Divas* is slightly different. It asks: what can we learn from the complex and contradictory careers of successful black women? Where do we find African Americans in this performative, "other-directed," narcissistic culture? What does African American stardom as a social phenomenon reveal about the aspirations of black folks in the twenty-first century? How have African Americans—in their struggle for inclusion in commercial entertainment—complied with dominant culture?

Film stars are exemplary palimpsests for reading the shifting values of a celebrity culture. In this early twenty-first-century moment, American popular culture grows increasingly celebrity-obsessed. From reality television programs and game shows that manufacture winners (e.g., *On the Lot, American Idol, The Bachelor, Flavor of Love, Making the Band, Who Wants to Be a Millionaire, Big Brother, Survivor, Dancing with the Stars*),[8] to pundit politics predicated on public perceptions of star personas,[9] to the wide world of professional sports,[10] Americans of all stripes are preoccupied with the fate of the famous.[11] This is not to mention the scores of biography pictures or reality programs that tease and titillate with the glamorous lives of the rich and (in)famous.[12] Even the socially disgruntled and psychologically disturbed (i.e., Colin Ferguson, Eric Harris, Dylan Klebold, and Cho Seung-hui)[13] seem to be striving for a kind of notoriety in death they could not achieve in life.

In our ordinary daily lives we are also presented with the possibility of becoming noteworthy, prominent, or exceptional. Embedded within our incentive system is the tacit promise of acknowledgment at some level. The prospect of achieving name recognition for professional expertise—whether artistic, athletic, intellectual, religious, or political—is one of the psychological rewards undergirding the American dream and pervading public discourse. Understanding American culture requires rethinking our national fascination with the "star system," as well as the multifaceted, contradictory meanings of stardom within the recently reconfigured military-entertainment-industrial complex.[14] Film stars are particularly useful templates for examining the functions of celebrity in American society.

In *The Dialectic of Enlightenment* and *Negative Dialectics,* Marxist theorists Theodor Adorno and Max Horkheimer offered a paradigm for analyzing film, media, and popular culture. They asserted that the phenomenon of mass culture has a political implication, namely that all the many forms of popular culture are a single *culture industry* whose purpose is to ensure the continued obedience of the masses to market interests. Entrenched in Adorno and Horkheimer's work was the notion that popular culture makes people docile and content no matter how difficult their social or economic circumstances. It provides a distraction that lulls people into complacency. An uncritical interest in, devotion to, and consumption of celebrity affairs (demonstrated by the commercial success of outlets *Movieline, Premiere, People, US, Entertainment Weekly, Jet, Ebony, Vibe, The Source, In Touch Weekly, Entertainment Tonight, Access Hollywood, Extra, Showbiz Tonight,* and *E! News*) is precisely what Frankfurt School theorists forewarned. In an era of postmodernity, which has thrown totalizing narratives into relief, readers might be inclined to view Frankfurt School theories as obsolete or uncomplicated.

In the 1990s, with the end of the Cold War, the initial expectation of many Americans was that the military-industrial complex would diminish and eventually fade away. Contrary to expectations, it has been reorganized and restructured. As Timothy Lenoir pointed out, the military-industrial complex has become the military-entertainment complex. Lenoir documented the history of war games and military simulations used for training, revealing the spinoff and adoption of key technologies by the entertainment industry. There has also been a flow of high-end technology and talented personnel from the military to the game entertainment industry.[15] This fusion between gaming technology concepts and blockbuster cinema was most profitably expressed in the *X-Men* films, *The Matrix* franchise, and the animation spinoff *The Animatrix*. In *The Matrix*'s dystopian vision of the future, the experiential world is actually a simulated reality created by machines in order to pacify, subdue, and harness the human population as an energy source. The trilogy films utilize and neutralize, mock and menace Frankfurt School theories, suggesting its creators had an eye toward cinematic self-reflexivity and political theory. The point is this: as we have become more appearance-oriented individuals, our society has become more entertainment driven and star focused.

The intensification of graphic violence and brutality in television (*The Sopranos; The Wire; CSI; The Shield; Rome; Dog, the Bounty Hunter; The First 48 Hours; Criminal Minds; America's Psychic Challenge*), the proliferation of reality shows, the expanding fan magazine market, the seeming racial/ethnic democratization of Academy Awards, the proliferation of award shows, and the integration of new entertainment technologies (iPod telephones, MP3 players, video games, the Internet) might be construed as the very phantasmal distractions from U.S. foreign and domestic policies (i.e., a dysfunctional electoral college, an overburdened health care system, inadequate environmental guidelines, growing militarism) Frankfurt School theorists anticipated. Many hope President Barak Obama is the neo(phyte) politician who can help deliver us from the postindustrial wasteland and the matrix of our other-directed imaginations.

As intertextual signifiers, stars expose the way the culture industry manufactures charisma and thereby creates a market (or fan base) of spectators conditioned to be moviegoing, fanzine- and game-purchasing consumer-citizens. *Divas on Screen*—like any analytical discussion of the cinema's broader relationship to American politics and culture—integrates Frankfurt School skepticism with more optimistic methodologies. Weber's notion of charisma and feminist film theory provide theoretical balance.

German sociologist Max Weber defined charismatic authority as one of three forms of authority, the other two being traditional (feudal) authority and legal or rational authority. Weber defined charisma as a certain quality of an individual personality, by virtue of which someone is set apart from ordinary people and treated as endowed with supernatural, superhuman, or at least specifically exceptional powers or qualities. These traits are not accessible to the ordinary person but are regarded as divine in origin or as exemplary, and on the basis of these qualities the individual is treated as a leader. However, for Weber, charisma is both an innate quality and artificially manufactured by society. It represents both creativity and the rationalization thereof. In works such as *Economy and Society* and in collections like *Max Weber on Charisma and Institution Building*, charisma is a flexible and invertible concept.

Weberian interpretations of charisma have informed star discourse in cinema studies for decades. Seminal scholarship in the discipline employs charisma to analyze stardom as a sociological phenomenon. Chief among such works—and central to the formation of this book—are two Richard Dyer titles: *Stars* (1979) and *Heavenly Bodies: Film Stars and Society* (1986). Dyer's publications were among the first books to take stardom as a sociological phenomenon seriously. In his essay on Paul Robeson, Dyer emerged as one of the first scholars to consider the complex and contradictory nature of African American celebrity.

Historian Donald Bogle's seminal study *Toms, Coons, Mulattoes, Mammies and Bucks: An Interpretive History of Blacks in American Films* (reprinted in 1992) is one of the most comprehensive discussions of African American representation in movies. Bogle covers many of the major film actors, but not in isolation or as unique phenomena in and of themselves. The book in which he closely examines the life of one person is *Dorothy Dandridge: A Biography* (1998), an exhaustive, well-researched volume that informed the Dandridge chapter published here in *Divas*. In his more recent publication *Bright Boulevards, Bold Dreams: The Story of Black Hollywood* (2006), Bogle returned to the project of African American Hollywood historiography.

If Richard Dyer's and Donald Bogle's work has been influential, P. David Marshall's has been instrumental. *Divas* is indebted to his theoretically rigorous *Celebrity and Power: Fame in Contemporary Culture* (1997). Marshall picks up where Dyer and Bogle leave off. He offers an updated discussion of Weberian charisma, fully integrating Weber's intellectual project concerning rationality and rationalization with Frankfurt School and Cultural Studies methodologies. He also writes about Oprah Winfrey and was one of the first of many scholars to take her celebrity seriously. In writing *Divas*, I wedded the analytical methods for theorizing stardom (as outlined by Dyer and Marshall) to African American historiography (as practiced by Donald Bogle).

The goal was to examine these women's careers in a way that is historical and theoretical. The feminist film scholarship of Carol Clover (particularly her notion of the Final Girl), Yvonne Tasker (on women as agents of narrative action), Marguerite Rippy (on the sexual commodification of black women), Kathleen Rowe (discussing the unruly woman), and Chris Straayer (defining the temporary transvestite film) enabled me to develop close textual readings against the grain of mainstream, patriarchal discourse. My analyses rely on the feminist foundations laid by these scholars. Their scholarship allowed me to rethink the contributions of African American women performers.

The word *diva* has origins in the Indian Sanskrit word *devi*, which means "goddess." It also derives from an ancient Italian word meaning "goddess" that originates from the feminine form of the Latin word *divus*, meaning "divine one." In modern usage, *diva* is a term with multiple meanings that have varied connotations. *Diva* has two common or familiar meanings. Webster's English

Dictionary defines *diva* as an operatic prima donna or as a very successful singer of nonoperatic music: a jazz diva. The word was originally used to describe great female opera singers, almost always sopranos. Soprano voices are traditionally classified into the subcategories of dramatic (rich and powerful), lyric (lighter), and coloratura (high and very agile). They are normally female but may also include boy sopranos (previously known as castrati), hence the cultural association with female performers. *Diva* is often used to positively comment on a woman's talent, performance style, or stage presence and has become a synonym for a famous or successful woman. Today *diva* may describe an extremely independent, talented woman and also apply to women in the classical arts.

The second set of meanings is less flattering. The word may refer to a person who considers herself (or himself) more important than others or who has high expectations of others and becomes angry when her standards or demands are not met. *Diva* sometimes carries a comical or negative connotation, implying a pop star who labels herself thusly and is arrogant, difficult to work with, high-maintenance, or otherwise demanding. In mainstream vernacular, a woman may be referred to as a diva, thereby suggesting she is especially dramatic or emotional. According to one popular Web site, a diva is a bitchy woman who must have her way exactly, or no way at all. She is rude and belittles people, believing everyone is beneath her. As such, she is selfish, spoiled, and overly dramatic.

Diva has become so charged with negative implications and association with prima donna histrionics that—to some—it is an epithet to avoid, a disparaging appellation. Take Karen Grigsby Bates's protective *Essence* article "Angela Bassett Is NOT a Diva!" as a case in point. Bates fondly describes Bassett as "serenely well grounded" and boasts that she possesses a "deep, throaty voice with the Florida twang of her childhood."[16] The careful emphasis on her down-home earthiness and southern drawl would hardly be necessary if Bassett—like so many African Americans—didn't have to apologize for her Ivy League education or ask fans to overlook her formal training and credentials. Bates was joined in this journalistic gesture by Hilton Als, who—one year later—wrote an eloquent article for *The New Yorker* and made a similar discursive maneuver.[17] "In conversation," he writes, "she indulges in many forms of black American colloquial speech, in the accents of her native St. Petersburg, Florida—'Mm-hmm,' 'Girlfriend,' 'You know what I'm sayin?'"[18] Describing her ability to move in and out of black vernaculars prefaces Als's discussion of her educational background. The point is simple: Bassett's publicists carefully avoided any connection with the term *diva* or any hint that she might be disconnected from her rural working-class roots. Such cautious public relations tactics help explain why some folks look askance at the word *diva* and the very notion of being one.

For *Divas on Screen*, I appropriated the term *diva* to refer to the way a performer's charismatic talents, performance style, and screen presence transcend the individual work (i.e., films, television programs, or comedy specials), instead becoming part of an extracinematic, extradiegetic public persona widely recognized and acknowledged by a national *and* international community of mass-culture consumer-spectators. In my formulation, the connotations are not negative or laden with notions of class privilege.

My divas of the big screen are analogous to divas in the popular music industry, in that both are exceptional or uniquely endowed with traits or talents. The assumption here is that these talents are both innate and manufactured by the culture industry. The current generation of black women in mainstream film and television has shattered part of the glass ceiling. Even if we find some of their work excessively commercial or explicitly mainstream, we can acknowledge the ways in which their careers have challenged the status quo at particular moments. These women enable us to articulate a new, more nuanced critique of African American representation in popular culture. Dorothy Dandridge, Pam Grier, Whoopi Goldberg, Oprah Winfrey, and Halle Berry are divas on screen because they are successful, self-possessed, self-aware icons of late twentieth-century Americana and avatars of new millennial multicultural sensibilities. In a longer study I would certainly include the likes of Abby Lincoln, Eartha Kitt, Cicely Tyson, and Angela Bassett, to name but a few.

The first diva addressed here is Dorothy Dandridge. The Dandridge chapter begins by placing her celebrity in the post–World War II context of 1950s American culture. Dandridge's status as a sexy film persona needs to be situated in terms of the decade's contradictory discourses regarding race and sexuality. She was an African American woman in a country that preferred European American women. She was a black woman in a society in which white feminine pulchritude and virginity were synonymous with piety and purity. Ironically, Dandridge was fashioned as a sex symbol in an environment that was relatively sexually repressive. These facts alone made her career difficult to navigate. Fortunately, for African American audiences, she represented something unique. For colored audiences, Dandridge was a sophisticated representative of African American beauty. Beyond the texts of her films, she represented class, elegance, and style. In black fanzines like *Ebony, Our World,* and *Negro Digest,* Dandridge's image and celebrity were not proscribed by the limits of the Hays Code. Her iconicity resonated differently with African American audiences, who brought their resistant and critical spectatorship[19] to the segregated balconies of American movie theaters in the 1950s.

Chapter 3 provides an examination of Pam Grier's rise to stardom through low-budget sexploitation and Blaxploitation pictures produced by offbeat production houses like American International Pictures (AIP). Formed in 1956 from American Releasing Corporation by James H. Nicholson and Samuel Z. Arkoff, American International Pictures was a low-budget production company. At AIP, Nicholson and Arkoff were committed to releasing independently produced, inexpensive films, primarily of interest to teenagers of the 1950s, 1960s, and 1970s. Beginning with a brief biographical account, this chapter recounts Grier's discovery and work at AIP. It traces the emergence of Grier's tough-girl screen persona, which emerged in the wake of—and possibly in response to—1970s feminism. Yet, like Dandridge, she encountered a series of contradictions in roles she played during her career. Grier's forceful screen characters were often contained and controlled by the narrative conventions of sexploitation and Blaxploitation cinema. I interpret this containment as a form of cultural backlash against the gains of the feminist movement, given the way these films evince an iconography of misogyny. Hence, this chapter addresses some of the aesthetic relationships between different forms of exploitation cinema.

The following chapter, "Goldberg's Variations on Comedic Charisma," is partially indebted to Kathleen's Rowe's indispensable book *The Unruly Woman: Gender and the Genres of Laughter* (1995). Rowe provides a paradigm for discussing Goldberg's performative penchant for menacing the dominant discourse with her unruly and defiant characters. Though a few published biographies on Goldberg have appeared (i.e., James Robert Parish's *Whoopi Goldberg: Her Journey from Poverty to Megastardom*), comparatively less has been written about her.[20] One wonders if this critical silence stems from the tension and discomfort evoked by her unconventional public and screen personae.

Having followed Oprah Winfrey's career closely for more than a decade, I have seen several books written on her life and career. However, this scholarship does not address her film work. My chapter culminates in a close reading of *Beloved*. It was one of the first essays on the adaptation of this novel to film and encapsulates some elements of Winfrey's charismatic capitalist persona. Furthermore, the scholarship on Winfrey has just begun to address her extensive entrepreneurship, diverse media outlets, complex international philanthropy, and cinematic endeavors.

The final chapter, on Halle Berry, brings *Divas on Screen* full circle by addressing the intimate, if posthumous, relationship between the late Dorothy Dandridge and the blossoming career of Halle Berry, acknowledging the ways Dandridge's career made Berry's possible. Without Dorothy Dandridge, the meteoric rise of Halle Berry simply does not make sense. This is an indisputable fact that Berry herself has acknowledged in interviews, in acceptance speeches, and in film projects she has chosen to produce. Some aspects of the relationship between Dandridge and Berry can be garnered from the biographies of Berry.

None of the previous biographies—whether they are about Dandridge, Goldberg, Winfrey, or Berry—absorb theoretical models and paradigms into their discussions. As a consequence, they fail to address the resistance of camp aesthetics; the implicit feminist sensibility in some of the films; the precise nature of these women's charismatic appeal; the manner in which these performers portrayed characters that menaced the dominant discourse; and the creation of a consumer culture that audiences negotiate. It is only by employing various theoretical tools that we gain a more comprehensive understanding of the multifaceted nature of their star personae, thereby grasping how they have become divas in their own right.

Dorothy Dandridge's
Erotic Charisma

For this reason above all Dorothy Dandridge is important.
I believe she is the only genuine black female star Hollywood
ever produced, if by star is meant that combination of an immediately seductive image with the larger-than-life projection of a
persona, the combination that also produced Marilyn Monroe.

—Karen Alexander

Some drew the seemingly inevitable comparisons between
Dandridge and Marilyn Monroe. In the popular imagination,
both appeared to be sensitive fragile women in a cutthroat film
industry controlled by men. Yet their lives—and the pressures
they had to live with—were often vastly different.

—Donald Bogle

The American cultural and political landscape of the 1950s was rife
with contradictions. As a decade, the 1950s were plagued by fear yet filled with
frivolity. The postwar era of relative economic prosperity led middle-class
Americans to believe the "good life" had finally arrived. Yet social injustice,
institutionalized racism, and bureaucratic mismanagement undermined the
promise of democratic freedoms, the enjoyment of civil liberties, and equal
access to opportunity. America was legally segregated by race (Jim Crow),
geographically stratified by class (in Levittown-like suburban enclaves), domestically divided by gender (through the cult of domesticity), unnerved by
McCarthyism (the Hollywood blacklist), and embattled with communism
(the Korean War). Ironically, many Americans maintained their faith in "the
dream," exhibited patriotic dedication, and displayed the jingoism accompanying the nation's postwar global privilege.

If there was one individual whose personal life and public career epitomized the unfulfilled promise of a profoundly conflicted era, it was Dorothy Dandridge. Too often film historians (Mills, 1991; Bogle, 1997; Conrad, 2000; Rippy, 2001) have narrated the abbreviated days of Dandridge in terms of the exploitation she endured at the hands of unscrupulous industry agents. While there was tragedy in her life and career, there was also much to celebrate and admire. Though stunted by the conservative ideologies of the era, Dandridge's celebrity legacy—which is currently Halle Berry's inheritance— paved the way for black women to portray glamorous, sophisticated leading roles in films marketed to mainstream audiences. More successfully than her contemporaries, many of whom were exceedingly talented (i.e., Fredi Washington, Lena Horne, Juanita Moore, Eartha Kitt, Louise Beavers, Abbey Lincoln, et al.), she became the first major crossover film starlet. With its air of bourgeois respectability, elegance, and sophistication, her persona broadened the image of black womanhood in the public sphere. Eisenhower-era African Americans connected with Dandridge because her élan contradicted segregationist notions of black inferiority. Her celebrity image—like that of Sidney Poitier—progressively negated Jim Crow ideology, which had dictated a discourse of black subjugation. This chapter examines her stardom in the context of 1950s America in an effort to understand how she became one of the first divas of the silver screen.

By examining the public discourse around Dorothy Dandridge's stardom, we gain a sense of how she became a *phenomenon of consumption* and an icon admired by African Americans, in the same manner as Marilyn Monroe and Rita Hayworth before her were admired and idolized by mainstream America. Through her celebrity, Dandridge was a phenomenon that helped instantiate African Americans as consumers in twentieth-century public discourse.[1] Dandridge's stardom existed in the context of America's changing race relations, but it is impossible to discuss her public persona without also considering how class functioned in the creation and solidification of her image. Heretofore the term *black middle class* has been utilized, but not in the traditional Marxist-Gramscian sense: as a hegemonic force assimilating to the mainstream and thereby alienating the masses of proletariat black folks from themselves. Instead, the black middle class is discussed here as a group seeking self-determination, economic independence, racial uplift, and broader representation in the media as entitled citizens.

Wherever consumption is linked with class aspirations, and celebrity is linked with consumption, famous people play a role in the formation of middle-class taste. By considering the star discourse revolving around Dandridge, we gain a sense of her as the contested terrain upon which competing cultural discourses of black middle-class identity and comportment played out.

In their study of 1950s American culture, historians Douglas Miller and Marion Nowak capture the irony of the era in their description of the disparity between recollection and reality. They discuss the return of repressive Victorian ideals that sharply contrasted with the expectations of modern life most Americans held as possibilities for themselves. Miller and Nowak are among numerous scholars and historians who have recorded the era as a period of complex cultural anxiety and self-denial. They write:

> The fifties witnessed much less happy nonsense, much more conformity. International tensions and conflicts were far greater than had been the case during the relatively isolationist twenties. The daily reality of the cold war caused persons to fear international communism, more importantly, internal communist subversion. Such fears put a premium on conformity. Bourgeois values reasserted themselves in a manner which would have pleased a twenties fundamentalist. Domesticity, religiosity, respectability, security through compliance with the system—that was the fifties.[2]

Miller and Nowak draw parallels between the 1950s and earlier periods in American history. They were not alone in their observations, as similarities between cultural trends of the 1920s and the 1950s are offered in much of the historical literature of the era (i.e., Ellis, 1954; Miller and Nowak, 1977; Oakley, 1986; Halberstam 1993), asserting that postwar periods engender social conformity out of national necessity. Scholars have suggested these are moments in which notions of national community are reconstructed and re-imagined. There is considerable evidence Americans turned away from the realities of the period (i.e., the bomb, the anti-Soviet Cold War, Truman's 1947–initiated witch hunts, and race riots) toward a wistful vision of themselves as happy homemakers, fatherly breadwinners, dutiful daughters, and obedient sons. As a consequence, socially designated roles and identity categories (i.e., race, class, gender, and nation) were more narrowly circumscribed than in previous, or subsequent, years.

Throughout the decade, the cult of domesticity determined many white women's lives. The men they married defined these women, as did the children they nurtured. Beginning in the 1940s and throughout the 1950s, for example, white women endured these oppressive expectations. Many married at younger-than-ever ages and bore as many children as their grandmothers. Masses of women attempted to conform to the dominant regimes of marriage, coupling, and reproduction. Among those of childbearing age, the most common response to the question of how many children were ideal rose from two to four.[3] Second-wave feminists argued that prevailing 1950s discourses of gender and sexuality took their greatest toll on women, holding them unduly responsible for the nuclear family's discontent as well as the uncertainty of modern life.[4] Nowhere was this discourse more evident than in Philip Wylie's 1942 work *Generation of Vipers,* in which he coined the term "Momism" to refer to excessive mothering and excessive devotion to one's mother. Wylie's thesis was later revived and repackaged in Hans Sebald's *Momism: The Silent Disease of America* (1976), which offered a sociopsychological study of the tactics, effects, and cultural, legal, and familial ramifications of domineering and manipulative mothering.

For African American women in particular, it was social activism—rather than marital status—that determined family interests. Black women nationwide organized alongside, and in the tradition of, extraordinary activists like Mary McLeod Bethune, Dorothy Height, Marian Anderson, Coretta Scott King, Fannie Lou Hamer, and Rosa Parks.[5] These women protested lynching, fought for voter registration, campaigned for the desegregation of armed forces, sought reform of the criminal-justice system, and organized black churches. During the 1940s, while black American soldiers were fighting armies of racial supremacists in Europe, their sisters, wives, mothers, girlfriends, and families were fighting the racist dictates of Jim Crow at home. The summer of 1943 echoed the summer of 1919 and proved particularly violent. Race riots erupted in Los Angles, Detroit, Philadelphia, Harlem, Beaumont, and other cities across the country. African Americans, who initially believed they had migrated to a promised land, found northern bigotry every bit as pervasive and virulent as in the South. But in the North they were not the only targets of white racism. The climate was violently hostile toward Filipino and Mexican Americans, who were targeted by white backlash against California's counterculture. Fueled by white supremacy, this backlash was predicated on the perception that Roosevelt's New Deal policies created greater economic opportunities for blacks and other ethnic minorities than it did for European Americans.

Film scholars have noted the relationship between generic conventions and historical discursive formations. Chief among such scholars is Michael Renov, who has analyzed the ties between female-oriented genres and postwar institutional discourses. In his essay "Leave Her to Heaven: The Double Bind of the Post-War Woman," he asserts that the years immediately after the war were confusing regarding the cultural messages shaping women's roles. Work versus motherhood presented one conflict. The ideology of motherhood, the cult of domesticity, and the tradition of black women's activism competed with the emergence of yet another image of womanhood: the sexually ebullient film-star pinup. This was an iconic spin-off of the calendar girl, who typified the image of seductive womanhood popularized in men's magazines before, during, and after World War II. The war sanctified the idea of the pinup, and though some movies concentrated on wholesome family entertainment, men plastered their barracks with inviting photos of film stars.[6] The contrast between sexy film stars and wholesome mothers was one of the decade's social paradoxes, but this contradiction would intensify as American corporate interests increasingly relied on sexuality to revive the financially struggling film industry.

For instance, the disappearing movie audience and the threat to filmgoing posed by television resulted in an economic crisis for the film industry.[7] This crisis played a key role in bringing sexually and racially explicit subjects to the screen. Titillating subjects were used to sell movie tickets, since Hollywood found itself in transition both technologically and thematically. In addition to providing the primary competition for film, television played a role in the demise of the Hays Production Code. As movie audiences opted for home entertainment, Hollywood producers began bending—then breaking—the self-regulatory code to lure paying customers back to theaters. Film producers knew sex and sensuality would sell movie tickets. Other sensational subjects, like miscegenation (*Duel in the Sun*, 1946; *Pinky*, 1949), racism (*No Way Out*, 1950), anti-Semitism (*Gentleman's Agreement*, 1947), homosexuality (*Suddenly Last Summer*, 1959; *The Children's Hour*, 1961), and drug addiction or alcoholism (*The Man with the Golden Arm*, 1955; *The Lost Weekend*, 1945), would sell movie tickets, too, but none so well as sex.

The 1950s film star was symptomatic of the sexual and racial contradictions in America. For example, Hollywood feature filmmaking, with Euro-American actors and themes, typically focused on the unmarried, innocent, or virginal ingénue who presented the "repressive sexual bind." Men were forbidden to enjoy her sexually, except in fantasy. Sex, in mainstream films of this era, was referred to coyly but rarely dealt with honestly. The projection of sexual innocence by performers Sandra Dee, Debbie Reynolds, and Doris Day—who laid bare the Oedipal fantasy of "daddy's little girl"—typified the contradictory ideals inherent in the regimes of sexuality.[8]

These contradictions—including the virgin–whore dichotomy—existed in African American cinema, too. In the 1940s, films like *Cabin in the Sky* (1943) propagated the dichotomy of "good girl" (Ethel Waters's character Petunia Jackson) versus "bad girl" (Lena Horne's Georgia Brown). Even Andrew L.

Stone's *Stormy Weather* (1943) positions Lena Horne's Selina Rogers as desirable because she's virtuous. With a few early exceptions (i.e., *Duel in the Sun*, 1946), it was not until the 1950s and 1960s that the repressive sexual bind linked sex with pathos, murder, and deviance (i.e., *Carmen Jones*, 1954; *Porgy and Bess*, 1959; *Island in the Sun*, 1957; *Band of Angels*, 1957; *Touch of Evil*, 1958; *Imitation of Life*, 1959; *The Unforgiven*, 1960; *Flaming Star*, 1960; *Rosemary's Baby*, 1968). In these films, unrepressed sexuality was punishable by death, social ostracism, abandonment, and disownment.

In addition to their emphasis on sexuality as taboo, women's films (from the 1930s through the 1950s) emphasized physical attractiveness and the dominant discourses of adornment. Many mainstream films divorced themselves from controversial issues and timely plots (i.e., the displacement of women's labor after the war, postwar family relations, birth control, and abortion). Instead, they became "how-tos" on white heterosexual romance, on catching and keeping a man, and on appearance and sex appeal. Examples include *Three Coins in the Fountain*, 1954; *Gentlemen Prefer Blondes*, 1953; *How to Marry a Millionaire*, 1953; *Seven Brides for Seven Brothers*, 1954; *Father of the Bride*, 1950; *High Society*, 1955; *The Catered Affair*, 1956; *Pillow Talk*, 1959; and *Boys' Night Out*, 1962. But beneath the veneer of fun, frivolity, and flirtation lay profound tensions relating to the regimes of sexuality (i.e., heterosexual monogamy, lifetime commitment, gender roles, and division of labor) exerting power over social life. Studios relied on the proven formula popularized by screwball comedies of marriage and remarriage, as the Doris Day–Rock Hudson pictures demonstrate. With double entendre and subtext, they hinted at homosexuality and called attention to the gender performativity of the bachelor's sexuality.[9] On the surface—where most audiences engage movies—these pictures played out cultural tensions around monogamy and appeared to resolve issues happily, with plots in which women tricked boastful bachelors into becoming obliging grooms. In so doing, these movies ultimately intensified the cultural pressure to marry. Not only did they emphasize the importance of marrying and mating, they suggested women who failed to wed would become lonely spinsters. Finally, they reified the dominant discourse regarding nonmonogamous, premarital, and interracial sex, depicting them as socially unacceptable.

Meanwhile, external signifiers of sexuality—which were growing in importance in the 1950s—entered popular culture and the public sphere. Popular images in film, television, music, and advertising stressed the secondary sexual characteristics of both sexes. Male consumers purchased products to accessorize their masculinity, while women—black and white—became the consumers of mass-marketed femininity. Whether it was hair straightening and bleaching creams for black women, or padded panties, contoured brassieres, and hair bleaching for white women, all women were increasingly fashioning themselves after images presented in the media. Film stars were central to this commercial enterprise. Spectators consumed film stars, and stars, in turn, influenced the self-fashioning of female fans. The film industry produced spectators as consumers of the films as well as the products of other industries (Gledhill, 1991; Stacey, 1994; Cohan, 1997; Negra, 2001). What makes Dorothy Dandridge so important—at this moment of burgeoning mass consumption—is that she was a star during the instantiation of the black American as consumer in the twentieth century. Consequently, her celebrity coincided with, and influenced, the American consumer's image and understanding of black womanhood.

Jackie Stacey noted that in the 1950s, when fashions and cosmetics increasingly became available as mass-marketed items, "the reproduction of self-image through consumption was perceived as a way of producing new forms of American feminine identity which were exciting, sexual, pleasurable, and in some ways transgressive."[10] Stacey's seminal study of spectatorship and consumption demonstrates that the body was a central topic in the articulation of the relationship between female stars and women spectators. Female film stars were not only bodies on display, providing ideals of feminine pulchritude and sexuality, they were utilized to sell personal products to spectators for their own self-improvement.[11] African American starlet Dorothy Dandridge, Euro-American actress Marilyn Monroe, and the anglicized Irish-Spanish celebrity Margarita Carmen Cansino (aka Rita Hayworth)[12] all functioned in this way.

Among these three, Marilyn Monroe embodied the image of desirability and nubile feminine sexuality for white Americans. She was mainstream America's quintessential sex symbol. Monroe personified the (stereo)typical blond bombshell, patterned after 1930s archetypes Jean Harlow, Mae West, Carole Lombard, Joan Blondell, and Ginger Rogers. The 1950s and 1960s imitators (i.e., Jayne Mansfield, Janet Leigh, Kim Novak, Tippi Hedren, Brigitte Bardot, and Sandra Dee) signified the forbidden pleasures of white female sexuality as it was repressed and represented. According to Richard Dyer, Monroe's image ought to be situated in the flux of ideas about morality and sexuality characterizing postwar America. The changing sexual ethics were in evidence everywhere. For example, there was the spread of Freudian psychoanalysis in the postwar era (registered particularly in the Hollywood melodrama), the Kinsey Reports on sexual behavior, Betty Friedan's *The*

Feminine Mystique, and the brooding, bad-boy machismo of stars like Marlon Brando, James Dean, and Elvis Presley. Monroe's combination of sexuality and innocence was part of this flux.

In many ways, Monroe was a sign of the times. The discursive regime concerning what constituted sexuality mattered a great deal. Because Marilyn Monroe acted out these specific ideas, and because these ideas appeared to matter, she was the charismatic attraction that seemed to embody what sexuality was taken to be.[13]

Enter Dorothy Dandridge

The 1950s also witnessed the emergence of African American starlet Dorothy Dandridge. She was a sex symbol whose life and death paralleled Monroe's, and the two have often been compared (Young, 1965; Mills, 1970; Bogle, 1997; Rippy, 2001). Dandridge's ascent to fame might have been slower and more difficult, but her troubled life and untimely death were equally mysterious. By 1935, she had already begun working in film (*The Big Broadcast of 1936* and *A Day at the Races,* 1937). In 1941, Dandridge danced alongside the famous Nicholas Brothers in a "specialty" musical sequence of the *Sun Valley Serenade.* This was not their first meeting. She and her sister Vivian played some of the same nightclubs where the brothers appeared. On September 6, 1942, she married Harold Nicholas, and together they had one child. In the late 1940s she made numerous television appearances, but it wasn't until the 1950s that she was cast in leading roles, which legitimated her screen career. Throughout her professional life, she appeared in more than twenty-seven feature films, ten soundies, four short films, and frequently on television.[14] An actress and a celebrity personality, Dandridge was as culturally important as any of her contemporaries—white, black, Asian, or Native American. She, like Hayworth or Monroe, defined a distinct brand of sexuality at a moment when sex was increasingly entering the domain of popular culture.

Several parallels may be drawn between Monroe's and Dandridge's personal and professional lives. Both women withstood deeply troubled childhoods. Both struggled with unsuccessful and abusive marriages. As performers they were personally discontent with their public personae (as fetishized sex symbols). Monroe shared with Dandridge the vexed position of being a female sex symbol in a religiously conservative, racially segregated, patriarchal visual economy and society. As a consequence, both encountered difficulties when attempting to obtain serious dramatic roles and be taken seriously by Hollywood executives as artists. Dandridge and Monroe were positioned similarly in terms of their iconographic significance. Sadly, both women died young, under mysterious circumstances, leaving the question of possible suicide looming but ultimately unanswerable.

In 1965, A. S. "Doc" Young pointed out some of parallels between their short lives and careers in an obituary article on Dandridge.

> In the context of their lives and times in the theatrical world, Dorothy Dandridge and Marilyn Monroe possessed a great deal in common. They were once students together in a Hollywood drama school. But little did they know that they were more than merely schoolmates, that they were in fact, "tragic sisters" under the skin. Both were blessed with rare beauty. Both were to be ranked during their lifetimes, among the world's five most beautiful women. And, besides, both possessed that coveted Hollywoodian quality called "it"— both were fully and roundly packed with sex appeal. Neither was satisfied with applause, fame and fortune gained principally from good looks. Both fought mightily to gain acceptance as talented artists, as performers, rather than as sex-goddesses men lusted for from one corner of the earth to the other. But neither was destined to succeed to a degree that was entirely satisfying. . . . Except that Dorothy Dandridge was Negro and Marilyn Monroe was Caucasian, both lived and died by cruel plots of fate or destiny, which were no less than verisimilar.[15]

As instructive as these similarities are, however, the key differences in their experiences, and the meanings of these differences, are equally informative.

More explicitly than Monroe, Dandridge was a celebrity whose personal life and public personae reflected the contradictions embedded in the sociocultural milieu of the decade. For the mainstream spectator, Dandridge represented exoticized black sexuality at a moment when race relations were particularly unstable, making her the symbol of sexual taboos and forbidden desires. Monroe became a sign of Americana by virtue of her Kennedy family associations. Unlike Dandridge, Monroe was not the figurative screen upon which discourses of miscegenation, race relations, and class mobility were played out. Thus it was Dandridge who symbolized black participation in the armed forces as an army wife in *Since You Went Away* (1944). She embodied miscegenation taboos as the sexual object of white male desire in *Tarzan's Peril* (1951), *The Decks Ran Red* (1957), *Island in the Sun* (1957), *Tamango* (1958), and *Malaga* (1960). She represented black middle-class upward mobility as a dedicated teacher in *Bright Road* (1953) and as a shop girl turned secretary in *Island in the Sun* (1957).

Dandridge's personal life was also emblematic of the social and political climate. The public record of Dandridge's personal life stands out as another indication of her significance. She was a key figure of racial integration and transgressive interracial relations. Over the course of her life she was involved in numerous interracial relationships, including affairs with actor Peter Lawton and with director Otto Preminger and a troubled, abusive marriage to nightclub owner Jack Denison. The difficult and unfortunate ways in which these affairs ended underscore the notion of Dandridge as a tragic figure (e.g., as the woman never really accepted by the white Hollywood society folks with whom she associated). Consequently, she is read as the sad concubine of a string of white Lotharios. Most of these relationships, however, ended for reasons that did not necessarily involve race but (with the exception of Otto Preminger, who made Dandridge his mistress and refused to leave his wife) for other reasons: new relationships, career demands, domestic neglect, abuse, alcoholism, or financial indebtedness. The abusive relationships she endured as an adult echoed the abusive treatment Dandridge experienced growing up. Uncontested by the two major biographies, and one posthumously published autobiography (Dandridge, 1970; Mills, 1970; Bogle, 1997), is the fact she was physically and sexually abused by her mother's lesbian lover.

Dandridge's stardom is best understood in terms of a confluence of personal and political events: namely postwar contradictions in U.S. international and domestic policies regarding race, sexuality, and nationalism, and a set of unusual family circumstances. As Robert Lightning notes, "An Oscar nomination to Dandridge in 1954 and the international publicity surrounding this achievement (including an appearance at the Academy Awards ceremony as a presenter, and subsequent appearance at Cannes at the opening of *Carmen Jones*) serves again to trumpet U.S. liberalism to the world as well as to drive local attention from alternative political models."[16] Lightning is correct in saying that Dandridge's token status (as the major female crossover celebrity) potentially functioned as a diversion from serious social issues. However, a more fluid understanding of the relationship between material base and ideological superstructure reminds us that African Americans read against the grain of the dominant discourse. In other words, Dandridge's international visibility was also a source of pride for African American spectators who relished in the achievements of her celebrity.

Much of the scholarship on Dandridge has focused almost exclusively on the construction of her as stereotypical sexual figure vis-à-vis white male costars. The existing work has discussed the starlet as either a stereotypical sex siren or as a subversive image of blackness in relation to white characters. Such dichotomous scholarship locks our reading of her celebrity into a Manichean binary structure, a simplistic politics of positionality. This emphasis on stereotypes precludes other ways of readings and understanding her stardom and black spectatorship, particularly as they relate to class aspirations and social mobility.

Elizabeth Hadley Freydberg's essay on Dandridge typifies American film scholarship with its tendency toward binary analysis, focusing on minority representation as either "negative stereotype" or a "positive role model."

> During the 1950s, however, Black people in "real life" were engaged in the struggle for Civil Rights in every American institution. Although Black women such as Rosa Parks, Ella Baker, Daisy Bates, and Autherine Lucy were at the forefront of struggle for integration, the most publicized image of the Black woman on the movie screen, was that of a whore played by Dorothy Dandridge in *Carmen Jones* . . . The screenplay *Carmen Jones*, written by Harry Kliner, produced and directed by Otto Preminger, with incredibly stereotyped music by Oscar Hammerstein II, is transplanted to a parachute factory in the American South during 1943. After "hair-pulling fights between black females, the inevitable barroom brawl, the exaggerated dialect, the animalistic passions and furies of the leads" . . . *Carmen Jones* embodies two stereotypes of Black women—those of whore and bitch.[17]

She aptly calls attention to the gulf between Hollywood's fictional representation of black life and the social reality of political activism in which black Americans were involved in the 1950s. But such readings omit black audience response to black films, leaving spectators out of the analysis. There was devotion among black spectators for Dandridge given the image of acceptable bourgeois beauty and womanhood she presented, which heretofore had not existed in mainstream media.

When queried about Dandridge, black women spectators often expressed pride. As adult women, these spectators weren't looking for role models. They simply enjoyed seeing black women on screen. Speaking about her experience watching *Carmen Jones* from the "Colored-Only" balcony of a segregated Nashville movie theater, Ruth Jeffries said:

> I had never seen a black woman in this kind of role. Not that the role was profound. But it was a major role in a movie shown in theaters around the country. She was pretty. She wasn't fat. She wasn't a Step-and-Fetchit model. I remember reading her response to the nomination in some magazine. She said, "You don't know how much this means to me." We felt that way too. Young, black adults thought she was great.[18]

Dorothy Veal, another African American spectator, said she appreciated the black subjectivity Dandridge brought to the big screen.

> I liked Dorothy Dandridge. First of all, she was a beautiful woman. I liked to look at her. And, I didn't feel—at the time—that she played demeaning parts. I didn't feel she was a Butterfly McQueen or a Hattie McDaniel. She was different. She wasn't shuffling. She didn't have a handkerchief. She wasn't a handkerchief head. She spoke English. She didn't roll her eyes. She wasn't what you saw in others. I felt comfortable. I don't remember cringing. You know when you see certain things you want to go under the seat. You want to cover your face. Oh, my God, you just wanted to cover your face. It upset me. I can remember Butterfly McQueen and Hattie McDaniel and Louise Beavers, Step-and-Fetchit and Mantan Moreland. I can remember them as making me want to just disappear, go up in a puff of smoke. I know didn't have that reaction with her [Dandridge]. It was the same thing with Lena Horne. I didn't have that feeling with her [Horne]. But then maybe it's because they looked more like me. I'm not saying that I'm beautiful. But I could relate. She wasn't a maid.[19]

These views typified those of young African American women in the 1950s. Moreover, scholarship in other fields confirms these views were typical of black spectators through the 1940s and 1950s. For example, Joan Nestle's research in queer studies reveals how black working-class audiences took visual pleasure in the memories and images of black stars and celebrities. Nestle's essay "I Lift My Eyes to the Hill: The Life of Mabel Hampton as Told by a White Woman" revealed Ms. Hampton's pleasure and pride in seeing black performers. Hampton saved her scarce resources to purchase tickets for Broadway plays and to follow the careers of Josephine Baker, Marian Anderson, and Paul Robeson. According to Nestle, Ms. Hampton was "creating for herself a nurturing family out of defiant African American women and men . . . Her lesbian self was part of what was fed by their soaring voices."[20] In seeking out these entertainers, black women sought the cultural images they longed to see.

By citing these viewpoints, I want to call attention to black audience responses as part of the social equation of black stardom. Historically, African American audiences have negotiated what Manthia Diawara eloquently termed "problems of identification and resistance." As Diawara demonstrated, "whenever Blacks are represented in Hollywood—and sometimes when Hollywood omits Blacks from its films altogether—there are spectators who denounce the result and refuse to suspend their disbelief."[21] By the same token, black spectators may choose to identify with particular aspects of a filmic spectacle (i.e., the star, the music, the location shooting) and reject other elements (i.e., a racist script, flawed direction, the editing, or point-of-view). This was particularly the case in Dandridge's day. To a greater degree, we ought to include black audience responses in analyses of black stardom. Otherwise, we risk producing discursive readings of African American culture void of African American experiences.

Alluding to the perceptions of audiences, but not actually citing individual women spectators, Donald Bogle made a similar observation about the aura of black stardom. He asserted, "the star was the embodiment of the audience's wild hopes for itself, its dreams of power, charm, and beauty . . . they had not yet had the pleasure of seeing Hollywood movies with such a charismatic figure (who looked like them) at the center. Dandridge came to touch on a dream of Black America for itself."[22] He describes Dandridge specifically as a reflection of the audience's human vulnerability. The glamorous aesthetic of classic Hollywood stardom and genuine talent were at the heart of Dandridge's appeal, *especially* to African American audiences.

To reintroduce audience response and identification is to counter scholarship that omits socioeconomic aspects of spectatorship from analyses of black representation. Recall that in 1950, only one-sixth of the Negro men in the Unites States were employed in occupations that identify them with the black bourgeoisie or upper middle class. The proportion of Negroes in professional and technical occupations (i.e., schoolteachers, preachers, physicians, dentists, lawyers, college professors, entertainers, embalmers, funeral directors, social workers, and nurses) was less than one-third as large as the proportion among white Americans. In 1949 the median income of Negro families was $1,665, or 51 percent of the median income of white families, which was $3,232. Only 16 percent of Negro families, as compared with 55 percent of white families, had incomes of $3,000 or more. The small proportion (five in every thousand) of Negroes whose annual incomes amounted to $5,000 or more included physicians, dentists, lawyers, entertainers, and businessmen.[23] Because African Americas were concentrated in lower-working-class jobs, they did not yet constitute a significant portion of middle-class America. Nineteen-fifties black audiences connected with Dandridge because she was a symbol of success in a society that allowed blacks few opportunities for advancement, much less "conspicuous achievement."[24] Her celebrity mitigated segregationist notions of black inferiority. In this context, the image of bourgeois womanhood progressively challenged white supremacy and racial subjugation. Dandridge's entrance into mainstream consciousness as a film personality—even with compromised roles—signified a change in the American cultural landscape. It indicated that future blacks might have greater access to the Hollywood dream factory. Black spectators were aware Dandridge was a unique screen idol. This is not to privilege spectator identification with Dandridge over Hadley Freydberg's analysis of her films and screen persona. But it is to suggest that alongside historical analysis and ideological readings, we ought to consider audience investment in stars as part of celebrity discourse.

Perhaps Hadley Freydberg took cues from predecessor James Baldwin, an author, activist, and pioneer of black studies. When Baldwin was writing in the late 1960s and early 1970s, black cultural critics emphasized structural and ideological analysis. Baldwin wrote several critical essays examining the contents of Hollywood films and the exclusionary machinations of the industry. His criticism was often published as a collection of essays. *Notes of a Native Son* (1955), for instance, contained an essay on *Carmen Jones*. Similarly, *The Devil Finds Work* (1976) was a book of film essays informed by the sensibility of the Black Arts Movement.[25] A rich tradition of African American literary figures writing essays of cultural criticism extends through and beyond Toni Morrison's *Playing in the Dark*. Just as important as ensuring Dandridge's position among the pantheon of American screen talents is the need to secure the intellectual genealogy of black film criticism often circumvented by variants of cultural studies. Baldwin critiqued the limitations placed on African American cultural production and black artistic expression.

Baldwin was fascinated by luminaries like Sidney Poitier, Dorothy Dandridge, and Harry Belafonte but took exception to their token status. In one essay on 1950s cinema, Baldwin argued: "*Carmen Jones* has Negro bodies before the camera and Negroes are associated in the public mind with sex . . . Since to the lighter races, darker races always seem to have an aura of sexuality, this fact is not distressing in itself . . . What is distressing is the conjecture this movie leaves one with what Americans take sex to be."[26] Baldwin challenged the way black cultural idioms were controlled by the Hollywood culture industry and were dominated by European cultural values. He criticized the stereotypical caricatures to which black actors were limited. His ideological insights led him to read black performance and performativity more closely, thereby deciphering how actors subverted restrictive contexts.

> It is scarcely possible to think of a black American actor who has not been misused: not one has ever been seriously challenged to deliver the best that

is in him. The most powerful example of this cowardice and waste are the careers of Paul Robeson and Ethel Waters. If they had ever been allowed really to hit their subtle stride, they might immeasurably have raised the level of cinema and theater in this country . . . What the black actor has managed to give are moments—indelible moments, created, miraculously, beyond the confines of the script: hints of reality, smuggled like contraband into a maudlin tale, and with enough force, if unleashed, to shatter the tale to fragments. The moments given us by black performers exist so far beneath, or beyond, the American apprehensions that it is difficult to describe them.[27]

Exemplified here, Baldwin provided seminal commentary on film and literature. However, much of his work—and the scholarship derived from it—discusses black popular culture in bipolar terms: as the negative stereotype versus the positive inversion of stereotypical images.

In more recent scholarship on Dandridge, Marguerite H. Rippy sought to recuperate the starlet's maligned screen persona. Rippy writes in light of the biographical material on Dandridge but critiques the patriarchal structures to which the star was confined. She also discusses the subordination of Dandridge's race to her gender, her blackness to her femininity. In some ways, she typifies the Baldwinian critical stance by claiming the star's persona/performances could subvert the otherwise racist context out of which they emerged. For instance, Rippy devoted her essay to reinterpreting Dandridge. Her intent was to offer an alternative to the fetishizing discourses of exotic sexuality.

> Her cinematic performances often challenged the normative expectations by replacing the common image of the victimized white female body with the image of a black female body victimized by masculine violence—both black and white. . . . This victimization of the black female body appears in several of Dandridge's films including *Tarzan's Peril* (1951), *Tamango* (1957), *Island in the Sun* (1957), *The Decks Ran Red* (1958), and her well-known *Carmen Jones* (1954). All these films portrayed Dandridge's interracial appeal as both inescapable and taboo, and specifically label these desires as tragically self-destructive to both desirer and desired.[28]

Throughout her essay, Rippy offers a rigorous explanation of the performance of cultural associations between femininity, sex, blackness and primitivism in Dandridge's work, noting that these were associations with which the star was uncomfortable. And she notes Dandridge's personal ambivalence regarding her objectification in the form of self-promotion. Overall, Rippy's discussion is compelling and instructive because it enables us to view the

Dorothy Dandridge, majestic as Melmendi in *Tarzan's Peril* (1951).

films—and Dandridge's persona—as something other than simplistically stereotypical. However, it also omits black spectator response and emphasizes
the actor's victimization.

By unpacking Dandridge's "persona"[29] through 1950s racial politics and
notions of primitivism, Rippy backgrounds other variables in the reading
of performance. She backgrounds *class* as a social category for interpreting

the star's major films. In so doing, historians and scholars omit patterns of star consumption and the ways black critics and audiences might have responded to and consumed Dorothy Dandridge. Recall that the 1950s marked the instantiation of the black American as a consumer recognized by the consumer-product industry sector. Stars were not only bodies on display providing ideals of feminine beauty—they were also utilized to sell products, particularly to female spectators.

I want to move beyond these studies—and the Baldwinian approach— by revisiting the biographies, scholarship, and public discourse circulating around Dorothy Dandridge's star persona. The conversations around her stardom demonstrate that her "charismatic appeal"[30] was a function of both her class position vis-à-vis the newly emerging black middle class, and her socially constructed sexuality tossed amid the rising tide of regulatory sexual discourse. This includes, but moves beyond, physicality as a basis for analyzing Dandridge's celebrity. It involves (1) considering extratextual industrial issues and (2) sociological dynamics of class as they informed her persona. We ought to interpret her sexualized charisma as a function of the intersection of race, gender, and class dynamics. Therefore, I view Dandridge's celebrity in terms of sexual appeal but by also taking class into account as a key variable in the construction of beauty and—by extension—sexual desirability. In focusing on class(ed) constructions of beauty and desirability, we follow the legacy of Roland Barthes to consider how celebrities enable people to mask awareness of themselves as class members, reconstituting social differences in the audience into a new polarity: pro-star versus anti-star.

Dandridge: Representative Black Beauty

In a comprehensive study of postmortem recollections of a film star, S. Paige Baty discusses the way celebrities can be viewed as *representative characters* (through which we approach the political and cultural conditions of our time) and as mass-mediated characters through which multiple meanings, references, and roles are remembered.[31] A representative character is a kind of symbol. It is a figure through which people in a given social environment organize and give meaning and direction to their lives. Representative characters are not only icons or symbols, they can be products or commodities that consumers purchase when they buy a magazine, watch a movie, or listen to music.

Dorothy Dandridge was a representative character. As the first black female movie star she was an altogether unique and unprecedented cultural phenomenon: a glowing figure of legend and glamour.[32] Despite Dandridge's controversial roles, she presented a bourgeois ideal, a point of reference and focus that gave living expression to a vision of life. As a result, she became a focal point of discussions in the black community about black beauty, femininity, middle-class aspirations, and upward mobility. Thus a component of Dandridge's success entailed the black community's consumption of her (and figures like Nat King Cole, Sidney Poitier, Harry Belafonte, Bill Cosby, Lena Horne, Eartha Kitt, and Abbey Lincoln) as representative of black bourgeois identity.

In fixing beauty types, stars define *norms of attractiveness.*[33] More prominently than her sisters in cinema, Dandridge solidified a public persona of respectable, black bourgeois womanhood, feminine beauty, and domesticity. Hers was an image that helped define, for a given group of people, what kinds of feminine traits, comportment, and public performance of womanhood were appropriate and fashionable to develop. In defining norms, standards, and behaviors with which audiences identify, stars become representative figures. As representatives, they are not only icons, they are also products and/ or commodities providing indexes of the metamorphosing body of political representation—the changing contours of the body politic itself as effected through the media.[34] Like her Euro-American counterparts (Rita Hayworth, Marilyn Monroe) Dandridge performed a specific function for black women spectators. She represented the dominant culture's ideal concept of black femininity, thereby playing a key role in the processes of identity formation.[35]

Dandridge's impact has been so broad that we still find traces of her persona in the self-fashioning and film roles of contemporary celebrities like Oprah Winfrey, Halle Berry, and Beyoncé Knowles. Actress Halle Berry has claimed Dandridge was her role model. Nowhere was this personal and professional self-fashioning more evident than in Berry's decision to produce (and star in) HBO Pictures' *Introducing Dorothy Dandridge* (released August 21, 1999). Publicity for the television special emphasized the physical similitude, the supposed spiritual connection, and the professional parallels between Dandridge and Berry. This publicity began at least two years prior to the film's television debut. For instance, in 1997 *Ebony* magazine ran a cover story captioned "Who Should Play the Tragic Star?" The list of potential actresses included almost every major celebrity, including Janet Jackson, Whitney Houston, Vanessa Williams, Jasmine Guy, Angela Bassett, and Berry, with Houston and Berry as frontrunners. But *Ebony* publicity favored Berry. It even included quotes offering Berry as the obvious first choice for the role. Take the following quotation from Dandridge's childhood friend Geraldine Branton as a typical example. According to *Ebony,* Branton said: "It will take

Dandridge was the image of glamour, beauty, and refinement.

a special actress to pull this off. She will have to be outstandingly beautiful and possess a vulnerability that very few people have . . . Halle Berry is nearly as beautiful and has shown some vulnerability. But the portrayal of Dorothy could be the toughest job for any actress."[36]

Evidence of Dandridge's representativeness can also be found in the self-fashioning of Oprah Winfrey. Winfrey has—to some extent—emulated aspects of Dandridge's star persona in an attempt to represent a similar brand of bourgeois comportment, those techniques of self-enhancement that Dandridge mastered (exercise, diet, hairstyling, fashion, and glamour).

Winfrey's most public attempt at such self-fashioning came with the production and release of *Beloved*, during which she presented herself as an alluring film actress, starring in a major Hollywood picture. In publicity stills for *Beloved*, she appeared in *Vogue* and *Woman's Day* dressed in ball gowns, coiffed and made up to look remarkably similar to Dorothy Dandridge. The *Vogue* layout not only revealed the impact of Dandridge on an already popular television talk-show host, it demonstrated the difference between visual codes for television and film stardom. Whereas TV stars dress to project the image of the everyday woman, the film star dresses to project an ideal of womanhood, an ideal to which women are expected to aspire. Embedded in Oprah Winfrey's self-fashioning as a film star are vestiges of the Dandridge discourse of representative beauty.

The film *Carmen Jones* and actress Dorothy Dandridge have had an impact on younger celebrities like Beyoncé Knowles. In 2001, Robert Townsend directed the MTV movie *Carmen: A Hip Hopera*, a contemporary remake of the 1950s version. The film starred Beyoncé Knowles as Carmen and Mekhi Phifer as Sergeant Derrick Hill, the corollary to Harry Belafonte's Joe. It also featured Mos Def as Frank Miller, an updated version of the character Husky Miller portrayed by actor Joe Adams in 1954. Though conceptually based on Prosper Mérimée's novel and Bizet's opera, this Def Jam audience film owed its greatest debt to the all-black-cast production. It modernized the story and setting by placing the fateful couple in urban rather than in rural America. It utilized the hip-hop style and vernacular trendy among youth audiences/consumers. And it featured two mainstream artists, reigning diva Beyoncé Knowles and hip-hopper turned actor Mos Def. It seems fair to say that Dandridge—and the films she starred in—were representative. She was a mass-mediated character through which multiple meanings, references, and roles are remembered.

Dandridge's Charisma

The notion of representative characters dovetails with Max Weber's notion of charisma. For Weber, a charismatic person is someone other people follow because of his or her individual qualities (i.e., strength, intelligence, beauty). "Charisma may be of two types: primary charisma is a gift that inheres in a person simply by virtue of natural endowment. Secondary charisma is produced artificially."[37] Dandridge's charisma was the composite of primary (i.e., innate gifts) and secondary (i.e., rehearsed effort, industry enhancement) talents. It was the intersection of physical endowments and the manufactured charisma produced by routine commercialism and publicity.

Dorothy Dandridge was both an entertainment charismatic *and* a representative character. She earned these distinctions because she represented the image of black beauty and womanhood African American audiences idealized. In this respect, she was more successful than Eartha Kitt at earning audience admiration and identification. Kitt was a charismatic entertainer but not a representative idol. Kitt cultivated a more political and polemical persona (i.e., one misunderstood by segments of the black public). As a consequence, she was perceived as iconoclastic, controversial, and self-absorbed. She rebuffed automatic or facile identification with the African American community.[38] An uncompromising individualist and international performer, Kitt viewed herself as a global citizen and a gifted cosmopolite rather than merely an African American celebrity. She thereby disrupted the identificatory relationship and feelings of reciprocity between herself and black audiences. She enjoyed more personal freedoms from accountability to the black communities but paid for these freedoms by limiting her fan base.

Dandridge, on the other hand, learned from childhood that she would suffer for failing to uphold shared standards of behavior and feminine propriety. Geneva Williams, her mother's longtime companion, abused Dandridge as a child. Referred to as Neva, Geneva raised Dorothy and her sister Vivian. She was given control of the girls and allowed to discipline them however she chose (Mills, 1970; Donald Bogle, 1997). As the sisters grew and entered puberty, Neva, whom they called "Ma-Ma," became obsessed with the girls' virginity, or the loss thereof. Daily, Williams pulled Dorothy aside, forced her to remove her upper garments, and then tightly bound up the girl's budding breasts with heavy muslin cloth.

> Apparently, paranoid that Dottie might be in the same [pregnant] predicament, Ma-Ma wanted proof that the teenager was untouched. Dottie protested that she had done nothing. But Ma-Ma was not satisfied. As Dottie lay on the bed, Neva suddenly lifted Dorothy's dress and ripped off her undergarments in order to examine her vaginally. Dorothy was shocked and frightened, unable to understand Ma-Ma's behavior. Having been taught to obey and respect this woman she felt emotionally paralyzed and unable to defend herself . . . Ma-Ma pushed her back on the bed and then forcibly examined her.[39]

Similar to other entertainers, her individual charismatic talents grew out of emotional difficulties and her personal desire to transcend the trauma of her youth. In this respect, she shares the personal profile of other entertainment charismatics (i.e., Billie Holiday, Elvis Presley, Marilyn Monroe, John Lennon, and Oprah Winfrey) whose experiences of childhood trauma were linked later in life—by their own admission—to hopes for fame and a desire to overcome early-life adversities. Within film studies, star analysis has presented considerable evidence that many film stars share the experience of having had an absent, or inconsequential, father figure. A large percentage of stars suffered decidedly unstable childhoods during formative years.[40] Out of the adversity of early life, many of these celebrities have fashioned a charismatic persona.

For example, Marilyn Monroe experienced the sensation of belonging to the universe as the first intimation of her charismatic appeal. In her autobiography, *My Life* (1974), she described herself as belonging to nobody and everyone at the same time, finding "the public" was her only home. Her admission that she belonged to the public ("because I had never belonged to anything else") was literally true, as she had been raised on public funds virtually from birth. Born Norma Jean Mortensen in Los Angeles in 1926, she never knew her father and hardly saw her mother, who was an institutionalized schizophrenic. She is one of many stars whose individual charisma grew out of a union between emotional difficulties and personal desires to transcend the trauma of youth. David Aberbach's description of Monroe's celebrity readily pertains to Dandridge. Aberbach writes:

> Her charismatic appeal seems to have emanated from the aura of public availability which surrounded her and which she cultivated . . . Her luscious persona belonging to the ocean and the sky and the whole world was largely her own creation, the blend of sexual allure, wit and pathos, the product of much calculation and art. She spent hours each day in front of mirrors with lipstick, powders and mascara. "There is not a single movement" she said, "not a single inflection in a line that I haven't learned by myself, working it over a thousand times" (Lembourn, 1979). She spoke of "the face that I've made," a face and an image she did not believe to be naturally beautiful but which she virtually willed into being. She transcended her roles, using them as showcases for moments of child-like wistful radiance, innocence and freshness. She was tragic and suggestive of unfathomable disturbance yet sweetened this image with physical beauty and the honey of sex. Her roles are memorable not for themselves as much as for her screen persona, and the fascination of her persona does not lie in the acting, fine as it often is, but in the hints of the real, vulnerable creature behind the mask.

Aberbach might easily have been discussing Dandridge's celebrity persona, since it was similarly moving yet equally rehearsed. It was the combination of self-invention, sexual allure, American racial pathos, careful calculation, and artistry. But it was her physical attributes that garnered the most attention and marked her as representative sign. More prominently than her predecessors, Dandridge fixed a physical image of black feminine beauty.

During the height of the studios' golden era (1929–60), Hollywood determined the standards of beauty for black, white, and Asian and Latina actresses. Lighter-skinned African American women like Fredi Washington were believed to be "mulatto."[41] Consequently, they had difficulty securing roles playing either black or white characters. Issues of representative skin complexion and norms of black attractiveness were passionately debated in Negro communities and black entertainment periodicals throughout the 1940s and 1950s. Take for example the article by New York's *Amsterdam News* staff writer Dan Burley. Writing for the *Philadelphia Tribune* under a pseudonym, Burley argued in defense of underrepresented lighter-skinned Negro entertainers: actors, singers, and dancers. Here he challenged use of disparaging colloquialisms like "high yellow," a vernacular term for lighter-skinned blacks.

> It is undeniable that the ban on the mulatto and those persons who can be identified as "high yaller" has been and is still unfair, cruel and grossly insulting. Many competent performers, some with Hall of Fame potentialities, are barred from show-world heights only because the white people who pay the bills want to see only those Negroes of whom they are sure. Although they have as much, if not more to contribute to the entertainment world, as any other members of the vari-colored conglomeration labeled as "Negro," the mulatto has been successfully discriminated against in amusement fields right down the line . . . Hollywood has never been brought around to see Fredi Washington advanced on a basis of her magnificent portrayal of the light-skinned daughter of Louise Beavers in *Imitation of Life*.[42]

Burley's arguments contrast markedly with the privilege historically associated with, and bestowed upon those with, lighter skin. Historically, lighter skin tones have been privileged and valued over darker complexions in both white and black communities.[43] This is an age-old issue with origins in the political economy of American slavery. There are longstanding critiques of this class conditioning in African American studies: in sociology (i.e., W. E. B. Du Bois's *The Souls of Black Folk*), in literature (i.e., James Weldon Johnson's *Autobiography of an Ex-Colored Man*),[44] in social psychology (i.e., Frantz Fanon's *Black Skin, White Masks*), and in some of the earliest black independent films (Oscar Micheaux's *The Homesteader*). The hotly debated issue of color and representativeness relates to assessments of Dandridge's physicality. The literature on Dandridge repeatedly cited her complexion as one of her most remarkable physical assets, as she was believed to possess the desirable complexion.

> Through her childhood, her skin color (which friends and associates in later years described in different ways) went from a deep burnt yellow to a startling golden brown, close to Vivian's but somehow richer, neither dark nor extremely light. "It was pure *café au lait*," said Dorothy's friend Geri Branton, "absolutely gorgeous." Her skin also would take to lights, camera filters, and makeup extraordinary well, and she would be blessed, like most great film stars, in having the type of beauty that could be heightened with makeup. During this era when light skin, keen features, and straight hair were valued in both Black and White America, Ruby considered the girls' complexions a blessing.[45]

Conversely, there were also those who maintained her skin was too fair to represent African Americans. Some believed she was not black enough. Take Nichelle Nichols's comments on attitudes toward Dandridge during the shooting of *Porgy and Bess* (1959) as one example.

> At that time, Dorothy Dandridge's delicate beauty was out of sync with the Black response . . . I think because she had very Caucasian features and a delicate body and a delicate demeanor she was made to feel she was not Black enough by people who were jealous of her, by some people on the picture who were jealous and by some people just in general who were jealous.[46]

Such comments exemplify how skin tone factored in discussions of black stardom and in norms of attractiveness as representative. From the spectators' comments, peer reflections, the black press, and her biographies we can extrapolate the significance of her physicality. Dandridge was considered beautiful because she provided an image of acceptable African American beauty that both white and black audiences accepted. But when placed alongside her contemporaries Lena Horne and Eartha Kitt, a socially constructed ("café au lait") paradigm of representative black feminine beauty—for which there was appeal—emerges.

Problematically, this paradigm narrowly defines acceptable notions of attractiveness. What's more, the archetype continues to inform standards of beauty in contemporary popular culture, as many of the recognizable marquee names of black performers are either biracial beauties or women of fair complexion (i.e., Halle Berry, Beyoncé, Jennifer Beals, Veronica Webb, Thandie Newton, Rosario Dawson, Alicia Keys, Mariah Carey). These women personify the Brazilian beauty standard, confirming what Robert Stam—in his work on syncretism—has called the "Brazilianization of American popular culture." Whereas a symbolic mulatto like Dandridge was once considered light-skinned by African American standards, her contemporary counterparts like Halle Berry are the celebrated icons of mainstream popular culture. The symbolic mulatto (or mixed woman) who once embodied the infamy of miscegenation now signifies the harmony of multicultural diversity.

One consequence of Euro-American colonial conquest is that greater economic value has historically been ascribed to lighter-skinned complexions. Light skin and aquiline facial features have long been concomitants of social mobility, or signifiers of racial pedigree, or interpreted as indicators of class status, especially for women in Western patriarchal cultures. Colorism, analogous to Gayatri Spivak's notion of "chromatisms," has been an issue throughout the African diaspora as a consequence of colonialism. Former slaves and colonized persons were subjugated to European aesthetic philosophies of beauty.[47] Frantz Fanon argued that centuries of color-caste conditioning and socialization resulted in black self-consciousness as a self-negating activity. He asserted the indoctrination of black self-denial manifested as a "corporeal malediction"[48] in which greater value was attached to lighter, whiter physiognomies.

Some social scientists claim the desire for lighter skin is nearly universal. Throughout Central and South America, Asia, and even Africa, society is prejudiced against those with dark skin, especially dark women.[49] The overvaluing of light skin and straight hair exists because it has been presented as the dominant aesthetic worldwide. Ella Shohat and Robert Stam point to the way idealized European beauty standards have been dispersed throughout the world. For Shohat and Stam, these standards "explain why *morena* women in Puerto Rico, like Arab-Jewish women in Israel, dye their hair blond, why Brazilian TV commercials are more suggestive of Scandinavia than the Black-majority country, why "Miss Universe" contests can elect blonde "queens" even in North African countries and why Asian women perform cosmetic surgery in order to appear more Western."[50] Self-estrangement from one's own body is partially a result of the mainstream media's dissemination of a hegemonic esthetic inherited from colonialist discourse.[51] Because skin color has long been synonymous with class status, it is easier to understand why Dandridge's complexion became a concomitant of her physical capital.

The social construction of Dandridge as a bourgeois beauty is also evident in the extradiegetic realm of publicity. In the black fanzine *Our World* she was described as "This nut brown singer with a lush body and a great lady manner, [who] has become the Queen of the country's swank Supper

Clubs."[52] Here she is scripted as the sign-bearing, sign-wearing body that in turn produces signs of black bourgeois comportment. It is difficult to view her films (or the public and scholarly discussions circulating around her stardom) without considering the significance of her complexion, the emphasis on her gracefulness, her characters' narrative struggles for respectability, and her conduct in manners. To this end, I spend the remainder of this chapter discussing the public conversations around her physicality and her film performances. These public conversations and movies reveal her communication of, and ability to signify, black bourgeois womanhood.

Reading black fan magazines from the 1950s, we gain a sense of how Dandridge was discussed and consumed by some black spectators, and of how her beauty was constructed as dignified, as elegant, as signifying bourgeois refinement. We also gain a critical sense of what Robyn Wiegman, in her research on race and gender, dubbed "black women's simulation of a white bourgeois womanhood."[53] I recognize the usefulness of Wiegman's analysis for discussing racial stereotypes in film. However, she uses the expression "black women's simulation of white bourgeois womanhood" without exploring its meaning and without suggesting black middle-class womanhood might have political significance or historical specificity. Nowhere is there exploration of why black women sought to achieve and maintain a standard of socially valued womanhood. Nor is there discussion of the way middle-class identity shielded men and women from the disciplinary surveillance of a white racist gaze in a racial state, thereby mitigating encounters with discrimination.

According to Evelyn Higginbotham, black bourgeois womanhood has been constructed—in part—out of a desire to be accorded the respectability, dignity, and courtesy more readily accorded white women in public spaces. Higginbotham provides a more nuanced discussion of black bourgeois womanhood. She charts organizations like the Woman's Convention, which was first formed in 1900 as an appendage of the National Baptist Convention. The Women's Convention opposed the social structures and symbolic representations of white supremacy through the "politics of respectability." The women's movement of the black Baptist Church emphasized reform of individual behavior and attitudes as a goal and a strategy for reform of the entire structural system of American race relations.[54] She points out that the women's movement in the black Baptist Church reflected and reinforced the hegemonic values of white America, as it simultaneously subverted and transformed the logic of race and gender subordination.

Discussing stardom, fanzines, and star biographies in the context of black bourgeois identity broadens our understanding of Dandridge's persona in two ways. First, it helps us understand the historical specificity of her celebrity: what might be considered stereotypical today was viewed differently by 1950s audiences. Second, it is also a matter of understanding that black stars knew their stardom as bittersweet, if not altogether oxymoronic. Dandridge knew her celebrity involved playing multiple roles: as an American, as a Negro, as a bourgeois woman, and as a historically gendered subject whose body signified the sexual excesses projected onto the black female body by a white patriarchal visual economy.[55] Chief among the many African American publications engaged in multifaceted discussions of her stardom were *Ebony*, *Our World: A Picture Magazine for the Whole Family*, and *Negro Digest*, to name but a few.

Black Fanzines: *Ebony, Our World,* and *Negro Digest*

Several of the black publications that cropped up after World War II reflected the new sense of optimism felt by many African Americans. After all, it was the black press (i.e., the *Pittsburgh Courier*, the *Amsterdam News*, the *Chicago Defender, The People's Voice*) that helped foster a collective political identity between 1827 and 1945. It was the black press that created the design of an eagle sitting on a banner that read: "Double Victory," calling for democracy at home and abroad. So black-issue oriented publications were essential to public and political discourse. Black-themed magazines would take this role one step further. These innovative magazines were an important phenomenon—a vital source for changing appraisals of beauty, identity, and lifestyle. They were founded in response to the emancipating effects the war had had on blacks for whom the magazines were intended.[56] Amid the post–World War II culture of consumption, advertisers began aggressively cultivating a black consumer market.[57] By the 1960s, *Ebony* enjoyed a striking expansion in sales and in page upon page of upmarket advertising, largely resulting from efforts to reach the black consumer.

Owned by a black family and produced by a mixed staff (of which blacks were a majority), *Ebony* boasted a readership of five million by the end of the 1950s. According to historian Arthur Marwick, the quality of the writing and photojournalism was relatively high; the tone was liberal, commonsense, strongly in favor of black civil rights, and deeply proud of black achievements within American society. The magazine epitomized the ideology of "the New Negro." For example, a 1956 editorial praising the Montgomery bus boycott organized by Reverend Ralph D. Abernathy emphasized the emergence of a new black community, empowered by its collective use of capital. Marwick notes that ten years later, in November 1965, in an article on what it called its "nativity," *Ebony* set out its position within the context of the slowly changing economic position of black Americans.

To "accent the positive" as *EBONY* has done, is to give Negro America a sorely needed psychic lift. Nowhere is this lift more in evidence today than in the advertisements of high caliber, which it has attracted to its pages within the last decade. When *EBONY* first began publication, it had never occurred to most national manufacturers of commodities, which millions of Negroes as well as whites buy, to place advertisements in Negro publications. When major firms did advertise in the Negro press, which was very seldom, it never crossed their minds to use Negro faces in the ads, or to picture black youngsters eating nation brand cereals, or colored people riding in an automobile, be it Ford or Lincoln, or buying a soft drink for their children. Now in *EBONY* there are strikingly beautiful ads of Negroes doing all these things.

Look at the handsome young brownskin couple extolling the delights of Coca Cola in full-page color, or the good-looking young Negro in the "Camel Time" ad, the stunning brown girl smoking a Newport, and those wholesome Negro families pictured getting into sleek shining cars. Twenty years ago, to expect to see such advertisements in a colored magazine would have been unthinkable. In the field of the American commercial, *EBONY* has been as much pioneer as was brownskin Matt Henson when he became the first man to set foot on the North Pole. That *EBONY* can now afford not only to have color covers, but feature articles *in color* inside the magazine is due to its determined and dogged assault on the white battlements of Madison Avenue advertising. It was not easy to make "the walls come tumbling down." But they did. Result: now even the *New York Times, Life,* and *The New Yorker* picture Negro models in ads—not of the once popular "ham what am" variety either.

Five years after the birth of *EBONY*, its publisher presented a series of authenticated facts to the advertising agencies that helped open their eyes to the dollar value of the Negro market. Nine out of ten *EBONY* readers carried life insurance. Four out of ten *EBONY* readers owned cars. Two out of ten in 1950 possessed television sets, and the same percentage bought pianos. One out of four had graduated from college and were potential culture buyers. *EBONY* had its circulation authenticated by the Audit Bureau of Circulations, and its contents indexed in the *Readers' Guide to Periodical Literature*. The result is that today *EBONY*'s advertising is voluminous, the format of the ads most attractive and, if they were to be one hundred per cent visually believed, *all* Negro Americans are good looking. Typical example, the charming *café au lait* couple at their lovely dining table advertising simplicity patterns. To see ourselves presented so handsomely in commercial advertising (which now has spread to other national publications) is a great positive achievement due to *EBONY*.[58]

The rhetoric of consumerism here is determined by the logic of American capitalism. It is a logic linking black consumer power and black cultural citizenship. What's remarkable is the extent to which the consumer-as-citizen ideology echoes or paraphrases the rhetoric of civil rights. Both are narratives involving the ideology of inclusion, the quest for fair treatment and equal access to opportunity. Whereas minority inclusion was not considered seriously elsewhere in mainstream culture, a variety of black periodicals wed civil rights principles to the discourse of the American dream. Here, in these magazines, African Americans are scripted as subjects deserving *inclusion in images,* the *right to civil treatment* in the shopping center, and an *equal opportunity to spend.* Unfortunately, commercial advertising is at odds with political protest. Advertising promotes a consuming vision, a consumptive lifestyle, and ultimately reduces social protest and social change. The dual functions of advertising consist of promoting consumption as an alternative to protest and turning alienation into a commodity.[59]

The same rhetoric of "inclusion," "rights," and "equal opportunity" influenced the coverage of the star system in black periodicals. The fanzines, for example, were imbued with the optimism of the era yet cognizant of American racism. They are one venue through which we can understand the oxymoronic nature of black stardom in the 1950s, the individual black star's relationship to African American spectators, and the star itself as a kind of commodity.

In 1954, *Ebony* ran several articles about the struggles of Negro models striving to "make it" in the fashion world. One article—titled "Can Negro Models Make the Big-Time?"—described how African American women had begun to receive more jobs in mainstream art, fashion, and advertising modeling. The author writes:

> The best that the average colored model could hope for prior to 1944 was an occasional stipend for posing as a servant in an ad. A non-white fashion model was indeed a rare bird. Today the picture has changed remarkably. More and better jobs have become available to Negro beauties in art, fashion and advertising modeling and there are straws in the wind that predict that colored models will someday be completely integrated at the top levels . . . Probably the most significant development today is that some white firms are hiring Negro models to display their products to white people . . . Modeling

fees for Negroes have risen along with the increased demand for their services. Five years ago, the average hourly pay to a Negro model was $5. Today, the average is $10, and a few earn $25.[60]

Elsewhere in the article, the author laments the paucity of black women currently able to earn enough money to make modeling a full-time career but emphasizes the gradual changes under way in the industry. Articles about the fashion industry ran alongside articles about the film and television industries. In 1955, *Ebony* ran an article captioned, "Do Negroes Have a Future in Hollywood?" It was similarly optimistic in its account of the gradual changes taking place in the film industry and cited Dandridge's successes as an example of the changing attitude toward colored actors.

> Almond-eyed Jeanna Limyou, *Ebony*'s alluring cover girl, is a sun-bronzed California teenager with a face and figure that could stop traffic on the Pennsylvania Turnpike. Only 17 years old, Jeanna is one of the most charming and talented youngsters in the new crop of Negro lassies seeking fame in motion pictures. Conceivably, her break could come soon for Hollywood is changing its attitude toward Negro actors and actresses. Movie people who only a decade ago would not dream of giving a Negro performer the "big build up" are doing an about face that holds real promise for the Negro stars of the future. Dorothy Dandridge got the glamour treatment in the highly successful (it grossed $5 million) *Carmen Jones* and both Dorothy and Lena Horne are in line for other good roles.[61]

This article and others articles like it positioned Dandridge as a representative character, as one who achieved an unprecedented level of exposure, glamour, and success. Hers was the career pattern and physical type young aspirants (like Jeanna Limyou) sought to emulate. She was the signifier that made black bourgeois womanhood visible. Dandridge and her contemporaries provided the context in which Limyou's "sun-bronzed" complexion became a primary feature of feminine pulchritude, a prized asset of physical capital.

The fanzines reveal that black women who sought to imitate her and to produce themselves as entertainment commodities admired Dandridge's career. Through feminine identification with Dandridge, spectators were encouraged to view themselves as potential models, actresses, and stars—thus as potential cultural products. This positioning of Dandridge lends credence to my claim that those black women film stars (i.e., Lena Horne, Dorothy Dandridge, Abbey Lincoln, and Cicely Tyson) were feminine idols even though black spectators recognized the profound limitations of their film roles. Nowhere was her physicality more closely linked to a commodified black bourgeois womanhood than in *Ebony*. Take for example the 1962 cover story captioned "The Private World of Dorothy Dandridge." A standard star layout, it places Dandridge at home amid beautiful housewares, domestic amenities, and accoutrements of material success. Clearly, the image of domestic perfection is being sold to black consumers. Robinson's article presented her as the picture of fame and a representative character. She is both extraordinary and part of everyday life.

> *A performer at five.* The scene opens with the star of the show: a honey-colored, brown-eyed beauty of surprising slimness and indeterminate youth. Clad in tailored slacks and bulky over-blouse. She sweeps down a winding stairway and into a sunken living room to extend her hand in greeting to a visitor . . . Except for the fact that her face would be instantly recognizable to millions, there is nothing in the scene which suggests that this is the private world of Dorothy Dandridge, one of the great beauties of our time, a sex symbol to magazine editors the world over, and Hollywood's first authentic love goddess of color.[62]

This is one example of how her complexion and physique were linked—in star discourse—to notions of black exceptionality, erotic sexuality, and a bourgeois lifestyle. This discourse portrays her as sharing the simple desires of the common citizen (home, domesticity, the American "good life") yet celebrates the qualities setting her apart from the average citizen.[63]

This type of promotion exposes a tension in celebrity discourse. Accommodating both the extraordinary and the everyday, star discourse must resolve domesticity and commercialized sexuality. But this tension was not particular to African American stars of the 1950s. It was an issue for Rita Hayworth and her contemporaries in the 1940s. And it appears to have been an issue more recently for young white celebrities like Jennifer Aniston and Brad Pitt. Star discourse reveals the material construction of sexuality. It discloses the way in which all sexual leisure and lifestyles ultimately become colonized by consumer culture. Such discourse deploys coded messages to further the commercialization of all commodity forms.[64] Star discourse creates a chain of signifiers linking sexuality and the body with the social and material accoutrements of bourgeois lifestyle and desirability.

The recognition of black and bronzed beauty (something we cannot take for granted) in American film contributed to a sentiment of optimism regarding the possibility of gradual institutional change. Trailing Jeanna Limyou's story, *Ebony* ran an article captioned, "Public Disapproval Ends Era of Uncle Tom Casting," followed by another story headlined, "Negro Market Is Too

Large to Offend." Citing the growing numbers of black moviegoers, the writer of the second article claimed surveys revealed as many as 3½ million blacks attending movie houses each week. Implicit in these stories and their headlines is a sense of optimism.

> The trend in Hollywood today is toward integrated casts. The pattern, Louella [Parsons] says, was set five years ago when Stanley Kramer filmed *Home of the Brave*, a controversial race theme movie about a mixed Army unit in which James Edwards had a key role. The picture set off a cycle of racial problem pictures, which opened the way for later films (*Unchained, The Egyptian, The Robe, The Ten Commandments, The Black Widow*) in which Negroes were given parts in which no attention was called to their color at all. They simply became "human beings."[65]

Such articles revealed the naive optimism embedded in the rhetoric of integration. Throughout black communities, moviegoers believed that once Hollywood integrated its movies, American society might follow. Obviously, this never happened and the optimism was false hope—as noted by Henry Louis Gates Jr. in Marlon Riggs's seminal documentary on the history of television, *Color Adjustment.* Nonetheless, articles in *Ebony, Our World, Sepia,* and *Cue* propagated the rhetoric of integration without questioning how this discourse promoted the misguided notion of "colorblindness." Implicit in the liberal ideology of colorblindness is the false notion that blackness is a handicap progressive whites should graciously overlook. It implies African Americans must undergo "de-negrification"[66] to be accepted by mainstream spectators. Some writers maintained that to be taken seriously by Hollywood, black actors needed to embrace the "assimilationist imperative," a euphemism that in effect meant cease being African American and start signifying the universal humanity associated with Euro-American subjectivity. In fact, this is precisely what actor Sidney Poitier attempted in films like *No Way Out* (1950), *Paris Blues* (1961), *Lilies of the Field* (1963), *Patch of Blue* (1965), *To Sir with Love* (1967), *In the Heat of the Night* (1967), and *Guess Who's Coming to Dinner* (1967).

However, this call for black actors to emphasize their transcendental humanity and downplay their historical blackness was articulated on screen (almost exclusively) in terms of blacks seeking relationships with whites and in terms of the taboo of miscegenation. One of the only American-made films of this era to escape the double bind of representation and still depict African American subjectivity in terms of its humanity was Michael Roemer's *Nothing But a Man* (1964). But Roemer's film was released more than a decade after stars Dandridge and Horne made their first major screen appearances. Dorothy Dandridge, Eartha Kitt, Lena Horne, and their fans broke the ground that later became fertile soil for Roemer's work to thrive. Dandridge was integral to the newfound sense of black identification with media images and the newfound optimism discussed as a transitional stage in Hollywood.

Stars presented as transcendental figures could also be used to sell products to female spectators.[67] The sense of integration-era optimism and black consumer-citizenship—symbolized by the employment of these women— also helped sell cosmetics and feminine products advertised in fan magazines. The fan discourse circulating around their careers informed the sale of commodities to those women who wanted to participate in an imagined black bourgeois community. In her work on the social construction of beautiful white film stars, Jackie Stacey notes that the body-as-commodity was a venue used to sell white Hollywood starlets to spectators. One characteristic of consumption practices among spectators of the 1950s in relation to stars is the centrality of the female body.

Following Stacey, I am asserting that the black film star's body is a venue through which black feminine identity is marketed to spectators. It is sold as an idea and as the composite of a variety of products. Horne and Dandridge were sold to African American women spectators as the sign-bearing, sign-wearing ideals to be emulated. Copying their look meant consuming the right products: cosmetics, fashions, and hairstyles. The class-conditioning commodities included hair-straightening techniques, skin bleaching creams, feminine hygiene products, and makeup.[68] Such items were advertised in *Ebony* info-adverts extolling the virtues of douches, lotions, hair pomades, bleaching creams, and the like. Moreover, in selling these items, these magazines propagated narrowly defined concepts of black beauty.

Ebony actively propagated this narrow notion of black beauty, linked as it was to the cult of black celebrity. For example, the magazine ran a story with photographs of black female celebrities shot by French photographer Philippe Halsman. At the time, Halsman was one of *Life* magazine's top photographers. He took many covers for *Life,* including the then-recent color cover of Dorothy Dandridge. The *Ebony* article with Halsman's images was audaciously captioned: "The Five Most Beautiful Negro Women." It featured Lena Horne, Dorothy Dandridge, Hilda Simms, Joyce Bryant, and Eartha Kitt as they lay seductively in satin and silk nightgowns with plunging necklines. The short text read:

When *Ebony*'s editors met to select five women to sit for glamour photographer Philippe Halsman, the acknowledged master at capturing the beauty of women on film, quite a controversy developed. It seems that after Lena Horne and Dorothy Dandridge, there was very little agreement. After long and sometimes violent argument, all agreed to limit the group to beautiful entertainers and the five shown on these pages comprised the final selection. In appearance, they offer a fascinating physical range. One thing they have in common is a striking, though different beauty. Lena Horne, Dorothy Dandridge, Hilda Simms, Joyce Bryant and Eartha Kitt are five of the most beautiful and talented women in America today.

Following each star's photograph, commentary from Halsman appears. These comments were his ruminations on each star's unusual enigmatic character and individual sex appeal. However, the contradiction here is that while each woman selected supposedly represents a distinct beauty type, they all look remarkably similar in pose, facial features, skin complexion, and dress. Fanzines *Ebony* and *Our World* emphasized the similarity between their physical types. These publications distinguished between the starlets, but often only in a battle-of-the-beauty-queens standoff, positioning one celebrity as more sophisticated, genteel, and representative than others.

In June 1952, *Our World* ran a cover article on Dandridge titled "Can Dandridge Outshine Lena Horne?" This feature placed the celebrity accomplishments of Dandridge and Horne in competitive opposition. Such articles mimic the dominant mythology of stars as persons belonging to a charismatic family or clan upon whom unique talents and gifts have been bestowed. Implicit in these star narratives is the notion that charisma is transferable from one generation of a clan to the next.

In this mythology, a genealogical language of black royalty (i.e., pedigree, ancestry, and birthright) is employed. For example, the *Our World* article used such terms, emphasizing that although Horne was a singer of renown, Dandridge—born to actress Ruby Dandridge—was somehow more aptly suited for stardom because it was part of her heritage. I read this scripting of Dandridge by the black press as a significant part of the production of black bourgeois imagery, as an aspect of the manufacturing of black aristocracy out of black celebrity.

> In the opinion of most columnists, she is fast moving into first place, a spot long occupied by Lena Horne and unchallenged by anyone. Every big magazine has featured Dorothy. Because of her solid bookings in some of the best night spots, some show people think that Dorothy will outshine . . . She feels

that Lena is a great performer, but they are two distinct types . . . There is however, a striking resemblance between Dorothy and Lena. Both have the ability to wear clothes, are beautiful women and can sell sex with a song . . . If Dorothy Dandridge is finally able to outshine Lena Horne, it won't be a matter of chance. Show business is in Dorothy's blood. She was born into it. Her mother, Ruby Dandridge, currently a radio actress on the *Beulah* show, was an actress when Dorothy was born. Dorothy has always loved the spotlight and has been preparing for a theatrical career all her life . . . Lena has done almost everything in her field and Dorothy Dandridge knows that outshining the most popular Negro female song stylist is no mean feat. She is, however, willing to try, if it doesn't destroy her freedom.[69]

The rhetoric of "hereditary charisma,"[70] celebrity birthright, and competition are also in evidence. Here, as elsewhere, there is a class-specific positioning of Dandridge as a normative beauty, as genteel and patrician. The language of descent employed here parallels the dominant discourse around her complexion as a signifier of innate nobility. These discussions lend credence to my claim that as the reigning black female star of the 1950s, she was upheld as the image of idealized modern femininity and defined this identity for black spectators despite audience recognition of and resistance to her roles and characters as mediocre.

Dandridge on Film

Fan devotion to Dandridge was a result of the urbanity and modernity she projected through her womanhood. But it was not only in the public discourse of her stardom that we find discussion of her exceptionality and representative bourgeois womanhood. Her star vehicles also evince the recurring theme of her exceptionality.

In movies like *The Bright Road* (1953), *Island in the Sun* (1957), and *Tamango* (1958), for instance, her characters stand out as liminal.[71] The definition of *liminality* employed here is derived from Victor Turner and Kathleen Rowe. Turner uses the term *liminal* to describe things associated with transitions, margins, and thresholds. He writes, "All societies carve out spaces or times that exist on the edge of normal activities and that are marked by contradiction and ambiguity. Often dramatic or performative, these spaces and times allow a society to comment on itself through experimentation and play." Liminality is never a permanent state but exists in relation to dominant or indicative time. Liminality, which includes spaces and times situated at the edge of everyday activity, is a concept readily applicable to forms of entertainment like cinema. The cinematic narrative is a distinct dramatic and performative unit with specific spatial and temporal limitations or conditions. In it, we find characters, plots, metaphors, and events signifying various types of liminality.

Liminality provides a framework for contextualizing Dandridge's screen characters, which were often positioned at the interstices between two distinct, segregated realms: the black (or African American) community and the white (or largely Euro-American) community. Her characters were usually set apart from the larger black community and positioned as extremely beautiful, exceptionally sophisticated, or sexually desirable. As such, they were often set apart from the larger black proletarian masses. Most of the supporting black characters in her films were more brown-skinned in complexion and working-class in origin, and they were rarely romantically or sexually involved (i.e., in *Carmen Jones, Island in the Sun, Tamango*). In more than one of these films, Dandridge's physical body signifies a particular class distinction in the narrative world of the film.

Robert Lightning has made a similar observation about her characters. He argues, "Her outsider status is given an *intra*racial class aspect." Lightning notes how skin color functioned in the construction of Dandridge (and before her, Lena Horne) as representative of a "burgeoning black bourgeoisie."

> That Dandridge is promoted as a sex goddess is not merely a matter of her being attractive but of the particular type of beauty she exhibits . . . the color coding of black women in films as early as *Birth*: The dark-skinned mammy is non-sexual and nurturing, the lighter-skinned Lydia passionate and sexual, and almost every black glamour star (however briefly) has been of the latter type: a black woman who also meets European standards of beauty. One might expand upon the mulatto metaphor here to describe certain post-war black stars (Dandridge and Poitier) who exhibit traits satisfying to a white bourgeois audience (Dandridge's beauty, Poitier's middle-class-ness).[72]

Lightning asserts that certain black stars were deemed acceptable because they were culturally assimilated and physically attractive, therefore less threatening. Consequently, he reads Dandridge as a symbolic mulatto.[73] Problematically, however, this "symbolic mulatto" conceptualization of her cinematic persona functions to describe and decode her liminality in racial terms. It fails, for instance, to provide an analysis of Dandridge's persona in black-cast pictures like *Bright Road* (1953) and all-black-cast movies *Carmen Jones* (1954) and *Porgy and Bess* (1959).

In *Bright Road,* for example—one of three pictures Dandridge made with Harry Belafonte—she portrays a dedicated young schoolteacher. This film was MGM's first black-cast film in ten years. It featured only one white actor, Robert Horton, as a doctor. Focusing on a segregated and secluded black enclave, the film depicts an insulated world in which one small African American community thrives. It presents an idyllic image of childhood innocence, kindly teachers, and primary education at a rural schoolhouse. In the film, Dandridge was made up to appear unmistakably prim, proper, and pristine, for the role of one of the first black professional women characters in a studio film.

According to Bogle, MGM's makeup supervisor William Tuttle devised a new pancake makeup base to give her *more* color. Later *Ebony* journalist wrote that this had been done so that she will be readily recognized by audiences as a Negro teacher. She looked darkened, not greatly so, but not quite as natural as she was to look in her subsequent black & white films *The Decks Ran Red* and *Malaga.* Natural or not, the make-up base heightened her pristine beauty, according to Bogle. *Bright Road* is nonetheless an important

Dandridge as Jane Richards is the image of respectable womanhood in *The Bright Road* (1953).

film, one often ignored by film scholars like Rippy who tend to emphasize the way Dandridge's characters were victimized by a racist patriarchal discourse. Indeed this is accurate. Dandridge portrayed many women who were victimized by black and white men. But in *Bright Road,* the character and circumstances are quite different. If anything, *Bright Road* is a film that—in its innocence and gentle romance—prefigures *Nothing But a Man* (1964), with equally beautiful leads Ivan Dixon and Abbey Lincoln. In the narrative of *Bright Road,* Dandridge's costume, makeup, and self-sufficient character cannot be interpreted in terms of the "symbolic mulatto" metaphor or read as belonging to the classic black victim. Rather, she functions here as the embodiment of bourgeois womanhood. Therefore, Lightning's model does not provide a template for reading the narrative relationships between her characters and other African American characters.

Whereas white feminist film theory articulates gender masquerade in terms of costume (dress, lipstick, high-heeled shoes), props (purses, cigarettes), and physical space (spatial arrangements of domesticity and motherhood) that function as fetish objects negating the putative lack of woman, I view Dandridge's complexion, physiognomy, and class affiliations as the fetish objects that negated the threat of her supposed "difference," for white audiences. Colorism in the black community meant it also made her appealing to African American audiences because these signifiers allowed her to affect the dominant facade (or mask) of bourgeois femininity, thereby rendering her a sexual object. She was able to embody and signify the cultural capital of the black habitus partially because—as mentioned—light skin in black communities has historically signified class mobility.

In the films *Carmen Jones* (1954)[74] and *Porgy and Bess* (1959),[75] both directed by the acclaimed auteur Otto Preminger (who was also Dandridge's controlling lover), her eponymous characters Bess and Carmen are also intermediary figures. James Baldwin was cognizant of the relationship between color and class in Hollywood cinema—and in Dandridge's films particularly. He made the compelling argument that color cast(e)ing in *Carmen Jones* revealed the film's ideological structure and Dandridge's liminal place within it. For Baldwin, *Carmen* was one of the most explicit, self-conscious weddings of sex, color, and social value Hollywood had ever turned out.

> A movie is, literally a series of images, and what one *sees* in a movie can really be taken, beyond its stammering or misleading dialogue, as the key to what the movie is actually involved in saying . . . Dorothy Dandridge— Carmen—is a sort of taffy-colored girl, very obviously and vividly dressed,

but really in herself rather more sweet than vivid. One feels—perhaps one is meant to feel—that here is a very nice girl making her way in movies by means of a bad-girl part . . . Harry Belafonte is just a little darker and just as blankly handsome and fares very badly opposite her . . . Pearl Bailey is quite dark and she plays, in effect, a floozie. The wicked sergeant who causes Joe to desert the army . . .[76]

Though Dandridge's Carmen is blameworthy, Baldwin argues that there's a relationship between her light complexion (and costuming) and the narrative's treatment of her character. For him, the three leads are indefinably pitiable (i.e., "not after money or jewels but something else, causing them to be misunderstood by the more earthy types around them"). In this respect, Baldwin sees her exceptional characters as sitting between a proletarian blackness and a black identity marked as middle-class and more conflicted.

There is still another way in which Dandridge's characters (Carmen and Bess) may be interpreted as liminal. In the narratives, both were ostracized from the fictional black communities. In these films, Bess and Carmen are "fallen" women. They are women of avarice or ill repute. In these films Dandridge plays "the bad girl" punished (i.e., via rape, death, violence). These physical abuses are often the consequence of failing to submit to conventional regimes of work, domesticity, religiosity, and monogamy. Like Carmen, Bess stands at the interstice between bourgeois propriety and complete indecency. The pulchritude of her characters often buys them temporary freedom from conformity to the routines of everyday life. But these characters ultimately meet their demise. Carmen and Bess each feel entitled to more moral freedom, recreational excitement, and material goods than they're given.

Like *Carmen Jones*, *Porgy and Bess* provoked intellectuals, critics, and artists (i.e., James Baldwin, Harold Cruse, and Lorraine Hansberry) to debate its representation of African Americans. The representations of southern black folk culture in *Porgy and Bess* resulted in the opera—and the motion picture—becoming the subject of considerable controversy.[77] Yet the story of *Porgy and Bess* is straightforward. Set in Charleston, South Carolina, at the turn of the twentieth century in a small black enclave called Catfish Row, it tells of Porgy (Sidney Poitier), a crippled beggar who travels about in a goat-drawn cart and who falls in love with Bess, a woman of uncertain reputation who is under the domination of a stevedore named Crown (Brock Peters). Before *Porgy*, Peters had appeared in only one other film. In *Carmen Jones* he played Sergeant Brown, a foil to Belafonte's Joe. In *Porgy and Bess*, Peters's Crown kills a fellow Catfish Row dweller after a craps game erupts in brawl. He flees but returns later to collect Bess. Only now he must confront Porgy, a love-struck cripple who has fallen in love with Bess. When he kills Crown, Porgy is hauled off to jail and Bess is enticed to New York City by the flashy gambler Sportin' Life (Sammy Davis Jr.). At the end of the film—and the opera before it—Porgy is heading to New York to search for her. Here, Dandridge portrays a pawn in a game of male desire. She is a liminal figure who stands between respectability and impropriety. She offends respectable womanhood (by virtue of her association with Crown) yet upholds and respects family values (in her domestic arrangement with Porgy).

In 1967 historian Harold Cruse was chief among the films' critics. Cruse viewed the entire arts scene as a white-dominated misrepresentation of black culture, the epitome of which was George Gershwin's folk opera *Porgy and Bess*. He viewed the opera—and its manifestation as cinematic Americana—as at the heart of a debate about the civil rights movement and "civil writers" subordinating themselves to the cultural values of the white world. According to Cruse, these European values were used to negate the Negro cultural equality and exploit black culture. Cruse wrote:

> In May 1959, following the successful opening of *A Raisin in the Sun,* its author Lorraine Hansberry debated Otto Preminger on a television program in Chicago, over what she labeled the deplorable "stereotypes" of *Porgy and Bess*. The film version of the folk-opera had just been released . . . This was not the first time *Porgy and Bess* had been criticized by Negroes. Ever since its premiere in 1935, it has been under attack from certain Negro quarters because it reveals southern Negroes in an unfavorable light. Hence Miss Hansberry's criticisms were nothing new or original. What *was* new, however, were the times and the circumstances. Miss Hansberry objected to *Porgy and Bess* because stereotypes "constitute bad art" when "the artist hasn't tried hard enough to understand his characters." She claimed that although Gershwin had written a great musical score, he had fallen for what she called the exotic in American culture: "We, over a period of time, have apparently decided that within American life we have one great repository where we're going to focus and imagine sensuality and exaggerated sensuality, all very removed and earthy things—and this great image is the American Negro."[78]

During this debate Hansberry also complained about *Carmen Jones*. According to Cruse, Hansberry weakened her argument on the subject of "artistic integrity" by wanting to know why no whites had been cast in this caricature of *Carmen*. The entire muddled question of integration in the arts loomed largest. Cruse maintained that Hansberry's whole debate was a waste of time except from the viewpoint of making noisy, superficial, integrationist propaganda. "The real cultural issues surrounding *Porgy and Bess,* as it relates to the American Negro presence, have never been confronted by the Negro intelligentsia," wrote Cruse. To criticize any play involving black Americans purely on ideological content was not enough. Hansberry presented further proof of Cruse's contention that the creative black intellectual does not possess a cultural critique of his own art, or art created for him by whites. "Most Negro criticism of *Porgy,*" he wrote, "has been of middle-class origin; hence a generically class-oriented non-identification was inherent in Miss Hansberry's views."[79]

Cruse demonstrated bias in his criticism of Hansberry when he offhandedly dismissed black audiences for seeing these productions. He said as much by writing, "Needless to point out, the film *Porgy and Bess* had its Broadway and neighborhood run, and hundreds of working-class Negroes (whom Miss Hansberry claimed she wrote about in *Raisin*), lined up at the box offices to see this colorful film 'stereotype' of their people."[80] Nowhere in Cruse's reading is there discussion of audience agency, resistant spectatorship, or the significance of these films for working-class black audiences in terms of class aspirations. This is unfortunate because black audiences have historically resisted and vocally responded to visual spectacles. Black audience interaction with religious, communal, and cinematic spectacles is a matter I discuss in following chapters on Pam Grier and Whoopi Goldberg. This notion of passive spectatorship does not accurately characterize black cinematic spectatorship, which—according to Manthia Diawara—has been interactive, resistant, and subversive of dominant narrative ideology since the silent era. Furthermore, implicit in Cruse's commentary is the belief that working-class Negroes were pitifully ignorant of, or willfully blind to, racial stereotypes on screen.

Black audiences may have enjoyed aspects of these movies (i.e., Dandridge as icon) despite depictions of black folk culture. Audiences may have taken visual pleasure in the presence of black stars on screen—as the respondents to my questions suggested they did—despite the implausible limitations of these screen characters and narratives. Therefore, it is entirely possible that black audiences resisted aspects of these films and accepted others. This possibility is underscored by the contention that stars mask people's awareness of themselves as class members by reconstituting social differences in the audience into a new polarity: pro-star/anti-star. Regardless of film politics, African Americans enjoyed seeing Dandridge in the movies.

In *Island in the Sun,* based on Alec Waugh's novel, Dandridge portrays another liminal figure standing at the threshold between diametrically opposed groups: the black workers and the white planter class. Typical of 1950s Hollywood cinema, designed to bring back the declining audience, it exploited the sexual and racial taboos of the 1950s in a salacious tale of miscegenation, adultery, denial, and betrayal. The film is thematically similar to Hollywood's genre of hysterical prairie/plantation social problem melodramas like *Duel in the Sun* (1946), *Pinky* (1949), *Giant* (1956), *The Searchers* (1956), *Band of Angels* (1957), *Flaming Star* (1960), and *The Unforgiven* (1960), all of which exploited themes of gender, race, class, nation, miscegenation, citizenship, and land appropriation.

The blacklisted Robert Rossen directed *Island in the Sun,* which paralleled two interracial love stories set in the British West Indies. The film's producer, Darryl F. Zanuck, chose the island of Grenada to depict the fictitious Santa Marta Island of Waugh's novel. According to film historian Thomas Cripps, novelist Alec Waugh intended *Island* as "a Caribbean metaphor for American racial tensions, and 20th Century-Fox purchased it in the same spirit—as much a crusade as a moneymaker."[81] Not coincidentally, *Island in the Sun* was a financial success, returning significant capital on its investment. Audiences must have loved its tropical setting since, according to Cripps, it earned 20th's biggest profit since *The Robe.* Donald Bogle confirms the film's financial record, reporting that it "earned a then healthy $8 million, out-drawing *The King and I* in many of the spots where [it] opened."

The picture starred Joan Fontaine as the lithe Mavis Norman, a guilty, liberal-minded white aristocrat who falls in love with Harry Belafonte's physically dynamic David Boyeur, a labor organizer and political pundit who threatens white rule of Santa Marta. Mirroring David and Mavis's transgressive, transracial desire are Margot Seaton (Dorothy Dandridge), an island shop girl turned secretary, and the British character Denis Archer (John Justin). In the film, Julian Fleury and his wife (Basil Sydney and Diana Wynyard) have two adult children, Maxwell (James Mason) and Jocelyn (Joan Collins). Jocelyn falls in love with Ewen Templeton (Stephen Boyd), the son of the governor of Santa Marta, Lord Templeton (Ronald Squire). But when she learns, through the investigations of a visiting American journalist, that she has black blood in her ancestry, she refuses to marry Ewen but continues to see him. Maxwell uses his family name and reputation to stand for the legislative council, opposing the popular native-born trade union leader David Boyeur (Harry Belafonte).

At the end of the film, Margot and Dennis elope (off-camera) and leave for London. The other successful heterosexual union occurs when the biracial Jocelyn (Joan Collins)—who later learns she's really white—marries Ewen Templeton, the young, rich officer with an exotic past life in the Middle East.

Jocelyn's brother, Maxwell Fleury, and his wife are left behind, as is David Boyeur, who wins the election and subverts white political dominance. Mavis and David end their sexless affair with "a parting played as though carved in stone," wrote Cripps. David's reasons for dismissing Mavis's affections in favor of kith, kin, and countrymen are articulated in his cold good-bye speech to her: "My skin is *my* country. Maybe the men looking at Margo [Dandridge] at some cocktail party in Bloomsbury or at a literary tea, well they'd envy Dennis Archer. Their own wives look sort of dull when she walks into a room. But if I were to walk in with you, or a girl like you, well . . . You'd forget yourself and call me a nigger—no, this is my world." Thus while Dandridge's Margot and Collins's Jocelyn (the not-quite-white women seeking bourgeois respectability) escape the sugarcane and coconut agrarianism in favor of modernized Europe, Belafonte's labor organizer David Boyeur—and the other racially coded characters elect to stay behind. In the verbal and visual lexicon of *Island,* we find the discourse of Dandridge's color emerging yet again. Her complexion is the capital purchasing free movement between racially segregated communities. Dandridge's Margot is granted social privilege as a function of physical capital.

Tamango (1957) similarly places Dandridge's character in the interstice between two opposing worlds. She moves between the free white world of those who *possess* capital and the captive black world of those who *are* capital: between the slaves and the slave catchers. The film, based on Prosper Mérimée's short story, with a screenplay by Lee Gold and Tamara Hovey, recounts a slave revolt onboard a ship en route from the African Gold Coast to Havana, Cuba, in 1830. The film's narrative parallels the development of the two original male protagonists: the Dutch captain Reinker (Curt Jurgens), commander of the slave ship *Esperanza,* and the eponymous Tamango (Alex Cressan), a captured African and leader of the rebellion.

Throughout the film, Jurgens's aged Captain Reinker is a merciless European slaver who has taken Aiche (Dandridge) as his mistress. Initially, she tries to dissuade the slaves from rebelling. Dismissed by the other slaves as "the white man's trash," Aiche begins to question Reinker's devotion and the reality of her circumstances. Out of spite against Reinker—whom she now thinks is tiring of her—Aiche helps the slaves planning rebellion. Learning of the captain's counterattack, she tries to stop their uprising, and when she cannot, she elects to die with her people in a last desperate affirmation of the right of human freedom.

Throughout *Tamango,* Aiche functions as a narrative go-between: she traverses between slaves and freemen, the captain and Tamango, blacks and whites, the private (bedroom) and public (ship deck). She is the currency, or valuable tender of exchange, between communities, ideologies, identities, and domains of narrative space.

Significantly, director John Berry was blacklisted like Robert Rossen. Subsequent to his blacklisting, he directed a documentary titled *The Hollywood Ten* to raise funds for HUAC victims before moving to France. Two versions of the film were made. The film was an Italian-French coproduction. One version, made in France in the English language by Les Films du Cyclope, was distributed in the United States by Hal Roach Distributing Corp. The other version was made for American audiences.

Writing his review for *The Product Digest* in 1959, Vincent Canby wrote: "*Tamango* is full of the same kind of larger-than-life emotions which made another Mérimée piece so effective when adapted as the romantic and melodramatic opera, *Carmen*." The story may have been based on another Mérimée narrative, but Dandridge was reportedly unhappy with initial scripts. Bogle wrote that "once Dorothy read the script, she became incensed. Instead of a shipboard rebellion, *Tamango* seemed a shipboard sex drama, tawdry and exploitative." Infuriated, she insisted her manager Earl Mills contact director and producer. She wanted to call off the picture. Since no one wanted Dorothy to leave the production, Berry agreed to changes. It was decided the film would do what *Island in the Sun* should have: film romantic scenes in two versions, a more explicit one for European patrons, another sanitized version for American audiences.[82] Because the interracial relationship was given physical expression in the form of gesture, kissing, and the like, the film was banned in France. As a result of its director being blacklisted, its overseas production history, and its subject matter, there is still much to uncover regarding *Tamango*, a film that is as enigmatic as its liminal star.

Dandridge is one of many women who successfully broke the racial barrier in Hollywood precisely because she was considered beautiful. Therefore, this chapter has examined the social manufacturing of her beauty as representative of black beauty. Dandridge is also an important icon for understanding black spectators and their class aspirations and identifications. Since so many black women have historically been denied the sense of "bourgeois respectability" in public and private spheres, I find in celebrities like Lena Horne, Dorothy Dandridge, and Eartha Kitt models of a particular masquerade or performance of black bourgeois beauty and feminine respectability, which heretofore did not exist.

This is not to negate the extent to which European physical ideals informed what was considered acceptable black beauty. Indeed, Anglo-American ideals (lighter complexions, small features) informed the construction of Dandridge as acceptable. Thus I'm not making a case for Dandridge's star charisma as independent of Anglo-American cultural hegemony. However, I'm asserting that Dandridge and her contemporaries found constituents in black audiences, in women who identified with and admired black female film stars. They had fans in women who took solace and found pride in images of glamorous black women on screen. Even though black audiences found Dandridge's roles lacking dimension, discourse in fanzines and structural analysis of films provide venues through which we come to a better understanding of the oxymoronic nature of black stardom and black audience identification with black stars. Part of Dandridge's success entailed how the Negro community consumed her as a representative of black bourgeois identity. Hers was an image that helped define, for a given group of people, what kinds of feminine traits, comportment, and public performance of womanhood were appropriate and fashionable to develop. As a film star, she represented physical ideals, donned the mask of femininity, and embodied the sexual charm that 1950s film stars were believed to possess.

Pam Grier

A Phallic Idol of Perversity and Sexual Charisma

You will note I am deliberately avoiding the recent spate of so-called black films. I have seen very few of them, and, anyway, it would be virtually impossible to discuss them as films. I suspect their intention to be lethal indeed, and to be the subject of quite another investigation. Their entire purpose (apart from making money; and this money is not for blacks; in spite of the fact that some of these films appear to have been at least in part, financed by blacks) is to stifle forever any possibility of such moments—or, in other words, to make black experience irrelevant and obsolete.

—James Baldwin

Black youth know that society at large does not respect pimps and racketeers, but there is a certain *charisma* about them in the ghetto.

—Dr. Alvin F. Poussaint

The movies are so rarely great art, that if we can't appreciate great trash, there is little reason for us to go.

—Pauline Kael

I got Coffy and Foxy Brown and Sheba from my womanhood.

—Pam Grier

The early 1970s screen persona of exploitation movie diva Pam Grier is best understood in the context of social and political events of that decade. In the final years of the 1960s, major social policy changes engendered the sexual liberation of American film culture. First introduced in 1960, the birth control pill became a symbol for societal change in the Western world. In November 1968, the second major change occurred: the restrictive Hollywood Production Code gave way to the new Rating Administration. The new classification system did not solve the problems Hollywood faced with censorship but relaxed preexisting codes that forbade any depiction of obscenity, sexual slavery, miscegenation, nudity, homosexuality, kissing, or references to sexual perversion. The third significant change was a shift in legal statutes. In 1969 the U.S. Supreme Court ruled in *Stanley v. Georgia* that people could read and look at whatever they wished in the privacy of their own homes. The U.S. Congress, in hopes of finding another approach to controlling what many considered a threat to traditional American values, authorized $2 million to fund a presidential commission to study pornography in the United States and to recommend what Congress should do about it. By 1970, the sexual revolution had shown its effects. Films were no longer subject to prior restraint, nor were they all appropriate for the same audience. These pharmaceutical, legislative, and industrial initiatives meant that even when sex, sexuality, and corresponding gender roles were not explicitly the subject of 1970s cinema, they were often just beneath the surface, informing the ideological tone, formal texture, or narrative structure of a motion picture.

At the beginning of the decade, growing distrust of government, struggle for civil rights, increased influence of the women's movement, a heightened concern for the environment, and enhanced space exploration confronted Americans. The antiwar movement became both more powerful and less cohesive between 1969 and 1973. Many Americans opposed escalating the U.S. role in Vietnam yet disapproved of the counterculture that had arisen alongside the antiwar movement. Leaders of pacifist movements became increasingly strident, greeting returning soldiers with jeers and taunts on public streets. Hippies, known for their long hair, casual drug use, and promiscuity, subordinated the clean-cut, well-dressed Students for a Democratic Society as movement leaders. The FBI's Counter-Intelligence Program (COINTELPRO), discovered in 1971, suppressed Black Panther Party activity.[1] Their efforts culminated in Angela Davis's indictment on murder and conspiracy charges. Protesting injustice, inequality, and U.S. militarism, musicians such as Joan Baez, Bob Dylan, Stevie Wonder, and Jimmy Hendrix performed songs that revealed the widening generation gap. And in 1973 the Supreme Court struck down state laws banning abortions.[2] Amid this climate of war, social realignment, and presidential impeachment proceedings, dystopian visions of American culture thrived.[3]

Books published in the 1970s revolved around the broad theme of humanity's alienation from its spiritual roots. John Updike portrayed characters trying to find meaning in a spiritually empty society on the brink of moral decay. Joyce Carol Oates wrote of the search for spiritual meaning. Kurt Vonnegut explored the loneliness of contemporary society and the power of hungry materialism pervading it. Author Toni Morrison emerged as one of the most poignant literary voices to narrate the black American experience as an *American* experience. Whereas literature addressed mounting alienation, popular culture wavered between realism and escapism.[4] On one hand, reality sitcoms like Norman Lear's *All in the Family*—white America's top-rated TV program for the first half of the decade—showed family life ridden with bigotry and strife. On the other hand, escapist fantasy, horror, and nostalgia pictures like *The Exorcist, Jaws, The Way We Were, American Graffiti, The Texas Chainsaw Massacre,* and *Saturday Night Fever* captured mainstream imagination. For African Americans, Blaxploitation offered both a hint of reality and a dose of fantasy by depicting institutional and individual incidents of racism while simultaneously offering the fantasy that—like Sweetback, John Shaft, and Cleopatra Jones—brothers and sisters could kick the Man's ass. Still, many others rejected such escapist fare and its crude depiction of black Americans in confrontation with the predominantly white power structure.

Amid this atmosphere of disaffection and rebellion, the voluptuous Pam Grier rose to prominence as an idol of perverse sexual pleasures in sexploitation pictures and as a vengeful, coffee-colored femme fatale in Blaxploitation movies. Her screen persona encapsulated the ethos of personal frustration, sexual liberation, and political upheaval permeating American society. In an interview with filmmaker Isaac Julien, Pam Grier acknowledged the direct relationship between the changing culture and her film roles. "Coffy was my mom, Foxy Brown was my Aunt and they were women who were very demonstrative but yet very feminine and knew how to use sexuality. The sexual movement was raging through the streets, shorts were getting shorter, skirts were getting shorter, and men's pants were getting tighter. People were throwing underwear bras out the window. We had Woodstock. You loved your naked body. So all of that was about who we were too. And, you could see that in film."[5]

As the freshness of 1950s and 1960s starlets Dorothy Dandridge, Eartha Kitt, and Abbey Lincoln faded, Pam Grier emerged as one of the new black female film stars. After all, the time seemed right for Grier to soar, since actresses like Dandridge had already broken some of the color-casting barriers. "Well, the 70s for me was the moment when we could really live out the freedoms and political gains won by the 40s, 50s and 60s," Grier told Isaac Julien. "I could come out here, and go to Beverly Hills, and the doors were open for me to go to night clubs and restaurants and be treated very equal." Grier ultimately became the next mainstream African American crossover phenomenon and sex symbol. Her onscreen persona, which combined brazen sexuality, physical strength, and Black Nationalist sentiment, informed the portrayal of action heroines in popular culture years after her early exploitation career had waned (i.e., *Posse*, 1993; *Original Gangstas*, 1996). Grier's trademark (i.e., her image as a bad-ass femme fatale) left an indelible impression because she embodied the 1970s attitude of cultural defiance manifested as a kind of Afro-kitsch.[6] The uniqueness of her screen persona explains her appeal to younger audiences and illuminates why Grier was able to make a late-1990s comeback (i.e., *Jackie Brown*, 1997; *Bones*, 2001) rather than fade into the shadows of film history like some of her contemporaries. Even today, Pam Grier is thankful to the younger generation of film and recording artists for rediscovering her early film work.

> The hip-hop nation found me and put me on a pedestal. Now I'm in the rap and hip-hop videos. I like the music. I dance to it. I work out to it. These young people could be my children. They love R & B. Snoop loves R & B. That's all he plays. He gets all his style and a lot of his sampling from R & B back in the day 'cause that's all his parents played. So, all of a sudden, Quentin said: "You know what? What you did, and who you were, what you represent . . . are still very important. And, these kids see something and feel something. Most can articulate what it was but many can't. They just like the fact that you stood up, you were a hero and who do we have to look up to now? There's you, you know. Black Jane Bond."

As a result of her unique persona and resurgent career, Pam Grier is—and will remain—a definitive icon of 1970s popular culture, an exploitation movie diva of the silver screen.

By confronting male authority onscreen and representing black women as both sexually and intellectually self-determined, Grier altered the depiction of black women in cinema. No individual actor can single-handedly subvert the exclusionary practices, institutional racism, heterosexist logic, ageist mythos, or nationalist tendencies endemic to Hollywood. Nor are Grier's superwoman characters defendable as socially minded portraits of real political figures. The exploitation roles she accepted were limiting, repetitive, and often-simplistic caricatures. But like other forms of kitsch and camp, they were popular, and as a consequence, they catapulted her to stardom. As the queen of Blaxploitation cinema, she—more than her contemporaries Tamara Dobson (*Cleopatra Jones*, 1973), Carol Speed (*The Mack*, 1973), Vonetta McGee (*Shaft in Africa*, 1973), Diahann Carroll (*Paris Blues*, 1961; *Claudine*, 1974), and Eartha Kitt (*Anna Lucasta*, 1959)—personified the sultry leading lady, slightly altering the screen image of black women as merely passive objects onto which stereotypes of the mammy, the sexual siren, and the comic Topsy have historically been projected. She belongs in the pantheon of radical 1970s film stars (i.e., Raquel Welch in *Myra Breckinridge*, 1970; Jane Fonda in *Klute*, 1971; Julie Christie in *McCabe & Mrs. Miller*, 1971; Faye Dunaway in *Chinatown*, 1974) responsible for the paradigmatic shift away from women represented solely as sexual *objects* of the gaze toward women as *subjects* propelling the narrative, working as active agents and intelligent investigators.[7]

Despite numerous star vehicles, television and Broadway appearances, and her late-1990s reemergence as a TV celebrity, there is limited scholarship or film criticism addressing Pam Grier's career. This critical quiet surrounds Grier and her African American contemporaries. Perhaps Grier's star vehicles received little scholarly attention because they were known for narrative simplicity, sexual sensationalism, and technical deficiency. As Eric Schaefer noted in his well-researched history of exploitation cinema, these movies "are usually thought of as ethically dubious, industrially marginal, and aesthetically bankrupt."[8] At the time of their release, African American artists and intellectuals like James Baldwin rejected the image of black life projected by these pictures. Perhaps Baldwin (wearied by the repetitiveness of Blaxploitation) read these films too literally, glossing over their *camp* elements. But to dismiss sexploitation films as crude or trashy precludes any examination of their form, their content, their appeal to spectators, or the relationship between high and low film culture. It also creates a double standard not applied to other exploitation subgenres and proves reductive for several reasons.

The question of the relationship of art to trash is not purely an intellectual dilemma, but a painful and baffling phenomenon of lived experience.[9] Philosophers long ago established that taste is an abstract sociological fiction. Studying taste as an independent abstraction, David Hume concluded that the beauty of objects exists in the mind of the beholder and is profoundly personal. Exploitation films are not high art by any beholder's observation. But viewing them as *camp*, we can better understand their appeal to spectators at particular historical moments. Further, the production conditions Schaefer outlines above describe virtually all Blaxploitation films, many of which (e.g.,

Shaft, Blacula, Superfly, Cotton Comes to Harlem) received critical, historical, and theoretical analysis in cultural studies (Neal, 2002) and African American screen studies (i.e., Cripps, 1990; Bogle, 1989; Guerrero, 1993; Hartman, 1994; Medovoi, 1998) despite their status as lowbrow entertainment. Production value has not deterred film historians or critics from rigorously considering the history of exploitation (Schaefer, 1999), sexploitation (Friedman, 1990; Hubner, 1992; Miller, 1994; Sullivan, 1995), pornography (Turan & Zito, 1974; Williams, 1989, 1993), teen exploitation (Doherty, 1998), horror exploitation (Weaver, 1988, 1993; Skal, 1993), or other so-called exploitative genres with low budgets, repetitive formulas, self-conscious acting, camp aesthetics, or technical clumsiness. Grier's films should be no exception.

The critical silence around Grier's work may reflect the layers embedded in her screen persona. Neither racial role model nor simple stereotype, Pam Grier's 1970s persona was multifaceted. Her screen characters fused feminist sensibilities, campy "butch-femme" aesthetics, Black Nationalist radicalism, and women's subjectivity. The ambiguity regarding the placement of Grier's persona is a function of the overlapping genres (i.e., action, cult, science fiction, sexploitation, Blaxploitation) and cinematic styles (realist and camp) of the films in which she appeared. She portrayed a monstrous femme fatale in the campy B science-fiction picture *The Twilight People* (1972), a vengeful femme fatale in Blaxploitation movies like *Coffy* (1973) and *Sheba, Baby* (1975), an action heroine in *The Arena* (1973), and an investigative detective–working girl in *Foxy Brown* (1974) and *Friday Foster* (1975). These exploitation films, with lewdly explicit sex scenes, gratuitous violence, and mundane dialogue, became cult-movie[10] sensations primarily because they expressed countercultural sentiments and because they projected audience fantasies of rebellion against authority, propriety, and social conventions.

In a discussion of cult cinema, Umberto Eco has offered an explanation of the way certain films emerge as cult objects.[11] For Eco, such pictures are not necessarily produced by word of mouth, nor are they necessarily classic films turned cult favorites like *Casablanca* (e.g., produced with large budgets, stars, and technical expertise, proving profitable). Cult cinema includes "outsider cinema" and underground cinema, bizarre films with low budgets, character actors, and remote locales. These movies are "born in order to become cult objects."[12] They make direct intertextual reference to other motion pictures, and they subtly allude to other films. The enjoyment of these movies is heightened for audiences familiar with film language and the repertoire of archetypes encoded by genre movies. Contemporary horror, for example, is self-referential and assumes horror-literate audiences (i.e., *Scream, Scream*

2, *The Blair Witch Project, Freddy vs. Jason, Final Destination 2, Scary Movie, Alien vs. Predator*). Pam Grier's 1970s characters and star vehicles were similarly shaped by cinema and subsequently shaped succeeding films. *Coffy* (Jack Hill, 1973), for instance, contained drug kingpin characters popularized by 1930s gangster movies like *Scarface* (Howard Hawks, 1931). *Friday Foster* (Arthur Marks, 1975) employed a plot structure made familiar by 1940s film noirs like *The Big Sleep* (Howard Hawks, 1946). *The Twilight People* (Eddie Romero, 1973) was produced on a shoestring budget, featuring cheap costumes, cheaper makeup, and cheesy special effects like the ones seen in 1950s science fiction features *Creature from the Black Lagoon* (Jack Arnold, 1954) and *I Married a Monster from Outer Space* (Gene Fowler, 1958). If her films were cult movies, then, by extension, Grier became a cult figure, representing what Christopher Lasch termed an "ego-ideal": the admired, idealized image[13] of this alternative pop-culture landscape.

Early 1970s cult films solidified her statuesque "Amazonian"[14] image and her specific brand of star charisma. The culture industries (i.e., film and advertising) packaged Grier as a woman possessing a kind of masculine— almost phallic—charismatic authority. The concept of *phallic charisma* used here to discuss Grier is simply a metaphor describing the combination of sexual bravura, physical prowess, and sassy attitude encompassed in her screen persona. By discussing Grier in terms of phallic charisma we gain a sense of her as both a *phenomenon of consumption* (consumed by audience-consumers) and a *phenomenon of production* (produced by industrial institutions like American International Pictures). Her unique brand of charisma enabled her—unlike other actresses from this period—to remain popular throughout the 1970s and stage a career comeback in the late 1990s. This chapter addresses her exploitation star vehicles. Pam Grier was both an object of the gaze *and* a subject of narrative action in films utilizing her as a vehicle of camp aesthetics.[15]

Grier's Biography: A Star Is Born at AIP

Pamela Suzette Grier was born on May 26, 1949, in Winston-Salem, North Carolina. She was relocated, just a few weeks after her birth, to Denver, Colorado. The family was moved to a military base in Swindon, England, where they lived during little Pamela's early childhood. When she was five, her father, a mechanic for the United States Air Force, was transferred to Travis Air Force Base in California. While she was growing up, her working-class family struggled. Years later Grier said, "We were never able to go to a store and buy clothes. My clothes came from Sears & Roebuck catalogues and we had hand-me-downs. I loved clothes from Goodwill because they were practically new," the actress recalls.[16] Part of Grier's youth was spent on military bases in the American South. During her childhood, Grier learned about and experienced American racism and racial discrimination.

> On the base, there's no race or gender. You're just military and you're all military and they take good care of you. There are buses and shuttles. Everyone lives next to each other and there are no racial problems. But when you're in the South and you come off the base, now its gets a little serious. We would go shopping and bring food and things home. But the city buses wouldn't stop to pick us up because we were Black. The buses would be half filled or have just a few people on them. We're standing there, its 110 degrees in the shade with humidity and bugs. They'd go right by us and we'd have to keep walking until the next bus stop and then maybe he'd stop. There weren't any black bus drivers. They were all white. Sometimes they would see us, and my mother, dragging. Then, they would stop.

Until the age of fourteen, Grier lived on various American military bases in Europe. When her family finally returned to the United States, they settled in Denver, Colorado, where the teenager was a foreign oddity to her new American peers. Speaking with a British accent, she was accustomed to afternoon tea and carried herself in a way others deemed pretentious and standoffish. Grier explained this cultural difference, saying: "Denver wasn't bad. It was rough. I wasn't very big then and I found that you had to fight all the time. You had to fight for your lunch money or act like you didn't have any. You had to put it in your socks or tape it under your shoes or something. It was pretty rough, especially for a young kid who had been sheltered on air force bases."

Following the death of her boyfriend, eighteen-year-old Pam entered Metropolitan State College in Denver. At this school her self-confidence flourished. Planning to become a doctor, she also entered the Miss Universe Beauty Pageant for prize money to help finance another year of school. A second runner-up, Pam still needed money for tuition. She entered a local beauty pageant in Colorado, in which she was the only black woman competing. She did not win but caught the eye of Hollywood agent Dave Baumgarten. The professional meeting with Baumgarten followed a failed romance with basketball star Kareem Abdul-Jabbar. With little reason to remain in Colorado, Grier accepted Baumgarten's invitation to accompany him to Hollywood. Initially, she declined, but her mother urged her to accept. Grier agreed, and Baumgarten set up a meeting. He became her agent, sent her to acting classes, and employed her as a switchboard operator with his agency. Once in Hollywood, Grier encountered old-fashioned but still prevalent institutional racism.

Auditions proved frustrating. Repeatedly, she encountered racial discrimination bolstered by Euro-American beauty standards. After readings and auditions, Pam was repeatedly rejected for petty reasons. One agent rejected her for not being "Negro enough." Another complained about "the gap between her two front teeth being too distracting on film." At times she was considered too thin, or, conversely, too fat. Grier's difficultly auditioning lends credence to the *tyranny of thinness* argument proffered by scholars Kim Chernin and Susan Bordo, both of whom discuss the unobtainable physical standards women—celebrity women, in particular—are expected to maintain.

Browsing through classifieds, Miss Grier noticed American International Pictures advertising for a switchboard operator. The job paid twenty-five dollars more a week than her current salary. She told the AIP personnel director she could operate the switchboard and was hired. Grier recalls:

> When I started working at AIP I knew I wanted to learn about the business because I wanted to be *in* the business. I started listening in on calls, and got to know a lot about what was going on . . . I wanted to see how things work, what makes a success and what makes a failure. When I relieved the production secretary, I would study the storyboards in the production room. I got to know who was doing what, where they were doing it, and how long it would take. Everything went click in my head. I was a little monster for the information.[17]

Her first small role was a part in *Beyond the Valley of the Dolls* (Russ Meyer, 1970). She had no idea what the film was about beforehand, and her part in *Beyond the Valley of the Dolls* turned out to be a small cameo. Thereafter she appeared onstage in James Baldwin's *Blues for Mister Charlie* and *Carnival Island* with the Ebony Showcase. Throughout the decade she sang background vocals for her cousin Rosey Grier, and for Bobby Womack and Lou Rawls, while also appearing in commercials. Her first leading role was in *The Big Doll House,* for which she also sang the theme song.[18]

Hearing discussion around AIP of casting for B movie producer Roger Corman, Pam seized the opportunity to audition. At the time, Roger Corman reigned as the most prolific producer of low-budget movies. His sixteen-year-tenure at AIP taught him film advertising strategies and the basic formula for making pictures inexpensively. During his career at the small studio, Corman learned everything he could from AIP's president James Harvey Nicholson and vice president Samuel Zachary Arkoff, and he perfected the formula of low-budget exploitation filmmaking across horror, science fiction, and teen-pic genres. However, Corman felt constrained by the standards and rules determined by Arkoff and Nicholson.

In 1970, Roger Corman formed New World Pictures, which produced and distributed exploitation movies as well as the sophisticated European art films directed by celebrated auteurs François Truffaut, Ingmar Bergman, and Federico Fellini.[19] Grier's role in *Beyond the Valley of the Dolls* revealed her potential to Corman, who was willing to cast her in New World productions. The early work at New World Pictures ultimately proved definitive for Grier, molding her nascent star persona.

Corman reproduced AIP's low-budget production strategy at New World Pictures. He kept overhead down, bypassed big-name celebrities to make salaries less crippling, and shot on location at inexpensive sites like the Philippines, where local labor was inexpensive. The writing of New World's scripts was also carefully supervised. The procedure always involved a writer bringing a story or idea to Corman, who then worked closely with the writer until details of plot and the various ideas were worked out to his satisfaction.

One of the primary story ingredients of New World's pictures was the sexual role reversal. The heroine and/or female protagonist was usually given traditionally masculine characteristics. She was a forceful protagonist. She fought physically with women and men. She scorned conventional authority and was a woman of few words, considering action superior to speech. She was the quintessential "phallic" woman. This super-assertive female— who exposed her breasts as readily as she brandished a gun—was a staple character constantly featured in Corman-directed and produced films (i.e., *Gunslinger, Swamp Woman, Teenage Doll,* and *Viking Women and the Sea Serpent*)[20] and later in several exploitation pictures. Grier explained that Corman's attention to social issues informed his filmmaking. "The women's movement was happening all over the world. . . . Roger Corman had been making films with predominantly women leads. He started focusing on putting women of color in these roles; you know, the biker-nurse type roles, the strong women movie roles. He had a lot to do with my beginning."[21]

Grier's Phallic Charisma

According to psychoanalytic theory, the fantasy of the phallic mother or woman originates in childhood. In the primary cognition process of infants, the contradictory concepts of phallic and nonphallic, castration and noncastration, coexist in a way that allows the boy child to maintain identity with the mother. Fetishism arises when a substitute object takes the place of the supposedly "missing" female phallus, serving to reassure the boy child—and later the adult male—that women are not much different from men and can be safely approached. When the fetish is a separate object, like a shoe or material like fur or leather (the feel of which may recall infantile closeness and intimacy with the mother), it appears to deliver control of the problematic missing phallus and assuage surrounding anxiety through disavowal. Fetishism may occur when part of the body (i.e., breast, thigh, hair, neck) is overvalued so much that it becomes more important than the whole—it is displaced through synecdoche. Breast fixation, for example, is fetishistic, and by transference upward, breasts assume phallic properties. In Eurocentric cultures where whiteness has historically been linked to notions of white supremacy and light complexions are given greater value, race and skin complexion may also become fetish objects. Slavery, colonialism, class, and caste stratification along color lines reveal race as a prominent bodily signifier. The racial fetish is unlike Freud's sexual identity fetish because "skin color functions as the most visible of fetishes."[22] Scholars W. E. B. Du Bois and Frantz Fanon long ago established that the black body occupies a unique ontological position in Euro-American cultures. The black (actor's) body—in this case Pam Grier's body—has historically been a site at which multiple fetishes (i.e., sexual and racial) were simultaneously objectified.

Sigmund Freud's theory of fetishism is problematic, particularly as a clinical phenomenon of sexual pathology and perversion. It is therefore limited in its application. But the central notion of the fetish as a substitute for the absent phallus enables an understanding of the psychic structure of disavowal and the splitting of conscious and unconscious belief.[23] Feminist theories of fetishism have been used to explain male audience fascination and identification with "phallic heroines": those fictional female action figures (i.e., *Lara Croft: Tomb Raider,* Ripley in the *Alien* quadrilogy, *Buffy the Vampire Slayer*) engaging in heroic activities generally considered the domain of their male counterparts. The phallic heroine is a variation of the phallic woman. As defined by J. Laplanche and J. B. Pontalis, the phallic woman is endowed—*in fantasy*—with a phallus. "Fantasy," in this context, is the illusory realm of narrative cinema viewed in a darkened room, which according to Christian Metz mimics the structure of human dreamscape. The image of a phallic woman has two primary cultural forms: (1) she is represented as having either an external phallus or phallic attribute, or (2) the woman has preserved the male's phallus inside herself. In general, the expression describes a woman with particular character traits (i.e., authoritarianism, subversiveness, and deceptiveness).[24]

Several of Pam Grier's characters were symbolic phallic heroines. Visually and narratively, the films placed emphasis on her body in such a way as to create an image of phallic femininity. The camera's close-ups of her buxom breasts; her use of phallic props in the mise-en-scène (i.e., guns, knives, razors, wires); her statuesque height; her racial identity as black and therefore supposedly tougher, and her narrative roles as aggressive women all enabled Grier to create a sexy, badass screen persona. Her identity as a black woman figured prominently in the way she was constructed—even fetishized—as a phallic heroine. The discursive myth of black women as bitchy matriarchs is coterminous with the racist notion that black women are tougher, stronger, more masculine, and/or more controlling.[25] Grier could be presented and marketed by the culture industries (i.e., film, television, advertising industries) as an aggressive woman because notions of black womanhood were already in place, actively constitutive of the dominant cultural ideology producing a discursive formation.[26]

This racist discourse, with roots in the political economy of slavery, re-emerged in 1965 with the Moynihan Report, which linked the socioeconomic problems of some black communities to a so-called matriarchal family structure.[27] During slavery and in periods of colonialism, and under the present authoritarian military state, the black family has been the site of political resistance to racism.[28] But the discussion of black pathology developed into a dominant discourse informing theories of black social relations. It became pervasive enough to inform ideas African Americans held about themselves. For instance, even Pam Grier unintentionally participated in the discourse of black matriarchy—as many of us have—when she told one reporter: "It makes sense strong women would come out of black films . . . The woman has always been the strength of most black families. Little black boys have always been scared of their mamas."[29] Clearly, Grier intended to emphasize the constructive ways African American women maintained family despite slavery, disenfranchisement, regional migration, and urban decay. However, her statement inevitably falls into dialogic relation with dominant discourse.

However, the cinematic fetishization of women characters as "phallic" is usually not racially specific. What's more, Pam Grier was not alone in playing aggressive character parts. Asian American and Anglo-American women also played ballsy figures in Arkoff's and Corman's (s)exploitation films. They were assisted in this by adhering to the campy performance aesthetics characteristic of AIP's exploitation pictures.

AIP Camp

Camp is generally understood as an aesthetic style in which humor and unserious or flippant behaviors are key features. It is a style of exaggeration, poking fun at or parodying traditional gender roles, characters, and modes of behavior. Camp reveals the artificiality of all identity categories (racial, gender, class, sexual, etc.) in American society by showing how unnatural these roles are. Camp is also an approach taking the so-called "natural" way of being (the "essence") and executing it excessively. It presents a self-conscious mimicry or mocking of behavioral codes by taking them beyond their traditional boundaries. One popular example of camp is *Da Ali G Show*. Host Sacha Baron Cohen (aka Ali G Indahouse) mockingly performs various identities with such subtlety as to fool only his on-camera interviewees and not the viewing audience.

Camp, which has existed for ages, gained wider currency in the 1960s with Susan Sontag's seminal 1964 essay "Notes on Camp." She pushed it beyond the aesthetic domain of the gay and lesbian community, spurring a host of critical investigations into camp as a mode of aesthetic engagement. In the intervening years, there has been a denunciation of Sontag's concept and a subsequent movement to reclaim it as part of oppositional queer aesthetics—a "queering of camp," as Fabio Cleto has suggested. As a humorous aesthetic sensibility, camp articulates double entendre in objects, persons, and dialogue. It amounts to the exaggeration of behavior in performance and the flamboyance of mannerisms susceptible to double interpretation. It may be the sensibility of failed seriousness, or the playful dethronement of the serious and the theatricalization of experience.[30]

A stylistic device used in exploitation cinema, "camping" intensifies the fetishistic, soft-porn atmosphere because, through it, filmmakers and actors exaggerate the sensory and parody the sexual. Grier's prison pictures contained enough nudity, lesbianism, and sadomasochism to be read as a kind of soft porn. Intercourse and vaginal penetration never occurred onscreen but were implied, suggested, or occurred in off-screen space. These films demonstrate the existence of a continuous pornographic tradition running through dominant culture.[31] Nonetheless, campy women-in-prison films—in all their strangeness and multiple marginality—present images of women and women's relationships seldom found in more mainstream genres. As Suzanna D. Walters notes: Women in this world live together, love together, fight each other, and fight back against the largely male system of brutal domination keeping them all down.[32]

These films are characterized by several elements including some lesbianism, violence between women, initiation of innocent victim to prison life, a turning point where innocent victim becomes conscious and rebels, struggle between prison authorities and inmates, riot, breakout and the inevitable shower scene. But within these broad structural elements, there is a great degree of variation. For example, while lesbianism is clearly a central element in this genre (and possibly one reason these films have any audience at all, given the prevalence of "lesbian" imagery in male-produced porn), it is alternately treated as mutual, loving romance and as violent, sadistic abuse.[33]

Predictably, lesbian scenes in Grier's star vehicles reproduced traditional gender binaries and hierarchies. The presence of these traditional roles suggests that the films were scripted to tickle heterosexual male fantasies of lesbianism but with campy humor absent from pornography. Many prison pictures express (hetero)sexual male desire but cannot be reduced to this alone. On the one hand, they articulate a form of objectification and male dominance over the apparatus of representation, evidenced by sexploitation's emphasis on action and on violence against women rather than on erotic sexuality. That heterosexual men rent pornography with hints of lesbianism more frequently than women (statistically speaking) suggests these films were really intended to titillate male viewers. On the other hand, within the binary dynamic of lesbian sadomasochism, these films posit female characters whose desire is freed from penile representation. Within the film, the tough lesbian fetishist—a character Grier often played—turns her own body into the unrelinquished phallus, or takes a phallic woman (another with a masculinity complex) as her desired object.

Grier's characters were the tough prison matrons that dominated delicate feminine prisoners. She delivered campy performances playing "butch" characters or strong-willed dykes who proudly displayed possession of a (symbolic) phallus, while her costars played the weaker femme characters, assuming the "compulsory masquerade of womanliness."[34] In *The Big Doll House* or *The Big Bird Cage*, a character's "butch" orientation was signified by her sexual forwardness, rigid comportment, lesbianism, and use of exaggerated innuendo. By contrast, submissiveness, demure demeanor, and naiveté indicated a character's "femme" orientation. The exaggerated, campy performance of sexual aggression was aided by the use of props (i.e., guns, knives, tools), costumes (i.e., low cleavage, short dresses, high-heeled shoes, sassy hairstyles), and feminized bodies (i.e., nudity) that created the alluring masquerade of "femme" versus "butch" gender roles. The embellished performance of sexuality, with which Grier became associated, marked her as a sexual idol.

Ironically, Pam Grier's authoritative characters were usually foiled in the denouement. Sexploitation's leading women characters were often disciplined as if antiheroines: the "bad girls" rarely—if ever—spared excessive punishment for their transgressions of the patriarchal social order. Principal and featured characters were shot, tortured, raped, maimed, or doomed to a life of prostitution and drug addiction. Whereas Blaxploitation films positively affirmed their target audiences' problack, antiwhite sentiments, sexploitation movies often reinforced promasculinist, antifeminist fantasies—an indication that heterosexual men might have been the target audience. This narrative containment of women was generically determined, but it was also necessitated by extracinematic discourses regarding attitudes toward women's labor, women's sexuality, and women's liberation. With respect to the demise of Grier's strong women characters, I agree with Pamela Robertson, who asserted that some forms of cinematic camp (i.e., *The Gold Diggers of 1933*) were produced at moments of antifeminist backlash and used anachronistic images to challenge ideas regarding women's changing roles in public and economic spheres.[35] My central point is that the ambivalent treatment of Grier's (s)exploitation characters was a reflection of larger societal tensions with 1970s feminism in general and strong women in particular. The second wave of feminist activism proves an important social context for interpreting the production and reception of Grier's screen persona as a campy, phallic idol of perversity.

Cultural Backlash and the Iconography of Misogyny

It is widely held that societal tensions reverberate in the cultural expressions of political movements. The suffragist movement, feminist activism, the Black Power movement, the civil rights struggle, and gay pride's Stonewall engendered or accompanied cultural consequences in the arts. In 1986, five years before the publication of Susan Faludi's *Backlash: The Undeclared War against American Women* (1991), art historian Bram Dijkstra published *Idols of Perversity*, a seminal study of the representation of feminine treachery in fin-de-siècle Western European culture. Confronted with a wealth of material, he examined the prevalence of these themes in *Evil Sisters* (1996), a subsequent study revealing parallel trends in twentieth-century visual culture.[36] It is significant that his work parallels the scholarship of art historian Elaine Shefer, author of *Birds, Cages and Women in Victorian and Pre-Raphaelite Art* (1990). A salient trend among this scholarship is the recognition of cultural backlash visited upon women at various moments of feminist achievement.

Since the publication of these books, Black British and postcolonial scholars have offered incisive readings of the relationship between the scopic practices of the nineteenth century and the disciplinary discourses of the body (Bhabha, 1994; Mercer, 1994; McClintock, 1995). Together with Dijkstra's and Shefer's work, this literature suggests a correspondence between nineteenth-century social-scientific discourses pathologizing womanhood and "images of misogyny" that emerged as backlash against early women's liberation and suffrage movements. Throughout the history of art, women have been compared to a storehouse of animal, vegetable, and floral objects. In nineteenth-century English (and Western European) art the favorite analogy was that of the bird. The association of "the woman" with "the bird in the cage" was a persistent and cherished image. According to Shefer, the bird-in-the-cage symbol allowed both artists and writers to preach "woman's mission" in society. This "mission" was a Victorian euphemism for "women's rights" and an issue that began agitating social critics by the mid-nineteenth century.[37] These avian Victorian portraits prefigured twentieth-century (and twenty-first-century) iconography (i.e., film, television, and advertising) in which the woman in the bird cage repeatedly appeared, both literally and figuratively.

Dijkstra draws an inverse connection between the publication of Nicholas Francis Cooke's *Satan in Society* and social gains made by women. Cooke and the British pre-Raphaelite painter William Lindsay Windus and their cohorts were representative of the writers, artists, and intellectuals who viewed the women's movement as "indicative of a perverse strain of delusion in the female mind." For these male intellectuals, feminine self-assertion represented a reversion to a more primitive stage of human civilization.[38] The new emphasis on women's education was also perceived as a threatening perversion of the status quo. Coincidentally, by the end of the nineteenth century, the number of women college students had greatly increased. Higher education, particularly, was broadened by the rise of women's colleges and the admission of women to formerly all-male colleges and universities. Some of the most prestigious women's colleges emerged during the latter half of the nineteenth century, the same moment Dijkstra addresses.[39]

What specifically concerned Nicholas Cooke and his contemporaries was the proliferation of female boarding schools, which Cooke viewed as an arena in which masturbation, sexual impulses, and female relationships might be routinely practiced or indulged. Interestingly, this single-sex environment parallels the penal enclaves presented in Grier's women-in-prison pictures. Nonetheless, Cooke believed he and his colleagues had found an "explanation for vice in the dangerous—one might even say incestuous—energies released by women who consorted with each other."[40] In this milieu, Dijkstra finds opposing trends: the "iconography of misogyny" emerging in cultural spheres (the salons of Europe and North America) concurrently with a more favorable response to women's education in the public sphere. Implicit in Dijkstra's analysis is the contention that this imagery flourished in reaction to the temporary instability of patriarchy at a moment of feminist achievement. The iconography of misogyny was evident in artistic images of feminine weightlessness, languidness, and fatigue, and feminine likeness to earthliness, repeatedly presenting (white) women as passive sexual entities inviting aggressive male sexuality.

> The turn-of-the-century painters, in creating these images of helplessly ecstatic women, were playing directly on their audiences fantasies of aggression and "invited" rape by depicting women who were extremely vulnerable and naked, usually sprawled flat on their backs in primarily sylvan surroundings, yet who appeared to be in the last throes of an uncontrollable ecstasy. Inevitably these paintings must suggest a perverse combination of intense sexual need and abject helplessness on the part of the women depicted. There is only one way in which these creatures can be joined: we must descend to their level, become part of their world of earth and trees, part of the preconscious universe, responsive to nature's barbaric invitation to engage in the purely sexual, purely materialistic ritual of reproduction . . . [41]

The recurring motif of spastic, uncontrollable, helpless women—as if their backs had been broken in some violent movement, so that they are now sprawled out as if paralyzed, having been made doubly vulnerable by their nakedness—characterized the male preoccupation (which developed during the nineteenth century) that women were born masochists and enjoyed rape. This dissection of the nineteenth century's social paranoia concerning women's sexual perversity suggests an inverse relationship between women's liberation movements and the representation of women in patriarchal cultures. We might interpret these artistic representations as concomitants of cultural backlash against a changing social and political climate.

There is a historical parallel between late nineteenth and late twentieth-century cultures in terms of political backlash. This parallel informs my reading of the relationship between the 1970s feminist movement and popular representations of women in 1970s sexploitation prison pictures. My notion of Grier's screen persona as "perverse" dovetails with Dijkstra's analysis of these painted figures as idols of perversity. Pam Grier played characters that were perverse for being authoritative and commanding yet sexually defenseless against male aggressors. Though they appeared at different historical moments, both the paintings and Grier's prison pictures presented spectacles of female sexual perversity: women who seemed to invite rape, enjoy physical abuse, long to be vanquished, and daydream of sexual abandon. In their imagery, the films evoke nineteenth-century visualizations of women. In their narrative content and semiotic registers, these motion pictures evince a similar anxiety regarding single-sex environments, women's sexuality, feminine bodies, and women as sexual beings because the films hinge on the same combination of sexual craving and abject helplessness, agency, and inactivity.

This historical context helps explain the publicity and marketing techniques employed by studios to advertise Pam Grier's films to theater owners and audiences. For instance, this context explains why press kits for prison pictures like *The Big Bird Cage* encouraged theater owners to "Set up your own picket line of pretty young girls carrying placards protesting life in *The Big Bird Cage*. Tie in Women's Lib and prison reform to get good coverage in your local news media."[42] Filmmakers, publicists, and studio advertisers produced these films and marketing campaigns with the intention of capitalizing on their oppositional relationship to women's liberation. These movies were designed to arouse and antagonize feminist sensibilities. Furthermore, this press kit proviso offers additional evidence that the target demographic for these films comprises spectators who will appreciate the film's adversarial relationship to feminist activism. It substantiates an application of Dijkstra's theory: misogynist imagery emerges in reaction to the instability of patriarchy at moments of feminist achievement.

Idols of Perversity: *Women in Cages*

Nowhere was Pam Grier more explicitly advertised as an idol of phallic perversity than in the salacious promotional trailers for her star vehicles. Trailers, press kits, lobby cards, and poster advertisements for exploitation movies exceeded the limits of decency, promising more sex, sadism, and violence than found in mainstream fare. These motion pictures guaranteed images of helplessness and women with intense sexual needs. For example, the press kit for *The Big Bird Cage* read: "Against the exotic background of lush valleys terraced with rice paddies, Pam Grier and Teda Bracci lead their teams of fellow prisoners in muddy battle in the action-filled story of desperate women, *The Big Bird Cage*." Or consider the *Women in Cages* trailer, which promised: "Innocent, young girls, held in cruel bondage! Sold to the highest bidder, to satisfy strange desires."

The movie *Women in Cages* (1971) marked the beginning of Pam Grier's sexploitation film career. Like many of these movies, it was shot on a low budget in the Philippines using Philippine extras as cast and crew to keep production overhead low. Pam Grier plays Alabama, a sadistic dominatrix and prison supervisor. The story begins aboard the ship *Zulu Queen*, a floating house of prostitution, topless dancing, and drug trafficking. Lost onboard, an innocent young white American, Carol Jeffries (Jennifer Gan), is mistaken for one of the ship's dancing dope smugglers. Apprehended for drug possession, she is falsely accused and sentenced to confinement at Gargel del Ingierno, a deplorable prison deep in the heart of an unnamed tropical jungle. At the penitentiary, Carol is strip-searched and housed with a motley crew of hostile cellmates including a dope addict nicknamed "Stoke" (Roberta Collins) and a merciless husband killer, Sandy (Judy Brown). Actors Collins and Brown were cast as these callous characters, but exploitation filmmakers, conscious of their predominantly male audiences, usually employed actresses who resembled models more than hardened criminals.

Typical of exploitation, *Women in Cages* is laced with sexual innuendo, lesbian sexuality, racial conflict, and social commentary. Even Grier's char-

Pam Grier portrays sadistic prison guard Alabama in *Women in Cages* (1972).

acter—intentionally named "Alabama"—invokes the history of race relations in the South.[43] Significantly, it is Grier's Alabama who seeks retribution for white racism. For instance, after celebrating five years in exile from the U.S., Alabama, the prison wardress, disrobes and reclines with her Philippine concubine Teresa (a prison inmate). She confides in petite Teresa that the new American inmates are "Typical of the racist bitches I left back in the States!" These expressions of racial hostility foreshadow Alabama's vengeful attitude toward white women and her sadistic fixation with them. When inmate Carol, called by her surname Jeffries, defies Alabama (telling visiting dignitaries about harsh prison conditions), the warden punishes her in a medieval-style den of torture cheekily called "the playpen." Despite being strapped down bare-breasted on a breaking wheel with legs splayed open, Jeffries insults Alabama, asking, "What hell did you crawl out of?" To which Alabama defiantly replies, "It was called *Harlem*, baby! I learned to survive and *never* have pity. This game is called survival! Let's see how well *you* can play it. I was strung out behind smack at ten and worked in the streets when I was twelve. You have a *long* way to go!"

As campy and comical as these scenes are, they rely on racial signifiers, on the visibility of Grier's blackness. Her blackness is semiotically and sociologically linked to her personal vendetta against systemic, structural racism. Offering a condemnation of American racism, this scene teases spectators with its half-serious discussion of race relations. For this reason, the film may be seen as belittling the analytical discourse of racism.

The seriocomic social commentary woven into titillating scenes of sexual brutality made the sleazy aspect of sexploitation more salacious. Such commentary wed racial antagonism to campy sadism. By manipulating racially charged sexual taboos, sexploitation pictures exposed the sexual fetish of racism. Racial prejudice (both antiwhite and antiblack) in these films functioned as a kind of obsession in which the racialized Other was semiotically charged with difference. Campy, cult cinema routinely employed racial fetishism and violence self-consciously by heightening spectator awareness of the social hierarchies being inverted. For example, Alabama's attitude toward Jeffries is a response to both Jeffries's race and gender privilege; it is a response to her whiteness and the historical precedent of safeguarding white femininity while exploiting black womanhood during slavery.

The racially charged violence against women enacted by females in *Women in Cages* is overshadowed by the violence against women perpetrated by men. Sexploitation narratives relied on a familiar formula. They allowed female prisoners to escape but only to encounter a greater barbarity immediately beyond penitentiary walls. In *Cages,* inmates Sandy, Stoke, Jeffries, and Teresa escape, taking warden Alabama hostage. Trudging through jungle bush, Alabama's hired trackers hunt them down. But Alabama falls behind when she's injured. Rather than helping her, the hired trackers ravage and assault her. Tying her bare-breasted, brutalized body to a tree, they move on to pursue the other fugitives. Teresa doubles back to Alabama's rescue, but after she unties her, their reunion is interrupted by another band of brutes that gang-rape and murder Teresa and Alabama.

While sexploitation is not necessarily intended for a male audience, these films are exceedingly misogynist in their treatment of women. The films create a world in which men dominate. Female characters in Grier's early pictures were literally (physically) punished for strides toward (a figurative) liberation; liberation metaphorically related to the women's movement and second-wave feminism. Images of prostrate, violated female bodies are pervasive in 1970s sexploitation and provoke a parallel between these movies and Dijkstra's reading of nineteenth-century images of prostrate women who were believed to invite sexual aggression. Scenes of helpless women played into the notion of "invited" rape by depicting women who were extremely vulnerable, naked, and supine. The pervasiveness of these images in film underscores my application of Dijkstra's claim that this imagery was a response to the instability of patriarchy at a moment of feminist achievement.

There are at least two ways of reading this recurring phantasm of "perverse" women being gang-raped and tortured by hordes of men in woody environs. On one level, this narrative construction fuels the homophobic logic that women and sexual minorities deserve whatever backlash or retribution heterosexist patriarchy allots for their noncompliance. On another level, an entirely different reading might interpret this scene—and by extension the entire film—as an outing or critique of heterosexual masculinity. After all, the parody of butch-femme roles within the prison and the burlesque play at binary sexuality within the prison reveal gender to be a performance, a masquerade. The masculine woman, as opposed to the androgyne, represents to men what is unreal about masculinity, while actors whose masculinity is overdone and dated invoke the dialectic between (past) imprisonment and (present) liberation that helped to inspire the sexual politics of the late 1960s.[44] The supposed "naturalness" of gender is rendered dubious if not debunked. The unmitigated brutality of male characters presents heterosexual masculinity as predatory, carnivorous, and ultimately destructive even for tough women like Alabama.

Like sexploitation, Blaxploitation relied on many of the same B character actors. Players Sid Haig, Margaret Markov, Teda Bracci, Robert Doqui, and

Katherine Loder reappeared in films directed by Jack Hill, Eddie Romero, and Roger Corman. This was partially due to the fact that the producers and directors were longtime colleagues who relied on the same cast of actors. Loder, for instance, who played prison wardress Lucian in *The Big Doll House,* later played the sadistic Madame Katherine in Jack Hill's *Foxy Brown.* Two levels of reflexive play and intertextuality operate here. First, the 1970s women-in-prison pictures reflexively alluded to women-in-prison films from the 1930s, 1940s, and 1950s released in the United States and the UK (i.e., *Prisoners,* 1929; *Ladies of the Big House,* 1932; *Ann Vickers,* 1933; *Women in Prison,* 1938; *Girls on Probation,* 1938; *Convicted Women,* 1940; *Good Time Girl,* 1949; *The Weak and The Wicked,* 1953; *Women's Prison,* 1955; *Blonde Sinner,* 1956).[45] Second, 1970s films were self-referential in their casting, rotating roles among the same actors. Such reflexive play was as familiar to audiences as Grier's symbolic function as an aggressive woman.

The Big Doll House

Pam Grier's next sexploitation film was *The Big Doll House* (1971). Set on a tropical Pacific Island, *Doll House* is about life at Prison del Inferno. Home to 150 women criminals, Inferno houses killers, prostitutes, and various enemies of the state—outcasts struggling against loneliness and frustration. Among the inmates are Harrad (Brooke Mills), a junkie and baby-killer; Bodine (Pat Woodell), the political prisoner; Collier (Judy Brown), the innocent new girl; and Grear (a Cormanesque homonym for Pam Grier), playing the controlling lesbian who refers to herself as "the Old Man." The moniker "Old Man" codes Grear as the patriarchal phallic figure relative to other women inmates. When Marni Collier, a deceptively sweet young killer, joins the inmates of cell number 3, she becomes the pawn in a struggle for power between blond Karen Alcott and buxom Grear, a feisty ex-prostitute. Their fight over sexual possession of one of the weaker girls establishes Grear as the dominant (fe)male figure.

At Inferno, Grear constantly rivals the psychotic prison wardress Lucian (Kathryn Loder). Lucian is a stereotypically drawn sadistic dyke (as signified by her boyish body, conservative hairstyle, Nazi-style uniform, and dictatorial manner), eager to punish any prisoner who defies her. Two of the prison's cigarette-and-candy vendors, Harry and Fred (Sid Haig and Jerry Franks), smuggle a letter to Bodine from her boyfriend Rafael, leader of the unnamed country's revolutionaries. The prison wardress discovers it. And, in an attempt to uncover Rafael's base of operations, Lucian punishes Bodine with unrelenting sadism in a secret cell while a hooded figure in uniform looks on.[46] When Alcott is caught relieving her sexual frustrations with Fred, Lucian punishes her in the same medieval cell. Dr. Phillips (Jack Davis), the prison physician, is incredulous when the girls complain about Lucian's abusiveness. Staging an escape, they start a food fight in the mess hall, overturning tables and throwing trays. But guards subdue the riot, and for punishment Lucian confines Alcott, Bodine, and Ferina to the "hotbox," a merciless steam room. In the final scenes, a shootout in the prison leaves few survivors. The heroin-addicted Harrad stabs Grear to death. Bodine is brutally shot down. Alcott takes her revenge by blowing up their escape truck. Only Collier escapes the nightmare.

The Big Doll House also presents a racialized, gendered economy of power and privilege in which white women are positioned as naturally feminine. There is a clear ethnic distinction between the butch Philippine prison guards and the mostly femme white inmates. Whereas the guards are stout, fully clothed, short-haired, and armed (i.e., visually coded as masculine), the prisoners are svelte and scantily clad, with long tresses and nubile bodies (i.e., visually coded as feminine). That the guards signify masculinity or butch womanhood and the prisoners signify femininity suggests that gender inheres in the role function itself. There is something about the victim-prisoner function that wants manifestation in racially coded conventions of femininity.[47] In this racialized visual economy, Grier/Grear stands out as a liminal figure positioned between the feminine white world of captives (prisoners) and the masculine, Philippine world of free persons (armed guards). Grier's symbolic liminality (as go-between traveling to and from two symbolically different gender poles) manifests in the film's narrative: she supplies inmates with heroin obtained from Lucian in return for being the prison snitch.

It is not only Grear's lesbianism or identification with the sadistic Lucian that suggests her difference, her perversity. Grear also prostitutes herself to male guards despite loathing men and male sexuality, as when she tries to bribe Harry with sex in exchange for drugs she can no longer obtain from Lucian. She lures Harry to her cell pretending to be a sex-starved, helplessly ecstatic, eager-to-be-vanquished inmate and allows him to fondle her breasts. When Harry predictably double-crosses her, she snaps "You're rotten, Harry . . . you know why? 'Cause you're a man! All men are filthy. All they ever want to do is *get* at you . . . But no more . . . I'm not gonna let a man's filthy hands touch me again!" In this scene Grear is semiotically coded as tough and perverse. Her status as a prostitute notwithstanding, she embodies the perverse combination of intense sexual need and abject helplessness Dijkstra's describes when analyzing the iconography of misogyny in Western art. The moment she signifies as sexually deviant, as an idol of perverse sexuality, the campy dialogue comments on sex and gender roles. Men are denounced as "filthy" and as capable of exploiting women even when women are most vulnerable. Finally, the intentional homonymic slippage between Grier and "Grear" strengthens the symbolic connection between the actor playing perverse characters (Grier) and the perverse onscreen characters she portrays (Grear). Such semiotic slippage fortified Grier's image in the popular imagination.

The Big Bird Cage

Trailers for Pam Grier's next film, *The Big Bird Cage* (1972), invited spectators to witness the spectacle of feminine abjection and sexual perversity by touting: "Abused by savage degenerates! Ravaged by vicious dogs! Punished by the terrible machine that maims tender bodies! Crippled, innocent young minds, denied the one thing that would make their lives bearable: their overheated passion bursts forth in a wild rampage of vengeance and destruction. A strange world in which men are only half men, and women who are *more* than all woman!" Upon advertising a strange world complete with *"women who are more than all woman,"* *The Big Bird Cage* trailer promised the spectacle of excessive femininity. At this cue, the trailer cuts to a scene in which the knife-wielding Pam Grier's tells Sid Haig, "I *told* you I was gonna cut it off if you tried to pull that shit on me!" Repeatedly, these sensational trailers highlighted Grier as the star and primary female force to be reckoned with in the movie. The trailers openly advertised her as the castrating, yet sexually exciting Amazon endowed with something extra. The notion of being more than all-woman is overtly linked to her physical aggressiveness and attempt to appropriate ("cut off") the symbol of masculine authority. Significantly, "cutting it off," or literal castration, is a goal one of Pam Grier's Blaxploitation characters will achieve as the ultimate act of retribution.

New World Pictures returned to the Philippines for the filming of *The Big Bird Cage* in which Grier portrayed Blossom, an undercover revolutionary posing first as a singer in a nightclub. One night, after performing, she and her bandit-revolutionary boyfriend Django (Sid Haig) hold up the club to obtain funds for their insurgent cause. They attempt to abscond with a hostage, the comely Terry Rich (Anitra Ford), known for her ability to swindle powerful politicians. When the authorities intervene, Terry is captured and sentenced to a government work camp outside Manila, a camp controlled by the sadistic warden Zappa (Andy Centenera). Given the film's geographi-

cal landscape and its pseudorevolutionary theme, it's probable that Warden Zappa is a campy caricature of Mexican revolutionary Emiliano Zapata
(1879–1919), champion of the poor, a land reformer, and a guerrilla fighter
during the Mexican Revolution and its aftermath.

At the prison campsite, inmates are deprived of so-called natural sexual
desires. For instance, the male guards are openly homosexual, which is the
warden's way of denying the women any temptation. This is yet another indication that sexploitation was self-consciously parodying sex and gender
roles. Heterosexual transgressors are disciplined with confinement to "the
Birdcage," Zappa's giant bamboo sugar mill with huge, dangerous grinders.
Prisoners are also sent there for failing to meet daily quotas in the rice and
sugarcane fields. Interned at the camp are several prisoners: the garrulous
Bull Jones (Teda Bracci), the leggy new girl Terry, and Mickie (Carol Speed),
a diminutive but sassy young black girl. But before Django and Blossom can
break into the prison and free their would-be comrades, they return to the
base for additional weapons and supplies.

Meanwhile, Django fails to make the rendezvous point, so a jealous Blossom threatens him. Witnessing her cocky possessiveness, a fellow revolutionary says: "If only we had more women like her, what a revolution we could
have!" This scene typifies the sexploitation genre's emphasis on aggressive
women situated in tropical locales in which an unnamed "revolution" is supposedly taking place. The need to recruit more women like Blossom propels
the diegesis. Blossom, Django, and comrades plot to infiltrate Zappa's prison
camp and liberate and then enlist the inmates. Once interned as an undercover inmate, Blossom demands that the other women submit to her authority but encounters resistance and racism. Fights between prisoners continually erupt, providing narrative justification for prurient mud-wrestling and
food-fighting scenes.

In keeping with the loutish spirit of camp, racial tensions between characters are garishly scripted in *Bird Cage,* as when one adversary taunts Blossom by asking her, "Where do you want to be buried, nigger?" Provoked
but not unsettled, Blossom dismissively responds, "It's *Miss* Nigger to you!"
Glibly insisting on the conventional title "Miss," rather than objecting to the
racial epithet "nigger," Pam Grier's Blossom shifts the linguistic balance of
power by evoking the arbitrary relationship between signifier and signified
in language. She demonstrates that the relationship between signifier (i.e.,
"nigger") and signified (i.e., any individual) is a result of a system of social
conventions specific to each society and to particular historical moments and
cultural contexts. There is no single, unchanging, or universal meaning. This

structural realization opens up meaning and destabilizes it by breaking any natural tie between signifier ("nigger") and intended signified ("Blossom"). By insisting on "Miss," Grier's character opens up language, unlocking the constant play of signs, signifiers, and signifyin(g). Such signifying enables linguistic slippage between and within words, thereby producing a totally new meaning. The dialogue for Grier's character Blossom audaciously vacates the derogatory moniker of its racist efficacy and ability to inflict emotional injury. By extension, the white supremacist viewpoint implicit in the utterance is temporarily vacated of power. This type of semiotic slippage and linguistic play typifies exploitation's campy verbal style and Grier's star vehicles.

While sexploitation pictures kept their racial politics cheeky, they relied on the brutal spectacle of gang rape as a narrative staple. In *The Big Bird Cage,* new girl Terry Rich—in trying to escape—encounters a rapacious mob. She wanders off into the woods, scantily clad in a prison gown, looking for a telephone. Helpless and needy, she comes upon a small cluster of huts inhabited by local men. They ambush her. Fortunately, but ambiguously, the rape of Terry is interrupted by a flamboyantly gay prison guard, Roccio (Vic Diaz), who has followed her into the woods. When Roccio finds her, he jokingly quips, "How come stuff like this [gang rape] never happens to *me?*" Reducing sexual identity to sexual activity, this flip, perversely campy dialogue is obviously misogynist. The joke trivializes the brutality of rape as sexual violence against women while simultaneously implying that gay sex is sadistic. Homophobia as a weapon of sexism reveals its effect on women's sexuality and women's liberation.[48]

Invariably, these rape scenes were shot from the viewpoint of male char-acter-perpetrators with reaction shots from female victim characters. Nearly seamless editing aligns gazing spectators with the male perpetrator's point of view. Yet the films do not fix spectators into static alignment with the ag-gressor/perpetrator. Spectator identification flips between alignment with the vicious mob-perpetrator and alignment with the female victim. The identifi-catory shift articulates sexploitation's ambivalence toward its women charac-ters—giving audiences the viewpoint of the woman being molested *and* the viewpoint of the attacker. Sexploitation's shifting point of view evokes Carol Clover's explanation of shifting identification in slasher films, a matter for detailed discussion later.

Close readings of these scenes reveal exploitation's backlash against, and ambivalence toward, women. Because these films move spectators in and out of identification with women characters, they challenge the idea of a fixed viewpoint. By extension, they challenge the notion of a purely masculine or feminist discourse or—for that matter—a coherent worldview. Instead, they present a mixture of conflicting points of view and visual forms (e.g., realism versus stereotype, narrative continuity versus didactic episodes), which disrupt the coherence of the dominant ideology by troubling conventional cinematic forms. Slasher, horror, and sexploitation films can become part of learning and struggle toward feminist or libratory consciousness because of the brutal treatment of female, gay, and lesbian characters. These movies preclude fixed spectatorial positions that can be set against the falsity of dominant ideology.[49] My central point is that Grier's sexploitation vehicles contained aggression and ambivalence toward female characters, an ambivalence encoded in the camera's point of view.

The financial success of Grier's prison pictures paved the way for her roles in Demension Films' *Twilight People* (Eddie Romero, 1972) and Metro-Goldwyn-Mayer's two releases *Hit Man* (George Armitage, 1972), and *Cool Breeze* (Barry Pollack, 1972). Studios recognized her marketability and fan following. Grier reportedly found this work rewarding because it engaged her enthusiasm for acting. She realized, however, the stylistic limitations of being locked into these films and their unserious camp aesthetics. "I didn't know how to be an actress," Grier lamented. "They said, 'Pam, you're an actress now.' I thought, am I? I don't think I'm a very good one because I don't think the movies are good."

Black Mama, White Mama

Until this point, Pam Grier's pictures had performed well with fans. But it was not until she portrayed incarcerated prostitute Lee Daniels in AIP's *Black Mama, White Mama* (Eddie Romero, 1972)—an exploitation movie thematically indebted to Stanley Kramer's *The Defiant Ones*—that white Hollywood executives began to notice her as an actress and box-office surefire. *Black Mama* was a financial success mainly because production costs were tightly controlled. Shot in the Philippine Islands, the shoestring production conditions proved challenging for all actresses involved. According to the film's press kit, the actors faced hardships in filming this prison adventure.

> From their living quarters in Manila, the cast and crew had to face a two-hour drive by limousine, then by jeep to the heart of a tangled forest. The roads were frequently hit by storms that left nothing but rivers of mud so the jeep rides were rough adventures in themselves. Much of the filming was done between rain storms. Several times the group was stranded for hours while

roads had to be rebuilt to permit passage. . . . Typhoid and cholera epidemics were sweeping parts of the Philippines while *Black Mama, White Mama* was being filmed and one of the stars, Lynn Borden, contracted "H" type typhoid. . . . The jungle adventure is the fifth motion picture of her recent credits which was filmed entirely in the Philippine Islands.[50]

The movie paired Grier with blond actress Margaret Markov playing Karen Brent, an idealistic guerilla fighter also interned at the prison. Together Markov and Grier made two of the first female interracial buddy films. *Black Mama, White Mama* (1972) and *The Arena* (1973) were transitional films for Pam Grier, as each broke with the prison-picture formula structure in which her characters were repeatedly killed in the final act. In *Black Mama* Grier's character literally sails off into the sunset with a small fortune in hand. In *The Arena* both she and Markov survive but Grier triumphs as the stronger of the two, walking away uninjured. Faithful to the novel on which it was based, *Black Mama, White Mama* used prison life as a backdrop for a story about two women—one white, the other black—on the lam.

At a women's detention camp somewhere in an unidentified jungle, a bus pulls up carrying a slovenly group of women prisoners. The setting is familiar, but *Black Mama* reverses Pam Grier's *Big Bird Cage* role as a revolutionary fighter, casting Markov as the political rebel. That night, Lee (Grier) rebuffs the sexual advances of matron Densmore (Lynn Borden), a sleazy blonde with lechery on her mind. We get an appreciation for the movie's sensibilities right away when we're treated to a lengthy shower scene, complete with Densmore peeping through a crack in the wall as Lee pleasures herself. This scene goes on for over two minutes, with the nude girls giggling throughout. When Densmore approaches Karen (Markov) with the same offer, she accepts, hoping it will facilitate her escape. Karen's acceptance angers Lee, and the two start fighting in the mess hall. As punishment for unruly behavior, they are stripped and sentenced to the "hot box." Upon their release from the hot box, Lee and Karen are chained together. Karen's guerillas ambush the bus, and the women escape.

Imitating the racial dynamic of *The Defiant Ones, Black Mama, White Mama* has Markov's Karen and Grier's Lee chained together at cross-purposes: Lee needs to retrieve a suitcase full of money hidden at one end of the island; Karen plans to rejoin her guerillas and continue fighting the revolution led by Ernesto (Zaldy Zshomack). Meanwhile, word of their breakout reaches island gangsters Ruben (Sid Haig) and Vic Cheng (Vic Diaz). Vic knows about the money Lee has hidden and dispatches gunmen to track her. As the women forage deeper into the jungle, stealing provisions from local farmers and villages, the police, led by Captain Cruz (Eddie Garcia), follow.

One key difference between *The Defiant Ones* and *Black Mama* is that Grier's Lee does not sacrifice herself for Markov's Karen the way Sidney Poitier's Noah Cullen does for Tony Curtis's John "Joker" Jackson. Throughout cinematic history, black characters have typically been sacrificed so their white costars/counterparts could live. Jeanine Basinger argued that this narrative pattern gained full expression in the World War II combat film.[51] We see vestiges of this narrative outline in contemporary horror and science-fiction films (i.e., *Alien 3, Scream 2*). Such patterns reproduced the stereotype of the dying slave from Harriet Beecher Stowe's *Uncle Tom's Cabin*. Tom is beaten, chased, insulted, and enslaved, but when he dies, he dies content because he has been loyal to his white master. *Black Mama* presents a racial role reversal with respect to this paradigm. Grier's Lee not only saves herself, she survives Markov's character Karen. In the 1970s, audiences enjoyed a reprieve from narratives of black sacrifice because exploitation films (sexploitation and Blaxploitation, in particular) broke this mold. *Black Mama* proved transitional in another way. It broke the generic pattern common in Grier's pictures. Sexploitation's women characters were rarely—if ever—spared excessive punishment for their transgressions of the patriarchal social order. In *Black Mama,* Grier's Lee ultimately triumphs rather than dies in the final reel.

That Grier's characters were often sole survivors is significant in terms of feminist film history and theory. These narrative endings are noteworthy because they suggest evidence of a precursor to Carol Clover's notion of the Final Girl. In a seminal study of slasher films as a subgenre, Clover defined the Final Girl in terms of horror film. There are parallels between the aggressive action heroines of exploitation and the Final Girls of horror pictures. Like the Final Girl, who looks for the killer, the exploitation heroine looks to satisfy her revenge against monstrous male villains. Much like the Final Girl of horror films, the exploitation heroine is—by the conclusion—aligned with the camera and audience. Like the Final Girl, the exploitation heroine is presented as tomboyish, or "butch," or somewhat androgynous (i.e., Jamie Lee Curtis in *Halloween*). And, like the Final Girl, who shares masculine qualities with the killer, the exploitation heroine shares masculine qualities with the sadistic villains and prison guards.[52] Grier was a phallic symbol par excellence. Her only contemporaries in this respect were predecessors who—a few years earlier—appeared in sexploitation pictures prior to Grier. The most notable example is Japanese-Filipino-American Tura Satana, who starred in *Astro Zombies* (1967), *Faster, Pussycat! Kill! Kill!* (1966), and *Doll Squad* (1973).[53] It was after Grier's initial success with Roger Corman that others began entering the scene. Making this observation, Grier told filmmaker Isaac Julien:

> I think after the first three or four films with Roger, other actresses said you know what, "I just wanted to be the prissy love interest. But I think I'm going to kick some butt too, make some money like Pam." So there were other actresses entering, from Tamara Dobson to Gloria Hendry. They started coming in and getting the work that I . . . [had] not turned down, but I was already hired to do a certain amount of work and I can only be in so many places at once. So, other actresses were doing pretty much what I was doing.

The Arena

Following *Black Mama, White Mama,* Grier starred in the Steve Carver–directed, Corman-produced picture titled *The Arena* (1973). Grier and Margaret Markov received equal billing in this low-budget but lavish—by Roger Corman standards—New World release. Filmed quickly and cheaply (for $75,000) in Italy by Carver, *The Arena* (released overseas as *La rivolta delle gladiatrici*) was dubbed a "mini-spectacle rip-off of Kirk Douglas's star vehicle *Spartacus*" (Stanley Kubrick, 1960).[54] Years later, in the summer of 1988, *The Arena* was re-released for the videocassette market under the more sensational title *Naked Warriors*. In keeping with the exploitive distribution strategies of its production, publicity material for videocassette store distributors enticed retailers with the following: "The competitive spirit of the [1988 Korean] summer Olympics will put your customers in the perfect mood for this Olympian-theme release."

Shot on location in Italy, *The Arena* is set during the decadent days of ancient Rome. In the opening scene, Roman soldiers scour the countryside, carrying off beautiful women to be sold as slaves. One of these captive women is the proud Bodicia (Markov), a Druid high priestess. Another is a voluptuous African woman named Mamawi (Grier). In the Roman town of Brundisium, the owner of a local arena where gladiatorial contests are staged purchases the women. By day, the women must serve patrons of the arena. At night they're obliged to warm the beds of fatally injured gladiators, or those sentenced to death. Internal dissension among the slavewomen erupts one day into a wild free-for-all in the kitchen of the owner's villa. Their masters, who see a chance to tickle the jaded palates of arena patrons, watch this impassioned but comic melee with condescending approval. Henceforth,

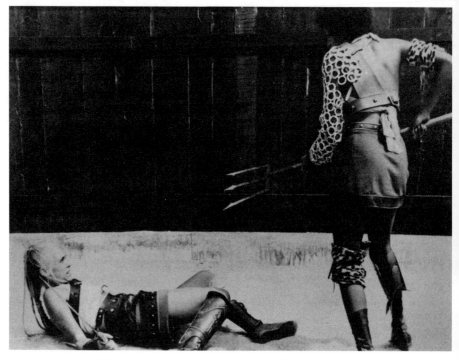

Grier (as Mamawi) and Margaret Markov (as Bodicia) are luscious gladiators in the *The Arena* (1973).

the women will be trained as gladiators and will challenge each other in the arena. The first fight turns out to be a farce. But soon blood begins to flow and the women are forced to fight to the death just like men. Horrified by this barbarity, Bodicia and Mamawi lead a revolt against their masters. Many of their sister slaves are killed in the uprising, but these two manage to fight their way through the labyrinths and beyond the city walls to freedom.[55]

Grier in Transition

Black Mama, White Mama (produced by AIP) and *The Arena* (produced by New World) were transitional films for Pam Grier. Precursors to her Blaxploitation films, these sexploitation-action roles maintained her forceful woman-warrior iconicity but downplayed the lesbianism prevalent in earlier pictures, making her image more mainstream and therefore acceptable to straight women and traditional African American spectators. In these later films, Grier's characters have more autonomy and control of their sexuality than that granted to costar Margaret Markov, who—by contrast—portrayed sexually vulnerable women. For instance, in *The Arena*, Bodicia and Mamawi (Grier) are brought into the harem, where they are expected to dance, entertain, and perform sexual services. Mamawi capitulates by belly dancing to stir the randy spectators. For resisting this degradation and refusing to charm the harem's male visitors, the proud, innocent Bodicia is raped while intoxicated onlookers become aroused. The message of this scene—and the film—is clear: cooperate or be punished. Both *The Arena* and *Black Mama, White Mama* reproduced the antiwoman backlash familiar from earlier sexploitation films. But Pam Grier's characters were gradually beginning to fare better in the narrative relative to her previous roles.

After completing *The Arena*, Grier landed a lead role in the Jack Hill–scripted and –directed movie *Coffy* (1973). The film's press kit hailed the picture's realism and Grier's firsthand knowledge of the subject. "Pam has seen the devastating effect of narcotics within her own family, so her depiction of the enraged Coffy is doubly real. She advised Jack Hill about the many situations and characters in the fast-paced drama. *Coffy* was filmed in and around Los Angeles, on actual locations. It has the ring of truth and the ring of bullets. It is a smashing story of retaliation."[56]

Coffy served as the bridge from sexploitation to Blaxploitation. Prior to *Coffy*, Grier had only costarred with Margaret Markov, Roberta Collins, Judy Brown, Sid Haig, and other B movie actors. She had not yet carried a film on her own as the principal star. In terms of style, *Coffy* repeated the campy, exploitation recipe. And, like her earlier films, *Coffy* was a hit. Following its financial success, AIP president Samuel Arkoff ushered out several imitations. All were produced with the same low budgets, gratuitous sex, requisite violence, and backbreaking shooting schedule, with Pam Grier campily playing various voluptuous vigilantes. As a result, Grier signed a contract with AIP, which subsequently featured her in *Scream, Blacula, Scream* (Bob Kelljan, 1973), *Foxy Brown* (Jack Hill, 1974/75), the racial drama *Bucktown* (Arthur Marks, 1975), *Friday Foster* (Arthur Marks, 1975), and *Sheba, Baby* (William Girdler, 1975). All were profitable, but the star was growing weary of these one-dimensional roles. She told one reporter: "My movies were the first they had done with a strong woman character, not to mention black. Once they saw the grosses, they wanted to do every one of them like that. I was angry. You can't give people the same thing all the time. You made money on one thing, so the next time you go for something a little better than you had before."

After completing work on *Friday Foster*, and fulfilling her contract with AIP, Grier left the studio. She later told reporters of her dissatisfaction with

Investigative working girl in *Friday Foster* (1975).

AIP. Lamenting Arkoff's provincialism to one interviewer, Pam said he was "someone who can't see past the cash register, someone who has a peanut brain."[57] Optimistic and eager to produce her own scripts, she established Brown Sun Productions. Speaking about the company, she told *Sepia* magazine: "I know I can make my company a success. I read the trades. I know I'm big. I can get investors and I'm going to make money the way I see fit. No mindless women, no dumb situations. I know I have to go slow but I'm going to sneak up on them little by little and then I'm going to create a monster. This girl is not just another body for the camera."[58] Unfortunately, Grier was unable to turn Brown Sun Productions into a profitable enterprise. Matters worsened when she also started having difficulty securing roles. After her contract with American International Pictures ended, her professional acting career began to dwindle. She received only supporting roles, like the character Regine in the *Mandingo* sequel *Drum* (Steve Carver, 1976), or the part of Mary Scott, the wife of Richard Pryor's Wendell Scott in Warner Brothers' *Greased Lightning* (Michael Schultz, 1977). William L. Van Deburg offered an explanation of the restrictions posed by exploitation films and an analysis of why women stars like Pam Grier had difficulty branching out beyond the genre. For cultural historian Van Deburg, the objectifying phallocentric gaze curtails and contains female performers.

> Female love interests in the Blaxploitation films sometimes acted as if they were attempting to join the pin-up goddess aloofness of Lena Horne with the overt sexuality of Eartha Kitt and Dorothy Dandridge. Some slyly witty femmes even managed to toss in a few stinging wisecracks à la Pearl Bailey. Most, however, were firmly fixed in the "phallocentric gaze," which students of modern film culture have identified as a major hindrance to the development of fully realized cinematic portrayals of women. In terms of both filmic representation and reception, male definition dominated. Attractive female characters in supporting roles were to be looked at, desired and possessed. At all times, they were expected to subordinate their own needs to the prerogatives of the male culture hero. Presented as passive, erotic objects pleasing to the hyperactive and voyeuristic male gaze, such characters contributed importantly to the creation of a Hollywood fantasy world in which the woman as ornament, victim, or spectacle could hope to influence events only through her sexuality. Her main concern—and what she did best—was to satisfy the patriarch's lusts and to boost male egos on both sides of the camera.[59]

While Van DeBurg aptly describes the sexual construction of icons like Grier, he describes them as passive objects when they are also active narrative agents and protagonists in these films. Scholars Pam Cook, Carol Clover, and Yvonne Tasker have demonstrated that both male and female spectators move in and out of an identificatory relationship with active narrative agents. Van DeBurg's literal analysis fails to account for exploitation's playful comic sensibility or women's aggressiveness or the way women turn their hostility against the male world, thereby parodying male violence as campy butch violence. His reading reductively maintains woman-as-object, precluding any notion of generic continuity between 1970s exploitation and 1990s action, horror, or neo-noir, replete as they often are with strong women characters.[60] Generic continuity from the 1970s to 2000s is traceable through filmmakers like Jonathan Demme, who coscripted *Black Mama, White Mama* (1972) and directed *Caged Heat* (1974) only to later direct *Silence of the Lambs* (1991). It is also traceable in the film-studies literature. Carol Clover, for instance, noted how films like *The Accused*, the *Aliens* quadrilogy, *Silence of the Lambs*, and *Thelma and Louise* are predicated on the "low-budget, often harsh and awkward but sometimes deeply energetic films that preceded them by a decade or more—films that said it all, and in flatter terms, and on a shoestring."[61] Clover is clearly referring to the exploitation films and their various permutations. Her thesis also applies to more recent films like *Domino* (Tony Scott, 2005).

From Idol of Perversity to Idol of Black Power

Riding on the coattails of *Shaft* (Gordon Parks, 1971) and *Sweet Sweetback's Baadasssss Song* (Melvin Van Peebles, 1971), Grier's Blaxploitation films placed her in a new but familiar context. She sustained the transition from sexploitation to Blaxploitation because the films were structurally and thematically similar. Whereas sexploitation presented a parodic gender masquerade ("A strange world in which men are only half men, and women are *more* than all woman!"), Blaxploitation offered racial masquerade, over-the-top performances of undefeatable black characters who were not taking shit from "the Man." Grier's tough persona, which had offered a sexual perversion of the patriarchal order, was shifting into a social subversion of the racial and patriarchal order. Her new characters deployed sexuality as a lure to foil the white criminals, black kingpins, and petty pushers responsible for drug-related despair, and prostitution in black communities. A reinvented phallic woman, she presented the "old masochistic male fantasy of subjection to a dominating femme fatale."[62] But this old dominatrix had a new political agenda.

Assuming different names (Coffy, Foxy Brown, Friday Foster, and Sheba Shayne), Grier personified fictional figures in the symbolic act of (black) national allegory.[63] As Benedict Anderson demonstrated, a nation is more than a geographical location. It is a consensual idea, a cultural and political construct, and an abstraction given form, unity, and meaning in the realm of discourse. The idea of nation is formulated and sustained by means of allegories or fictions that incarnate and dramatize the conflicting forces at play in the construction of nationhood. Pam Grier's protagonists carried the symbolic weight of post–civil rights black national identity in cinematic texts that functioned as metaphors for the pitfalls of inner-city life. For instance, in *Coffy*, she plays the eponymous night nurse turned vicious vigilante; a woman eager to right the wrongs committed against black community and civil society. Reflecting on these characters, Grier said: "Women of the 70s had to do a lot of things because of the wars. They had to do a lot of things that men were supposed to do. If you didn't have a man at home, you did it. So, I brought that into the films. Coffy, Foxy Brown and Sheba were independent women that did things because there wasn't a man around."[64]

When the film begins, Coffy plans to kill everyone responsible for destroying her eleven-year-old sister Lu Belle (Karen Williams), who lost her mind after she was introduced to dope. Her vigilante spree begins with the seduction of a small-time pusher named Sugar Man (Morris Buchanan). She blows Sugar Man's head off with a sawed-off shotgun. Forcing his hireling to overdose, she explains her plot to avenge Lu Belle. For Coffy, Lu Belle's fate is symptomatic of the exploitation of poor black folks by organized criminals. She confesses to her friend Officer Carter Brown (William Elliot) that the problem is more pervasive than she initially believed. From a prostitute named Priscilla (Carol Lawson), Coffy learns that a big dope distributor and pimp, King George (Robert Doqui), works for Las Vegas drug lord Vitroni (Allan Arbus) and that Vitroni is hooked in with police through Carter's crooked white partner McHenry (Barry Cahill). Despite sympathizing with her motives, Carter urges Coffy to relinquish her vendetta. "Why kill some junkie who's paying for his own habit? He's only part of a chain that reaches back to some poor farmer in Turkey or Vietnam. What good would it do to kill one of them?"

Superficially political dialogue, sprinkled throughout Blaxploitation movies, typified the genre's cursory nod to social problems and political issues (e.g., women's liberation, Black Power, drug addiction, prostitution). Jack Hill and Roger Corman (among others) made a routine practice of weaving social issues into exploitation narratives because this recipe worked successfully in precursors *Shaft* and *Sweet Sweetback's Baadasssss Song*. Filmmakers sought to captivate politicized black audiences already galvanized by civil rights activism, Black Panther protests, Stokely Carmichael's speeches, "free Huey Newton" rallies, the murder of Fred Hampton, and the arrest of Angela Davis. The films operated according to a Manichean schema: black self-determination (a fusion of Black Pride, Black Power, and Black Nationalism)[65] coalesced to defeat white villainy. Brilliantly sporting dashiki shirts, kente cloth, bell-bottom pants, and well coiffed afros, black actors playing these protagonists (Shaft, Coffy, Cleo, and Sweetback) signified nationalist sentiment through their performance of the *esthétique du cool*.

Encoded through performance and costume, the *esthétique* was demonstrated by a character's cool pose, a chameleon-like ability to fool the unsuspecting, a commitment to ferret criminals, and a black aesthetic.[66] *Esthétique* dictated eschewal of black bourgeois values (and concomitant excesses) in favor of characters supporting a working-class black community (i.e., *Blue Collar*, 1978). For decades, African Americans assimilated to mainstream American culture. Unquestioned assimilation ended for a cross-section of 1960s and 1970s progressives. Younger African Americans rejected middle-class mores and embraced the experiences of blacks from inner-city ghettoes. Youth-oriented counter-culture began valorizing anti-establishment ideologies. Participants of the underground economy (pimps, sex workers, and drug traffickers) were suddenly valorized as real, as authentically black, and as untainted by collaboration with white patriarchal capitalist society. These professional hustlers decided that if they had to comply with market forces, they would do so as part of their own illegitimate network—an economic system they could control. Ironically, these outsiders unwittingly collaborated with "the system" they sought to subvert by trafficking in an illegitimate but globally recognized underground economy.

The 1970s notion of an *esthétique du cool* was not universally embraced. As early as 1972, critics began questioning the sociological value, representational authenticity, and financial exploitation of Blaxploitation pictures. First, there was B. J. Mason's 1972 *Ebony* cover story titled "The New Films: Culture or Con Game?" Next came the 1973 *New York Times* article "Is It Better to Be *Shaft* than Uncle Tom?" Pearl Bowser's essay in *Black Creation* suggested, "The Boom is really an Echo." Even celebrity interviews lamented the repetitiveness of these pictures. Take Patrick Salvo's *Sepia* article titled "Pam Grier: The Movie Super-Sex Goddess Who's Fed Up with Sex and Violence" as a case in point. But box-office revenue, not intellectual commentary, determined production. Audiences enjoyed the *esthétique,* the heroine's perseverance and her sense of righteousness. They appreciated her ability to fight the power structure despite the campy aesthetic with which that fight was presented.

Not only did audiences respond at the box office, they also responded to the star herself. Nowhere was audience appreciation more evident than in the fan mail Grier received.

> I have fan mail that you read and sometimes I almost weep from what women were getting out of it. They were saying I was doing and saying what they wanted to say. My family said I was just playing us in our daily activity, in our daily quest for respect, to hold on to our dignity and just try to verbalize our integrity. It was so refreshing to hear that and to know that the guys didn't feel their place in society was being taken over by strong women. It was never to take the place of a man, take away his job. It was like, well, if you're not here, I'm not going to let the house burn down. I have to protect myself and the family and the kids.[67]

The narrative of *Coffy* exemplifies the way Grier's Blaxploitation characters achieved revenge against those white criminals exploiting working-class black communities. In one of two showdowns between Coffy and drug dealer Vitroni, she delivers another classic revenge speech for which Blaxploitation stars and characters were venerated. Posing as Jamaican prostitute Mystique, Coffy deceptively agrees to service Vitroni, knowing his Achilles heel is a sadistic sexual fetish for beautiful women.

"Get on the floor and crawl over here!"
"Oh, please, I know I'm not good enough for you. But let me touch your white body just once."
"Crawl over here! I'm not gonna hurt you, just crawl, you black bitch."

Black and white audience sympathies are readily aligned with Grier's Coffy not only because Vitroni's the villain, but also because his sexist and racist behaviors render him even more deplorable. This scene supplies another example of exploitation cinema's emphasis on the fetish of sexual racism. In a typical seduce-and-betray scene, she corners him, pulls out the pistol hidden in her bag, and taunts: "So, you want me to crawl, white motherfucker?" Unfortunately, Coffy's attempt to teach Vitroni a lesson is thwarted when his henchmen suddenly intervene. She returns later to kill him and his hirelings, giving them the generic vigilante sendoff. Her victory furnishes the predictably binaristic spectacle of subversion: good black woman defeats evil white man.

In addition to legitimizing Grier's acting by enabling her to jettison the residue of seedy sexploitation, *Coffy* exemplified Blaxploitation's racial revenge motif in which black women were vigilante-survivors hunting white male criminals. This new victim-survivor's quest for justice inverted the racial and gender hierarchies of mainstream vigilante cinema popularized by white male stars Charles Bronson, Chuck Norris, and Clint Eastwood.[68] The appearance of female vigilantes in recent action films (i.e., *Kill Bill, Kill Bill 2*), neo-Blaxploitation (i.e., *Undercover Brother, I'm Gonna Get You Sucker*), horror (i.e., *Scream 2, The Ring*), and neo-noir (i.e., *Jackie Brown*) suggests structural continuity between old and new films as well as the existence of cult cinema's intertextual archetypes— preestablished, frequently reappearing types recycled by innumerable texts, provoking déjà vu in the spectator.[69] Grier's career as a subversive phallic femme was predicated on her narrative function as an intertextual archetype. Her characters' rancorous remarks resonated with those of other characters in similar situations, evoking the same satisfaction audiences derived from similarly triumphant vigilantes. *Coffy*—like other Grier pictures—succeeded in becoming a campy cult film not because it is *one* movie but because it is *the movies*.

Foxy Brown

Foxy Brown (1974), a sequel to *Coffy*, was based on the same narrative formula and catalogue of intertextual archetypes. Both were directed and scripted by Jack Hill, and both yielded significant returns at the box office. *Foxy Brown* grossed $2.46 million in domestic rentals. Once again, Grier plays the epony-mous lead whose mission is to defeat predatory drug kingpin Steve Elias (Peter Brown),[70] the villain responsible for the death of her undercover nar-cotics agent boyfriend Michael Anderson (Terry Carter) and her younger brother Link (Antonio Fargas).

Cornered at a local taco stand by Eddie (Tony Giorgio) and Bunyan (Fred Lerner), two members of a local dope ring, Link frantically phones Foxy. As the assassins are closing in on Link, Foxy appears, opens up a can of whoopass, wreaks havoc on the dealers, and takes Link to her apartment for safekeeping. Later, when Foxy brings home her lover, Michael, who has had his face altered to prevent recognition by the mob, Link identifies him. Trying to improve his position with the mob, Link phones Miss Katherine Wall (Katherine Loder), head of the local dope and prostitution ring. Kath-erine passes the information to her lover-henchman Steve Elias, who sets up an ambush to kill Michael. An enraged Foxy decides to go undercover and infiltrate the syndicate. She ingratiates herself with Miss Katherine and becomes part of her high-class call-girl operation. Her first appointment is to accompany one of Katherine's most experienced girls, Claudia (Juanita Brown). Their mission: satisfy and bribe a local judge to release members of Miss Katherine's gang who are awaiting trial.

But just as Foxy prepares to strike against Katherine and Steve, she's cap-tured and sent to the "Ranch," a filthy backwater farm where she is tied, drugged, and repeatedly raped by two slovenly racists. As film scholar Ed Guerrero noted, villainy is linked to racist sexism in *Foxy Brown*. Guerrero aptly noted how this scene evokes memories of black women's plight under slavery, since it contains visual references to the plantation, including a mo-ment when Foxy is lashed with a bullwhip. Guerrero's observation under-scores my thesis that sexual racism is endemic to exploitation cinema. When Foxy eventually escapes, she persuades a handful of militant youngbloods to join her fight against drug lords by convincing them that her cause is not only personal but the plight of all black people.[71] This is yet another example of how writers, directors, and producers of Blaxploitation cinema exploited the sentiments of politicized black audiences to garner box office revenue.

The image of sleazy racists and grubby sexists violating the heroine justifies the narrative's rape-revenge crescendo. After enlisting the righteous young brothers to help her exact revenge, she plans the ultimate reprisal: to castrate Steve with a hunting knife. The castration obviously occurs off-screen but is powerfully staged nonetheless. And its significance is underscored when Foxy personally delivers Steve's member (now placed in a pickle jar) to his

Grier as Foxy Brown (dir. Jack Hill, 1974).

lover, Katherine, who, upon recognizing his genitals cries out, "Steve!" Foxy's revenge has literal and figurative significance. It is a literal expression of Foxy's personal triumph over Steve (i.e., the penis) and a figurative expression of the black community's collective victory over a criminal figurehead (i.e., the phallus). It's also a symbolic appropriation by Foxy of the proverbial phallus. Symbolic order is restored: the corrupt Law of the deviant father is subverted by the righteous ways of the black mother. Steve's physical castration metaphorically endows Foxy with phallic properties.

Foxy Brown's retaliatory castration anticipates the classic rape-revenge scene of Meir Zarchi's cult film *I Spit on Your Grave* (1977).[72] Generically speaking, *Foxy Brown* is a harbinger of rape-revenge films and ought to be considered a cinematic antecedent for its plot structure. Both films' protagonists (Jennifer and Foxy) are the antithesis of their perpetrators. Foxy is an urban-based, northern, black female who abstains from drug use. The perpetrators are rural, southern, white male drug abusers. Jennifer is similarly juxtaposed against her perpetrators. She's an educated, urban-based journalist who is viciously attacked by country bumpkins. Just as the assault on Jennifer is an act of so-called generosity toward one of the group members, "a gift" to Matthew, so Foxy's confinement to the "Ranch," where she's drugged and abused, is a gift to "the [good old] Boys" on the farm. Both women ultimately achieve vengeance in the form of physical castration. And both *I Spit on Your Grave* and *Foxy Brown* are intertextual archetypes, films produced in relation to other films with the purpose of becoming a cult objects.

Friday Foster and *Sheba, Baby*

Yaphet Kotto (whose first film credit is *Nothing But a Man*) costarred with Grier in *Friday Foster* (Arthur Marks, 1975), her seventh appearance in an AIP feature release. Based on the popular syndicated adventure comic strip of the same name, *Friday Foster* casts Kotto as an intrepid private eye and Grier as a high-fashion model turned photographer. Together they find themselves in a situation fraught with political intrigue and murder. The film also features stars Godfrey Cambridge, Eartha Kitt, Scatman Crothers, and Ted Lange, aka "Jr." of the popular television show *That's My Mama*. Director Marks wrote the screenplay, and Orville Hampton penned the story. But despite fine performances from Kotto and Cambridge, *Friday* turned out to be hackneyed.

By the time AIP released the last films under Grier's multipicture contract with the studio (*Sheba, Baby*, 1974; and *Friday Foster*, 1975), the generic recycling of her vigilante vehicles was well worn. Every aspect of *Sheba, Baby's* production indicated generic exhaustion. Not only does Grier appear emotionally removed in the film, the supporting cast is weaker than her usual costars (Sid Haig, Katherine Loder, and Vic Diaz), who in the past had executed campy performances to infuse these pictures with a unique combination of kitsch and comedic levity. By 1975, the campy qualities were either gone or so worn that critics and audiences stopped supporting these pictures. Biographer and film historian Robert Parish summed up the situation saying that audiences, "satiated with the Blaxploitation formula, and baffled by the tentativeness of this new entry, were not enthusiastic about *Sheba, Baby*. The grosses were down to $1,000,000 in domestic film rentals."[73]

Nostalgia for Herself: "Kit Porter Is a Real Motherfucking Diva!"

When her contract with AIP expired, Grier stopped receiving roles and professional offers commensurate with her industry experience. It was not until 1977 that she would again be in front of the camera, opposite Richard Pryor in *Greased Lightning,* directed by Michael Schultz. Four years later, she played the giggly homicidal prostitute Charlotte opposite Paul Newman in the police drama *Fort Apache, The Bronx* (Daniel Petrie, 1981). Speaking about this film Grier recalls, "I really felt like I had done something in that." But having been a film star and exploitation movie diva did little to protect Grier from the realities of being African American in a predominantly white society. After the filming was complete in 1981, Pam was accosted by two police officers outside her Beverly Hills home.[74] Despite her status as a celebrity, Pamela Grier—like Dorothy Dandridge before her—was not free from the reality of racist surveillance in America.

Her performance in *Fort Apache, The Bronx* notwithstanding, the 1980s yielded little more than minor roles in small films like *Something Wicked This Way Comes* (1983) and *Above the Law* (1988). Dissatisfied with these minor roles, Grier turned to the theater. She appeared in productions of *Frankie and Johnny,* for which she gained seventy-five pounds, and a production of *Fool for Love,* which earned her an NAACP Image Award in 1986. The actress declared: "As long as I can do one play a year, I'm happy . . . The nineteen eighties were pretty boring in terms of the movie offers I was getting, and that's when I discovered that working in the theater was a great way to keep developing my acting skills." While developing her acting skills in the theater, Grier finally realized she was always meant to be an actress. "My confirmation came after I did *Frankie and Johnny.* I think acting became very important to me then because until then, I kept thinking I wanted to end up behind the camera."

In 1988, Grier's acting career was unexpectedly interrupted when she was diagnosed with cancer.

> My doctor gave me 18 months to live. My whole life changed. I became a different person at that point. I was cut up and felt I was going to be a castrated female after the surgery. There was transposition of organs, all kinds of things for radiation purposes, to save me. There were days where I thought, "Should I live? Should I die?" I had to take it one step at a time. After two years, I realized I was okay. I remember I stopped wearing my Rolex, which I used to wear because you would get help in stores faster, people would wait on you quicker. Minnie and I joked about it: "We're gonna get waited on today." I took it off

after that, and I haven't worn it since. I just wanted to bring more truth to my life. I survived a wall, and didn't need a Rolex to say anything about me.

With the 1980s slump and her bout with cancer behind her, Pam Grier began working again. First she secured a substantial role in *Original Gangstas* (Larry Cohen, 1996), which reunited her with fellow Blaxploitation stars Fred Williamson, Jim Brown, Ron O'Neal, and Richard Roundtree. Unfortunately, *Gangstas* was met by mediocre reviews and had a less than stellar performance at the box office, earning a domestic total gross of $3,718,087. Next the star played yet another tough, phallic femme, the dangerous transsexual Hershe Las Palmas in John Carpenter's *Escape from L.A.* (1996). This film fared better at the box office than *Gangstas* but was not a major role for her. Following *Escape,* she starred as divorced mother Louise Williams in the science fiction comedy *Mars Attacks!* (Tim Burton, 1996). Fortunately, *Mars* performed reasonably well, grossing $37 million domestically and $63 million overseas for a worldwide total of $101.3 million.

Grier took smaller roles in *Fakin' da Funk* (Timothy A. Chey, 1997) and *Strip Search* (Rod Hewitt, 1997) before starring in Tarantino's *Jackie Brown* (1997) and Ernest R. Dickerson's *Bones* (2001). The fact that she successfully obtained these roles evidences the longevity of her star persona. None of her 1970s contemporaries have reemerged to assume leading (or prominent supporting) roles in mainstream, theatrically released pictures. For Grier, featured roles in *Original Gangsters, Jackie Brown,* and *Bones* utilized the aura of her 1970s screen persona to create a feeling of nostalgia for that decade.

Jackie Brown is a perfect example of postmodern nostalgia. According to Pam Grier, the "role of a lifetime" emerged with Quentin Tarantino's third film, based on the Elmore Leonard novel *Rum Punch.* One of Grier's most enthusiastic fans, Tarantino wrote the screenplay adaptation of *Rum Punch* as a star vehicle for the actress he had admired since his adolescence to play the novel's Jackie Burke. As homage to Grier's most famous role, *Foxy Brown,* Tarantino changed the character's name to Jackie Brown. *Jackie Brown* not only reanimated the myth of the phallic woman striving for revenge, it also reinvented Grier's former persona. *Jackie* recharged Grier's screen persona and snowballed into new projects: Ernest Dickerson's horror film *Bones* and, later, a role as Kit Porter on Showtime's lesbian soap opera *The L Word.*

Both *Bones* and *The L Word* utilize the aura of Grier's 1970s persona, but in different ways. Set in the present day, *Bones* tells the history of one African American neighborhood crippled by organized crime; the film's plot is reminiscent of Grier's earlier work. In a series of flashbacks, we return to 1979, when Jimmy Bones (Snoop Doggy Dogg, aka Cordazer Calvin Broadus), an admired neighborhood protector who personified the *esthétique du cool,* is betrayed and brutally murdered by a corrupt white cop (Michael T. Weiss) and his henchmen. When Jimmy dies in his home, his lavish brownstone becomes his tomb and the neighborhood he once protected is brutally exploited by drug dealers. Twenty-two years later, the neighborhood is a ghetto and his home a gothic ruin. When four young deejays turn the house into a nightclub, they unknowingly release Jimmy's tortured spirit, freeing his repressed, vengeful soul. Jimmy's ghost sets about exacting revenge. His killers meet their deaths quickly, unaware of the gruesome fate before them. With each new victim, the terror mounts, and Jimmy's vengeance spins out of control, ultimately threatening everyone, including his former lover, Pearl (Grier).

Historically it has been uncommon—in mainstream commercial movies— for older women to be coupled with or cast as the love interests of younger men. Between Pam Grier and Snoop Dogg there's a twenty-two year difference. But their coupling is consistent with the film's narrative and the imaginary world it pictures. *Bones* seeks to re-create the countercultural aura, soulful atmosphere, and phonic ambiance of the 1970s. It relies on the persona of Grier to conjure its flashbacks. Inscribing Snoop Dogg as a badass, Shaft-like figure requires the accoutrements, props, and paraphernalia associated with the 1970s. In this instance, Grier functions in exactly that capacity. *Bones,* like *Jackie Brown* before it and, to a lesser degree, *The L Word* after, harnessed the aura of Grier's former persona. This nostalgia for the past cinematic presence of Pam Grier is the clearest indication she was a definitive cultural icon of the 1970s.

Even *The L Word,* which utilizes Grier modestly as a supporting character, implies that her character Kit Porter, a recovering alcoholic in a twelve-step program, was once a soul diva. To do this, it again links her with Snoop Dogg, who plays Slim Daddy, a successful hip-hop artist and music producer. She is related to the main cast of characters through her half-sister Bette (Jennifer Beals), the fair-skinned, corporate lesbian curator monogamously involved—during season one—with Tina Kennard (Laurel Holloman). In the first season the social world of *The L Word* revolved around Bette and Tina's closely knit group of lesbian girlfriends, including newcomer Jenny Schecter (Mia Kirshner), a college grad who moves to LA to shack up with her boyfriend Tim Haspel (Eric Mabius). Bette and Tina bring Jenny into contact with their wide swath of single girlfriends, including closeted tennis player Dana Fairbanks (Erin Daniels); trendy magazine writer Alice Pieszekci (Leisha Hailey); and a promiscuous love-'em-and-leave lesbian lothario[75] named Shane McCutcheon (Katherine Moennig).

Snoop Dogg (Jimmy Bones) and Grier (Pearl) are reunited lovers in *Bones* (2001).

While this lesbian soap opera doesn't invoke the political militancy of Grier's 1970s Blaxploitation image, it does call to mind the soulful sisterhood always embedded in her screen persona. On the show, Kit's music career gets a boost when Slim Daddy decides to sample one of her old hits on his new record. Through Slim Daddy, the TV viewing audience is made cognizant of

Kit's cultural relevance. While shooting the music video for their song, Slim Daddy reminds a frustrated director not to forget his place.

> *Kit:* I love the song. And, I really want to be in the video. But I can't be in it like this. When I stopped drinking I promised myself I would never make a fool of myself again.
>
> *Slim Daddy:* It's my bad. I put the girls in the video cuz I thought this is what you wanted. I thought this was your thang.
>
> *Kit:* You did that for me?
>
> *Slim Daddy:* Yeah.
>
> *Kit:* Listen, it's not about the girls. It's just that . . . well, hell, I'm not twenty. And, I ain't nobody's hoochie. So, why am I puttin' myself through all this? If they don't like me and my song, this is not gonna convince them.
>
> *Director:* Sorry to interrupt. But I have to keep shooting. Are you in, or not?
>
> *Slim Daddy:* Excuse me, Kit. If it wasn't for Kit Porter, wouldn't none of us be here. Wouldn't be no song. Wouldn't be no video *for* you to shoot. So, what you *meant* to say was, you 'bout to sit yo' ass over there and figure out how to get this right. Right!?

What makes this scene interesting is its double articulation. It has diegetic (narrative) and nondiegetic (nonnarrative) significance. At the diegetic level, it articulates the difficulties encountered by older women artists trying to speak through a youth-dominated music video vernacular. Kit knows the concept for the video is wrong for her. Yet the narrative world of the TV show is consistent with the African American tradition of paying respect to blues, R & B, or Motown artists who preceded hip-hop. At the nondiegetic level, the scene resonates with the real-life screen career of Pam Grier. Contemporary artists ranging from Quentin Tarantino to Snoop Dogg (not to mention writers of *The L Word*) recognize their debt to the pop-culture legacy of Grier and her contemporaries—those on whom they rely to evoke that "old-school" feeling. Here the term *old school* is not only a reference to 1970s funk, it also refers to traditional dating practices. For example, when a cross-dressing drag king named Ivan (Kelly Lynch) begins romantically pursuing Kit, Bette warns, "She's courting you, old-school, and you're letting her!" Throughout, *The L Word* displays similar signs of nostalgia in narrative genuflections to Kit's/Grier's memorable past. Take the nightclub scene, in which Slim Daddy opens Kit's act, saying, "Kit Porter is a real motherfuckin' diva," as a case in point.

Having moved on to new projects in both television and film, Pam Grier's screen career continues to evolve. Yet because of the cultural impact of her early work, she still functions as one of the definitive and enduring icons of 1970s soul music, badass attitude, and sheer elegance. On the strength of her earlier screen persona she became an entity that evokes the aura of the 1970s in contemporary films. In *Jackie Brown, Bones,* and *Original Gangsters*—a film whose very title suggests a return of the past—Pam Grier is a semiotic sign of the reemergence of the past in the present, a true diva of the big screen.

Goldberg's Variations
on Comedic Charisma

It is scarcely possible to think of a black American actor who has not been misused; not one has ever been seriously challenged to deliver the best that is in him.

—James Baldwin

[Whoopi] Goldberg's unique success is to have avoided both female stereotypes. Indeed, cinematically she is not really constructed as a woman at all—neither nurturer nor siren, the faithful drudge of the ante-bellum South or the funky chick born to walk the wild side of the city's mean streets, her movie persona is more in the tradition of asexual coon entertainers such as Amos and Andy or Bill Bojangles Robinson. The coon, a lovable black buffoon, the lighthearted cousin of the harassed but ever faithful Uncle Tom, has roots as old as Hollywood itself.

—Andrea Stuart

Whoopi Goldberg is an atypical film and television star. She's the image of physical excess, iconoclasm, and rebellion in an industry preferring its women contained, controlled, and submissive.[1] Her stardom, itself a source of controversy and ongoing critical commentary, evokes feminist criticism of the 1970s, when writers like Molly Haskell and Laura Mulvey analyzed the limited roles available to actresses working within the patriarchal structures of Hollywood. Haskell faulted the industry for perpetuating "the Big Lie": mythic fantasies of marital bliss and conjugal euphoria, which ignored the facts and fears arising from an awareness of "the End"—the winding down of love, change, divorce, depression, mutation, and even death itself. While Goldberg's films (excluding *Boys on the Side,* 1995, and *How Stella Got Her Groove Back,* 1998) have not dealt with the end stages of love or life, neither have they perpetuated the Big Lie. As a black woman, she's been excluded from conventional romantic comedies. In diegetic contexts, and in the extradiagetic world, the comedienne has commented on her exclusion from traditional romantic couplings. She is one of the few female stars whose entertainment persona is not predicated on traditional notions of femininity, nubile sexuality, and happy-ever-after endings of heterosexual union. Evoking roguery rather than romance, Goldberg's celebrity calls to mind Kathleen Rowe's suggestion that the comedic, "unruly" woman is a *transgressive* figure who disobeys, confronts, and menaces the patriarchal order.

This chapter analyzes the semiotics of Goldberg's star persona. While her early career was built on standup comedy routines like *The Spook Show* (1983) and its Broadway version, simply titled *Whoopi Goldberg*, her current star persona is predicated on a long career of leading film roles in *The Color Purple* (1985), *Jumpin' Jack Flash* (1986), *Burglar* (1987), *The Telephone* (1988), *Sister Act* (1992), *Sister Act 2: Back in the Habit* (1993), *Corrina, Corrina* (1994), *Eddie* (1996), and *The Associate* (1996), to name only a few. An analysis of all her films is beyond the scope of this chapter. Instead, the critical commentary circulating around Goldberg's discursive subjectivity motivates my readings of select cinematic performances. The films I have chosen were central in the formation of her star persona. Viewing Goldberg's characters as always already problematized by the lingering specter of racial stereotypes, I locate the ways her diegetic and extradiegetic personae resist and even undermine privileged categories of identity and defy her marginalization. By foregrounding the political register and witty dimensions of her work as a comedienne, I discuss Goldberg's stardom in terms of a series of transformations that menace conventional categories of race, gender, and sexuality. My central argument is that her charismatic comedy is rooted in a transgressive repertoire through which she disrupts the dominant social order as presented in these narratives.

Webster's unabridged dictionary defines *comedy* as "any type of play or motion picture with more or less humorous treatment of characters, situation, and non-tragic ending." It also defines comedy as "the art, technique, or theory of writing, producing, or acting in such plays or motion pictures." Generally speaking, *comedy* refers to the genre and subgenres of film comedy and to the generic maneuverings of filmed slapstick or farce. Here the term *comedy* refers to Goldberg's specific *comedic idiolect* or repertoire of humorous and carnivalesque routines. In her routines, she continually shifts, critiques, and signifies on the existing hierarchies (i.e., race, gender, class) as they are reflected in society and the entertainment industries. Though her critiques sometimes failed to achieve intended goals and subvert hegemonic structures, her distinct brand of humor-based celebrity is a form of comedic charisma.

There are two opposing readings of Goldberg's screen persona. The first critiques her "negatively" as a reincarnation of stereotypes like Topsy, mammy, and the coon.[2] The second describes her more "positively" as a performer who subverts type. Michael Rogin articulates the first position, saying that *Corrina, Corrina* "re-inscribes the icon of the black mammy in the white/Jewish household—a recognizable and perpetuated image of African American women today." Readings of the film *Burglar* (1987) support Rogin's position. In the film Goldberg played a street-smart but clownish ex-convict referred to as a "pickaninny" by Ray Kirschman (G. W. Bailey), a white male character to whom she's financially indebted. And readings of more recent films like *Girl, Interrupted* (1999), in which Goldberg plays sanitarium nursemaid to Valerie Owens, are similarly censuring.

However, Lisa Anderson expresses the second position, stating that films like *Corrina, Corrina* "subvert audience expectations by using a standard mammy situation and reshaping it." My reading falls squarely between the poles presented by Anderson and Rogin. I maintain that while the specters of stereotypes seem to haunt her characters in *Ghost* (1990), *Sister Act* (1992), *Sister Act 2: Back in the Habit* (1993), and *Bogus* (1996), these pictures—and her roles in them—have been unfairly criticized as caricatures modernizing the coon image. They are also films in which she menaces the dominant discourses of womanhood, femininity, nuclear family, and class boundaries.

Anderson and Rogin present valid albeit reductive readings of Goldberg's persona. Rogin echoes Donald Bogle, who has long rejected Goldberg as a romantic film personality. The challenge of accepting Goldberg as a romantic lead came to a head during the production of *Fatal Beauty* in October 1987. The comedienne resisted defeminization by fighting to keep her character Rita Rizzoli's love scenes in the film. The bedroom scene was eventually cut despite the star's protesting. After the film's completion, Goldberg quipped that "had her character been a prostitute and Sam Elliott's character left fifty dollars in the bedroom, the scene would not have been cut from the film."[3] As Yvonne Tasker notes, Goldberg's image in *Fatal Beauty* as both a hypersexualized and a desexualized cop is related to the history of racial representation, in which discourses of sexuality have been mapped onto the black female body.[4] As Tasker's comment suggests, we cannot read Goldberg as either sexual *or* desexual but as both simultaneously.

Readings that interpret her characters according to such binaries fail to consider the instability and flexibility of gender categories, particularly in

Whoopi Goldberg with *Fatal Beauty* costar Sam Elliott.

comedy. These criticisms omit the generic conventions of comedy and the instability of identity within the genre, which often flaunts a carnival-like atmosphere positing most identities as unstable. Closer readings of her star vehicles demonstrate the way her characters—and the situations in which they are placed—trouble supposedly stable gender categories, critique notions of white identity, question whiteness as a social formation, and identify white racism.

Burglar is one film that comments critically on racism. Goldberg plays a female version of characters played by Richard Pryor and Eddie Murphy, comedians who pioneered mainstream audience acceptance of audacious, cocky African American actors employing crude language and acerbic patter to deliver real and unspoken truths about American race relations.[5] In the film, white divorcee Cynthia Sheldrake (Lesley Ann Warren) hires female ex-convict Bernice (Whoopi Goldberg) to commit a simple robbery. Cynthia needs Bernice to "steal back" jewelry taken by her miserly ex-husband. Bernice is double-crossed when Cynthia actually frames her for murder. Throughout the movie, characters comment on the racism implicit in a professional white woman's ability to frame a black working-class woman for homicide. The film calls attention to the overtly racist police practices and bigoted officers who presume Bernice's guilt. Bernice even comments on these circumstances. As if evoking the cacophony of competing social discourses concerning black criminality, black recidivism, and rates of incarceration, Goldberg's Bernice critiques the assumption of her guilt as a counterpoint to police discussions that link blackness and criminality. Nonetheless, this is one of the films—and Bernice is one of the many characters—that film critics cite as exemplifying the coon caricature. Simply put, there are moments in Goldberg's films—and aspects of her roles—that resist subservience to white patriarchal authority and challenge the unilateral assumptions of her identity. We can read her films in terms of the polyphony of competing social discourses they present and the workings of comedy as a genre, while also considering Goldberg's function as a chameleon-like comedienne.

Comedy as a genre is not necessarily concerned with representative types. In his seminal study of wit and its relation to the unconscious, Sigmund Freud asserted that comedy is an assertive genre. Because humor depends upon a perception of events or behaviors as unexpected or incongruous, the individual who publicly points up such inconsistencies issues a statement about the status quo.[6] This is a fundamentally assertive social function. Unlike drama and melodrama—or genres indexing reality through their use of the discourses of sobriety, comedy deals with people who cultivate extremes—either as excess or defect, as too much or too little. One aspect of comedy is that characters and situations are often out of proportion, disharmonious, and incongruous with their circumstances and are therefore funny. The character "types" in comedy are often not realistic portraits of average wo/men in everyday situations. When they are ordinary people, these characters are catapulted into extraordinary complications, bizarre misunderstandings, freak accidents, and unbelievable coincidences, and they offer a peep into the possibilities of chaos and mayhem from which they usually recoil.[7]

Goldberg performs extraordinariness through her comedic idiolect of performance traits. These traits include gestures, expressions, movements, and postures for which a given performer becomes known.[8] The comedienne's idiolect is unlike that of the dramatic actress, since it necessitates an ability to convey flexibility, extremity, awkwardness, and transformation. Her comedic idiolect and cinematic atypicality are performance characteristics she shares with comediennes Lily Tomlin, Danitra Vance, and Tracy Ullman, all of whom presented audiences with an arsenal of characters. Moreover, Tomlin, Vance, Goldberg, and Ullman have portrayed two genders, different generations, and various ethnicities. Placed in the context of her peers, we recognize Goldberg is not the first (or the only) comic whose gender identification (i.e., femininity) is considered flexible and/or questionable. Roseanne Barr, Ellen Degeneres, and Lea DeLaria are celebrities whose iconoclastic politics, public roles, and unusual comedic idiolects have functioned to destabilize their feminine gender masquerade. In part, this destabilization is a function of the Freudian notion that wit and humor are aggressive (read: masculine) expressions of repressed feelings, expressions, and desires. Wit is often related to aggression, hostility, and even forms of sadistic behavior.[9] It necessarily disrupts the fragile gender masquerade of conventional womanliness.

Wit and various forms of humor enable performers to be verbally aggressive, outwardly hostile, and even jokingly sadistic in performance. Verbal wit and physical humor require the performer to move beyond behaviors deemed feminine and perform the extreme, obscene, assertive, and unusual in such a way that the performance necessarily destabilizes supposedly fixed gender categories. This is certainly plausible if we consider women's comedy as an assertive, aggressive, or intellectual response to their subordinate position in patriarchal societies.

For example, Kathleen Rowe discusses the way Roseanne Barr "fashioned her Domestic Goddess persona out of clichés in U.S. culture about the fat, noisy, vulgar working-class housewife in order to make those clichés both visible and positive."[10] Barr has intentionally cultivated an idiolect (obnoxious facial expression, uses of voice, gesture, and ways of walking) in tandem with her eponymous leading character's obesity, vulgarity, and working-class lifestyle. Her performative idiolect successfully communicates these traits in such a way as to render the character realistic, sensible, and intelligent. However, the same comedic clichés concerning fatness and vulgarity also serve to desexualize Barr, because they are beyond the scope of manners (i.e., body maintenance, refinement, obedience) considered conventionally feminine behaviors.

Like Roseanne Barr, Whoopi Goldberg fashioned a menacing comedic persona out of racial clichés about nappy dreadlocked hair, attitudinal behavior, dark skin, and working-class blackness, making these clichés visible, positive, insightful points for launching critiques. For instance, one of Goldberg's early stage routines was based on a little black girl who fantasized about having luxurious long blond hair. Through the black child's self-loathing desire for whiteness—evoking Pecola Breedlove from Toni Morrison's *The Bluest Eye*—Goldberg subtly casts aspersions on a society conditioning young people to accept socially constructed notions of Euro-American beauty. Through her comedic persona, she identifies and challenges the predominance of Euro-centric aesthetics. Revealing black body consciousness as a negating activity[11] in an American sociocultural context, she points to the psychological distortions implicit in an African American identity based on Euro-American concepts. The sociopsychological commentary issued by this character in Goldberg's repertoire is reminiscent of Frantz Fanon's discussion of the "Fact of Blackness" in *Black Skin, White Masks* (1967). Fanon articulated some of the ways in which blacks in the Antilles developed a negative self-image as a result of their encounter with the white, colonizing world. Like his predecessor Albert Memmi, Fanon outlined how this sense of inferiority came into being through an encounter with the white colonizer.

The troubled gender identities of Roseanne Barr, Ellen Degeneres, and Whoopi Goldberg demonstrate that associations between gender, sex, and desire are themselves predicated on the hyperrational, patriarchal social order of Western societies. All three female entertainers are positioned as "less feminine" because (as comediennes, working-class women, lesbians, or nonwhite persons) they occupy marginal subject positions and possess idiolects expressing these subject positions. Being active rather than passive, daring instead of dainty, public as opposed to private, and vulgar rather than virginal, they call attention to the false polarities defining (*wo*)men in relation to men. Their public personae and performance traits manifest the social and discursive constructions of gender, as well as the binaries upon which gender dimorphism is predicated.

Judith Butler claimed the presumption of a binary gender system implicitly retains the belief in a mimetic relation of gender to sex whereby gender mirrors sex. Nowhere has this mimetic relationship between sex and the signifiers of gender been more apparent—and more regularly inscribed—than in the cinema. Within these terms, "the body" becomes a passive medium on which cultural meanings are inscribed, or the instrument through which an appropriative and interpretive will determines a cultural meaning for itself. Gender in comedy is doubly performative. It involves a certain amount of play, of mutability in how we perform, and in how we inherit, gender discourse. Whoopi Goldberg occupies a liminal position relative to the "heterosexually ideal genders."[12] Her liminality in this binary system is a function of performance. Goldberg functions—in some of her films—as the literal and figurative instrument or medium for expressing the flexibility of culturally determined performances of gender and sexual identity. While we might agree that aspects of Goldberg's identity are problematic (i.e., she's been "defeminized" or "desexed" by the narratives, that her racial identity invokes historical constructs and tropes of blackness) we can also acknowledge that it is sex—as it relates to race and gender—that is inherently unstable.

Thus far, this chapter has addressed the way wit and comedy preclude comediennes like Goldberg from being constructed as conventionally feminine. However, I have yet to address the way the social construction of beauty excludes Goldberg, instead dismissing her as physically unattractive or even ugly. It seems equally important to complicate the notion of Goldberg as unattractive and scrutinize the assumption of her undesirability. Doing so requires interrogating these categories.

Reading her persona as the embodiment of an unattractive, and therefore desexed, stereotype is as reductive as reading film star Dorothy Dandridge solely as sex siren, or as one-dimensional as viewing media mogul Oprah Winfrey as a mammy figure. Over time these readings have overdetermined and negated the complex ways African American women celebrities produce themselves as subjects complicit with—yet also in opposition to—dominant cultural ideologies of race and gender. These readings are legitimate and parallel Donald Bogle's interpretive study of Hollywood. They also dovetail with the concomitant critique of Hollywood's Eurocentric aesthetic philosophy and photographic technology, which privileges white skin and white women rather than women of color.[13] Few of the critics who argue that Goldberg is desexualized bother to challenge the light-skin privilege bestowed upon actresses Halle Berry, Thandie Newton, Vanessa Williams, Lisa Bonet, and others. Nor do they mention brown-skinned performers such as Alfre Woodard, Debbie Morgan, and Angela Basset. Ultimately, the issue is not whether Goldberg is beautiful and therefore sexually desirable but that her physiognomy doesn't conform to the widely held standard of beauty operating within mainstream white America and in African American communities. For example, in a February 7, 1995, interview with Lea DeLaria of *The Advocate,* Goldberg responded to questions regarding her ability to work in the industry despite her unconventional appearance.

> I don't have to be beautiful. I can be really big, I can be wrinkly, because it's all about the work. It's not about: "Oh we put you in this movie because you're

really great to look at." So, I hope I will be doing the same stuff that I've always done. I'm only interested in conquering what I'm interested in . . . the
intricacies of an actor. I want to be Brando, I want to be Bette Davis. I want
to be De Niro. I want to be Pacino. I want the essence of those people. I want
the essence of what they do to be the foundation . . . I can't think about that
[the powers that be] because then I would have to hear the static of "Your
nose it too big, your ass is too big, you're too dark, you're too light, your hair
is too weird, your feet are too long . . ." You know? Who the fuck wants to
hear that?[14]

Goldberg's liminal position reveals the extent to which notions of femininity and feminine beauty are still predicated on bodily signifiers (fair skin
complexion, straight hair texture, low weight, and youthful appearance)[15]
that communicate a mimetic relationship between gender and sex whereby
Eurocentric ideas about the genitalia (and body) are supposedly mirrored
in the face.

Sociologist Charles Herbert Stember examined the putative mimetic relation of gender to sex whereby gender and sex are mirrored in bodily signifiers. He questioned why the characteristics of face and hair (the upper part
of the body) played such a crucial role in determining a woman's sexual
attractiveness—even among other women. Stember concluded that the focus on women's facial beauty occurs because the face has symbolic meaning.
That in some way the face stands in metonymically for the woman herself
in a way that other parts of the body do not. Speaking about the face as an
object of beauty in Euro-American cultures, Stember asserts that the face
must not suggest the taboo lower parts of the body. He writes:

What it must convey to be attractive, it seems, is the *opposite* of what exists in
the lower part of the body—"dirt" in its widest sense: excretion, bodily odors,
and the general character of the genital-urinary-excretive areas. As Germaine
Greer commented in discussing the image of the ideal woman: "Her essential
quality is her castrated-ness. She must be young, her body hairless, her flesh
buoyant, and *she must not have a sexual organ.*" Any hint in the all-important
upper part of the woman that there lurks in the lower part an odoriferous,
slimy dark, wet organ in between her legs, or to be precise, between her organs
of excretion, tends in a very important sense to render her less attractive sexually. Her physical "attractiveness" in a real sense is based on her facial features
diverging as far as possible from anything suggesting the genital area and its
adjacent organs of excretion. The notion that facial features must be perceived
as "anti-genital" throws light on the criteria of female beauty found to have

such widespread currency. It explains the existence of a hierarchy of female beauty in which the black woman appears at the lower end. It is not alone her skin color, noted earlier, conceivably associated with the color of excrement, but her thick lips and wide nostrils, suggesting the vulva itself. The hair of the black woman as well is in texture much like pubic hair, and carries the same association. The black woman, in other words, projects in her face, hair, and skin—her upper half—the explicit image of her lower half, which is why, as Grier and Cobbs have observed, she is considered "ugly."[16]

Stember intends this commentary as a deconstructive analysis of the devaluation of black women's physicality. However, he inadvertently reifies and reproduces the ethnocentrism implicit in such assessments by failing to unpack other relevant variables factoring in the equation. The suggestion that black women's faces more readily evoke their genitalia is exceedingly racist and laughably ethnocentric. He fails to examine the racism and ethnocentrism implicit in such a statement. Stember also disregards the significance of the political economy of slavery, the historical overvaluation of white female sexual purity, the masculine vantage point from which he's articulating his analysis, and the European psychosocial association of whiteness with purity and blackness with filth. These cultural components factor into the devaluation of black womanhood and black women's physicality.

To Stember's credit, however, his analysis dovetails with critical theory (i.e., Julia Kristeva, 1981; Céleste Derksen, 1994), film and television studies (i.e., Barbara Creed, 1993; Kathleen Rowe, 1995), and cultural anthropology (i.e., Mary Douglas, 1966; Mary Russo, 1994) that analyze notions of the female body as abject, as filthy, as threatening, as comedic, as grotesque, and in terms of the carnivalesque divide between upper and lower regions of the body. Stember's work also dovetails with Butler's critique of the mimetic relation of gender (femininity and desirability) to sex (genitalia and intercourse) whereby ideas about the gendered body (i.e., femininity) are supposedly mirrored in sex and sexuality (i.e., penetrability).

Whoopi Goldberg manages to subvert categories of beauty in her repertoire because she possesses a talent for bodily transformation in comedy—a *comedic charisma of transformation*. Whether in drama, comedy, or "dramedy," her charismatic authority derives from her playful corporeal performance of various identities, which interrupt and destabilize the status quo with subversive rebellion. Her *charismatic comedy of transformation* has much in common with the discourses of carnival, or what Mikhail Bakhtin terms "the carnivalesque."

Carnival and the Carnivalesque

In *Rabelais and His World,* Mikhail Bakhtin wrote of the liberating effects of European festive folk culture. For example, in Rabelais's work, the material bodily principles, (i.e., images of the human body with its food, drink, defecation, and sexual life) play a predominant role. Images of the body are offered in an extremely exaggerated form. For this reason, he is associated with an aesthetic of *grotesque realism.* The material bodily principle in grotesque realism is offered in its ever-popular festive and utopian aspect. In grotesque realism, the body is deeply positive. Bakhtin noted how "universal, democratic and free" carnivalesque laughter was for "the people" in preindustrial and precapitalistic cultures.[17] In *Rabelais,* "laughter becomes the form of a free and critical consciousness that mocks dogmatism and fanaticism."[18] Carnival was an all-encompassing time of sanctioned freedom and transgression when masquerading, role reversal, games, eating, drinking, copulation, and almost any unusual behavior was permitted. Many view Bakhtin's discussion of the carnivalesque as a study of class conflict over hierarchies of power. My analysis of the carnivalesque (in Goldberg's films) is a study of racial and gendered conflict over racialized and gendered hierarchies of power.

In his discussion of the carnivalesque in cinema and literary comedy, Andrew Horton maintained that pre-Oedipal comedy[19] has much in common with a spirit of carnival. He acknowledges that American cinema has no direct relationship with a carnivalesque culture as seen in medieval Europe. However, there is a degree to which the carnivalesque atmosphere and subject matter are manifest in American film comedies. Horton maintains that Bakhtinian theories facilitate analysis beyond subject matter—having implications for form and structure. I concur with Horton, as I see an atmosphere of the carnivalesque structuring aspects of American cinema, especially in Goldberg's films. Further, I see an aesthetic of grotesque realism manifest in her charismatic comedy of transformation. Kathleen Rowe similarly refers to the Bakhtinian carnivalesque in her examination of gender and the genres of laughter in television,[20] and her insights instruct my reading of Whoopi Goldberg. Just as Roseanne Barr is a force of incisive political commentary, revealing the social order and the difficult aspects of working-class women's lives, so Whoopi Goldberg's comedic charisma transgresses the status quo and offers a critique of gendered racism.

Rowe parallels Bakhtin's grinning pregnant hags and the figure of the *unruly woman.* The unruly woman represents a special kind of excess differing from that of the femme fatale. She is willing to offend and be offensive. Described as too fat, too funny, too noisy, too old, and too rebellious, the unruly woman unsettles social hierarchies, crosses social boundaries, and appears in the genres of laughter, or those sharing common structures of liminality[21] and inversion. The unruly woman embodies the spirit and form of carnival parody, freedom, and celebration: what Bakhtin explains as the essence of the carnivalesque. She is in the state of becoming. Associated with beauty and monstrosity, the unruly woman dwells close to the grotesque. The figure of the unruly woman contains potential for a feminist appropriation, for rethinking how women are constructed as gendered subjects in the language of spectacle and the visual.[22] The trope of the unruly woman is analogous to the comedienne and therefore evident in the cinema (and the screen persona) of Whoopi. Rather than view Goldberg as a sexless coon caricature, we can consider the ways her characters are rebellious. Her rebelliousness, her vulgarity, her attitude, and even her blackness are the rule-breaking characteristics that upset the civility, temperedness, and whiteness associated with order in daily life. Unsettling hierarchies and crossing boundaries, she is unruly in nature and nonconformist in appearance.

The comedienne's chosen celebrity name, "Whoopi Goldberg," is a case in point. Her name literally and figuratively disrupts the patriarchal order with its comedy of transformation and its carnivalesque qualities. First, it literally disrupts—as all pseudonyms do—the form of social organization in which the father, as head of the family and familial descent, is reckoned in the male line through the father's surname. Second, it disrupts figuratively and metaphorically because the name is predicated on ideas of playful disguise. Third, her name invokes grotesque realism as well as the digestive and sexual functions of the body.

The first part of her name is derived from the common colloquialism *whoopee cushion* and concomitant jokes about flatulence, indigestion, and the uncontrollable nature of the lower stratum. A playful term for the industry of stand-up comedy from which she emerged and for revelry, it nonetheless has origins in her biography. The actress admits it derives from her own flatulent tendencies. But *whoopi* also has sexual connotations. The phrase *making whoopi* has long been a euphemism for sexual intercourse and for fooling around. Through a chain of signifiers, this name invokes the material body, the flesh, the foul matter eliminated from the body, and corpulent excess.

Consonant with the grotesque realism we find in her name—and by extension her screen persona—images of the human body as multiple, bulging, oversized, protuberant, and incomplete. The openings and orifices of her carnival body are emphasized in an image of corporeal bulk with the orifices (mouth, flared nostrils, anus) yawning wide and lower regions (belly, legs, feet, buttocks, and genitals) given priority over its upper regions (head, spirit, reason). In her name we hear the displacements as effected between the high/low image of the physical body and other social domains. This grotesquely real body is always in the process of *becoming*. It is a mobile and hybrid entity, outgrowing its limits, obscenely decentered and off balance, a figural and symbolic resource for parodic exaggeration and inversion.[23] The name Whoopi symbolizes these excesses, this obscenity, and her transgressive tendencies, on screen, on stage, and in the playful-parodic hosting of the seventy-first and seventy-fourth annual Academy Awards ceremonies.

The second part of her pseudonym, Goldberg, is derived from an extended family tree. According to biographers, she drew upon her family tree and came up with a distant relative who was Jewish and went by this name. Use of the traditionally Jewish family name proved an effective attention-grabbing gimmick, making her stand out immediately from other entertainers. The surname Goldberg invokes disguise by alluding to the Jewish and Irish traditions of racial border crossing common in minstrel entertainment.[24] That Goldberg's own genealogy includes the Jewish Diaspora introduces yet another category of carnival: hybridity. The surname brings into play the racial hybridity of her family tree. Hybridity is a hallmark of carnival. Therefore, both parts of her pseudonym introduce aspects of the carnivalesque: indecency, impropriety, masquerade, pretense, border crossing, and hybridity. Her celebrity name invokes the disruptions of patriarchal social order with its suggestion of modes of transformation and racial crossing. It prefigures transgressions of the bourgeois social order by implying and expressing the willingness to offend and be offensive. The name signifies an idiolect—a repertoire of unruly, unfeminine, unrestrained, and undisciplined behaviors typifying her persona.

Comedic Carnival on Film

I have based my concept of Goldberg's *comedy of transformation* on her screen characters, many of which straddle binaries through a comedy of shifting subject positions. The character transformations vary across texts, but Goldberg's films implicitly and explicitly involve movement between diametrically opposed categories of identity, including gender binaries. These characters often disrupt the static, essentialist notions of blackness at the level of the signifier. In several of her star vehicles we see manifestations of this transgressive comedy of carnivalesque transformation. This includes, but is not limited to, *The Telephone* (1987), *Ghost* (1990), *Sister Act* (1992), *Sister Act 2* (1993), *Boys on the Side* (1995), and *The Associate* (1996).

Goldberg's one-woman Broadway stage routine, *The Goldberg Variations*, marked the beginning of her acting career.[25] The stage material initiated her technique of signifyin(g) within the performance, to constitute a performance within the performance—a definitive characteristic of Goldberg's comedic and dramatic acting. Exploring Goldberg's performances in the aforementioned films adduces my claim that her charismatic comedy of carnivalesque transformation is a comedy that reappropriates, signifies, and critiques categories of identity as well as her own liminality.

The Telephone—an improvisational, one-character-driven movie—was the first film in which Goldberg transposed the grotesque realism of her stand-up comedy to screen. Directed by Rip Torn, *The Telephone* was released after Goldberg played an abused housewife in Spielberg's *The Color Purple* (1985); portrayed Terry Doolittle in Penny Marshall's *Jumpin' Jack Flash* (1986); played a reformed cat burglar in Hugh Wilson's 1987 film of same name; and was an undercover cop in Tom Holland's *Fatal Beauty* (1987). None of these earlier, mediocre movies (with the exception of Spielberg's *Color Purple*) did much to develop Goldberg's career. Some failed miserably both critically and financially. For example, *Fatal Beauty* was a commercial failure as well as a poorly constructed film. Made at a cost of $18 million, it grossed a meager $4.7 million in domestic film rentals in the United States and Canada.[26]

A low-budget feature, Torn's *The Telephone* was no exception to this pattern. Written by screenwriters Terry Southern, Academy Award–winning co-screenwriter of *Dr. Strangelove;* Harry Nilsson; and Goldberg, the movie was a string of a half-dozen character routines for Goldberg to perform. It was partially based on Jean Cocteau's 1930 one-woman drama *La voix humaine.* Before the film's release, *Telephone* was tied up in legal battles between Goldberg and Torn over the final editing. Once finally shown in limited release, it was critically disparaged as "claustrophobic," as "self-inflicted character assassination," and as "monumentally unfunny." All the film's characters revolve around a schizophrenic young woman alone in her apartment. *Telephone* tells the story of a lonely, eccentric, unemployed actress, disconnected from reality. Holed up in her apartment, she amuses herself with a zebra-striped telephone: ignoring threatening phone calls from creditors, arguing with a girlfriend, waiting for an ex-boyfriend to call, and pranking the Catholics' call-in confession line by pretending to be an Irish priest.

Despite its litigious production history, limited release, and negative reviews, *The Telephone* is a film worth rereading. My contention is that critics confused tragic content and comedic form, consequently misreading and undervaluing *The Telephone*'s social commentary and Goldberg's performance strategy. The film, curiously named for the zebra-striped phone in the protagonist's apartment, is not a comedy but a dark and cynical picture of a black woman's isolation and alienation. It employs Goldberg's comedic repertoire of transformation to convey the circumstances engendering the character's psychosis. In the first of three acts, Vashti Blue (Whoopi Goldberg) amuses herself with a repertoire of make-believe characters and phone conversations with friends.

In the second act, her agent Rodney (Elliott Gould) and his girlfriend Honey Boxe (Amy Wright) interrupt Vashti's evening routine. When they arrive, Vashti entertains them. Rather than perform, she shows them a tape of her new stage work. But when Rodney dismisses Vashti's performance art as trashy, she rebels against his onslaught of derisive remarks and continual sexual harassment. She rebels by performing the "dance of the seven flatulences," pretending to break wind on and around Rodney while saying: "The first flatulence is dedicated to dickhead producers. The second flatulence is dedicated to asshole agents. These flatulences were made just for you, Rodney!" Angry over Rodney's imposing nature, critical dismissal of her artwork, and inability to secure her jobs, she rebels against his physical presence, his artistic sensibility, and his entertainment-industry authority.

Throughout *The Telephone,* Goldberg's Vashti performs various characters and routines. Vashti's characters are familiar to audiences because they are like Goldberg's earlier standup routines, in which she played characters within characters. Much of her standup was not scripted but improvisational. The scenes are uniquely Goldbergesque because she's exceptionally capable of performing-the-rebellious-performer and because they are typical of her rebellious repertoire of the performing self. They are typical of what Christy Burns—in another context—referred to as "humor against the springboard of social propriety and tendency to retrieve sources of bodily embarrassment such as shit, snot, and gaseous expulsions to produce a comic cringe."[27]

Here she portrays a character performing rebellion against her social, physical, artistic, and economic negation. Her character Vashti uses the performance (therefore, performance within performance) to signify on social marginality with what Stallybrass and White have called the "literal openings and orifices of a carnival body," with an image of corporeal excess, with her yawning anus, and with lower regions now given priority because her upper regions (i.e., her artistic ideas) have been rejected. The "dance of the seven flatulences" is a figural and symbolic resource of discursive parody in the film. It is an exaggeration and inversion of the power dynamic between actor and agent, between labor and management. As *The Telephone*'s narrative progresses, Vashti's grotesquely real body becomes increasingly rebellious against her desperate financial circumstances.

In the third and final act of *The Telephone,* a telephone serviceman (John Heard) visits Vashti's apartment. His goal is to repossess her phone. Shocked by her resistance, he questions her refusal to release the phone: "You mean you actually developed an attachment to this phone? It looks like something you'd have phone sex with!" This is an implicitly racist remark, because it is the zebra pattern on the phone that semiotically links anonymous, uninhibited (phone) sex with animalistic, primitive passions. Embedded in his statement are tropes of primitivist discourse that hinge on a chain of signifiers linking Africa's indigenous wildlife (i.e., zebras), sexual activity, and nonwhite persons in the lexicon of primitivism. Within the logic of primitivist discourse, so-called "primitives" are akin to our untamed selves, our "id" forces—libidinous, irrational, violent, and dangerous. Primitives exist at the lowest cultural levels.[28] In making such a remark, the serviceman dismissively places Vashti at the lowest level (culturally and physically) by alleging her simplicity, irrationality, and base nature.

Rodney's earlier aesthetic rejection is repeated in the serviceman's physical repossession. Together they form a double articulation of her artistic and financial poverty. Vashti pleads with the repairman. Begging him not to remove the phone, she exclaims: "Without it, I don't exist!" The irony of her statement becomes clear when spectators discover that her phone has already been disconnected. In a retaliatory gesture against the serviceman's insistence that she's disconnected, she fatally stabs him in a desperate attempt to hold on to her fantasy of engagement with the outside world.

Vashti's violent retaliation in response to the repossession performed by the serviceman is reminiscent of Radio Raheem's violent retaliation in response to Sal's demolition of his radio in Spike Lee's *Do the Right Thing* (1989). What Vashti Blue and Radio Raheem share is a personal identification with "stylized conversational performance" (i.e., rap music and performance art) as techniques of the self. In an essay on the dialogics of rap music, Elizabeth Wheeler incisively notes the politicization of rap music derives from its social realism. Wheeler writes, "You cannot [truly] hear rap music unless you acknowledge the split between two Americas: one getting rich, the other getting evicted." Wheeler defends the aesthetics of rap music as informed by social and grotesque realities.

My argument here is that the phone is to Vashti Blue as the radio is to Radio Raheem: the veritable symbol-object of the individual's performative connection with the world. Sal's attack upon the radio, and—by extension— Raheem's rap aesthetic, parallels the serviceman's attack upon the telephone and—by extension—Vashti's performance art. Coincidentally, both films end with a homicide. The film's abruptly violent conclusion underscores the interpretive mistake of viewing *The Telephone* as comedy. Ending with a homicide, it presents a bleak portrait of a woman's life and the attempt to use comedy as a means of personal-feminist resistance against the negations of bureaucratic consumer culture.

In consumer culture, the body functions as a commodity form. The body's value in the marketplace, particularly the entertainment industry, is commensurate with its phenotypic and aesthetic conformity to dominant ideals of beauty. Vashti's inability to produce herself as conventional commodity-spectacle in a visual economy renders her unemployable, invisible, and nonexistent. The film's narrative evokes—by metaphor—Guy Debord's often quoted statement that spectacle grasped is both the result and the project of existing (ideological) modes of production: "In all its specific forms, as information, as propaganda, as advertisement or as direct entertainment consumption, the spectacle is not a collection of images but a social relation among people mediated by images. It is the omnipresent affirmation of the choice(s) *already made* in production and its corollary consumption. The spectacle's form and content are identically the total justification of the existing system's conditions and goals."[29]

The social relations among people as mediated by images situate Vashti on the periphery, preventing her from having access to modes of production. Goldberg's character Vashti therefore rebels with unruly violence against her proletarianization,[30] her increasingly lowered standard of living, and her consequent invisibility at the hands of agents, managers, servicemen, and the communication-culture industries. She rebels against what cultural critic Michele Wallace has elsewhere (and in another context) described as "invisibility blues," the phenomenon of black women being denied critical and artistic voice in popular and mainstream American culture.[31]

Subsequent to *The Telephone*, there were other films in which Goldberg offered a carnivalesque performance of rebellion. *Ghost* (1990) was the next film in which Goldberg performed her carnivalesque rebelliousness. Directed by Jerry Zucker—who gained notoriety for producing slapstick comedies like *Airplane* (1980), *Police Squad* (1982), *Naked Gun* (1988), *Naked Gun 2½: The Smell of Fear* (1991), and *Naked Gun 33⅓: The Final Insult* (1994)—*Ghost* proved a major star vehicle for Goldberg. It became the surprise summer hit of 1990. According to Goldberg biographer James Robert Parish, the film was produced on a budget of $25 million and grossed $218 million in forty-one weeks at the box office. Its soundtrack sold over 500,000 copies, and Paramount Home Video enjoyed a record of 595,000 preorders from North American retailers alone. In addition to its financial success, *Ghost* earned Goldberg an Academy Award for best supporting actress. On March 25, 1991, the night of the sixty-third annual Academy Awards, she became the second black woman in history to win an Oscar. While the Academy Awards are really an indication of commercial viability rather than artistic merit, *Ghost* nonetheless demonstrated Goldberg's improving ability to render a performance within performance.

The narrative of *Ghost* revolves around New York banker Sam Wheat (Patrick Swayze) and his potter girlfriend Molly (Demi Moore), who have recently moved into a swank Manhattan loft. Although the two are in love, Sam fears commitment to marriage. One night, on the way home, a mugger murders him. Stunned to discover he's dead, his spirit remains alive and attempts to contact Molly. Because she is unable to hear him, he seeks the assistance of phony spiritual medium Oda Mae Brown (Goldberg) but discovers that she's not a phony, after all. She can actually hear and speak to him.

Within her performance of character Oda Mae Brown, Goldberg makes a clear distinction between the supposedly *real* interactions with the spiritual world Sam inhabits and the obviously phony con-artist interactions she knowingly and self-consciously performs to earn a living. The false spiritual relationship is performed differently from that of the real liaison she makes with Swayze—especially at those moments when Swayze's is not in the frame. Even the narrative and dialogue foreground this dualistic performance, as Demi Moore's Molly must learn to distinguish between Oda Mae's performative personality and her actual communicative interactions with Sam.

An analysis of Goldberg's performance in *Ghost* evokes the literary scholarship on signifying by Henry Louis Gates Jr., for whom signifyin(g) has several meanings. As a principle of language, signifyin(g) is not the exclusive domain of black people. However, as an African American term and rhetorical device it (1) refers to the ability to speak with innuendo, (2) can mean the mocking of a person or a situation, (3) denotes speaking with the hands and eyes, and (4) is the language of trickery, of words achieving direction through indirection. Gates offers that historically, when African Americans mentioned signifyin(g), they were referring to a "style-focused message, styling which is foregrounded by the devices of making a point by indirection and wit."[32] Signifyin(g) as a structural component of performance applies to literary, musical, and visual texts. In *Ghost,* and later in the *The Associate,* Goldberg's expressive use of voice, gesture, and costume function as modes of signifyin(g) that critique the actress's placement between what Judith Butler

The happy medium between *Ghost* costars Demi Moore and Patrick Swayze (1990).

calls the heterosexually ideal genders. She performs a masquerade of femininity through a comedic play of costumes used to defeminize her body. I will to return to Goldberg's performance in *Ghost* later in this chapter when I consider the film alongside *The Associate*.

Sister Act

Emile Ardolino's film *Sister Act* (1992) is another text in which Whoopi Goldberg's character—and by extension her screen persona—becomes associated with carnival transgressions. Her rebelliousness, noisiness, vulgarity, and

attitude are viewed as the rule-breaking behaviors upsetting the social order and transgressing the rules of everyday life in the narrative world of the
film. Importantly, her blackness (i.e., her racial otherness) also functions as
a signifier of menacing cultural difference and deviance.

During production, Goldberg's menacing relationship with studio chief
Jeffrey Katzenberg paralleled her character's menacing behavior in the film.
According to press reports, the comedienne fought for many changes in
the final script: plotline changes, the perspectives and grievances of real
nuns, concerns about how women are treated in the church, and an ex-
tended relationship between herself and the other nuns. It became common
knowledge throughout Hollywood that Goldberg was fighting a battle with
Disney management over the shape and progress of *Sister Act*.[33] Unlike *The
Telephone, Sister Act* was a huge financial success and earned the actress a
Golden Globe nomination in the Best Actor category and a People's Choice
Award as Favorite Movie Actress. Despite negative reviews in the press, the
film grossed $139.4 million at the domestic box office in the United States
and Canada. The production history behind the film reveals the irony of the
movie as a major star vehicle for Goldberg. Fortunately, actress-singer Bette
Midler turned down the role as the lead, fearing audiences might not accept
her—a Jewish woman—as a Catholic nun. This created an opportunity for
Goldberg to star in the role.

In the film, Goldberg plays Deloris Van Cartier, a Vegas casino showgirl
and the girlfriend of gangster Vince LaRocca (Harvey Keitel). When she witnesses Vince's execution of an employee, Deloris seeks the authorities and
agrees to testify against LaRocca. First, however, she must wait for a court
date. In the interim, officer Eddie Southern (Bill Nun) places her in a witness protection program. He hides Deloris in "the safest place in the world
. . . the last place Vince will look for her." The hiding place is St. Catherine's
Convent, home to an order of traditional women-religious who have literally cloistered themselves away from the secular world and their immediate
surrounding neighborhood. The unlikely notion that an African American
lounge singer would/could live harmoniously with an all white order of nuns
is the structuring gag or *peripeteia* of the film narrative.[34]

I maintain that this is the peripeteia of the film because it structures the
reversal of Deloris's situation in the plot from misfortune (i.e., hunted homicide eyewitness) to comic fortune (i.e., peaceful inhabitant at a convent).
This relatively easy change of fortune, or transition, occurs contrary to the
likelihood that these racially and culturally dissimilar women could live together harmoniously, making their situation humorous and surprising. The

peripeteia of *Sister Act* surprises spectators by contradicting our culturally grounded ideas concerning which situations are plausible or implausible. The balance between plausibility and implausibility, rationality and irrationality renders peripeteia into narrative comic surprise for spectators. The absurd idea of living among a community of all-white nuns is a situation Deloris rejects outright, telling Eddie she can't live where "there's nothing but a lot of white women dressed as nuns!" Yet it is this masquerade of religious womanhood that ultimately protects her from vengeful villains.

The words and images constituting the jokes of *Sister Act* also derive meaning from discourses external to them. In other words, the peripeteia is constitutive of social discourses defining our expectations. Goldberg's character Deloris (aka Sister Mary Clarence) utters phrases and critiques that have meaning because of the social discourses of which they are already a part. For example, Deloris's exclamation about the absurdity of living among white nuns calls attention to Christianity as a Eurocentric discourse of whiteness. She implicitly identifies the racial hierarchy within Christianity generally and in the Catholic Church specifically.

Implicit in this is the knowledge that Christianity (though it initially developed out of Judaism and in North Africa) became the religious export of Europe. It developed in relation to the Manichean dualism of "black" versus "white" that has been mapped onto skin color difference. Thus it has been mapped onto the whitening of the image of Christ and the Virgin in painting, and it has been mapped onto doctrines of racial superiority and imperialism.[35] Knowledge of this racialized religious tradition is implied in the character's rejection of her living assignment. She rejects the suggestion that she live among a community of white women-religious—women who might always perceive her as representative of sinful black "otherness." To summarize, her rejection of the white convent is a double-voiced utterance articulating (1) an implied knowledge of a European religious tradition and (2) the uneasiness of her position as a secular black American woman within it.

In the film, first impressions prove offputting: Deloris startles Mother Superior (Maggie Smith) with her carnival-colored casino clothes and bushy afro-styled hair. And Mother Superior immediately rejects the idea that anyone could conceal someone like Deloris, saying: "That is *not* a person you can hide, that is a conspicuous person, designed to stick out!" If the balance between plausibility and implausibility is partially what transforms the peripeteia into comic surprise, then *Sister Act* is funny because it balances the implausible notion that someone like Deloris Van Cartier could credibly wear the mask of religious womanhood. The absurdity of her living among the nuns combines with Goldberg's parody of bodily awkwardness. Her successful charade or "passing" is a temporary transformation, which articulates a fiction of essential identity.

From the moment of her arrival at St. Catherine's Convent, Deloris and Mother Superior are rivals, each seeking to control convent life. Throughout the film, they are coded as polar opposites. Deloris is flashy, garish, loud, and excessive, with her tawdry clothes, careless comportment, vulgar language, and daring demeanor. Conversely, Mother Superior is staid, subtle, quiet, and repressive with her restrictive habit, priggish manner, careful diction, and authoritative stance as astute head mistress. Their rivalry is aesthetically communicated via color in the mise-en-scène, language in the dialogue, and songs on the soundtrack—all of which convey their difference in terms of a series of racial and religious dualisms: white/black, spiritual/physical, mind/body, stasis/movement, closed/open, classical choir/gospel rhythm. For example, at their first communal dinner, Deloris is falsely introduced to the community of nuns as Sister Mary Clarence, a woman "eager to accept a more disciplined life." Deloris rebuffs this by mocking their mealtime prayers. Thus begins a competition for power maintained throughout the film's narrative between Deloris's secularisms and carnivalesque subversions of convent(ional) Catholic order on the one hand, and Mother Superior's sanctity and attempt to maintain spiritual bureaucratic authority on the other.

Playfully, the term *order* has its own polyvalent reverberations in the narrative of *Sister Act*. First, it refers to the ecclesiastical community of members under religious rule, required to take solemn vows. Second, it refers to the rank and class of persons in this community—Mother Superior being the most senior and authoritative. Finally, it references the regular or harmonious arrangement of daily life, the state of peace and freedom from confusion or unruly behavior with respect for laws. Goldberg's Sister Mary Clarence introduces carnival by transgressing the ecclesiastical order: she replaces Mother Superior as the most authoritative, she breaks curfew rules by which they organize their daily routine, and she introduces danger, profanity, and confusion into the sacred space of religious domesticity. Her successful subversion is the primary pleasure of the text. Initially, Mother Superior appears to control Deloris's life, insisting that she don a habit, assigning her a religious pseudonym, controlling her activities, determining her hours, confining her to convent grounds. Ultimately, it is Deloris who gains control over the internal machinations of convent life via the choir, earning the admiration of the rank-and-file nuns, successfully bringing the public into the private cloistered community, secularizing religious rituals.

Deloris's reversal of fortune is synonymous—in the narrative—with the aesthetic triumph of her dynamic black popular gospel over Mother Superior's lifeless European classicism. Initially assigned to instruct the choir as a punishment for rowdy behavior, Deloris is given the Herculean task of revitalizing an inert, discordant group. She teaches the nuns popular songs with religious lyrics and gospel renditions of classical favorites. Their successful performance of these songs is another source of comedic and visual pleasure for spectators because it reproduces the peripeteia structuring the film to create the feeling of utopia characteristic of musical films. Prepared and then sprung at anticipatory moments in the film, the peripeteia hinges on spectator expectations regarding the unmusical nature of the choir contrasted by their newfound musicality (i.e., an ability to carry popular tunes). These scenes effectively balance the implausible notion that Goldberg's Deloris transformed nonsingers into competent performers with the plausible idea that most people can carry popular tunes given minimal musical training. That these women might actually harmonize is merely an extension of the gags or jokes, and Deloris is the comedic venue through which these gags are rendered musically in the narrative.

Goldberg's character Deloris becomes the vehicle through which the narrative introduces popular gospel music. In turn, this music structures the narrative's ideological tension between Deloris as counterculture opposing Mother Superior's dominant culture. The music's semiotic function in the narrative is best understood in light of gospel's troubled history and quest for legitimacy. According to ethnomusicologist Horace Boyer, the term *gospel music* originally referred to a type of song and to a style of piano playing. Gospel singing is still distinctive for its treatment of four elements of music: timbre, range, text interpolation, and improvisation.

Originally rejected by some black communities, gospel music did not begin to make an impact on the public until the 1920s. Carried from the South to the northern states by migrants during the 1930s and 1940s, it gradually attracted more performers and a larger audience. By the mid-1940s it was accepted as one of the several types of black religious music. The years 1945 to 1955 witnessed the rise of American gospel music from shabby storefront churches to gospel-group extravaganzas with singers of extraordinary control and nuance. The late 1960s and early 1970s brought gospel into the Roman Catholic Church and, through television and recordings, into the homes of listeners around the world.[36]

However, throughout gospel's history and rise to mainstream popularity, black and white communities have doubted its religiosity, viewing it as secular rather than sacred. Some ethnomusicologists explain the sacred-secular divide as a consequence of gospel's cultural origins in Negro spirituals: as music created for religious services and activities without formal structure. Gospel music has been predicated on the concept of a spontaneous songfest comprising simple melodies capable of much embellishment to a text of few words, which could support repetition, leaving spaces for the reiteration of words by the congregation and freeing the soloist for the textual interpolations. The purpose was not to entertain, not to satisfy, not to merchandise, but to express the pent-up emotions of the participants. But this articulation of gospel has led to some essentialist misconceptions and inferences. This has led to the problematic perception of gospel as more emotionally expressive, less severely repressive, less artistically complex, and has furthered the idea it possesses a special "earthiness." More specifically, there is still the troubling belief that gospel retains a so-called primitive element differing drastically from the Western European aesthetic. The rapid vibrato, rhythmic improvisation, and changing tempos of gospel song contribute to this perception.

The history of gospel is relevant to its narrative function in the movie *Sister Act*. Although Mother Superior is pleased by the choir's vast improvement, she's disdainful of Deloris's gospel sound. She disapproves of the songs, viewing them as secular rather than sacred. However, Deloris's polyphonic harmony proves charismatic, bringing bystanders into the empty—nearly defunct—church to increase weekly mass attendance and uplift the dour spirits of the repressed nuns. Deloris's marginal and subversive art, therefore, enjoys an adversarial relationship to Mother Superior's power and to the official Catholic Church culture, thus reincarnating the spirit of carnival in the narrative.[37] That Goldberg's character turns a punishment (i.e., instructing the choir) into a reward (i.e., enjoyable performances) adds personal insult to Mother Superior's injured sense of aesthetic judgment. Even as Sister Mary Clarence, Goldberg's Deloris creates the possibility of subversive pleasure with her carnivalesque amalgamation of sacred and secular idioms: "highly" sacred classical music and "lowly" secular popular melodies (coded as European and African American, respectively) undergo hybridization in their performance of music medley.

Hybridization is an essential characteristic of carnival. In Bakhtin, carnival is presented as a world of heteroglot exuberance, of ceaseless overrunning and excess where all is mixed. Hybridization produces new combinations and strange instabilities in a semiotic system. It generates the possibility of shifting the terms of the system itself by erasing and interrogating the relationships constituting it.[38] Hybridity is an especially threatening category of carnival, not only because the hybrid entity is considered mongrel, impure, and grotesque, but also because moral panic is produced by the idea of promiscuous mingling of high and low.

The emotional resonance of *Sister Act* hinges on the symbolic power of the soundtrack. More specifically, it hinges on the emotive and corporeal sign-function of Deloris's popular black gospel music. By virtue of carrying the emotional weight of the film and its position as antithetical to "white music," gospel recalls the primordial role of music in culture as discussed by Nietzsche in *The Joyful Wisdom*. Deloris's gospel music functions in much the same way Nietzsche claimed certain musical forms can: by "calling the entire symbolism of the body into play, triggering the pantomime of dancing, forcing every member into rhythmic movement."[39] This is manifest in the film in Deloris's dancing nuns, who step out of choir formation to dance along with their solo parts. However, the emotive sign-function delegated Deloris's hybrid black music manifests the duality of carnival discourse.

This emotive sign-function problematically repositions "black" music as the more primitive, animal, and elemental component of hybridized popular music. Implicit in the strict separation of the European Christian music and (African American) secular music is an attempt to maintain the moral wholesomeness coded as a Christian aesthetic. Here the nun is reproduced as the archetypal symbol of innocence—and also of corruptibility—evoking the concept of first temptation/sin and the loss of Eden in Judeo-Christian cultures. Mother Superior rebuffs hybridity in music, and the pantomime of dance, as threatening the moral virtue of the nuns, who might be corrupted by the polyphonic rhythms offered by Deloris.

However, the new combination of musical styles in *Sister Act*'s narrative gives rise to new, enlivened social dynamics in the convent and—by extension—the parish at large. Deloris's musical direction erases the primacy of the old tradition and implies a new, more reciprocal relationship between mainstream and religious cultures. Rather than position these varying traditions as antithetical and incongruous, the film repositions them—initiating the resignification of gospel, demonstrating the two traditions as complementary. This is facilitated by the narrative's reliance on the *logic of multiculturalism*, in which low culture not only troubles high culture, it also reveals high culture as dependent upon low culture for its own contemporary relevance.

Notions of musical harmony and hybridity in *Sister Act* function as a metaphor for concordant relations in the social realm. They are metaphors for the realization of mellifluously orchestrated social relations among persons of different racial, religious, and class backgrounds. Therefore, *Sister Act* could be read as a *narrative of multicultural assimilation* in which the ability to absorb difference into the dominant order, and the ability of these women to harmonize, is a metaphor for the utopian realization of multiculturalism and the process of multicultural education, in which music is the common idiom. By the film's conclusion, even Mother Superior has been persuaded: she acknowledges and embraces the charismatic pleasure of Deloris's hybrid gospel-classical music and reformulates her views concerning the distinction between musical traditions.

That the film's narrative sentimentality (i.e., the fantasy of harmonious multiculturalism) is linked to the semiotic function of black popular music as creating the utopian sentiment suggests we read *Sister Act* as a comedy *and* as a musical. The film shares some of the attributes Richard Dyer assigns musical films in his discussion of these pictures as a form of utopian entertainment. A term with multiple meanings, *utopian* refers to the ideal conditions of social organization and political schemes. Utopianism maintains the belief in the perfectibility of human society. A utopian sensibility is contained and conveyed in the euphoric feelings of communal harmony, unity, contentment, and synchronicity. Entertainment may present utopian worlds, spaces, or moments of utopia within their narratives. Music may function as one of the many semiotic codes and/or conditions of this utopian sensibility.

According to Dyer, there are three main tendencies of such narratives: first, some musicals keep narrative and musical numbers separate. Second, some musicals retain the division between narrative dilemmas and musical numbers as escape but try to integrate the two with certain devices. Third, there are musicals that dissolve the distinction between the narrative and the music, implying that the world of the narrative is already utopian.[40] *Sister Act* retains the division between narrative as a set of problems (i.e., dearth of churchgoers, a bad choir, a financially indebted convent, Deloris's need to hide) and musical songs as escape from those problems, while integrating the numbers into narrative through typical transitional devices (e.g., the well-known cue for a song). Rather than completely dissolve the distinction between narrative and musical number to imply that the world of the narrative is already utopian (as found in musicals including *Jesus Christ Superstar, Hair, and The Wiz*), *Sister Act* situates Goldberg's Deloris/Sister Mary Clarence as (1) a menacing source of carnivalesque gospel music, (2) the figure that facilitates the transition between narrative and number, and (3) the retreat from the convent's repressive bureaucracy. She functions much the same way in the film's sequel.

Between starring in *Sister Act* and its sequel, the actress-comedienne appeared in a handful of other films, including Gail Singer's *Wisecracks* (1992), Darrell James Roodt's *Sarafina* (1992), Gene Quintano's *National Lampoon's Loaded Weapon I* (1993), and Richard Benjamin's *Made in America* (1993). Yet none of these films provided the same kind of platform for Goldberg to perform her repertoires of various characters and charades. In 1993, Disney approached Whoopi about making *Sister Act 2: Back in the Habit,* which would repeat the formula of its predecessor but without director Emile Ardolino, who was now dying with AIDS. *Sister Act 2* was to be directed by Bill Duke. An African American director, Duke was familiar with the subjects and themes structuring the narrative: the aspirations of disaffected inner-city black and Latino youth. Duke would also have greater sensitivity for the film's multicultural sensibility.

Sister Act 2: Back in the Habit

There are two important distinctions between *Sister Act* and its sequel, *Sister Act 2: Back in the Habit.* First, there is the extent to which *Sister Act 2* more heavily relies on the generic conventions of the musical by integrating additional music into the film and by casting professional singers (i.e., Lauryn Hill), whose narrative function is restricted to music. Second, the sequel places greater emphasis on music as metaphor for its ethos of multiculturalism conveyed through polyphonic harmony. Situating the story in an inner-city high school and the surrounding area, the sequel goes a step further by literalizing its emphasis on multicultural education. The narrative device of multicultural education sets the stage for the emphasis on diverse musical forms whose harmonic blending structures the utopian sensibility of the narrative. *Sister Act 2* expresses more emphatically a *narrative of multicultural assimilation,* in which the ability to absorb many differences into the dominant curricular order, and the ability of the students to harmonize, creates a sense of utopia.

At the beginning of *Sister Act 2,* the nuns find Deloris in Las Vegas working her own show. They've traveled there at Mother Superior's behest to return Deloris to the convent, where she again becomes Sister Mary Clarence. Her assignment: rejuvenate the decaying inner-city Catholic school and discipline the undisciplined teens with her uplifting (read: carnivalesque) spirit. As the music teacher, Deloris organizes a street fair–fundraiser, coaches the school's musically talented teens, and disciplines the unruly students. Paralleling the narrative of *Sister Act, Sister Act 2* foregrounds the charismatic function of Goldberg's comedy of transformation.

The film creates another venue for her idiolect of body movements, hand gestures, elaborate costume transformations, vocal inflections, and eye-rolling sarcasm. These are the means for expressing a repertoire of defiance against the school's administrative order. Whereas in *Sister Act* her character's defiance was directed at the authority of Mother Superior (and the dominant European culture), it is redirected in the sequel at the school administration's authority and at defiant teenagers (and their rap-dominated subculture). Deloris's identity as a black woman, and former rule-breaking menace, place her between narrative poles: the all-white administrative teaching staff, ill-equipped with their Eurocentric curriculum, and the rabble-rousing black and Latino teens eager for multicultural perspectives on life and music history.

To achieve the liminality between generational and racial poles, Goldberg's Deloris performs the role of an empathic nun while breaking the bureaucratic school board's rules. Once again she is a character within a character. She criticizes the immature behavior of the teens and mocks their juvenile, clannish

Gospel hip-hop, a metaphor for multicultural education in *Sister Act 2: Back in the Habit* (1993).

nature. By asserting the carnival right of criticism and mockery, she earns their respect. Her carnival mockery of their adolescent behavior parallels the process of signifyin(g), mimics the structure of "playing the dozens" and "dissing." Her "dissing" them into order is a mode of signifyin(g), which depends heavily on humor and the bravado of exchanging insults in a game of one-upmanship.[41] As the only black teacher, Goldberg's Sister Mary Clarence employs this mode of discourse as evidence of her cultural blackness, as evidence she can speak youth vernacular, and as proof she can relate to their experiences.

Between filming *Sister Act* and its sequel, Goldberg also appeared in the screen comedy *Soapdish*. When the possibility of a *Ghost* sequel fell through, Goldberg joined the cast of Herbert Ross and Aaron Spelling's parody of daytime soap operas. *Soapdish* provided Goldberg the opportunity to be costumed in a sophisticated and mature manner. More specifically, it offered her the opportunity to dress in a conventionally feminine manner, as opposed to dressing solely for laughs or for her repertoire of comedic transformation. This film raises the issue of costume and its function in creating her screen personae.

In addition to scrutinizing the narrative function of her characters, I want to consider the narrative function of costume in creating her screen persona as rebelliously comedic. Goldberg's reflections on *Soapdish* prove revealing. According to biographer James Robert Parish, when the film's costume designer Nolan Miller and the star met, she solicited his assistance with wardrobe.

> Nolan would later reflect: "I think Miss Goldberg has been dressed up for films in the past, but it was always to make everyone laugh, to be funny. And this time she was dressed seriously as a woman. And I think it was a wonderful feeling for her, and she liked it." She not only thought Miller was "very, very cool," but he taught her "That I could actually look any way I chose and be elegant. You know all of those women [on screen] who had great style and class—I could be part of that if I chose to be."[42]

These comments from Miller and Goldberg express the extent to which her narrative function as comedienne, her liminal characters, and her figural status as a menacing presence of carnival have mandated comedic costuming. These reflective statements evoke one of feminist film theory's major interventions regarding the status of gender categories: namely, that femininity is a masquerade. Masquerade is a product and function of vestments, accoutrements, and props worn to effect the disguise of gender difference. Vestments are also easily discarded to reveal similarities between genders. Goldberg's comic costuming in films must be viewed in light of the feminist articulations concerning gender's social construction.

As an actor whose corporeal playfulness—both diegetic and extradiegetic—is augmented by outlandish costumes, Goldberg has issued a menacing critique of dominant categories of identity from the liminal space of unruly womanhood. This unruliness has been mapped onto the visual text of her performing body through garments, hairpieces, garish makeup, colored contacts, and ill-fitting dresses. I maintain that these vestments defy conventional wisdom regarding appropriate fashion and the bourgeois standards of taste, comportment, beauty, and elegance to which women are expected to conform. The performative use of costume has enabled Goldberg to challenge the boundaries of gender, sexuality, and even race.

Ghost and *The Associate* are two films in which Goldberg strikingly conveys her comedy of transformation. The narrative structures of both these films (and her changing identities within the texts) reveal this brand of charismatic comedy. Her performative use of costume, gesture, and voice inflection enables us to see separation between the physically sexed body and gender as a product of props and aids. Therefore, I would like to return to my reading of *Ghost* and to a reading of *The Associate* to explain the ways in which narrative structure and performance coalesce in her rebellious idiolect.[43]

The Associate

In *The Associate* (1996), Goldberg effectively demonstrates her comedy of carnivalesque transformation as a comedy of gender transvestism. She plays two characters, or a character within a character, much like she did in *Ghost*, in which she acts out male and female gender roles/differences and—to a lesser extent—male and female sexual desire. Her performance of gender identity (and heterosexual desires) in these films recalls other cinematic texts in which a single actor performs opposing male and female genders. Such performances remind us of what film theorist Chris Straayer has aptly described as the "temporary transvestite film."[44]

In describing gender-coded behavior in cinema, Straayer explains that the transvestite is a figure often adopting the opposite sex's gestures and behaviors, either "naturally" or for parody. These gender-coded behaviors and gestures are often used to remind the film audience of the character's "original" gender and also to suggest the threat of exposure in the diegetic world. Straayer writes:

> Sometimes obvious male characteristics, such as a hairy chest or even a beard, contribute to a subversive and contradictory play of signification. The disguise

in temporary transvestite films, then, is both transvestism and cross-dressing. Within the terms of the narrative, the disguise is sufficient to trick other characters. Therefore, I have chosen to use the term transvestite to describe the generic *plot* of these films. However, because the disguise is inadequate to trick the film audience, its extradiegetic operation is that of cross-dressing.[45]

Straayer's understanding of temporary transvestite films informs my reading of mainstream and avant-garde cinema with this pattern. The vast range of roles and pictures that manifest some aspects of this structure include Dustin Hoffman's role in *Tootsie* (1982), Jaye Davidson in *The Crying Game* (1992), Robin Williams in *Mrs. Doubtfire* (1993), Tilda Swinton in *Orlando* (1993), Wesley Snipes in *To Wong Foo: Thanks for Everything, Julie Newmar* (1995), Hilary Swank in *Boys Don't Cry* (1999), and the Wayans Brothers' performances in *White Chicks* (2004). What these films have in common is the temporary cross-coding and adoption of gendered behaviors and sexual desire. Straayer's paradigm is as applicable to these films as it is to my reading of Goldberg's performance in *Ghost* and *The Associate*.

Straayer's model offers an alternative reading strategy. It is an alternative to theories proposed by other feminist film scholars and cultural theorists. Straayer suggests that parody is another way of reading gender and costume play. Since I'm reading *Ghost* and *The Associate* as comedies of gender masquerade through the bodily play of costumes used to feminize and defeminize the star's body, Straayer's model proves appropriate.

Many other feminist film theorists (influenced by Laura Mulvey) offer analyses of gender masquerade through Freudian and Lacanian psychoanalytic theories of cinematic fetishism. Recent revisions of Mulvey's paradigm cling to the notion that dominant cinema speaks a discourse of male oedipal desire and fetishism. Feminist film theorists deconstruct the conventional codes of femininity as a form of gender masquerade, which disguises the body. Classical Hollywood masquerade is said to emerge as the process in which the woman uses her body to disguise herself. According to this logic, femininity is merely a masquerade of accessories: fetish objects. For Joan Riviere, feminine masquerade is the defensive attempt to hide the possession of masculinity with excessive accoutrements, feathers, and props. Mary Ann Doane employed Riviere's analysis to argue that masquerade is the woman's attempt to construct a distance between her and a sexual identity created for her by patriarchy. For Gaylyn Studlar, "women's costuming is an inevitable reflection of the fetishistic process disguising woman's castration, rendering her difference harmless."[46] According to these feminists, the gender mask functions as a disguise in femininity, distancing and destabilizing the patriarchal gaze. Problematically, these models are always linked to Freudian psychoanalysis and theories of castration anxiety.

Furthermore, these theories do not readily explain the *comedic* gender masquerade or the race(d), gendered constructions of the body. Because she is African American, Whoopi Goldberg's womanliness is always already considered questionable. And, within her comedy routines, she shows the mask of femininity to be a farce. Goldberg's masquerade in *Ghost* and cross-dressing in *The Associate* fall outside psychoanalytic paradigms because her characters are never passive figures and they are rarely sexual objects of the male gaze.

To read her performances as Oda Mae Brown of *Ghost* and Laurel Ayers of *The Associate* as moments of temporary transvestism is to consider how these roles signify on the desexualization of Goldberg's screen image in particular and black women's sexuality in Hollywood films generally. If Goldberg's status as a comedienne is a partial explanation for the desexualization of her screen persona, then placing her work in the historical context of black women's representation in popular entertainment resituates the sexuality of her screen persona. Certainly, the construction of black female sexuality as aberrant, and therefore in need of social regulation, textual censorship, or narrative containment, does not originate with the cinema.

As the scholarship of African American feminists and historians (i.e., Hazel Carby, Patrica Hill-Collins, Cheryl Harris, bell hooks, Hortense Spillers, and Michele Wallace) has shown, the ideology of deviant black sexuality informed the political economy of slavery as well as the racial politics of labor relations after the Civil War. Long before sociologists and politicians devised policy that perpetuated theories about the existence of black matriarchs, slave owners argued black women were not *real* women, in an attempt to justify the political economy of slavery.[47] Throughout the nineteenth century, socioeconomic and cultural vectors converged in constructions of blackness, particularly the black female body. This systematic desexualization moved into mainstream American culture with minstrelsy.

Minstrel theater of this era was largely a transracial, transvestite theater in which white men cross-dressed as black women. The influx of Irish and Jewish immigrants increased the numbers of Americans who were the subjects of racial scrutiny, as they struggled to fashion themselves as "white" Americans. Shifting demographics coincided with changes in the economic organization of the country that resulted in the redefinition of gender roles. For David Roediger, the white working class—disciplined and made anxious by a fear of wage-labor dependency—began to construct an image of the black population as "other," as embodying the preindustrial, erotic style of life white workers loathed and longed for. Roediger asserted the same white workers who attacked wage slavery to distinguish themselves from black labor enjoyed imitating blackness on the minstrel stage.

This theatrical tradition was one of the primary ways European immigrants fashioned their own notion of white masculinity against a fiction of black womanhood. White men masked themselves as black women to display and ridicule insatiable female sexual appetite and the weaker sex's pretensions to independence. Michael Rogin writes: "Far from challenging rigid sexual divisions, 'minstrel-drag' ridiculed women who crossed gender boundaries; the aggressive minstrel caricature of women made grotesque female bodily desire and the moral authority of domestic ideology."[48] Borrowing Straayer's concept of temporary transvestism, I would add that early minstrelsy was not only a temporary stage of unstable gender identity, it was also a temporary stage of unstable racial identity.

Goldberg's performances in *Ghost* and *The Associate* invoke minstrelsy through an inversion of the ignominious tradition of transracial transvestism. Throughout *Ghost,* for example, Goldberg's phony spiritual medium, Oda Mae Brown, is physically excessive. Goldberg performs her character Oda Mae as buffoonish and as clowning in a way that calls attention to the limits of gender masquerade. Her corporeal style—gesture, walk, and voice—create an excessive, parodic representation of working-class womanhood. This performance is intended as gender parody but is also set against the "heterosexually ideal genders." The film juxtaposes the gendered bodies of Whoopi Goldberg's Oda Mae and Demi Moore's Molly as opposing physical types (the strength of a broadly built, working-class black woman is juxtaposed against the emotional fragility of streamlined, yuppie femininity). Black working-class identity is coded and conveyed through voice inflection, gesture, and movement—a variety of "techniques of the body" that are comically coded as antithetical to upper-class white womanhood.

Goldberg's expressive use of bodily techniques recalls Barbara Stanwyck's archetypal performance of distinctly working-class womanhood in the classic maternal melodrama *Stella Dallas* (1937). As Linda Williams remarked of Stanwyck, the actress's body fails to signify femininity because the fetishization is unsuccessful despite the presence of numerous props for the exaggeration of feminine presence.[49] Goldberg, with her huge wig and gaudy, bright-colored, outdated clothes, "parodies the 'natural' spectacle of women's corporeal excess, as simultaneously too much and never enough."[50] While generic and historical vectors may construct Goldberg as unfeminine, her performance of black working-class womanhood (here coded as masculine through techniques and juxtapositions) renders the notion of a fixed femininity farcical.

Goldberg's feminine charade is significant in the narrative of *Ghost*. The lack of femininity and class sophistication evidenced by Goldberg's Oda Mae reveals the gap between her gender masquerade and her physically sexed body. This gap positions phony medium Oda Mae as a false woman (i.e., wearing makeup and hairpieces) or as falsely feminine—and therefore more masculine—in relation to the naturally feminine (i.e., makeupless, overalls-wearing, clay-molding sculptor) Molly. The division between these women along lines of race, gender performativity, and class is relevant to the narrative at the moment of its emotional climax, when Goldberg undergoes gender transformation. Offering her own body as the physical vessel through which Sam's spirit and Molly's body connect, Oda Mae allows Sam to "use her body" to be with Molly one last time. Sam passes into Oda Mae's body, physically reuniting with Moore. *Ghost* aligns the black woman's erotic gaze with white male heterosexual desire for white women. In *Ghost* we have the representation of black female corporality as a comedic threshold, a liminal site, or an interstice, which functions in the narrative as a site for the realization of white sexual fantasies.

This scene presents the most threatening moment of temporary transvestism in the film. Beginning with the sexual embrace of two women, it quickly cuts away from their interlinked bodies and then cuts back to show spectators Sam and Molly embracing. Suspending disbelief, audiences are expected to believe Sam is actually inside Oda Mae's body. This scene is potentially threatening to heterosexuality because it initially presents the possibility of lesbianism (i.e., the sexual embrace of Goldberg and Moore) rendering Sam—and, by extension, heterosexual union—unnecessary for narrative closure. However, the potential threat of lesbianism is overturned by the temporary transvestism. The possible lesbian love scene is turned into heterosexual scenario in the shot of Sam and Molly embracing. Whether intentional or inadvertent, the primary effect is the same: a teasing of audiences with the possible threat of interracial lesbian love (a theme Goldberg returned to in *Boys on the Side*).

The secondary effect is the positioning of the black female character as interchangeable with the white male character. The film literally visualizes the culturally and historically inscribed gender slippage between black women (as supposedly emasculating, phallic, and masculine) and ideas about white men (as virile, rugged, and sexually desirable). Thus Goldberg's Oda Mae is transformed from a woman who fails to signify natural femininity into a woman who can embody and signify masculine virility. This same kind of gender slippage is evident in other Goldberg vehicles.

The Associate also inverts the tradition of transracial transvestism. Within the film, Whoopi's character Laurel Ayers is a dedicated and ambitious banker. The victim of gender discrimination, Laurel is passed over for a promotion in favor of another associate who enjoys career advancement because he is white, heterosexual, and male. She quits and starts her own firm, only to realize the powerbrokers on Wall Street still refuse to take her seriously. To break the glass ceiling and enter the "old boys'" network, Laurel creates the fictitious company figurehead Robert Cutty. Cutty is an old white man who serves (in absentia) as the CEO of her investment firm until Laurel is forced to produce Cutty in the flesh. To do so, she must actually become him, undergoing transracial transvestism.

While biographer Robert Parish insists that the buildup to seeing Whoopi's character transformed into an eccentric-looking white man is the main suspense of the movie, I maintain that the moment of her unmasking is the suspenseful climax. Up until the unmasking, Goldberg performs the gender charade of white masculinity, suggesting both womanliness and manliness are gender masquerades. These masquerades invoke Straayer's description of temporary transvestism as a disguise sufficient to trick other characters but inadequate to trick the film audience. At the moment of unmasking, when the characters are let in on the secret, she reveals the gap between gender and the physically sexed body in a racial and gender striptease.

This reappropriation of transracial transvestism is a moment of signifiyin(g) on the denigrating discourse of black representation in minstrelsy. Goldberg's masquerade is a disruption at the level of the signifier. When she dons the Cutty mask, Whoopi revises the signs of blackness by performing whiteness. Within the fictional narrative she abandons bodily gestures and vocal tonality believed to signify blackness, replacing them with signifiers of white masculine comportment. Whether Goldberg, dressed as Cutty, could actually pass for a male in the extradiegetic "real world" is less relevant than the way this comedy of temporary transvestism is signifiyin(g) on minstrel in the reel world—suggesting through resignification that gender binaries are expressed through performances of race and gender.

There are multiple ways of reading Whoopi Goldberg's celebrity persona. Her screen, standup-stage, Broadway, and television appearances (i.e., *Hollywood Squares, Whoopi* [the NBC Tuesday-night sitcom], and *The View*) demonstrate the various texts and intertexts in which her discursive comedic persona manifests. I have argued here that some media critics have resisted examining the ways her screen persona is rebellious and challenging. Through her comedy she resists dominant cultural notions of gender binaries and moves far beyond some of the limitations of racially stereotyped caricatures like Mammy or Topsy. My intervention with this essay was to examine the way a black comedienne challenges the boundaries and menaces borders.

The 2003 television sitcom *Whoopi* continued the tradition of Goldberg's earlier film work. Making jocular mention of Saddam Hussein or raising the prospect of an undiscovered Iranian missile system might seem to be a sitcom's kiss of death. It might seem unlikely, even impossible, for a show with such commentary to be a presumptive fall-season hit. But Goldberg tried once again—in the context of the show—to challenge mainstream sensibilities. In the sitcom she played Mavis Rae, an irascible Manhattan hotelier who savors her memories as a chart-topping R&B singer while dealing with family, friends, and customers in today's New York City. Living at the hotel with Mavis is her brother Courtney (Wren T. Brown), a man who is the opposite of his sister. Whereas Mavis is loud and liberal, Courtney is conservative and dates a white woman named Rita (Elizabeth Regen). Rita is the kind of black-identified white woman who uses black vernacular freely, listens to rap music, dresses in hip-hop gear, and is considered "blacker" than her African American boyfriend. Courtney and Rita are examples of the way Goldberg's comedy sets the stage for a critique of rigid identity categories, showing them as unstable and untenable. The program also pushed the envelope regarding what's considered acceptable on network television. Goldberg's Mavis poked fun at President Bush's malapropisms and mispronunciations of simple words like "nuclear," and she was not afraid to chastise people in interracial relationships. Far from politically or environmentally correct, Mavis Rae was also an unapologetic chain smoker. In fact, the program's pilot episode began with a cigarette joke. A hotel guest reminded Mavis that "secondhand smoke kills." Her rapid-fire retort: "So do I, baby . . . walk on!"

Oprah Winfrey

The Cathartic, Charismatic Capitalist

> While the nature of charisma precludes the existence of a
> standard predictable charismatic personality, the greatest
> political charismatics are not unlike artists. They use their
> followers as "material" to raise politics to the level of art.
>
> —David Aberbach

> Winfrey's 42 years have encompassed all the American
> nightmares—poverty, child abuse, drugs, racism, obesity—
> and all the redeeming features of the American dream: a
> giddying rise to fame, a third home in Aspen, fitness train-
> ing, [and] constant cathartic release of her inner demons.
>
> —Richard Thomas

> She has talked of ending her program in the next year or two
> and moving on to other projects, but her charismatic appeal
> is unlikely to diminish. Oprah is probably the greatest influ-
> ence on the adult population . . . she's almost a religion.
>
> —Fran Lebowitz

In the mainstream press, Oprah Winfrey has repeatedly been dubbed "the world's most powerful woman." As television talk-show host, she is the female equivalent of the nation's most beloved anchorman, Walter Cronkite. A media producer, she is the third woman in history to own a major production company and sound stages, following in the footsteps of Mary Pickford and Lucille Ball.[1] Together her talk show and magazine have resulted in the "Oprah Effect,"[2] influencing the careers of authors, the consumption of novels, the reception of films, and the dissemination of self-help techniques, making her the most influential bookseller in the United States and possibly the world. As the wealthiest female entertainer in the world, she became the first female African American billionaire.[3] Winfrey continues to exercise cultural authority as a producer of internationally popular media in a global mediascape; as an advocate of self-management technologies; and as sponsor of new media personalities like nationally syndicated relationship therapist Dr. Phil McGraw, personal money-manager Suze Orman, and professional motivator Iyanla Van Sant.

Yet despite Winfrey's personal and professional successes, questions are continually raised as to whether she is the embodiment of a recycled stereotype: a reconstituted mammy figure providing a successful media enterprise with a familiar cultural icon as its figurehead. As some critics have bluntly asked: Is Winfrey a powerful cultural influence, or is her popularity the result of similarity between her image (as a compassionate, full-figured, sexually nonthreatening black woman) and good old Aunt Jemima? For instance, in her discussion of images of black women in popular culture, sociologist K. Sue Jewell has asserted that "Oprah's large size was consistent with the mammy image." For Jewell, Winfrey's viewers were unaware of the subconscious correlation between the large stature of an African American woman and her credibility and capacity to provide comfort to adults and children. She writes: "Despite the fact that Oprah Winfrey has demonstrated her proficiency as a talk show host and actress, it is still the case that cultural images that symbolize African American womanhood continue to impact upon her" and other high-achieving women.[4] Jean-Christophe Agnew made a similar comparison between the talk-show host and the Aunt Jemima trademark, which recently received an upscale makeover. "What are we to make," asked Agnew, "of a figure like Aunt Jemima, whose 100–year old kerchief was finally removed from her head during her most recent makeover . . . now she is said to look like Oprah Winfrey."[5]

Such questions and comments abound in both the scholarly literature on Winfrey's stardom (Masciarotte, 1991; Shuttuc, 1996; Marshall, 1997; Abt and Mustazza, 1997; Illouz, 1999; Young, 2001) and in the familiar context of the television program itself. While appearing as a guest on her show, relationship therapist Dr. John Gray flippantly addressed the very issue that may belie the mediated myth of Winfrey's star image. During a supposedly cathartic role-play, Gray jokingly noted her professional success came at the expense of personal sacrifice when he suggested to the audience that she served as the surrogate mother of America's lost adults. Dr. Gray said: "Now you just feel Oprah's arms around you like your mommy's. Imagine your mommy holding you. And she's going to say loving things to you like she says to everybody all the time. She's the mother of America. [audience laughs] That's why she didn't have time for her own kids. She can't have kids. She's taking care of all the other little lost children."[6]

In the context of the television program, Gray's comments have a cultural significance of their own. On one level, his remarks inadvertently lend credence to the notion that as a cultural icon, Winfrey can be interpreted as a metaphorical mammy. After all, in American folklore, mammy was never depicted as taking care of her own children. Instead, she worked tirelessly and professionally as the caretaker of other people's children. This is not to say that *mammy* and *mommy* are indistinguishable signifiers. However, it is to recognize the implicit linguistic slippage and the (mis)conception of Winfrey as one who resembles the mammy figure. In American folklore and popular culture (i.e., literature, theater, film, television), the mammy figure has been a sexually nonthreatening, economically disenfranchised fixture of plantation family life, evoking nostalgia for the "old days" of the antebellum South.[7]

It is not only in the context of the show that the issue of Oprah's mammification has been addressed. Gloria-Jean Masciarotte suggests that a facile application of the mammy stereotype to Winfrey's star persona[8] negates the double-voiced nature of Winfrey's celebrity sign. For Masciarotte, this double-voiced celebrity manifests the problematic of representation between what is represented and what it signifies. She argues that the conflicting and confusing evaluation of Oprah's "person" depends on her double-voiced public identity as a large black woman: the matriarch of difference, the phallic mother, the sign of negativity in bourgeois, white patriarchy. And, at the same time, as a rich, glamorous television producer/star: the patriarch of representation, the Law, the signifier of transcendental capitalist subjectivity.[9] I concur with Masciarotte's first assertion that Winfrey's celebrity sign is a multivalent signifier. However, Masciarotte comes to a dubious conclusion. Problematically, she concludes that Winfrey-as-star speaks from the position of that which is abjected by culture, thereby never transcending the materiality of "negative aesthetic evaluation" to be figured as a metaphysical vehicle by which spectators transform the limits of fixed subjectivity.[10] Masciarotte writes:

> It is important to note that the sign of Oprah Winfrey traverses not only race and gender but also declines these determinates within the cultural politics of body and presence . . . her media sign cannot deny the inherent abjection of her differences. The result of her over-determined subjectivity is manifest in the televisual and media gossip that delights in her battles with food, her troublesome relationship with a good-looking guy that foregrounds and (according to the common wisdom of white patriarchal aesthetics) contradicts

her own more "mammy-like" appearance and function, and her fluctuating hairstyles and fashion choices.[11]

P. David Marshal (1997) also asserts that the emergence of Oprah Winfrey as a television celebrity is built on a series of binarisms that work to differentiate her presented subjectivity. However, Marshall's and Masciarotte's analyses of binary constructions prove reductive on two counts. First, this binary analysis resurrects Cartesian dualism, which places the mind—engaged in spiritual contemplation—in a position of hierarchical superiority over the corporeal nature of the black star's body. Second, such analyses diminish the significance, as does other scholarship on Oprah, of the unconventional aspects of Winfrey's career. Consider, for example, her book club's cultural capital; her access to modes of television and film production; her ability to influence the conditions of her stardom; her authority as an arbiter of middle-class American taste and her influence over consumer society's *cult of the body*. As an activist, she has challenged corporate exploitation of consumers during her involvement in the anti-beef industry campaign. And, in the film industry, consider her willingness to embrace (and render cinematic) the complex and traumatic legacy of slavery in her production of Toni Morrison's novel *Beloved*.

Emphasis on the Oprah-as-mammy metaphor obscures the aspects of Winfrey's iconographic status that align her with the dominant social order. These analyses position her as a reconfigured stereotype, when she is actually the reigning representative of America's disciplined, heteronormative, and bourgeois body. She is America's leading representative of late twentieth-century (and early twenty-first-century) technologies of self-embourgeoisement. Winfrey's weight-maintenance programs, her "well-dressed" body, and her conventionally styled hair inform her iconographic status—her star persona—as the nation's leading representative of transforming, modernizing self-help technologies. Who better than an Oprah Winfrey—a woman who has struggled with the stigma of weight, race, class, gender, and wavy hair—to demonstrate the transforming effects of technology on the self as methods of embourgeoisement?[12]

My reading of Winfrey's celebrity sign employs the Oprah-as-mammy metaphor as a point of departure rather than a conclusion. Winfrey's celebrity sign is not merely double voiced, it is also charismatic. She is charismatic, in part, because her celebrity is a sign based on transitions from the site of abjection to the site of assimilation, from anonymity to fame, from poverty to prosperity, from culturally insignificant to successful producer of mass-mediated signs. Her celebrity is predicated on a Horatio Alger narrative of success. Thus Winfrey speaks not only from the position of abjection, but also from that of someone who has transcended abjection through self-realization and entrepreneurial spirit. Her continued appeal is based, in part, on her self-promotion as a representative of every woman's—or every American's—ability to overcome social, psychic, sexual, and socioeconomic adversity/abjection.

The goal of this chapter is to offer an explanation of Oprah Winfrey's celebrity charisma. I maintain that she signifies a type of star charisma rather than political charisma. However, there are political aspects to her stardom. Her celebrity sign is multilayered. One layer of her charisma could be described as "cathartic charisma." In the pseudotherapeutic format of talk television,[13] she has played the role of America's therapist, which is different than merely functioning as a mammy figure. Since Winfrey's celebrity charisma is linked to her role as friend, confidante, personal healer, and cultural therapist, I characterize her star persona as signifying cathartic charisma. What becomes evident in this examination of Winfrey's star charisma is that her charisma is limited to consumer culture. The commercial limitations of her stardom were clearly demonstrated by the film *Beloved,* which failed financially despite the fact that she utilized her star charisma to propel the production, promotion, distribution, and exhibition of the project.[14]

During the thirteenth national season of her show, Winfrey introduced a "Remembering Your Spirit" segment to the existing format. In the newly revamped program, which was dubbed "Change Your Life TV," the host dedicated the closing segment of each show to consultations with professional ministers of New Age religion and newfound spirituality. This renewed spiritual sensibility would eventually permeate the star's other projects. For example, Winfrey told novelist-playwright Pearl Cleage that her role as Sethe in *Beloved* helped her to see her role on *The Oprah Winfrey Show* more clearly. She stated: "We will bring in more experts and emphasize the spirit. Every day we will have a segment called 'Remembering Your Spirit' to encourage viewers to go after their soul's desires. I want my work, all my work—movies, books, television—to be a light in people's lives."[15] No sooner did the "psychospiritual Reformation"[16] of the program prove popular among her audience than synergistic product tie-ins were marketed through Oprah's Book of the Month Club. For example, Amazon.com dedicated a separate Web page to books featured during the "Remembering Your Spirit" closing segment of the program. Popular titles included Judith Handlesman's *Growing Myself: A Spiritual Journey through Gardening* (1996), Sarah Breathnach's *Simple*

Abundance Journal of Gratitude (1998), Gary Zukav's *The Seat of the Soul* (1990), Naomi Levy's *To Begin Again* (1998), Alice Walker's *By the Light of My Father's Smile* (1998), Julia Cameron's *The Artist's Way: A Spiritual Path to Higher Creativity* (1995), and Frederic Brussat's *Spiritual Literacy: Reading the Sacred in Everyday Life* (1998). Clearly, spirituality was being appropriated and commodified into a variety of feel-good, self-help technologies.

Critical of the program's pseudoreligious format—namely, its concomitant shift from self-reference to self-reverence—*New York Times* media critic Jeff MacGregor described the new format as little more than aptly timed programming. MacGregor objected to the "hourlong interpretation of the Gospel-According-to-Oprah . . . [s]hot through with the usual platitudes of New Age unmeaning."

> It is a self-help anthology, presented with the missionary zeal of someone who's already got hers. Thus it is about nothing so much as Ms. Winfrey herself, and her pilgrimage toward a more rewarding state of Oprahness. Given our nation's endless search for the short cut to our better selves, it is a brilliant programming move. Which is not to say that Oprah's quest for human betterment is insincere, but rather that she has again anticipated the next pang of her audience's appetite. Oprah was among the first to book the sort of pathological sideshows that daytime is so roundly criticized for today. She was also among the first to abandon them. Her regular appearance in the financial monthlies as one of the highest paid/most powerful people in entertainment are based on more than her performance as television's most beloved ubiquitous empath. She is a shrewd businesswoman. Thus, like many gurus and circuit riders before her, Oprah has found a way to shamelessly market the history of her own misery and confusion as a form of worship. She is helped in this enterprise by a stable of experts, each appearing in rotation to explain for us the metaphysics of joy and sorrow and 401–K plans.[17]

The program's commodification of spirituality does not mitigate the fact that Winfrey's "Remembering Your Spirit" segment enables the program to function in the precise way critics implied the show, *Oprah!*—and by extension, the celebrity, Winfrey—could not: as vehicles for self-evaluation and metaphysical contemplation—however faddish—and as positions from which these might transpire. In fact, the show undermines the Cartesian dualism informing analyses of Winfrey's stardom.

I am suggesting that the religious tenor of *The Oprah Winfrey Show* (i.e., Oprah's Angel Network, "Remembering Your Spirit") reveals a relationship between the cult of the body and the cult of the soul in consumer culture.

Second, the addition of this religious segment to her program demonstrates a cultural link between therapeutic talk television and the prevailing atmosphere of heightened concern with moral character specific to late twentieth- and early twenty-first-century American culture.[18]

Winfrey has figured as a vehicle by which spectators transform the limits of fixed subjectivity. She represents a position from which audiences adopt the disciplinary tactics of body-soul maintenance—of spiritual introspection and dietary self-moderation as techniques of the self and as modes of personal uplift. Therefore, it is little wonder that Oprah Winfrey's celebrity charisma grew in effectiveness and became more spiritually oriented over the last decade of the twentieth century. The growing popularity of her charismatic celebrity has paralleled millenarianism and the rise of the therapeutic ethos in American life. Historical evidence suggests that during approximately the past three centuries, a therapeutic sense of self has prevailed in capitalist societies. The "history of capitalism is also the history of the elaboration and intensification of the therapeutic imperative."[19] The intensification of the therapeutic ethos has dovetailed with millenarianism. Winfrey's appeal—and by extension, her cultural authority as an arbiter of bourgeois heteronormativity (aka "good taste")—is a function of a celebrity sign that hinges on performing self-improvement, self-styled success, and the realization of the black bourgeois body through "technologies of the self."[20]

Thus there is a context for Winfrey's celebrity: late 1990s America witnessed the apotheosis of a form of cathartic mass entertainment—not unlike televangelism of the 1970s—that promised to deliver the product of spiritually fulfilling, "change-your-life TV" and self-improvement technologies. Winfrey's unique popularity as a talk-show host is a concomitant of her ability to present, perform, and personalize self-improvement in a charismatic and cathartic manner. To adduce this, I maintain first that Weberian notions of charisma illuminate aspects of Winfrey's celebrity. Second, I chart the historical origins of the "therapeutic ethos" in contemporary American culture (Lears, 1980; Grodin, 1991; White, 1992; Peck, 1995; Cloud, 1998). This therapeutic ethos emerged as a modern historical development shaped by the turmoil of the turn of the twentieth century.[21] It also informs the postmodern consumer culture out of which her celebrity emerged. By considering the emergence of the therapeutic ethos, I am suggesting cultural parallels between the modern religious sentiment of late nineteenth-century America and late twentieth-century manifestations of New Age religiosity present in the context of contemporary televangelism of which *Oprah* is an extension. The aim is twofold. First, the goal is to demonstrate that Winfrey's dominance in the talk-show arena—and, by extension, her celebrity—is not fueled by the similarity between her persona and the mammy icon. Rather, it is fueled first by her ability to recognize—and thereby commodify—cultural trends in the form of body-soul maintenance and self-help techniques before her competitors. Second, her dominance is a function of the program's amalgamation of cultural trends: the therapeutic ethos, as well as televisual consumerism as mass entertainment. Oprah Winfrey is the star player in the self-disciplining, spiritual-health education movement.

Winfrey's Charisma

Richard Dyer's seminal text on stardom advanced discussions of celebrity because it brought multiple theories of stardom (i.e., semiotic models of communication and behavioral/manipulation models) into dialogue with one another. Dyer's *Stars* (1979) was one of several examinations of the star system to acknowledge instances of stardom in which individuals who were given full promotional treatment still did not "make it" in the film industry. His observation suggested that film scholars needed to conceptualize why some stars become social phenomena and others do not. He was also one of the first scholars to demonstrate that sociologist Max Weber's (1864–1920) theory of charismatic authority has relevance for film studies, particularly star phenomena. More recently, P. David Marshall (1997) joined Dyer in his application of Weberian notions of charisma to the cinema, thereby conceptualizing social and ideological aspects of stardom.

Charisma may also grow out of the creative union of an emotional (and/or physical) disability or trial and unusually developed gifts or talents that counterbalance the adversity. Gifts of leadership may come to fruition through a correspondence between the charismatic's ideal inner world (i.e., religious contemplation, desire for fame, career aspirations) and an adverse external social, political, or economic reality. Theoretical articulations of charisma are sometimes bound by this very paradox: does crisis in the social order create the individual leader whose particular charismatic talents are thereby awakened, or does the charismatic individual engender the social change by his or her extraordinary behavior (Aberbach, 1996) or actions?

Like the charismatic figure, the celebrity demarcates an area of social life and identification that is fundamentally irrational. Weber's hypothesis concerning the resolution of irrationality into bureaucratic rationality offers a useful model for studying the "resolution" of celebrity status into rationalized forms in contemporary culture. The institutionalization of Winfrey's program, as a daily commercial ritual, regulates and routinizes the innovative possibilities of the program and the leadership potential of her celebrity. Given the artifice of the program, the commercial nature of the show, and its wholly routine structure, Winfrey should be categorized as an entertainment charismatic.

Entertainment charismatics are people who respond to adversity in their lives through a reaction formation. According to Freudian psychoanalysis, a reaction-formation occurs when an unconscious, unacceptable impulse or feeling (that would cause anxiety) is converted into its opposite so it can become conscious and be expressed. For example, a person adopts a set of attitudes and behaviors that are the opposite of his or her true dispositions. Winfrey's talents as a charismatic persona have come to fruition despite the adversity of an impoverished childhood spent in the segregated South on a Mississippi pig farm, a troubled adolescence during which she was repeatedly incestuously abused, and her inner aspirations to become a famous actress.[22] Her individual charisma has grown out of the union between personal difficulties and her inner desire to transcend the trauma of her youth. In this respect, she shares the profile of other entertainment charismatics (i.e., Billie Holiday, Elvis Presley, Marilyn Monroe, Dorothy Dandridge, John Lennon) whose experiences of childhood trauma were linked later in life—by their own admission—to feelings toward fame and a desire to overcome early-life adversities.

> The weaknesses of charismatics such as Charlie Chaplin, Marilyn Monroe or John Lennon often spring from early family loss or deprivation, leading to low self-esteem, depression and the blockage of feeling. But the weakness does not predominate. In fact, it creates an urgent need to develop unusual strength in other areas. This strength is drawn from positive conditions following the trauma coupled with natural gifts and a creative outlet. In the struggle to overcome or to master his weakness, the charismatic artist uses the media to recreate himself, to enhance his worth in his own eyes and in the eyes of his society or nation or entire world. Not having belonged to a secure home, he may find or create a home within an abstract entity such as the Public or the Universe.[23]

Jib Fowles has made a similar observation in his work on stardom. He claims that a stereotype exists about the families of stars. The father is either absent or inconsequential, while the mother pushes the performer onward to glory. A large percentage of stars do seem to have suffered a decidedly unstable life during the formative years. Thought to be a stereotype, this condition does, however, receive some confirmation in various star studies, as a disproportionate number of stars have apparently emerged from difficult childhoods.

Winfrey's celebrity sign is a composite of primary and secondary charisma. It is the intersection of individual efforts and talents and the *manufactured* charisma produced by a routine commercial program. Her star charisma is the institutionalization of her individual persona by the bureaucracy of syndicated television and magazine publishing.

Her program, for example, provides personal advice, pop psychology, and spiritual leadership. Filling societal roles traditionally assigned charismatic functionaries, *Oprah* and Winfrey disseminate self-management tactics (e.g., spirituality, body management, financial advice, fitness tips, relationship strategy, and personal hope) in a manner similar to clergy, personal gurus, and therapists. *The Oprah Winfrey Show* relies on Winfrey's charisma to convince studio and home audiences of the quasireligious transubstantiation of bodily techniques into life-improving practices.

The concept of charisma, as applied to stars, combines an understanding of the star's social function with an understanding of ideological function.[24] Dyer rightly cautions, however, that even though there is correspondence between political power and star charisma, problems arise when transferring the notion of charisma from political theory to film theory, because the star's status depends upon her or his *not* having any institutional political power. Marshall (1997) advanced Dyer's argument, asserting that in contemporary culture there is convergence in the source of power attributed to the political leader and film celebrities. I would add that this dynamic also applies to television celebrities. Both forms of subjectivity (political celebrity and star celebrity), sanctioned by the culture, enter the symbolic realm by providing meaning and significance for the culture at large.[25] It is useful to think of the nexus between political charisma and star charisma in terms of the relationships between stars and specific instabilities, ambiguities, and/or contradictions in the culture. The relationship between political charisma and star charisma—in particular the question of how or why a given person comes to have "charisma" attributed to her or him—is a function of the star's ability to be an outlet for social or political tensions. Winfrey's celebrity is not an outlet for sociopolitical tensions, since her cultural power is primarily limited to the realm of consumer culture. More specifically, it is limited to the realm of body and self-maintenance in consumer culture. She has used her show to highlight political issues (e.g., occasionally hosting political candidates or incumbent politicians). In doing so, she's allowed the program to bring a wider audience to political issues.[26] However, it is primarily in the arena of consumer society's body maintenance that she has charismatic authority. I am arguing that she provides an outlet for a multitude of society's moral tensions concerning bodily, psychological, and spiritual self-maintenance (i.e., adultery, abortion, RU-486, genetic engineering, sexual abuse, pedophilia, incest, rape, and cosmetic surgery).[27]

Before determining the relationship between Winfrey's star persona and the social milieu, it is necessary to consider the specific televisual context in which she became famous.

Weber, TV, and the Body

Weberian notions of charisma apply to television's personality system, as well. While Winfrey's celebrity has been constructed in film, it is primarily through television that she developed a star persona and a celebrity sign for which there is *charismatic devotion*.[28] Television genres classified as nonfiction—news, current affairs, talk shows, and variety game shows—are significantly structured in and around various manifestations of the television personality. Each of these genres is developed and organized around a central persona or personae. The news "reader," the current affairs "anchorman," the talk-show "host," the variety program "headliner," and the quiz show "master of ceremonies" are essential to their programs' action, pace, and thematic directions, and they provide their on-air personalities as a crucial aspect of the programs' televisual identity.[29]

The early twentieth-century expansion of biographical stories in popular magazines marked a shift away from the *idols of production* as primary educational models to be imitated toward *idols of consumption*. Parentage, personal relationships, friendships, and domesticity abound as thematic structures through which the heroes and celebrities of magazine biography are revealed in their "private lives"— a format not unlike that used in the fan magazine for the star system.[30] Yet, in this context, the star does not cease to be special but combines the exceptional with "the ordinary," the ideal with the everyday (Morin in Dyer, 1979: 25; Ellis, 1982).[31]

Within television's personality system, Winfrey is an idol of consumption. She functions as an educative model, one who presents and applies techniques of daily living and personal management. She and, by extension, her show are consumed as both exceptional and as part of everyday life. Having transcended abjection, she speaks from the position of the common woman. Having achieved celebrity, she serves as an idol of consumption and as a disseminator of disciplinary techniques for achieving and maintaining the bourgeois body. Her advocacy of the vast range of dietary, slimming, exercise, and cosmetic body-maintenance products evokes Foucault's analysis of the historical process by which bodies have been disciplined and normalized. We are reminded that through organization, regulation, and movement, our bodies are trained, shaped, and impressed with the stamp of prevailing historical forms of selfhood. For example, studies of prevalent eating disorders and breast implants demonstrate that women are spending more time on the management and discipline of their bodies than in years past.[32] Increasingly, as men become the targets of body-maintenance consumer products (i.e., Viagra, Rogaine, weight loss products), they feel the increasing disciplinary pressure, as well.[33] Winfrey figures prominently in this equation because, as an idol of consumption, she is a model of cyclical body maintenance.

Winfrey's charismatic appeal is rooted in her television program's successful presentation of self-help, body-maintaining techniques. These techniques help expand the market for such commodities. Within consumer culture, the body is a vehicle of pleasure: it is desirable and desiring, and the closer it approximates the idealized images of youth, health, fitness, and beauty, the higher its exchange value.

As a talk-show host, Winfrey's value (popularity with audiences) is partially derived from her having streamlined and glamorized herself, thereby embracing idealized images of youth, health, and beauty. She, like millions of Americans, desires to conform to idealized images of youthfulness, health, and beauty. The host represents scores of women (Caucasian and women of color) worldwide who struggle with existing hegemonic and Eurocentric images of youthfulness, healthiness, fitness, attractiveness, and spirituality and who hence identify with her. She therefore represents a global model for assimilation of conventional, bourgeois techniques of body and soul. In the late 1990s and the early years of the twenty-first century, this meant she adopted the disciplinary *cult of fitness,* in which mind-body health/healing is not so much a biological imperative linked to survival as a social imperative linked to status, prestige, and display. The body enters a competitive logic expressing itself in an unlimited demand for medical, dietary, surgical, cosmetic, and pharmaceutical services. For example, Winfrey continually speaks of having cosmetic surgery to make her breasts perkier, her arms thinner—and possesses the physical features millions of women worldwide covet. She routinely calls attention to her (on-again, off-again) successful diet and fitness practices.

As an African American woman, she is not necessarily resistant to the dominant beauty–body–mind cult of womanhood in consumer culture. Conversely, African Americans are greatly influenced by the images of comfort, convenience, machismo, femininity, and sexual stimulation that bombard consumers.[34] Her complicity with conventional beauty standards was evident when she admitted on her show that all her life she desperately longed to have "hair that swings from side to side." Ironically, such confessions make Winfrey more charismatically appealing, as viewers identify with her identification with the consumer cult of the body, the desire to increase their physical exchange value and their feelings of self-worth. Thus the star's commercial roles as an idol of consumption and a model of body maintenance demand that she charismatically uphold—if not personally embody—conventional beauty standards to propagate an image of the commercially obtainable, physically and spiritually disciplined, bourgeois body.

However, her willingness to adhere to conventional beauty standards has led critics to question her commitment to blackness and black cultural forms. Some have castigated her capitulation to hegemonic constructions of femininity and described her work in terms of its erasure of blackness. But the assumption of Winfrey's white identification (her nonblackness) is predicated on profoundly essentialist notions of blackness and on essential signifiers of the "black" body. Toni Morrison referred to the tendency to essentialize physical characteristics of blackness as *metonymic displacement*: the process by which color coding and physical traits become metonyms that displace rather than signify black character. The Jheri curl, the afro, dreadlocks, braids, and "nappy" hair are all examples of physical traits that have displaced African American character in favor of an image of blackness in the visual world.

In the script of Winfrey's celebrity, her straightened hair and commercial commitment to a class-specific (read: bourgeois) rather than a race-specific (read: African American) audience might metonymically displace her blackness in the cultural realm. But even this metonymic displacement of her blackness is not tantamount to an erasure of her blackness unless it is an erasure of the essentialist and hegemonic signifiers of blackness that proscribe and delimit blackness to signifiers, stereotypical devices, or comical conventions.

Further, the "Winfrey-as-white-woman" critique negates the reality of the black bourgeoisie, which historically has enjoyed greater diversity in modes of self-fashioning. These critiques also negate the impact of hair and body management technologies on colored bodies, suggesting that African Americans should not explore the range of self-fashioning options available to postmodern subjects. We might do better to construe techniques applied to Winfrey's body as part of a larger African American "discourse of adornment" rather than as a mere "whitening" of her person. After all, Madame

C. J. Walker, the first African American woman millionaire, did not simply cease to be "black" after inventing a hair-straightening chemical process. Thus Winfrey's adoption of commercial, bourgeois techniques of the self is linked with other life-changing transitions that make her celebrity sign the nexus for these discourses of mind, body, and soul.

Winfrey's celebrity as a charismatic talk-show host is the convergence of her professional aspirations (news anchor, actress, talk-show host) and the cultural gravity of millenarianism, which began—in the late 1970s and early 1980s—to pull popular culture toward the spectacle of New Age televangelism as inspirational talk television. Her charismatic appeal has been especially effective at this moment of late twentieth-century economic prosperity tempered by millenarian anxiety, a zeitgeist in which technologies of self realization are inextricably linked to the quest for spiritual salvation. Therefore, parallels between Winfrey's star charisma and the televangelist's star charisma become evident in a historical context.

In 1979, cultural critic Christopher Lasch observed that the 1970s retreat from community and communal responsibility resulted in a climate of narcissism. The climate of late 1970s capitalism, Lasch insisted, "is therapeutic, not religious." People long not for personal salvation, but for the feeling, the fleeting illusion, of personal well-being, health, and psychic security. Lasch contended that even the radicalism of the 1960s served—for those who embraced it for personal rather than political reasons—not as a substitute religion but as a form of therapy. He writes: "Narcissism appears to represent the best way of coping with the tensions and anxieties of modern life, and the prevailing social conditions therefore tend to bring out narcissistic traits that are present, in varying degrees, in everyone."[35]

Nowhere is narcissistic self-indulgence, met by the desire for community, more obvious than in the context of *Oprah!* Winfrey's promotion of bestselling money maven Suze Orman is a case in point. It typifies the show's psychospiritual approach to various forms of self-help. Orman, one of the experts appearing on rotation in the 1998–99 season, promised to change our lives by enabling viewers to clear up financial debt.

> *Winfrey:* Starting today, you, too, can commit to become truly rich and free of all the money worries that control your life. I know it sounds like pie in the sky, but it's not. By the millennium—make that your goal. And if you haven't been following our crash course in financial freedom with Suze over the last few months, it's not too late to get up to speed. Here's a look at some of the steps that we've covered, starting with ways to remove blocks to your own

personal wealth with real people just like you. First, Suze asked everyone to get in touch with an early childhood money memory and connect it to their money problems today. Then Suze showed us how fears about money can block financial freedom. And how to place those fears with what she calls a "new truth."

After several exercises and interventions with a group of young adults who formed a financial freedom team with Orman, to get control over their debt, the program concluded with the financial wizard reiterating her new truth and millenium mantra:

> *Orman:* Each and every one of us needs to take a vow that we're going to walk into the millennium financially free, powerful, the powerful beings that we were meant to always be. . . . Oprah—that's right—you've been trying to do it every day on these shows by remembering your spirit. By remembering who you are. How do you remember who you are every day? That's where the truth comes in. You start your day by saying that you are more, by feeling that you are more, by reconnecting to who you really are. . . . Let's seriously walk into the new year, the new millennium, powerful, financially free, knowing that we all have what it takes to do it. Please have faith in who you are and what you can create. Let's start there today.[36]

Orman's amalgamation of pop psychoanalysis, investment strategy, and millenarian sentiment lends credence to Lasch's otherwise cynical argument. However, I would qualify Lasch's remarks to assert that the contemporary moment is both therapeutic *and* religious, evidenced, in part, by Winfrey's celebrity sign. Within television's personality system she personifies societal roles that enable Americans to imagine a community in which viewers cathartically cathect[37] narcissism: matriarch (i.e., "the mother of America"), confidante (i.e., to whom we confess), fashion consultant (i.e., arbiter of taste), trainer (i.e., fitness guru), healer (i.e., redressing old wounds), teacher (i.e., educator of social mores). Winfrey's fans ironically believe they are therapeutically purging themselves of various deleterious fixations and addictions by merely reinvesting psychic energy elsewhere: newfound frivolities and organizations.

This is particularly ironic. It is ironic because viewers simply exchange one fixation (financial indebtedness to material items reflecting their self-worth) for another technique of self-aggrandizement (narcissistic cathexis). Personal financial mismanagement, for example, is replaced by a therapeutic commodity-technology of the self—in this case, Orman's book. It is additionally ironic because the therapeutic methodologies employed are themselves endlessly tautological: the purgation of destructive narcissism occurs through a supposedly constructive fixation on oneself. And finally, what becomes clear is that this confessional narcissism is a *communal narcissism* that feeds the individual's narcissistic self-interest and the desire to belong to a community whose members share this interest in the self.

Lasch's cultural history of therapeutic narcissism prefigures the work of T. Jackson Lears, who historicized the shift from a quest for salvation to self-discovery, offering that the rise of the "therapeutic ethos" was a modern phenomenon. Understanding the relationship between Winfrey's cathartic charisma and neoevangelicalism[38] (i.e., the growing political strength of the religious right, the popularity of New Age religion, the rise of religious cultism) necessitates revisiting Lears's contextualization of the "therapeutic ethos" and considering its historical relationship to modern notions of charisma.

From Salvation to Self-Realization

If we acknowledge that the issue-oriented talk show is the primary venue through which television hosts advertise and promote consumption of goods and services (i.e., self-help techniques, media celebrities, films), then we are prepared to consider the ramifications of the argument that advertising cannot be considered in isolation. Rather, advertising's role in promoting consumer culture can be understood only within a network of institutional, religious, and psychological changes. Lears suggested that a unique convergence of events in late nineteenth-century American culture led to the quest for health becoming a secular and self-referential project, rooted in peculiarly modern emotional needs.

Social historians have demonstrated that for the educated bourgeoisie of the late nineteenth century, reality began to seem problematic, something to be sought rather than merely lived. Feelings of unreality stemmed from urbanization and technological development, from the rise of an increasingly interdependent market economy, and from the secularization of liberal Protestantism among its educated and affluent devotees. Americans encountered the anonymity of the city and the modern comforts of city living. Yet researchers found these comforts did not produce healthy people, since the most "comfortable" people were also the most anxious, falling victim to nervous disorders.[39]

Adding to technological changes of the urban setting was another source that accounted for these symptoms. The interdependent national market economy laid claim to concepts of the self. As more people became enmeshed in the market's web of interdependence, liberal ideals of autonomous self-hood became more difficult to sustain. For entrepreneurs as well as wage workers, financial rise or ruin came to depend on policies formulated far away, on situations beyond the individual's control. Large bureaucratically organized corporations were becoming the dominant models. Jobs became more specialized, more interdependent, and personal autonomy became more problematic. In a society increasingly dominated by bureaucratic corporations, one dealt with people rather than things; "personal magnetism" began to replace character as the key to advancement. After the turn of the century, success manuals prescribed what sociologist David Riesman called "modes of manipulating the self in order to manipulate others." The successful man or woman has "no clear core of self, only a set of social masks."[40] From lowbrow success literature to the realm of high theory, Americans began to imagine a self that was neither simple nor genuine, but fragmented and socially constructed. Overall, the modern self of unreality stemmed from a variety of sources and generated complex effects but helped to generate longings for bodily vigor, emotional intensity, and a revitalized sense of selfhood. Lears writes:

> To a bourgeoisie suffering from identity diffusion and inner emptiness, the creator of the therapeutic ethos offered harmony, vitality, and the hope of self-realization. The paths to self-realization could vary. One might seek wholeness and security through careful management of personal resources; or one might pursue emotional fulfillment and endless "growth" through intense experience. These approaches were united by several assumptions: an implicit nostalgia for the vigorous health allegedly enjoyed by farmers, children and others "close to nature"; a belief expert advice could enable one to recover that vigor without fundamental social change; and a tacit conviction that self-realization was the largest aim of human existence . . . Rooted in personal dilemmas, the therapeutic ethos nevertheless provided a secular world view that well suited the interests of corporate proprietors and managers in the emerging culture.[41]

Lears sums up his argument by claiming the therapeutic ethos was rooted in a reaction against the rationalization of culture—the growing effort, first described by Max Weber, to exert systematic control over "man's" external environment and ultimately over "his" inner life. By the turn of the century, the iron cage of bureaucratic "rationality" had begun subtly to affect even the educated and affluent. Many began to believe their sense of autonomy was being undermined and that they had been cut off from intense physical, emotional, or spiritual experience. The therapeutic ethos promised to heal the wounds inflicted by rationalization. The nature of control varied: scarcity therapy addressed anxieties; abundance therapy addressed aspirations. The main point is that longings for reintegrated selfhood and intense experience were assimilated by both therapeutic and business elites in the emerging consumer culture.

Lears provides the historical context in which Winfrey's celebrity charisma may be understood as evidence of late 1990s America witnessing a resurgence of charisma as *cathartic charisma,* as neoevangelicalism in mass entertainment. He adds credence to my thesis that the growth of Winfrey's popularity has coincided with a rising tide of salvation as self-realization, of spirituality as therapy. The apotheosis of her celebrity sign—itself inextricably linked to her function as the charismatic sponsor of new techniques of the self—suggests links between contemporary postmodern culture and earlier modern moments (1890–1920) at which the advertising of new modes of selfhood promised new forms of invigoration, revitalization, and enchantment.[42]

The vast scholarship on mass-mediated religion, the electronic church, and televangelism confirms my notion that there is a relationship between modernity's religious ethos (the modern quest for charisma) and postmodernity's new charismatic spirit (the postmodern search for self-realization, self-rediscovery). Such scholarship includes Razelle Frenkl's *Televangelism: The Marketing of Popular Religion* (1987), Stewart Hoover's *Mass Media Religion* (1988), and Quentin Schultze's *Televangelism and American Culture* (1991).[43] Hoover, for example, claimed movements and media of the "left" in the 1960s and movements and media of the new religious, politically active "right" in the 1980s have their sources in traditional religious institutions brought on by modern life. For Hoover, the "crisis of modernity" is based in the ongoing evolution of late industrial and postindustrial society, where traditional structures have been undermined by physical, social, and economic changes.[44] The scholarship of Hoover et al. reveals parallels between television charismatics like Winfrey and televangelists Pat Robertson, Oral Roberts, and Jerry Falwell. In her ability to fuse new therapeutic and New Age religious technologies of self-maintenance as secular entertainment, Winfrey's charisma is homologous to that of a 1970s–1980s televangelist.

Evangelical Cultism, TV Charismatics, and the Entrepreneurial Spirit

There are three parallels between Winfrey's charismatic celebrity sign and the charismatic celebrity of the televangelist. More specifically, three parallels can be drawn between the cultural phenomenon of *Oprah* and the phenomenon of televangelism. I will draw these comparisons now to further adduce my two-part claim that (1) Winfrey's celebrity sign is best characterized by my notion of her cathartic charisma; and (2) Winfrey's celebrity is part of the reemergence of the modern therapeutic ethos as the postmodern culture of millenarianism. Hereafter, I refer to these three parallels as the cult of personality, the spirit of American business, and the "resolution" of irrational aspects of celebrity status into rationalized forms in contemporary culture.

In *Televangelism and American Culture,* Quentin Schultze describes human charisma as a natural reflection of the communicative talents of a magnetic personality and people's real need for authoritative figures they can trust. Gifted leaders, whether in civil rights movements or religious revivals, help people transcend the limitations of individual hopelessness and powerlessness. Personality cults are the unfortunate perversions of the inherently human quest for authority.[45] Schultze demonstrates that evangelical charismatic personalities often attract uncritical believers who submit to the authority of their leader far more than to the authority of tradition, the church, or the Bible. This kind of charisma may not be particularly spiritual. He asserts that televangelists share some of the same charismatic qualities of other celebrities, including show-business personalities. "Today's American culture is the soil and television is the fertilizer, for personality cults of all kinds, from political heroes to sports celebrities and entertainment stars. Gossip magazines thrive on these personalities. So does the contemporary Christian music industry. Even evangelical book publishing is greatly affected. Like show business, evangelical mass communication of all kinds now resembles the Hollywood star system. . . . Televangelism is an important seedbed for the growth of American personality cults.[46]

Schultze's argument is credible and suggestive. It suggests a pattern in the process by which the television industry manufactures its personalities. The fact that Winfrey's personality cult has expanded as a partial consequence of the show's growing spiritual content leads me to draw two conclusions. First, it leads to the conclusion that the bureaucracy of the television industry rationalizes the irrational need people feel for magnetic personalities they can trust and with whom they, as spectators, can identify. Second, it provides additional evidence for my thesis that Winfrey's celebrity sign has a charismatic component. The talents or charisma she brings to the job of host, however, are consequently routinized, "depersonalized" and manufactured by the culture industries as pseudo-charisma. Thus the scholarship on mass-mediated religion brings me to the crux of the first parallel: the popularity of Winfrey's program, coupled with the charismatic devotion of her fan following, suggests similarities between evangelical charisma and Oprah's cathartic charisma.

The second parallel I want to draw between Winfrey's charisma and the televangelist's charisma involves the *spirit* of American business; it involves the relationship between business and religion or what Nicole Woolsey Biggart has—in another context—called *charismatic capitalism.*[47] Once the original Protestant ethic stressing initiative, competitiveness, and perseverance spread to America, it was consonant with the rise of industrial capitalism. Rags-to-riches stories—like Winfrey's—and biographies of the captains of industry who put together industrial empires, like her Harpo Productions, were popular best sellers in the 1880s. Winfrey has been able to reinvigorate the Protestant ethic with the *spirit* of capitalism. In this sense, her charisma signifies a return to an earlier modern moment in American history. The central point is that the relationship between business and religion is part of the American cultural fabric.

In his text, Schultze asserts that televangelism as an institution is increasingly based on techniques of modern marketing. He bases this on the well-documented fact that throughout history Christian churches have typically been enmeshed in the business practices of the day. Further, he views televangelism as the modern American version of such financial and religious entanglements. Not coincidentally, Schultze's work is based on Weber's landmark study *The Protestant Ethic and the Spirit of Capitalism,* an examination of the relationship between an entrepreneurial ethos (e.g., business) and religious practice (e.g., religion). In this context, Schultze uses the term *entrepreneurial spirit* to signify on the solicitous business practices of televangelists Jim Bakker, Pat Robertson, and Oral Roberts. Biggart and Schultze demonstrate that throughout the history of the United States, business and religion have shaped each other's characteristics. Their work provides contemporary examples of such institutions: direct selling organizations on the one hand, and televangelism on the other. Explaining the spiritual version of planned obsolescence, Schultze writes:

> In fact, in many evangelical circles the conversion experience, the moment of accepting Christ as one's personal Savior, is the essence of the faith. As church services repeat the formulaic altar calls and "re-commitments" over and over again, faith becomes, like a consumer product, something that can be lost and found from one minute to the next. As with the purchase of new clothes, which for a short time create a sense of personal newness and identity, the cheaper versions of popular evangelicalism transform faith into little

more than a transient feeling or momentary decision . . . While churches and televangelists have adopted many business techniques, business in turn has borrowed the evangelistic rhetoric of salvation. Consumer advertising promises to save the distraught public from bad breath, inferiority, boredom, loneliness, unhappiness, unpopularity, sexual unfulfillment and all the other "sins" of American life.[48]

Schultze accurately captures the way consumer culture has harnessed religion. In doing so, he also unknowingly provides a description of the way Winfrey's program works. He captures the way she markets self-help programs and techniques such as Suze Orman's money-management strategy. In essence, the larger argument he makes about televangelism can be made of the business of quasi-religious talk television—particularly of *Oprah,* with its "Remembering Your Spirit" segment that might more aptly be titled "Remembering the Protestant Ethic and the Spirit of Capitalism." The business savvy with which media critics like MacGregor cynically discredit Winfrey is better understood as the culmination of an ongoing American cultural phenomenon dating back to the 1970s, with deeper roots traceable to modernity.

It is no accident that at the same moment media scholars were making links between mass-mediated religion and consumer culture—a sure sign of televangelism's decline—another wedding of religion and consumerism took place. Nowhere was this shift clearer than in the ratings war. In the late 1970s, just as the electronic church was sinking into a ratings slump, the daily religion of talk television was riding the tide of rising ratings. Shortly thereafter, *Oprah* began to surpass *Donahue* in the race to become the nation's leading talk show with the most popular host. Schultze's analysis evinces a debt to Max Weber's and T. Jackson Lears's work. However, this does not diminish the significance of his contribution: the most popular televangelists were notable for their personal charisma *and* natural salesmanship. Therefore, the spirit of American business is both what Winfrey's celebrity sign symbolizes—in her personal embodiment of the Horatio Alger narrative[49]—and what Winfrey herself proselytizes, in the *Oprah!* ministry.

This brings me to the third, and final, parallel between Winfrey's celebrity charisma and the televangelist's charisma. As mentioned earlier, the charismatic figure is like the celebrity because each demarcates an area of social life and identification that is fundamentally irrational. Recognizing that Winfrey and the televangelist are both salespeople begs the question: what does their merchandise have in common? My point is that while their merchandise assumes different names, characters, dispositions, and behaviors (i.e., Christ,

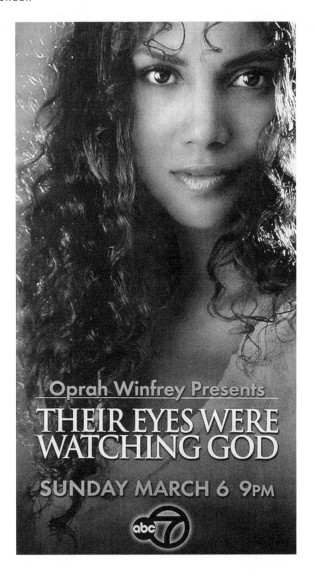

Halle Berry stars in her second Oprah Winfrey–produced made-for-TV-movie adapted from literature.

abstinence, forgiveness, dieting) their product is the same. Winfrey, like the televangelist, is in the business of selling hope. Whether in the form of salvation or self-realization, the product is hope that the inevitable future will be more promising, more enjoyable, more spiritually fulfilling than the present. In this sense, watching *Oprah*—like watching Pat Robertson—may offer the same irrational but participatory pleasures as, for example, playing the lottery, which guarantees nothing but provides optimism. This parallel is particularly salient when we consider how Winfrey's celebrity charisma is routinized. Like each prayer, each self-help technique is invested with the promise of delivering some kind of quality or condition for self-improvement. The internal aspects of Winfrey's cathartic charisma are thereby depersonalized and routinized. Now that these qualities are available for purchase, are transformed into external qualities, items, and routines (i.e., books, manuals, programs, techniques of the self), they become transferable, personally acquirable, and attachable to the ordinary wo/man regardless of the individual person involved. This transference is an example of how the charisma embedded in Winfrey's celebrity sign is depersonalized by the culture industries. Film, television, and book-publishing industries rationalize the irrational consumer desires of her audiences—their unquenchable thirst for new, life-changing products that *Oprah* the program and Winfrey the person endorse.

Nowhere was this more evident than with the synergistic promotion of the film *Beloved*—a film that itself has been linked to the religious sentiment present in *Oprah*.[50] As part of the promotional campaign, Winfrey granted interviews to a variety of women's magazines, appearing on their covers. Claiming her *Vogue* cover was the realization of a life-long dream, Winfrey promoted the magazine cover—promoting the film—on her talk show, during which she surprised select audience members with head-to-toe makeovers from *Vogue*'s employees. These "total" makeovers supposedly enabled the audience to participate in the sensational glamour of haute couture. When, in reality, the culture industries (the magazine-publishing, film, television, cosmetics, and fashion industries) were on *Oprah* collectively working to rationalize as obtainable the irrational and unobtainable fantasies of millions of women consumers who desire to live in the dreamscape inhabited by television and Hollywood stars.

The best barometer of Winfrey's success in this endeavor can be found in the record number of newsstand sales. In a 1999 *New York Times* article, Alex Kuczynski reported that stars who trade on Hollywood magic (read: charisma) have been pushing celebrity models off women's magazine covers and selling better than ever. Kuczynski wrote that "the shift from supermodel to Hollywood stars as public personalities on magazine covers is the latest sign of Americans' obsession with celebrity." *Vogue* magazine featured only one model on its cover since August 1998, according to editor-in-chief Anna Wintour. The magazine is expecting final numbers to show a huge jump in its usual newsstand sales of about 500,000 for its covers of Oprah Winfrey and Hillary Clinton.[51] Both the makeovers and the magazine sales demonstrate how the transference of star charisma embedded in Winfrey's celebrity sign is rationalized, routinized, and depersonalized by the culture industries.

Beloved

Though the term *magical realism* has been used primarily to categorize a Latin American literary practice, it is also relevant, I would argue, to the African American novel *Beloved*.[52] Mingling the mundane with the fantastic, Toni Morrison's Pulitzer Prize–winning novel[53] superimposes one perceived reality upon another, treating the fantastic as quotidian. It uses magic and fantasy to recuperate the real and reconstruct histories that have been obscured or erased by political and social injustice.[54] Gabriel García Márquez, whose *One Hundred Years of Solitude* epitomizes the magical realist style, locates the roots of magical realism in the African Caribbean coast of Colombia. The notion of magical realism persists because it retains explanatory value, but also because it describes the common historical and cultural conditions shared by African and Latin American authors. Such writers are familiar with transition, border crossing, and ambiguity, as well as with the mingling of capitalist and precapitalist modes within societies that have been postcolonial since the nineteenth century. They deploy the carnivalesque-grotesque— one complex theme of magical realism—to convey the notion of unfinished metamorphosis, the idea of something aborted, or incomplete. In *Beloved,* Toni Morrison uses magical realism as the structuring device to syncretize the supernatural with a realistic historical perspective. *Beloved* addresses the historical moment at which a newly manumitted African American community found itself between slavery and freedom, horror and relative happiness, antebellum tradition and Reconstructive modernity. In the filmed adaptation of *Beloved,* aspects of magical realism and the carnivalesque-grotesque[55] come to the forefront in ways that complicate the cinematic text.

On October 16, 1998, Touchstone Pictures released the Harpo Films/Clinica Estetico Production of *Beloved.* Directed by Jonathan Demme, the film starred producer Oprah Winfrey as Sethe and Danny Glover as Paul D. Oprah Winfrey worked on the adaptation of *Beloved* to film for over a decade, having purchased the film rights shortly after the book was published in 1987. Although Winfrey considered producing *Beloved* as a theatrical feature a "personal triumph," the film was considered a commercial failure (by Hollywood industry standards) for earning $24 million at the box office against a $65 million investment. When the additional $15–20 million for marketing and advertising campaigns[56] are considered, the film's production deficit was larger still. *Beloved* continues to return incremental profits as a video rental, but with only one Oscar nomination—for Best Costume Design—it was unlikely to gain much momentum as a rental commodity. Herein resides the crucial difference between the novel and the film: as the product of commercial culture (and society) the Hollywood commodity must earn a profit. To make a profit, it *must* entertain consumers. Where a novel can sell 20,000 volumes and yield a reasonable return, the film must reach millions.[57]

It is a long-standing truism that there exists no valid correlation between box office performance and artistic value, and *Beloved*'s box office performance is certainly not an indication of the film's artistic merit. In the 1940s, Frankfurt School Marxists Max Horkheimer and Theodor Adorno challenged the correlation between conspicuous production and cash investment in the culture industry. Investment, they argued, bears no relation to the meaning or merit of the products themselves.[58] In the 1960s, political modernisms and revolutionary "Third Cinemas" demonstrated that Hollywood films are popular precisely because they are ideologically complicit with dominant ways of seeing and understanding.[59] Political modernism offered a theory of countercinema—an independent and avant-garde praxis motivated by political concerns and by the critique of illusionism. Manthia Diawara, Clyde Taylor, and Michele Wallace critiqued ideological forms of signification and spectatorship in mainstream films.[60] These scholarly communities (i.e., the Marxists, modernists, Third Worldists, and African Americanists) proved that ideology involves not only the "message" of films, but includes forms of looking and hearing, as well as the biases in perception and identification that spectators bring to the cinema. And it is the aesthetic and ideological challenges to forms of signification and spectatorship that make *Beloved* as text and event so complex and interesting.

As an object of mainstream film criticism, *Beloved* fared poorly. In the mainstream press, *Beloved* was the subject of extensive media promotion. Media concentration escalated into a contentious debate about the impact of canonized literature on feature film production. Contradicting the media hype, several reviewers faulted *Beloved* for infidelity to its source novel and especially for its inability to translate the complexities of the original narrative. Historian Natalie Zemon Davis wrote: "In the movement from the miraculous prose of Toni Morrison to the screen, the story of *Beloved* has lost some of its breadth, complexity and imaginative range."[61] But we should be wary of moralizing and reductive readings, situating literature as miraculously highbrow and film as degenerately low-grade. Many of *Beloved*'s reviewers—proponents and detractors alike—failed to take into account the complicated conversion process by which a novel becomes a screenplay and the screenplay, in turn, becomes a film. This conversion is an artistic endeavor involving the *aesthetics of transcription* from novel to film, or part of what has been called "the dialogics of adaptation."[62]

Advising against reductive approaches focusing on "fidelity" to the source material, Robert Stam proposes "intertextual dialogism" as an analytical paradigm that sees adaptation as part of "the infinite and open-ended possibilities generated by the discursive practices of a culture, the entire matrix of communicative utterances within which the artistic text is situated."[63] Dialogism is an appropriate framework for evaluating film adaptation, as it facilitates analysis of the diverse extradiegetic texts, discussions, and ideological debates informing the critical discourse about a film adapted from a novel. Stam's insights dovetail with Pierre Sorlin's and Robert Rosenstone's discussions of historical film. Most books and reviews on the subject of history in film compare the events in film with a written description of those same events, presupposing the written description as always already more accurate and superior. But this approach implies two problematic, logocentric assumptions: first, that the practice of written history is the only legitimate way of understanding the relationship to the past, and, second, that written history mirrors reality.

Intertextuality is also an appropriate framework for interpreting a multivocal, magically realist novel like *Beloved,* which engages the interweaving of time frames, states of consciousness, discourses, linguistic codes (e.g., standard English, rural black vernacular English, black feminist discourse, black patriarchal discourse),[64] and genres (slave narrative, gothic, horror, historical melodrama). This matrix of utterances encompasses history as a discursive formation and its dialogic relationship with literature. This section of the chapter examines the adaptation of *Beloved* from novel to film through the prism of intertextual dialogism. The communicative utterances within which the film *Beloved* is immersed, meanwhile, include (but are not limited to) the media campaign around the film (which shaped the commercial reception and public discourse); the intertext of Winfrey's boundless celebrity (which helped bring the film to fruition but adversely affected its reception); and the competitive Euro-American-centered cultural terrain upon which African American films must forge a marketplace for themselves.

Toni Morrison gathered source material for *Beloved* from fragments of slave narratives she discovered while editing *The Black Book* (1974), a scrapbook of African American history. Particular historical details came from the real-life story of Margaret Garner, a slave, who in January 1856 escaped from her owner

Archibald Gaines in Kentucky, crossed the Ohio River, and sought refuge in Cincinnati. Gaines and a party of officers pursued her. Margaret Garner, her husband, Robert, and their four children were surrounded and overtaken. Realizing hopes for their freedom were bleak, Garner seized a butcher knife and with one stroke cut the throat of her little daughter—probably the most "beloved" of them all. Garner chose death for herself and her child rather than return to the state of chattel slavery. Implicit in the "herstory" of *Beloved* is a fusion of the past and the future in a single act of death. Garner was tried *not* for attempting to kill her child, but for the "real" crime, of stealing property—herself and her children—from her master. In *Beloved*, Morrison leaves some of this historical material behind, for although Sethe kills her child, Beloved, Sethe is freed and ostracized from the black community.[65]

In the 1970s, historians began reexamining both the status of family life under slavery and the variegated forms of resistance to slavery, ranging from subtle sabotage to outright revolts. Earlier schools of scholarship saw slavery as devastating to black family life and genealogy, yet newer research on the history of women and family examines how African Americans tried to lessen or outwit the dehumanizing effects of slavery. Although slaves had no formal right to marry or develop kinship ties, for example, running away constituted a major challenge to the slave system. Family loyalties were factored into the decision to flee and risk patrols, dogs, recapture, punishment, and harsher enslavement. Reviewing this history, Morrison read extensively about slavery, abolitionists, fugitives, and Cincinnati in the mid-nineteenth century.[66]

Morrison rewrites African American history as literature in her novels. The dialogic relationship between literature and history evident in her work reverberates with Hayden White's claim that history, too, is a form of *écriture,* an interpretive form of narrative emplotment. Historians choose, on aesthetic grounds, different plot structures by which to endow sequences of events with various meanings.[67] Morrison has often stated that the history and literature of the United States are "incoherent" without an understanding of the African American presence. Much like Jewish Holocaust literature—also known for its forms of magical realism—*Beloved* gives expression to intricacies, erasures, and surrealist disjunctions of conflicting histories. The film *Beloved,* for its part, reflects on these disjunctions through innovative formal techniques (expressionist, surrealist, magical, and postmodern techniques) in order to re-vision what is meant by history.

Given Morrison's literary objectives and Winfrey's personal commitment to the historical material, Jonathan Demme seems an unlikely choice of director for surrealist-experimental African American cinema. Directors Julie

Dash (*Daughters of the Dust*, 1991) or Charles Burnett (*To Sleep with Anger*, 1990), for instance, would seem like more obvious choices, especially since both are well known for successfully mingling the mundane, the spiritual, and the historical realms in magical-realist renditions of African American cinema. This is not to suggest that directors' racial identity essentially determines their ability to effectively direct a film. It is, however, to note that *Beloved* was Demme's first historical film to address African American issues, although he had made two documentaries about the black diaspora in other contexts (*Haiti: Dreams of Democracy*, 1987; and *Cousin Bobby*, 1991).

Winfrey's decision to select Demme as director articulates one of the tensions in making and marketing an experimental-historical black film that is part slave narrative, part magically real ghost story, and part maternal melodrama. The film innovatively combines disparate genres, nonlinear narrative construction, and an Afrocentric vision of American history to create what is in some ways an avant-garde film. Winfrey and the producers (i.e., Ronald Bozman, Kate Forte, Gary Goetzman, and Edward Saxon) may have been compelled to employ an A-list white male director whose Hollywood status and commodity-sign value would lend the picture prestige and name recognition and would balance its art-house qualities with a commercial trademark.

Unfortunately, Winfrey failed to anticipate the extent to which this directorial decision could adversely affect the film. Selecting an A-list director certainly endowed the film with Hollywood industry name recognition and lent it the aura of auteur cinema, but it also raised questions regarding cultural authenticity and experiential credibility. For instance, was Demme familiar with the politics of racial representation and the necessity for re-visioning African American history? Was it clear that this film presented a series of intellectual relationships between literature and historiography? Would Demme understand Toni Morrison's long-term professional project of examining the social constructions of blackness? While some white directors have represented African American subjects beautifully on screen (Michael Roemer's *Nothing but a Man*), there are those topics that are simply too sensitive to ever be completely free of cinematic essentialism. After all, even Steven Spielberg felt he needed to remind the viewing public he was Jewish and therefore an insider uniquely qualified to represent the horrors of the Holocaust in *Schindler's List*.

Revising constructions of African American history and identity constitutes an essential form of resignifying for Morrison. As she argues in *Playing in the Dark*, it is the examination of constructions of literary "blackness" that make it possible to discover the nature—even the tacit grounds—of literary "whiteness."[68] Morrison's criticism of literary whiteness broadens the critique of intellectual Eurocentrism by foregrounding the biases inherent in Euro-American literature and literary criticism. Second, this critique underscores the intertexual relationship between African American literature and American historiography; it reminds us that judgments about data, verifiability, argument, and evidence are always constructed and historically situated. Third, her literary criticism serves as an intertext for film criticism. By examining cinematic blackness, we can begin to dismantle the hegemony of cinematic whiteness. *Beloved* exemplifies the way African American history written as cinematic narrative can present an intellectual and ideological critique of dominant cinema.

The novel and film versions of *Beloved* begin with tropes of dismantled blackness. The narrative opens precisely where Toni Morrison's other narratives end: with the individual and the community sundered. This point of narrative departure forms an aesthetic link between Morrison's other works of fiction: the recurring emphasis on protagonists and characters who are separated from the larger community. Having learned of the infanticide, the black Cincinnati community has turned its back on Sethe (Oprah Winfrey) and her remaining family.

When the film starts, Sethe's two sons, Howard (Emil Pinnock) and Buglar (Calen Johnson), take their belongings and leave their haunted home in turmoil. The film then flashes forward eight years to the summer of 1873. Until this point Denver (Kimberly Elise) and Sethe have lived at 124 Bluestone Road alone, isolated from society. One summer day, Paul D (Danny Glover) walks into Sethe's front yard, and together they recount the years since escaping Sweet Home plantation. After a few days, Paul D agrees to live with Sethe and Denver, beginning a new life. As the summer moves into autumn, Paul D and Sethe grow closer. But their newly laid plans to bond as family are thwarted by the arrival of a mysterious young woman, Beloved (Thandie Newton).

Beloved offers the strongest expression of the harrowing experience individuals undergo at the hands of the community even while trying to be reconciled with it.[69] Separation from the community is almost always a consequence of some appalling, horrifying, or unrepresentable act. The unrepresentable—or what Morrison terms the *unspeakable*—manifests itself prominently in the author's other novels (i.e., *The Bluest Eye, Song of Solomon*) in the form of betrayal, abuse, and the presence of ghosts.[70] Maintaining much of the novel's plot structure, the film revolves around Morrison's female protagonist, Sethe. The central narrating voice, in both the novel and the film, belongs to

Sethe, since the story revolves around her maternal confrontation with the incarnated ghost of her murdered woman-child daughter, Beloved.

The tropes of unspeakable and unrepresentable acts render *Beloved* particularly challenging material to adapt to screen. A novelist's portrayal induces us to imagine characters and events. A film, by contrast, designates specific performers, props, settings, and landscapes. The selection of these signifiers imposes limits, restricting the imagination each spectator brings to the cinema.[71] In making *Beloved,* director Jonathan Demme not only manipulated concrete signifiers, he also concretized magical and supernatural events already unrepresentable, unspeakable, or difficult to signify. *Beloved* as a film therefore assumes a double "burden of representation," beyond that incumbent upon a novel.

The eponymous Beloved (Thandie Newton) instantiates this unrepresentability. Morrison wrote Beloved as a supernatural character that transcends epistemological and ontological bounds. "In magical realist texts," as critics point out, "ontological disruption serves the purpose of political and cultural disruption: magic is often given as a cultural corrective, requiring readers to scrutinize accepted realistic conventions of causality, materiality, motivation."[72] As the fulcrum of magical realism, Beloved as character is an oxymoronic literary construction that troubles convention and captures the paradox of uniting opposites. Simultaneously a corporeal presence and an ethereal ghost, she is also the matrilineal connection between indigenous black Africa and colonizing white America. As a symbol, she is the haunting avatar of many Beloveds—generations of mothers and daughters hunted down and stolen from Africa. A parapsychological epiphenomenon of slavery, invulnerable to barriers of time, space, and place, Beloved is both vacant and omnipresent.[73] As Sethe's offspring, she incarnates the newly formed black collective body, a hopeful populace reborn on the cusp of Reconstruction and bent on democratic participation.

Regrettably, critics hastily dismissed Thandie Newton's performance of Beloved as campy and farcical. Some cited Newton's Beloved as proof of the novel's untranslatability, an inevitable calamity in the passage from novel to film. But Newton's performance should not be dismissed as an inevitable betrayal of the source material or as a symptom of the film medium's intrinsic incapacity to capture the characterological complexity. The disparity is actually a matter of emphasis rather than translation. Precisely because the film foregrounds Beloved's actual return, her physical presence, and her life with Sethe, she becomes less the symbolic ghost of the written text than the corporeal reality of the film. More specifically, the film calls attention to the growth and development of her body, to its fluids and functions. She is Sethe's unformed, uncontrollable woman-child, blurring the boundaries between self and other.

To understand Beloved's prominent function in the film, it is useful to discuss her corporeality in terms of Mikhail Bakhtin's notion of the grotesque body and Mary Russo's notion of the female grotesque. Their notions of the grotesque inform (and overlap with) the category of magical realism. For Bakhtin, the unfinished and open body (dying, bringing forth, and being born) is not separated from the world by clearly defined boundaries; it is blended with the world, with animals, with objects. The grotesque body is an incarnation of this world at the absolute lower stratum, as the life of the belly, the reproductive organs, and the acts of defecation, copulation, conception, pregnancy, and birth.[74] "Bakhtin found his concept of the grotesque embodied in the laughing pregnant hags of the Kerch terra-cotta figurines, which combine senile, decaying flesh with fresh new life, conceived but as yet unformed."[75] In the enslaved body, which was a vehicle for white enjoyment and coerced festivity, one finds a negative, nonfestive version of Bakhtin's grotesque. For in the carnivalesque pageantry of the coffle, the enforced dancing on slave ship decks, and the obligatory live stepping on auction blocks, we see spectacles of black pain, which entangle terror and enjoyment.[76] Perhaps because the magical realism of the story is encoded into the story narrative itself, both the novel and the film share equally in these twin realms of the carnivalesque and the grotesque.

Mary Russo critiques Bakhtin for failing to incorporate the social relations of gender in his semiotic model of the body politic. Bakhtin's grotesque, pregnant hags for Russo remain underanalyzed, representing only paradox: in effect, pregnant death, senility and nubility, aged and new flesh. Within Russo's feminist perspective, the female grotesque can be used to destabilize idealizations of female beauty and realign desire, disrupting the familiar world, and, I would add, to introduce the state of cognitive dissonance typical of Beloved. I interpret young Beloved as a grotesque female body, one in the process of becoming. Beloved's arrival even coincides, it is implied in the novel, with carnival in the narrative (p. 235). At first she is the haunting ghost, but she later materializes into the grotesque corporeal body, representing the return of the repressed and the reemergence of Sethe's horrific maternal past as an irrepressible present. Once impregnated, she grows like the pregnant hag whose body symbolizes both young life and aged death. Beloved's continual physical metamorphoses parallel the narrative's aesthetic traversals between carnivalesque and grotesque realms.

The trope of the female grotesque aptly describes mother and daughter, as Beloved's grotesque body mirrors Sethe's. Toni Morrison's text and Akosua Busia's screenplay are replete with examples of abused, enslaved bodies. Sethe's body exemplifies the subjected, abused, and tortured corpus. In the film, the abuses endured by her are particularly visible. She is on display as the primary object of terror and victimization. Her body, bloodied feet, pregnant womb, swollen back, and incontinent bladder constitute what Saidiya Hartman terms the *scene of subjection*—the site of terror and violence perpetrated under the rubric of pleasure, paternalism, and property. We can extend Hartman's concept to an analysis of the film. The abuses perpetrated against Sethe—both overtly and covertly—constitute the very mise-en-scène of subjection in the film.

Recall, for example, Amy Denver (Kessia Randall), who stumbles upon pregnant Sethe (Lisa Gay Hamilton) as she lies stranded in the woods oozing, bleeding, birthing, and lactating with a blossoming cherry tree on her back. Throughout the novel and film, Sethe's body is associated with beasts of burden, blended with the world of animals. Schoolteacher chastises his nephews for beating Sethe as if she were a horse (149). Learning of the infanticide, Paul D tells Sethe she's "got two feet not four" (165). At one point, Schoolteacher tells the boys to write Sethe's "human characteristics on one side, and her animal characteristics on another" (193). Then there is the terrorizing day "two boys with mossy teeth, one sucking on [her] breast the other holding [her] down," took her milk (70). All of these incidents are foreshadowed by the description of Sethe's arrival at Sweet Home. When she arrived, "The five Sweet Home men looked at the new girl and decided to let her be . . . They were young and so sick with the absence of women they had taken to calves" (10). These incidents in the story evoke the grotesqueries of slavery, as written upon the enslaved body. Moreover, these incidents parallel the way Sethe literally and figuratively bestowed them upon baby Beloved's body (i.e., "with one stroke of the knife"). Taken collectively, these textual moments evoke the magical realist intermingling of man and beast, trading places within the slippery hierarchy of a grotesquely carnivalized world.

As a consequence of the film's emphasis on Beloved's developing self, Newton's performance does seem campy and comedic rather than solemn and severe. But the sounds and images of young Beloved drooling, defecating, burping, vomiting, and mumbling are clearly intentional, even unavoidable. Whereas readers of the novel move quickly through descriptions of Beloved's offensive physical fluidity, spectators of the film are confronted with lingering, embodied spectacles of her amorphousness, her protuberances, triggering a much more visceral kind of disgust. The grotesque body in cinema is usually a generic concomitant of slapstick comedy (i.e., Jerry Lewis's and later Eddie Murphy's *The Nutty Professor*); it is not usually a dynamic component of historical melodrama, therefore rendering Newton's performance "excessive" and difficult to assimilate. Newton's Beloved stands out as generically incongruous with other aspects of the film. Whereas descriptions of Beloved's grotesque body in the novel are simply components of the verbally constructed character, the live performance of Beloved's grotesque body in the film enters into intertextual dialogue with other performances in *Beloved*, which by contrast appear more measured. Her performance also enters into dialogue with other genres and individual films in which the grotesque is synonymous with comedy and/or horror.

As a film, *Beloved* dialogues with the vast genre of maternal melodramas also known as "women's films" and specifically with a subset of films functioning as a counterbalance to the dominant male genres, called "the woman's weepie."[77] These Hollywood genre films typically depict women as subordinated to the Law of the Father. Tragic mother-daughter melodramas have enjoyed commercial success in American theaters since the 1930s. In the transcription from novel to film, director Jonathan Demme, producer Oprah Winfrey, and screenwriter Akosua Busia were cognizant of the novel's potential relationship to classical Hollywood films scripted to address predominantly female audiences. As a film, *Beloved* could be categorized as an African American maternal melodrama (rather like such films as *A Raisin in the Sun,* 1961; *Sounder,* 1972; *Crooklyn,* 1994). Like classical melodrama, *Beloved* reveals how the mother strives to gain unmet gratifications by establishing an intimate relationship with her child. Sethe's yearning to merge with her children as love objects exposes this desire as excessive, uncontrolled. The social, moral, legal, and racial system is unable to accommodate her excessive love, a point Paul D expresses when he says: "Your love is too thick . . . what you did was wrong, Sethe" (165).

One key difference between *Beloved* and classic melodrama is that it overturns the trope of the sacrificial mother. Here the mother's personal sacrifice is the life of the child itself. Another important difference between *Beloved* and Hollywood's typical tragic maternal melodrama is that the latter usually exploits sensational or sordid subjects like sexual jealously (i.e., *Mildred Pierce*), class mobility (i.e., *Stella Dallas*), the tragic mulatto (i.e., *Pinky, Imitation of Life, Lost Boundaries*), interracial marriage (*Guess Who's Coming to Dinner*), or transracial adoption (*Losing Isaiah*) in ways complicit with the dominant ideology. The denouements of these pictures—mainstream and African American—inevitably reassert the Law of the Father, since the mother is ultimately revealed as excessive, overbearing, or somehow inadequate.

Because of the painful memory of slavery, *Beloved* approaches its maternal themes with more solemnity than most filmed melodramas. It raises questions of historiography in the context of maternal melodrama by treating the brutal genealogical legacy of slavery with high artistic seriousness. The cinematic *Beloved* even deploys a level of gravity and impact that surpasses the literary *Beloved.* After all, the cinema has a greater capacity to engage various senses and synthesize antecedent arts.[78] These resources for expression enable it to attain more emotional weight when the arts are synthesized with generic coherency. Whereas the novel offers description, the film presents mise-en-scène. More effectively than the novel, the film graphically (and acoustically) presents horrific representations of brutalized black bodies, of the enslaved body as the inscribed surface of historical events. Sounds of whips cracking, sights of bloody skin flayed open, nooses around necks, and the imprint of the chokecherry tree on Sethe's back momentarily conjure up the horror of chattel slavery in ways unavailable to novels. Even Baby Suggs's (Beah Richards) sermonizing plea for recovery and celebration of the black body are more vivid in the film than the written depictions of sermons at the Clearing.

One problematic consequence of the film's narrative emphasis on the tragic domestic drama, however, is the partial erasure of Paul D's (Danny Glover) post–Sweet Home survival story. Paul D's role in the film is limited to that of the man who reenters Sethe's life, who drives the ghostly spirit out of 124 Bluestone Road, and who later is in turn "moved out" by Beloved. His post-slavery traumas are abridged in the motion picture in favor of emphasis on Sethe's self-sabotage, trauma, re-memory, and guilt. Consequently, *Beloved* as a film becomes a "woman's film," focusing on efforts by Baby Suggs, Denver (Kimberly Elise), and Sethe to transcend the trauma of the past still threatening in the present.

Paul D's internment experience in Georgia, and his work on the chain gang, carefully described in the novel, is notably absent from the film. In the novel, Morrison recounts that Paul D was sent to prison after trying to kill Brandywine, the man to whom Schoolteacher had sold him. Brandywine was leading him, in a coffle with ten others, through Kentucky into Virginia. "He didn't know exactly what prompted him to try—other than Halle, Sixo, Paul A, Paul F, and Mister. . . . but the trembling was fixed by the time he knew it was there" (*Beloved*, 106). Just as Sethe's relationship with Beloved represents the link between many mothers and daughters, Paul D's incarceration and work on the chain gang represents the literal and figurative link between himself and many African American men who shared an abusive history of internment during Reconstruction. His subjugation at the hands of Reconstruction-era correction officers parallels Sethe's subjection at the hands of antebellum authorities. Relaying "his story" and setting it in Georgia is central to the historiographic intervention Morrison initiates.

Historians continue to unearth the relationship between slavery and mass incarceration. Prior to the 1920s, African Americans convicted of breaking the laws—petty and grand—in the New South found themselves "farmed out" to the highest bidder and destined to labor for the duration of their sentence or their life, whichever came first. Convicts built railroads, mined coal, manufactured brick, forested lumber, paved roads, and picked cotton. According to Alex Lichtenstein, convict leasing remained the predominant form of punishment until the closing years of the nineteenth century and contributed to the region's industrial expansion and postbellum economic transformation.[79] Various states, including Mississippi, Tennessee, Florida, and Alabama, relied heavily on convict-lease (chain gang) penal systems. The penal system in the New South was not only a corrupt system of labor recruitment, control, and exploitation; it was also suited to the political economy of a postemancipation society. "From a purely penological point of view, the convict lease was a fiscally conservative means of coping with a new burden: ex-slaves were emancipated from the dominion of the slaveholder only to be subject to the authority of the state."[80]

Benefiting from the scholarship of literary critics and legal historians such as John Edgar Wideman, Randall Kennedy, Horace Cayton, and St. Clair Drake, Loïc Wacquant writes: "On the morrow of Emancipation, Southern prisons turned black overnight, as 'thousands of ex-slaves were being arrested, tried and convicted for acts that in the past had been dealt with by the master alone' and for refusing to behave as menials and follow the demeaning rules of racial etiquette."[81] The racial disproportionality in U.S. imprisonment can be understood only against the backdrop of the full historical trajectory of racial domination in the United States.

Morrison recounts the internment experience of Paul D as a way of recuperating the historical experiences of incarcerated black men. Sexual abuse was a routine concomitant of this imprisonment. Thus the author recounts the daily practice by which black inmates were forced to fellate white prison guards (e.g., "Hungry, nigger?" *Beloved*, 108) as a way of re-presenting a variant of sexual racism that has long been suppressed. Enslaved men (and newly freed men) were sexually vulnerable both to the wanton abuses of their owners and to those operating as punitive agents for the state. Hayden

White's assertion that narrative broadly defined "has to do with the topics of law, legality, legitimacy, or more generally, authority,"[82] calls attention to the strong political intervention implicit in this aspect of Morrison's text.

The filmmakers may have omitted Paul D's story from the screenplay for any number of reasons. Including Paul's story material might well have earned the film an NC-17 rating from the Motion Picture Association of America. Second, some of the novel's material had to be eliminated to narrow the film's scope. Third, *Beloved* was made to appeal to female audiences. Retaining something of Paul D's perspective, however, enables the film to preserve facets of the gendered multivocality of the novel and the "multivalence of subjection" as endured by Morrison's characters.

When the film actually does include Paul D's perspective, it is rendered through unrestricted narration and perceptual subjectivity. The latter refers to the internal and psychological; it includes thoughts, dreams, fantasies, and sensory experience. Although both the novel and the film are multivoiced, the film is more adept at showing spectators the internal psychological states of characters. Flashbacks to Sweet Home, haunting memories, and encounters with ghosts, for example, are communicated in the film via focalized perceptual subjectivity. When Paul D first enters the house at 124 Bluestone Road, for example, the camera aligns the spectators with his point of view. What we see is his inner-subjective experience of the ghostly presence in Sethe's home. As he walks through the corridor, it appears as if he's walking through the annals of slave life at Sweet Home. Demme reportedly borrowed this eruptive memory technique from the death camp flash memories of Sidney Lumet's *The Pawnbroker*, forging a subliminal link between two forms of holocaust. First, Paul D sees visions of family and friends bloodied and chained. Then he's startled by the image of Sethe's murdered daughter. Finally, he takes his last steps through a barn door to enter her home. Throughout the foyer he's confronted with flesh-and-blood memories of abuses perpetrated on the plantation. Here the film develops the synthetic properties of the medium (i.e., closeups, wide angles, zoom-in shots, props, makeup, ambient sound, and point of view) to rouse our horror at the atrocities of slavery, by conveying a subjective experience. In the novel, by contrast, Paul D's entry into Sethe's home is described rather understatedly:

> Paul D tied his shoes together, hung them over his shoulder and followed her through the door straight into a pool of red and undulating light that locked him where he stood.
> "You got company?" he whispered, frowning.

"Off and on," said Sethe.

"Good God." He backed out the door onto the porch. "What kind of evil you got in here?"

"It's not evil, just sad. Come on. Just step through." . . .

She was right. It was sad. Walking through it, a wave of grief soaked him so thoroughly he wanted to cry. It seemed a long way to the normal light surrounding the table, but he made it—dry-eyed and lucky. (8–9)

While this description aptly details Paul D's actions, it does little to convey the subjective experience of his character or communicate his startling encounter with the ghostly presence haunting Sethe's home. Here the film effectively enlivens the original source material by synthesizing the various antecedent arts into focalized perceptual subjectivity. Because spectators are aligned with Paul D's perspective, they momentarily share his fear, dismay, and terror. This amplification suggests that film—rather than being inferior to the novel—can actually enrich written texts in ways that go far beyond what a prejudiced view would have us believe about the film medium.

Literary critics have discussed the way the novel created an aesthetic by playing against and through the cultural field of postmodernism. Both *Beloved* the film and the novel are polyperceptual: they engage numerous voices and narratives by telling and retelling the same event from Sethe's, Denver's, and Paul D's perspectives.[83] Like the novel, the film is innovative in linguistic ways that originate in the black tradition of oral narrative.[84] It mixes vernaculars and modes of response. Thus another key difference between the novel and the film is that the latter translates narrative voice into focalized perceptual subjectivity, bringing spectators and characters into closer relation.

The film manifests another hallmark of a kind of resistant postmodernism. By eroding the boundary between high (literary) culture and mass television or popular (low) culture, the film collapses a boundary, for example, between Toni Morrison, the erudite cultural producer and Nobel Prize winner, and Oprah Winfrey, the TV icon and arbiter of bourgeois taste. The novel's story of slavery (invoked by Beloved and endured by Baby Suggs) is premised on "the absence of power, the quest for self-determination, the loss of a homeland, and of a language."[85] But the film—at the level of its production, at least—comes wrapped in the aura of Winfrey's career success, as media mogul, a career marked by the presence of power, the realization of self-determination, the existence of a cinematic language. As producer and star in the transcription from novel to the screen, Winfrey's approach is "inevitably partial, personal and conjectural."[86] In what follows I explore the reception of *Beloved* in general and the impact of Winfrey's star persona on the media's response to *Beloved* in particular.

Do the Media Matter?

The critical discourse around the film *Beloved* influenced the reception of the picture. More specifically, the reception presents another set of texts with which the film exists in dialogic relation. Three salient issues regarding the media coverage stand out. First, the media saturation appeared to backfire: the excessive hype hindered rather than helped the film financially. Second, the racial polarization of the critical discourse indicated blatant ethnic and racial partisanship in film reporting. Third, the African American press coverage (in an attempt to overcompensate for, or preempt critical dismissal of *Beloved* by the white mainstream press) was overly celebratory. Contrasting the various public dialogues about the film contextualizes *Beloved*'s box-office performance. It also reveals how reviewer commentary became part of a discursive struggle over the reception of dramatic black films by critics and audiences.

The reviews and promotion of *Beloved* revealed distinct trends and, more specifically, two types of media coverage: promotional magazine stories (i.e., in *Vogue*) and evaluative film reviews (i.e., in *The New Yorker*). By and large, evaluative reviews appearing in the mainstream news publications (the predominantly white press) were respectful of the efforts to bring *Beloved* to fruition but overly critical of the final product (these reviews were found in *The New Yorker,* the *New York Times,* the *Village Voice, Variety,* and *Sight & Sound*). Conversely, commentary in African American periodicals (*Ebony, Jet, Essence,* the *Amsterdam News*) was uncritical and explicitly celebratory. A concerted effort on the part of black-issue-oriented publications (and African American journalists working at predominantly Euro-American publications) was aimed at encouraging audiences to support *Beloved*.

However positive the African American media campaign may have been, that support did not translate into ticket sales or approval from black audiences. Not only did African American audiences fail to support the film, a larger black bourgeois community denied the film artistic recognition. This aesthetic negation was clearly articulated at the 1999 NAACP image awards. Despite receiving six nominations, *Beloved* lost to *How Stella Got Her Groove Back* (36 percent) which took Outstanding Motion Picture over *Beloved* (17 percent), *Down in the Delta* (15 percent), *Enemy of the State* (22 percent), and *He Got Game* (10 percent).[87] So, despite the film's relatively high production

Oprah Winfrey, Thandie Newton, and Kimberly Elise star in *Beloved* (dir. Jonathan Demme, 1998).

values, its positive reviews in the black press, an expensive advertising campaign, a story based on a Pulitzer Prize–winning novel, and a cast of stars, *Beloved* was unable to gain recognition from African American audiences.

The mainstream press coverage began with a *Time* magazine cover story featuring the film's star-producer in costume. As *Time* covers are usually reserved for persons (and events) reflecting the tenor of the zeitgeist, the cover itself seemed to mark a milestone because (like the *Time* cover featuring recording artist Lauryn Hill with the caption "Hip Hop Nation"), it appeared to substantiate the claim that black cultural idioms are continually moving from margin to center. Oprah Winfrey's image on the cover marked a milestone because it announced that a theatrically released African American film about the legacy of slavery and the reality of Reconstruction was a significant cultural event.

The four *Time* articles in this issue were so celebratory as to prod *The New Yorker* critic David Denby to begin his censorious review of *Beloved* by admonishing *Time* magazine. Denby wrote: "Weeks before the movie opened, *Time* unfurled the ceremonial bunting in a journalistic package so elevated in tone that the magazine seemed awed by the importance of its own coverage. When the public gets a proper look at the movie, the bunting may turn out to be a crêpe." While Denby's dismissive tone is certainly problematic, he was correct in predicting audience response. As the *Time* magazine cover demonstrated, the Disney Company was banking on the cultural capital invested in Winfrey's celebrity sign. Clearly, the studio, director Jonathan Demme, and Oprah Winfrey herself were under the false impression that charismatic devotion to her celebrity would translate into audience enthusiasm—in much the same way that a book "translates" into a screenplay. The pun-based headline of *Time*'s cover, "The Beloved Oprah," itself hinged on linguistic slippage between Winfrey's televisual and film personae, even as it paralleled the textual shift from novel to film. But what Disney, Demme, Winfrey, and others failed to realize is that Oprah's celebrity charisma constitutes entertainment charisma, not political charisma. Motivating black, white, and other ethnic audiences to support postmodern, avant-garde-inflected black cinema is fundamentally a difficult political and aesthetic challenge.

Beloved-as-film, more than *Beloved*-as-novel, elicits a particular political and ideological sensibility of viewers, a sensibility generally not found at the multiplex. In fact, rather than help the film, this kind of media coverage—like the casting of a TV celebrity instead of a trained actress—clearly hindered the film by discouraging viewers who erroneously dismissed it as more of Winfrey's self-indulgent commercial populism. Media saturation made it difficult to separate Oprah's making of *Beloved* from the commercial self-help agenda presented on *The Oprah Winfrey Show*. More than one reviewer commented on the connection between themes addressed on the show and Winfrey's interest in producing the novel as a film. *The Village Voice* critic Jim Hoberman suggested the movie might well be a platform for the issues Winfrey pursues in the context of her show.

> *Beloved* is less Oprah's vehicle than her time machine. Even more than Morrison, Winfrey—who sees herself as a medium for the spirits of specific Negro slaves—has assumed the role of a tribune. *Beloved*'s oscillating tone and close-up driven absence of perspective become more coherent once the movie is understood as an epic version of *Oprah!*—a show in which the star naturally shifts between autobiographical confession and maternal advice, reliving personal adversity and offering the model of her own empowerment as New Age therapy.

Writing for the *Chicago-Sun Times*, Roger Ebert echoed Hoberman's observations: "Her whole persona is about controlling her own destiny—owning herself. No wonder she was powerfully attracted by *Beloved*, which is about a woman who tastes 28 days of what freedom feels like and is willing to kill her daughter rather than see her taken back into slavery."

Writing for the British Film Institute's glossy *Sight & Sound,* Charlotte O'Sullivan made a similar observation. Even Winfrey herself made connections between her talk show and the film when she shrugged off criticism of *Beloved*'s limited commercial appeal by contending that America's current race problem is rooted in its failure to honestly confront its emotional issues and history: "If you don't acknowledge the pain in truth, then you carry forward the pain in distortion . . . It's no different from your own personal history and wounds. If you don't heal your personal wounds, they continue to bleed. And so we have a country of people who have continued to bleed."[88] Thus in her own proselytizing plea, Winfrey pursued the project as a partial extension of the themes, ideas, and technologies of self-help presented on the program. Her appeal thus manifests the intertextual impact of television stardom on an American literary classic.

On one level, the *Beloved* project was cultivated from a progressive desire to provoke American audiences to consider the dehumanization at the core of the nation's foundation. On another level, the film was based on a profoundly naive and commercial premise: that viewers would heed Winfrey's clarion call to "heal" the American family of its dysfunctional race relations. And that all that was necessary for this "healing" to occur—if not begin—was for the "mother of America" to tell her adoring public to go see this film. However, if it is naive for a celebrity like Winfrey to expect audiences to support an aesthetically and ideologically progressive project, it is worth asking another question: what does it take to get audiences (mainstream and ethnic) to support innovative, historically audacious black films?[89] What does it take to motivate African American audiences to support films other than *Blade* ($23 million) or *How Stella Got Her Groove Back* ($29 million)—films that earned more in two weeks than *Beloved* earned during its entire theatrical run?

The tension around *Beloved*-as-epic emerged in the racially polarized struggle for discursive control of its reception. Consider, for example, reviews by the African American *New York Press* critic Armond White and *The New Yorker* reviewer David Denby. White's complimentary review lauds every aspect of the film. White correctly notes, "Demme achieves in a commercial format what avant-gardists Carl Dreyer, Jean Cocteau, Maya Deren and Jean Genet could communicate to their intimates." But White's praise of Demme rises only to eventually fall into the trap of simplistic racial and aesthetic essentialism, as when he offers Demme's "black heart" as the explanation for his sensitivity to African American cultural idioms. White's own paradoxical racial essentialism is implied in the statement that lumps together dissimilar black-oriented films like the aesthetically innovative *Beloved* and the narratively conventional Steven Spielberg film *The Color Purple.* He writes:

To be inured to the faces in *Beloved* is to be indifferent to the lives they represent; their history, ethnicity and humanity. There's no way around the fact that film critics are pitifully subject to affirming themselves by praising such questionable talents as Woody Allen, Merchant Ivory or this week's Atom Egoyan. When films with African-American subject matter like *The Color Purple, Amistad* or *Beloved* are dismissed while trash like *The English Patient* or *Titanic,* or *Your Friends and Neighbors* is praised, it only means that white people are loving what has historically been their cinematic privilege.[90]

While we ought to be skeptical of White's appraisal of Demme, he makes a valid argument about the hegemony of Euro-American cinema and white film criticism, which participates in the exclusion and erasure of black cultural production. White describes what Cornel West has aptly described (in another context) as a history of "racist bombardment at the level of aesthetics." Moreover, White's sensitivity to the role of film criticism in the reproduction of taste rearticulates the fact that film criticism—a concomitant of cultural criticism—is always already a political enterprise.

If mainstream critics were unfairly disparaging of *Beloved,* this disparagement raises several questions. Was *Beloved* a poor adaptation? Were critics racially biased in their evaluations? How could the film have been cast or directed differently? The deeper we probe, the wider the critical divide. In opposition to White, for example, David Denby demonstrated considerable political partisanship in his assessment. The author of a polemical book against multiculturalism, Denby's dismissal went so far as to challenge the validity of multicultural education. For Denby the question was far greater than whether this was a successful adaptation. In his view, excessive praise for Toni Morrison's novel forced what he saw as the ogre of multiculturalism to raise its ugly head. In *The New Yorker* Denby wrote: "*Beloved* is not an event to be enjoyed; it's an event to be endured, rather like the dedication of a new building on the Washington Mall . . . Still, media attention of this proportion is bound to electrify the Morrison industry in the universities and the schools; one can only squirm in sympathy for all the seventeen-year-olds who will be forced to sit through the movie."[91]

It is hardly surprising that a critic with Denby's conservative sensibility (and traditional readership) would dislike *Beloved,* especially since he refers to the novel as "ornery." Translation: angry black women produce angry black novels that make conservative viewers uncomfortable and are therefore unworthy of critical praise. Denby's comments questioning Morrison's rightful place in the American literary canon indicate cultural backlash and crude intellectual protectionism. As if inspired by Allan Bloom's *The Closing of the*

American Mind, Denby attempts to protect the genealogy of Euro-American cultural capital—the very cultural hegemony for which Armond White overcompensates. Denby's review underscores the important intervention of Morrison's literary criticism. Her book *Playing in the Dark: Whiteness in the Literary Imagination* eloquently critiques such assumptions, accepted by literary historians and circulated as knowledge. This perspective maintains that traditional, canonical American literature is free of, uninformed by, uncontaminated by the four-hundred-year-old presence of African Americans. "The contemplation of this black presence," Morrison writes, "is central to any understanding of our national literature and should not be permitted to hover at the margins of the literary imagination."

Denby seems unaware of Morrison's argument in *Playing in the Dark,* an argument that could also be extrapolated to cinema and popular culture. Contemplating the black-diasporic presence is also central to an understanding of our national cinema. Late 1990s and early twenty-first-century cinema is replete with representations of menacing black drug lords, gang leaders, welfare mothers, crack addicts, violent prisoners, pushy pimps, and hooligans. Egregious examples from popular cinema include Tony Scott's *True Romance* (1993), Quentin Tarantino's *Pulp Fiction* (1994), Darren Aronofsky's *Requiem for a Dream* (2000), Steven Soderbergh's *Traffic* (2001), and Todd Solondz's *Storytelling* (2002), to mention only a few. In cinema today we still see films that present menacing black characters as the primary threat to supposed white innocence. A century after W. E. B. Du Bois declared, "The problem of the twentieth century is the problem of the color-line," we are still addressing "the relation of the darker to the lighter races."

While dialogue over the aesthetic merit of the film in mainstream publications was profoundly biased, discussions in the African American press were naively uncritical. Aside from Armond White's review, there was little in the African American press (with the exception of Talise Moorer's *New York Amsterdam News* review) of substance. Moorer acknowledged the film's significance, situated it historically, yet questioned casting decisions while still encouraging viewers to see the movie.[92] Writing for *Essence* magazine, Pearl Cleage published a fluffy interview with the star, which recounted Oprah's "journey to make the film," described the project as "her labor of love," and explained that "re-enactments of slavery" helped Winfrey prepare for the role. These production experiences turned out to be part of Oprah's process of spiritual self-renewal. And, Cleage reported, this religious sensibility would now permeate the star's other projects. Black press coverage allowed the intertext of Winfrey's stardom to govern evaluation of the film.

Aware of *Beloved*'s limited commercial viability, Winfrey asserted that this film was her "gift" to the black community. "I give it as a gift, and I know that every person who receives it and really gets it is transformed in some way." Articles in the Johnson Publications (*Ebony* and *Jet*), chronicled her so-called journey. These emphasized the challenging shift Winfrey made from an epistemological to an ontological understanding of slavery during the process of *Beloved*'s production. For example, in *Ebony* magazine, Laura Randolph wrote of Winfrey "that her emotions were so raw it surprised her. After all, [Oprah] knows Black history almost as well as she knows the book. "I thought I knew it," Oprah says, "but what I have come to know is that I had just intellectually understood it—the difficulty, the sorrow, the pain. You can talk about it on an intellectual level, but during the process of doing *Beloved*, for the first time, I went to the knowing place."[93]

Unfortunately, media coverage in African American publications can also be dismissed as publicity—engaged less in the quest for discursive authority than in propagating the culture of black celebrity. Film criticism becomes a form of ethnic cheerleading. In some ways, Oprah Winfrey's journey to the terrible place of "knowing" slavery may undermine a basic premise of the book. It may undermine Morrison's premise that slavery was so epistemologically dissimilar from twentieth-century life as to confound the mind with the unfathomable reality that would lead a person to choose death over life. Fortunately, the film successfully communicates this premise even if Winfrey's experience making the film does not. Further, *Beloved* the film communicates something profound about black modernity born of revolutionary struggle against the political economy of slavery.

Beloved as a novel and as a film presents a rich and revolutionary story. It articulates a reconstructive feminist voice within the fields of revisionist history, contemporary fiction, and feature film. *Beloved* is the product of, and a contribution to, a historical moment in which African American literature, historiography, and film production are in a state of fervid revision.[94] Morrison (in her novels and criticism) and Winfrey (in her show and making of *Beloved*) are signifyin(g), albeit quite differently, on academic and aesthetic traditions. For these reasons, I think the best way to interpret the cinematic *Beloved* is as a reconstructive text, seeking to open up new dialogues and new filmmaking possibilities. Viewing the film merely as a political football blinds us to its intellectual and aesthetic intervention against Hollywood's global hegemony.

Halle Berry
Charismatic Beauty in a Multicultural Age

> Movies are the place where the
> fundamental national ideals are set up.
>
> —Clyde Taylor

> The most identifiable similarity is that we're both
> two black women trying to make it in an industry that
> doesn't make much of a place for people like us.
> Dorothy was trying to carve a niche for a black leading
> lady back in 1953, and I'm still trying to carve that
> same niche in 1999. We share that struggle.
>
> —Halle Berry

Dorothy, Halle, and Oscar

In an era of multiculturalism, transnationalism, and globalization, mass media circulate among increasingly fragmented, multiracial audiences. Genre evolution and film star systems are driven by industry sensitivity to transnationality, multifocality, and syncretism.[1] Hybrid subjectivities, immigration narratives, and even biracial identities deterritorialize and deessentialize the process by which spectators imagine communities and experience cinematic narratives. Contemporary celebrities are simultaneously local and global, national and transnational, racially identified yet socially hybridized. The celebrity of Halle Berry, who is biracial but identifies as African American, exemplifies the way media in general, and cinema in particular, utilize bifurcated subjectivities to reach growing multiethnic populations. Her starring role in *Monster's Ball* (Marc Forster, 2001)—which angered many because of its particular depiction of an interracial relationship—garnered an array of awards from institutions on both sides of the Atlantic. In 2001 she was nominated for a Golden Globe and an AFI (American Film Institute) award for acting. Shortly afterward, she won the Berlin Silver Bear and the Best Actress Oscar at the seventy-fourth Annual Academy Awards.

The Oscar ensures Berry's place in the Hollywood pantheon. Historians will remember her as one in a long line of African American entertainment industry "firsts." The William Foster Photoplay Company of Chicago was—by most accounts—the first black-owned movie production house (circa 1911). Oscar Micheaux's *Birthright* (1918) was the first black-directed feature-length African American film. Hattie McDaniel was the first black woman to receive an Oscar for her supporting role in *Gone with the Wind* (1939). Sidney Poitier became the first black man to receive an Academy Award for his performance in *Lilies of the Field* (1963). Forty years later, Halle Berry became the first African American woman to win Best Actress. These achievements are cause for African Americans to observe, but with skepticism. After all, the Academy of Motion Pictures Arts and Sciences typically rewards the most commercially profitable pictures. Their designation as marketable in the global entertainment economy means these pictures comply with dominant ideological frameworks, as these structures and practices are recuperated within a film's diegesis. Market demands on commercial cinema explain why award-winning films are rarely—if ever—politically progressive or socially groundbreaking. Invariably, these pictures reveal the economic base and its relationship to the cultural superstructure.

The ensuing chapter examines Halle Berry's screen persona, which itself is a text shaped by career maneuvers fortuitously well synchronized with the zeitgeist. Her celebrity—like that of her predecessors—raises as many questions as answers. Foremost among such questions is whether her screen persona reproduces racial stereotypes (i.e., the jezebel, the tragic mulatto, the welfare queen), many of which predate the invention of the cinematic apparatus and overdetermined African American representation in literature and theater. Berry's African American critics fault her for "selling out" to the establishment by reproducing racial stereotypes about black women in mainstream film and popular culture. This chapter complicates such criticisms by considering the polyvalence of her star persona. This polyvalence propels discourse on representation beyond racial binaries into questions of hybridity and multiracial identity. For Dorothy Dandridge, Pam Grier, Whoopi Goldberg, Oprah Winfrey, and Halle Berry, succeeding in the predominantly white, heterosexist, capitalist patriarchy of Hollywood or network television required capitulation, complicity, compromise, and contradiction. These women are necessarily complex figures—profoundly Du Boisian in their double and conflicted consciousness about the film industry yet completely assimilated in their drive to succeed as crossover stars in mainstream America. Of all the celebrities discussed here, Berry has enjoyed the most conventional career trajectory, gradually rising through the ranks with a steady stream of respectable motion-picture vehicles. She has obtained a wider variety of film roles than any other African American–identified actress in U.S. history. This is an accomplishment in and of itself, because it may enable the next generation of actresses to exceed existing institutional boundaries. Having sustained a lucrative film career as an award-winning actress, Berry deserves recognition as a diva of the American screen.

As a consequence of winning the Oscar, Halle Berry's celebrity status has soared. She avoided the notorious "Oscar curse," becoming an A-list leading lady.[2] But it was not the Oscar alone that solidified her stardom. Her professional traversal from small roles (i.e., *Jungle Fever*, 1991) to niche-audience films (i.e., *Executive Decision*, 1996; *The Rich Man's Wife*, 1996; *B.A.P.S.*, 1997) to social-problem pictures (i.e., *Losing Isaiah*, 1995; *Bulworth*, 1998) to high-concept summer blockbusters (i.e., *X-Men*, 2000; *Swordfish*, 2001; *Die Another Day*, 2002; the campy *Catwoman*, 2004; *X-Men: The Last Stand*, 2006) was a process involving several career-building movies, a few television mini-series, and one decisive biography picture.

The HBO biography movie *Introducing Dorothy Dandridge* (Martha Cooliage, 1999) was more influential than any other film or accolade in advancing Berry's career. Despite its status as a made-for-TV-movie—or even perhaps because it was widely seen on TV—it established a cultural connection (in the minds of viewers, producers, and spectators) between Halle Berry and the late Dorothy Dandridge. Historian Donald Bogle, scholar Marguerite Rippy, and biographer Christopher Farley are among the researchers and celebrity watchers to suggest that Berry greatly benefited from portraying the late 1950s starlet. Farley summed it up well:

> *Introducing Dorothy Dandridge* was a case where the death of one star helped give birth to another. Playing a screen legend is a bid at immortality; however, it is usually a losing one that makes the living actor seem small by comparison. Halle, by showing as much sexual charisma, charm and acting ability as Dandridge, posed this silent question: Isn't she just as big a star? Ironically, Dorothy Dandridge provided Halle Berry a better part than Halle had ever gotten in her life or Dandridge had ever gotten before her death.[3]

Ebony magazine journalist Walter Leavy agreed with Farley. For its sixtieth-anniversary issue, *Ebony* published Leavy's cover story on the new trio of Oscar winners: "Denzel, Halle & Jamie: Celebrate 60 Historic Years of Civil

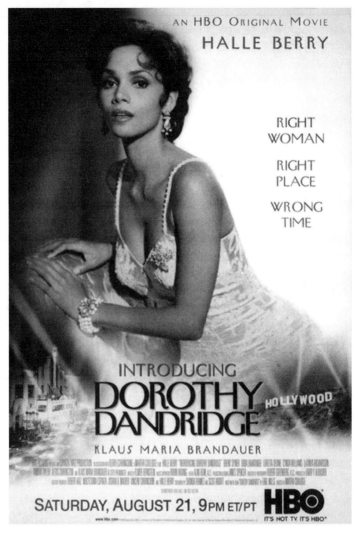

Halle Berry portrays Dorothy Dandridge in the HBO special *Introducing Dorothy Dandridge* (dir. Martha Cooliage, 1999).

Rights, Movies and More!" He suggested she demonstrated her versatility across many films but it was her role in *Introducing Dorothy Dandridge* that legitimized her as an actress, a role she claims was made for her because she and Dandridge had so much in common. "There were so many commonalities between us," Berry observed, "that I feel it was meant for me to bring Dorothy to life so that we all could have a greater understanding of who she was . . . It reminded me how easy I have it today . . . What she had to endure was mind-boggling . . . While making the movie, I realized I have no reason to complain about anything."[4]

Berry's seven-year effort to make the film, and her willingness to help finance the TV movie, speaks volumes about her passion for—and recognition of—the picture as a definitive career maneuver. From a professional standpoint, the numbers of spectators who watched the movie mattered less than what it accomplished for its leading lady. It legitimated Berry as an actor (in the eyes of production executives and Motion Picture Academy members) by associating her public persona and professional ambitions with Dandridge's screen persona and civil-rights struggle for inclusion. Furthermore, it simulated a familial or genealogical relationship whereby Berry became the descendant-beneficiary of Dandridge's Hollywood legacy.[5] *Introducing Dorothy Dandridge* articulates the semiotic relationship between diegetic and nondiegetic elements of an actor's persona. The diegetic (or narrative) content of Dandridge's turbulent biography was symbolically and semiotically linked to the nondiegetic (or nonnarrative) celebrity persona of Berry. During the classical Hollywood studio era (circa 1930–60), stars routinely portrayed important historical figures whose magnitude or prominence had a residual effect on their own public personae.[6] On a lesser scale, but with the same effect, *Introducing Dorothy* enabled Berry to augment her role in American film history.

The African American–oriented Johnson Publishing Company magazines *Ebony* and *Jet* helped solidify the Berry-Dandridge connection with promotional articles similar to Leavy's. Take the article "Halle Berry: On How She Found Dorothy Dandridge's Spirit and Healed Her Own" (*Ebony*, March 1999) as a case in point. From the preproduction press coverage through to Berry's Oscar acceptance speech, she continually reminded viewers that she was the continuation of Dandridge's lineage, the realization of Dorothy's deferred dreams.

Awarding Berry the Oscar made for an interesting moment of redress for the systemic exclusion of women of color from mainstream motion pictures and nationally recognized award-granting institutions. Even her acceptance speech implied as much. Token moments of inclusion and recognition— Cicely Tyson's Oscar nomination for *Sounder* (1973), Whoopi Goldberg's Golden Globe for *The Color Purple* (1986), Goldberg's and Oprah Winfrey's Oscar nominations for *The Color Purple,* Denzel Washington's many accolades for *Glory* (1989) and *Training Day* (2002), Cuba Gooding's Oscar for *Jerry Maguire* (1997), and Jamie Foxx's Oscar for *Ray* (2005)—siphon off and

An elated couple, Oscar winners Halle Berry and Denzel Washington strike a pose for the paparazzi.

diffuse assertions of institutional racism that accrue after decades of excluding ethnic minorities, particularly black women, from Hollywood filmmaking.

Discourse and activism protesting exclusion and misrepresentation date back to the early days of silent cinema, when, in the pages of the NAACP newsletter *The Crisis,* W. E. B. Du Bois protested the depiction of African Americans by whites in blackface in David Wark Griffith's *The Birth of a*

Nation (1915). Du Bois's critical project was revived periodically over the intervening years by various critics and again in the 1990s with the rebirth of Independent Black Cinema and outspoken filmmakers like Spike Lee (*She's Gotta Have It,* 1986), Robert Townsend (*Hollywood Shuffle,* 1987), the Hudlin Brothers (*House Party,* 1990), Julie Dash (*Daughters of the Dust,* 1992), Mario Van Peebles (*New Jack City,* 1991), Carl Franklin (*One False Move,* 1992), and Darnell Martin (*I Like It Like That,* 1994). Barring the NAACP image awards, their films made little impact at nationally recognized, revenue-generating award ceremonies, and many filmmakers have had difficulty securing subsidy for subsequent projects. The African American response to this situation has involved a series of critical articles in national periodicals.

On March 18, 1996, on the eve of the sixty-eighth annual Academy Awards, the film industry received some unflattering publicity. Journalist Pam Lambert, author of a *People* magazine cover story, "Hollywood Blackout," indicted the industry for its contradictory practice of saying all the right things but continuing its exclusion of African Americans. Lambert referred to this exclusion as a national disgrace. The statistics, she argued, tell the story. African-Americans constituted 12 percent of the U.S. population [in 1996] and 25 percent of the moviegoing audience, but only one of the 166 nominees at the Academy Awards was African American—a live section short film director. Of the Academy of Motion Picture Arts and Sciences' 5,043 members, who nominate and choose the Oscar winners, fewer than 200—or 3.9 percent— were African American. Only 2.3 percent of the Directors Guild membership was black, according to the guild's 1994 figures. A mere 2.6 percent of the Writers Guild was African American. And blacks accounted for less than 2 percent of Local 44, a four-thousand-member union that includes set decorators and property masters.[7]

Lambert's article was published almost concurrently with Reverend Jesse Jackson's open letter to the entertainment community titled "From Selma, Alabama, to Hollywood, California: A Thirty-One-Year Struggle for Fairness and Inclusion in the American Dream." Reverend Jackson eloquently tackled the issues. The paucity of nominations for people of color, he argued, is directly related to the lack of films featuring the talents of people of color. Reverend Jackson likened the practice of excluding minorities to Jim Crow laws enforcing racial segregation.

> Today, the adversary is not a group of racist individuals but institutions that continue to lock out people of color from significant levels of participation and decision-making. The same coalition of conscience that tore down the

cotton curtain of American apartheid must pull down the celluloid walls in Hollywood. Just as segregation—legal forms of apartheid—defined the rules of behavior for both whites and Blacks in the South, Hollywood's films and television industry defines how we see ourselves and each other. Our present and future generations should be seen as part of a multiracial society, a Rainbow Coalition.[8]

Jackson's letter reanimated the consumer-citizen discourse of inclusion that emerged in the mid-1950s alongside Dorothy Dandridge's civil rights–era celebrity. Halle Berry acknowledged this history of exclusion when she accepted the Oscar on behalf of Dandridge, Diahann Carroll, and the many others who have been overlooked and underemployed.

One quantitative difference between 1950 and today is that the numbers of ethnic minorities in film and television have increased. From the late 1960s through the 1970s, Blaxploitation revealed African American–oriented films as profitable. In the late 1980s and early 1990s, New Black Cinema reopened this market-driven debate. Whether it was Eddie Murphy's star vehicle *Coming to America* (1988), returning $300 million worldwide; Spike Lee's *Do the Right Thing* (1989), multiplying its budget to earn $26 million; or John Singleton's *Boyz n the Hood* (1991), earning $57 million on a $6.5 million budget, these films made money.

In the multicultural new millennium, a fresh cohort of musicians, rap artists, dancers, and playwrights entered the media market. Ice Cube helmed *Barbershop* (2002) and *Barbershop 2* (2004), the first of which earned $75 million on a $22 million budget. The Will Smith and Martin Lawrence star vehicle sequel *Bad Boys 2* (2003) garnered $262 million worldwide on a $170 million investment. And Tyler Perry's *Diary of a Mad Black Woman* (2005) grossed $50 million on a budget of $5 million.[9] This is not to mention the range of television sitcoms like *The Bernie Mac Show, The Dave Chappell Show, Eve, Girlfriends, Half & Half, The Hughleys, Soul Food,* or Tyler Perry's *House of Payne,* which have also diversified African American representation.

The evolving but continued cinematic marginalization of African Americans, Arab Americans, Asian Americans, Hispanic Americans, and Native Americans matters because mainstream mass media help to set the national tone through the dissemination of popular entertainment narratives. Works of entertainment are always both works of art and of ideology. As Richard Dyer notes, any entertainment carries assumptions about and attitudes toward the world, even if these are not the point of the thing. "The fact that an entertainment entertains does not let it off the hook of social responsibility, does not make up for sexism, racism, or any other deleterious ism."[10] The ideological function of mass media is evident inside Hollywood and outside the United States. Western European nations are becoming aware of their growing multiethnic, immigrant populations and grappling with ethnic heterogeneity. Only in the wake of the 2006 riots in the Parisian banlieues did leading French broadcaster TF1 dare to promote black newscaster Harry Roselmack (from the French-owned Caribbean isle Martinique) to the role of anchorman. Riots brought "cultural racism"[11] into focus. In Holland, Germany, and Scandinavia, minority groups are openly pressuring for more exposure in and access to mass-media and entertainment industries.[12] Globally and locally, in national and transnational media landscapes, celebrity and star images serve as "representative characters": definers of power and identity for a society. Once among the A-list of globally circulating Hollywood stars, Berry became part of an industrial constellation. Her crossover appeal epitomizes the way hybrid, exilic, and diasporic subjects, working within hegemonic social structures, negotiate the social antinomies of identity.

From Tragic Mulatto to Biracial Beauty

In *Hollywood Fantasies of Miscegenation,* Susan Courtney examined the upsurge of films in the 1950s flaunting transgression of the miscegenation taboo. Filmgoers in the 1950s witnessed a greater variety of mixed-raced couples than had been on the screen before. These were not solely black-white interracial relationships but ran the gamut and included Mexican, Asian, and Native Americans involved with white or European Americans. On the surface, these films expressed liberal sentiments regarding racial integration by exposing subtle slights, prejudice, and bigotry as daily practices. Catering to the sensibilities of a predominantly white audience, however, these movies inevitably redeemed the status quo, never finding faulty the social structures or belief systems that were preconditions for inequity. Creating and sensationalizing salacious narratives about illicit interracial relationships was the surest way to bring audiences back to movie theaters during an era of increased competition from the new medium of television.

From the pre–Hays Production Code era to the post-code rating system, in film after film (*The Birth of a Nation,* 1915; *Duel in the Sun,* 1946; *Pinky,* 1949, *Lost Boundaries,* 1949; *Imitation of Life,* 1934/1959; *Tamango,* 1957; *Band of Angels,* 1957; *Island in the Sun,* 1957; *Touch of Evil,* 1958; *Flaming Star,* 1960; *The Unforgiven,* 1960; *Quadroon,* 1972; *Angel Heart,* 1987; *Devil in a Blue Dress,* 1995; *The Human Stain,* 2003) the miscegenation taboo was figuratively encapsulated and literally embodied by the trope of the tragic "mulatto/a in the narrative."[13] The mulatto—about which volumes have been written—is typically envisioned as female. She is revered for her beauty yet ostracized for her alterity, her radical inassimilable difference and refusal to be contained by racial segregation. Within the context of literary and cinematic narratives, the mulatto's unfulfilled struggle for acceptance epitomized the pitfalls of transgressing the miscegenation taboo. At a societal level, these social-problem pictures (and their source novels) functioned as national allegories and sexual morality plays. They were key sites in the production of national discourse on sexuality, policing behavior by dramatizing the dire consequences of defying antimiscegenation legislation mandated by the racial state's governing apparatus. More effective than external policing, these films functioned in an educative capacity, teaching audiences to internalize self-regulating behaviors.

To her credit, Halle Berry has avoided typecasting in "tragic mulatta" roles (i.e., Lisa Bonet playing Epiphany Proudfoot in Alan Parker's satanic thriller *Angel Heart,* 1987), which Berry might easily have gravitated toward given her own biracial background. Her mother, Judith Berry, is Caucasian. Her father, Jerome Berry, is African American. Though her acting career has included racially mixed characters (i.e., the lead in the TV movie *Queen*), she prevented these pictures and her biracial identity from overdetermining or defining her public persona. Instead, Berry thanks her mother for empowering her with a sense of pride in her African American identity and for her healthy racial consciousness. Sharing these convictions in one interview Berry said, "If you're a white mother or father, and you have a black child—you have to make the effort to educate that child as to who they are and where they came from . . . You have to give them some of their culture back, educate them about their history, prepare them to be black American in a racist society."[14] With current trends in immigration and interracial coupling, Black Pride has taken a back seat to mixed-race pride. After all, there have been interracial relationships—coerced and consensual—resulting in mixed-race persons since before slavery. Most African Americans are racially mixed. How else could we account for the range of complexions, features, and hair types among African Americans? But in the late 1990s (circa 1997), when California parents began petitioning (via grassroots organizations like Project RACE) for additional categories to be added to the census, the notion of biraciality entered mainstream discourse.

Despite African American self-identification, Berry's biraciality is a salient component of her cinematic assimilability and commercial success. As a biracial person she is situated in a comparatively privileged position relative to many African American actresses. The privilege derives from her propinquity to whiteness in a society where color consciousness has shaped race relations.

The contemporary politics of skin color in America exists as a vestige of three distinct but interrelated events: the scientific creation of unequivocal racial categories during the Enlightenment; the trans-Atlantic slave trade; and the political economy of American plantocracies, which determined patterns of racial segregation, integration, and assimilation for decades after Reconstruction. The racialization of slavery—designed to support colonialism and safeguard the privileges of colonizers—occurred in connection with the growth of the world market and the rise of capitalism. Marx deals with this in outline in *Capital*, which Eric Williams takes up and analyses in *Capitalism and Slavery*. Scholars across various fields (e.g., the phenomenology of Maurice Merleau-Ponty, the psychology of Frantz Fanon, the sociology of Pierre Bourdieu, the labor history of Alex Lichtenstein, the anthropology of Ann Laura Stoler, the critical race theory of Cheryl Harris, or the legal theory of David Theo Goldberg) have demonstrated that race, class, and color consciousness impact the value modern nation-states assign to bodies and behaviors.[15] Because bodies are racially categorized and these categories are endowed with varying degrees of and "forms of capital,"[16] race and color figure prominently in the valuation of bodies as objects of desire. From such scholarship we know that "the very concept that a body possesses or reveals 'a color' is indebted to the privileging of vision and its attendant systems of representation that measure and quantify differences of skin hue and tone."[17]

The Color Complex, or Why Can't a Black Actress Play the Girlfriend?

As the authors of *The Color Complex: The Politics of Skin Color among African Americans* (1993) have demonstrated, there is a convoluted history behind color bias within the African American community that mirrors society at large.[18] In mainstream American film culture this semiotic bias has meant that browner-skinned actresses like Sheryl Lee Ralph, Angela Bassett, Lela Rochon, Regina King, and Kimberly Elise are often overlooked, underutilized, or bypassed in favor of their lighter-skinned sisters. These women are cast in films as wives, girlfriends, and significant others, but their opportunities are fewer. African American women are not alone in experiencing such discrimination. Asian and Hispanic American women have similarly been subjected to the commercial industry's longstanding color hierarchy. The construction of white femininity was so meticulously managed during the studio era from the 1920s through the 1950s that even classic Hollywood starlets like Rita Hayworth—born Margarita Carmen Cansino—struggled with studio Anglicization and the process of literally whitening her complexion, lightening her hair, and altering her overall image.[19] Puerto Rican actress Rita Moreno similarly faced color bias throughout her career.[20] The history of Hollywood makeup artistry reveals the common practice of darkening or manipulating the complexion of various white stars and celebrities,[21] to enable them to play mixed-raced characters (i.e., white stars Anthony Quinn, Elvis Presley, Audrey Hepburn, Jennifer Jones, Eli Wallach, and Natalie Wood). African American actors were also required to alter their complexions with makeup. Fredi Washington was required to darken her skin for the role of Udine in *Emperor Jones* (1933) so that audiences would not mistake her for white and think Paul Robeson was embracing a white woman. Nina May McKinney, Dorothy Dandridge, Lena Horne, and many others were forced to darken their complexions for various roles. The salient difference between blacks and whites altering their complexions is this: whereas white actors altered their complexions to broaden career opportunities and portray mixed-race characters or other races, black women were usually instructed to darken their skin so as not to be mistaken for white and thereby violate the miscegenation taboo, even after the Hays Code was defunct. Furthermore, darker-skinned characters—whether portrayed by blacks or whites—were often the nefarious, tragic, or untrustworthy evildoers in the picture.

Colorism exists today not only as a vestige of an ignominious American past, but as a quotidian practice in the present. Just below the threshold of consciousness, it lingers as a ubiquitous part of the transnational imaginary, omnipresent yet naturalized almost to the point of imperceptibility. Nowhere is this more evident than in the visual culture of mainstream American cinema, where the semiotic construction of good and evil has been given a particular color or hue. In the imaginary reel world, where desirability and sexuality are socially constructed by dominant culture, it is inevitable that commercial cinema will reflect the American racial hierarchy in the selection of signifiers.

Richard Dyer articulates a similar point in his seminal study of the representation of white people in Western culture. Examining photography and film, he critiques movie lighting conventions as part of a larger ideological system of communicating and inculcating values, beliefs, and codes of behavior that are integrated into institutional structures of the larger society. Dyer describes the use of light in the process of constructing images of white women in cinema. White women in film, he argues, are typically bathed in, and permeated by, light. The connotations of light and dark are unmistakable: their luminescence emphasizes virtue and desirability. For example, the southern U.S. ideal of womanhood intensified in the period after the Civil War. The celebration of the Victorian virgin in the cinema with stars Lillian Gish and Mary Pickford was part of a bid for the respectability of cinema as a medium. "The white woman as angel was in these contexts both the symbol of white virtuousness and the last word in the claim that what made whites special as a race was their non-physical, spiritual, ethereal qualities."[22]

Dyer's argument becomes more convincing when paralleled with empirical evidence provided by anthropologists Catherine Lutz and Jane Collins in their study of the semiotics of race, gender, and nationality in photography.[23] As a consequence of this shared visual vernacular, or collective semiotic, contemporary actresses of color (e.g., Asians, African Americans, Hispanics, and Indians) still contend with idealized constructions of white femininity upheld by the culture industries as the standard. Consequently, most film roles are still envisioned with white actresses in mind. Halle Berry, however, is one of the few African American actresses to cross the proverbial color line without adversely affecting her celebrity or alienating her fan base.

In the African American community, color preference subsided with the Black Pride, Black Power, and Black Arts movements of the 1960s. Many African Americans jettisoned hegemonic beauty standards. But the cultural revolution was uneven, incomplete, and unable to withstand what Cornel West has described as "racist bombardment at the level of aesthetics." In the multiracial, multicultural, and transnational new millennium, contemporary media (film, television, video, music, Internet)—and, by extension, society at large—embrace a wider range of corporeal schemas and skin complexions as physically attractive, sexually desirable, commercially marketable, and professionally promotable. In film, however, including African American–directed cinema, color has had an impact on casting. The impact of race and colorism on casting specifically, and filmmaking generally, has been important enough for various directors of color to address in silent films like those by Oscar Micheaux; in more recent comedies like *Hollywood Shuffle* (Robert Townsend, 1987), *School Daze* (Spike Lee, 1988), and *Mississippi Masala* (Mira Nair, 1991); and in progressive documentaries like *Coffee Colored Children* (Ngozi Onwurah, 1988) and *A Question of Color* (Kathe Sandler, 1992).

Physical appearance is an essential part of any celebrity's commercial appeal and mainstream marketability. The body is an especially loaded symbol in the overall structure of representation that serves to organize society.[24] Yet racism and colorism—because they are peripheral to majority discourse—are aspects of the commercial star system that celebrity biographers, entertainment journalists, and even film scholars circumvent. Acknowledging the impact of racism and colorism on the culture of celebrity requires also acknowledging that star charisma is not necessarily innate. Charisma (in its various forms as strength, beauty, wit, sex appeal, athleticism, and catharsis) is as manufactured by the culture industries as it is intrinsic to the individual.

By considering the physical body one of the categories constituting Berry's star persona, we can contextualize her celebrity as a social phenomenon. The body constitutes part of the star's idiolect: his or her unique set of performance traits.[25] In scrutinizing the body as polysemic signifier, we can appreciate how Berry has utilized, benefited from, and been disadvantaged by the Eurocentrism of an American racial hierarchy that places Euro-Americans at the top, Asian and Hispanic Americans in the middle, and African and Arab Americans at the bottom.

While her biraciality has been a component of her privilege and resultant marketability, Berry has also been subjected to racism and color prejudice—personally and professionally. For example, she's been rejected for roles because she was considered "too dark." Berry is unlike some actresses (i.e., Fredi Washington, Jennifer Beals, Lonette McGee, and Katherine McGee, or Latina stars like Jennifer Lopez, Eva Mendes, Kate del Castillo, and Sofia Vergara) who can pass for European. Like Dandridge before her, she's in a unique position.

Berry's iconicity fills a specific demographic niche. As a biracial woman, she subverts conventional racial categories designated by modernity and the racial state. Neither black nor white, neither dark nor light, she is bronzed beauty, a woman whose coffee-complexioned biraciality facilitates her marketability as multiracial celebrity sign that can be packaged, commodified, and sold to a transracial demographic of media consumers (i.e., African American, biracial American, Afro-Hispanic American, and even white American). She represents the newer brand of pop idols: those whose physicality articulates the instability, mutability, and flexibility of racial categories in an era of increased interracial marriage, global multiculturalism, and transnational migrancy. As P. David Marshall notes, celebrities represent subject positions that audiences can adopt or adapt in their formation of social identities. Each celebrity represents a complex form of audience subjectivity that, when placed within a system of celebrities, provides the ground on which distinctions, differences, and oppositions are played out.[26] Marshall's comment was echoed eight years later (with nuanced specificity) by Mary

Beltrán. According to Beltrán, the new ethnically ambiguous protagonist embodies contemporary concerns regarding ethnicity and race relations with respect to the nation's burgeoning cultural creolization and multiethnic population.[27]

Statistics on shifting demographics portend the continued mixing or creolization of American society.[28] In popular culture, increasing numbers of artists and entertainers embody the demographic trend toward amalgamation. That's because from 1970 to 1997, the number of multiracial children quadrupled to more than 2 million. "Between 1990 and 2000, the Census revealed the white U.S. population decreased from 76 percent to 69 percent. By 2050, half the United States' population will be classified as something other than white. In fact, non-Latino whites already make up less than half of the total population of 48 major cities, including San Diego, Boston and Philadelphia. Non-Hispanic whites already are a minority in the entire state of California."[29] In Colorado, for example, young people were the largest age group describing themselves as multiracial in the 2000 census. In 2002, African Americans made up 13.1 percent of the U.S. population and Hispanics 13.4 percent. Both groups are growing, but the Latino population, boosted by high immigration rates, is growing considerably faster. Attracting less attention are the countless encounters, interactions, and intermarriages that take place every day as African Americans and Latinos, among others, live and work together in urban and rural areas. Increasingly, the U.S. is a nation of color.[30]

The growing number of young celebrities and public personalities who either genotypically identify as biracial or phenotypically appear racially mixed is both a reflection of and a response to shifting demographics and their concomitant effect on popular culture (i.e., Jessica Alba, Lisa Bonet, Rosie Perez, Jennifer Beals, Veronica Webb, Vin Diesel, Rosario Dawson, Mariah Carey, Beyoncé Knowles, Thandie Newton, Lenny Kravitz, Nicole Ari Parker, Boris Kodjoe, Alicia Keys, Shemar Moore, Tracee Ellis Ross). It is not clear that they all have equal access to portray characters of various ethnicities the way—for example—Vin Diesel does. "In what seems to be Hollywood's version of the 'one-drop rule,' the majority of these multicultural actors (who are part African American) play African American characters rather than different ethnicities."[31] Even Halle Berry plays African American characters most of the time. But the fact that she has been routinely offered a range of scripts and characters across the racial spectrum, including racially unidentified characters (as in *The Rich Man's Wife*), is a consequence of shifting demographics that have resulted in the creolization of the population.

The trend of utilizing bifurcated subjects to reflect the growing multieth-nicity of the national community extends beyond commercial cinema and into advertising, music, and television. In the music industry, multiraciality is evident in the mixed-race girl bands like the Spice Girls or the Pussycat Dolls[32] and the "not-quite-white" boy bands like the Backstreet Boys, 'N Sync, and 98 Degrees. On one hand, these groups epitomize a "we-are-the-world" approach to pop music celebrity, literally and figuratively celebrating racial harmony. On the other hand, these musical groups conform to the logic of dominant culture by suggesting—in typical United Colors of Benetton iconography—that the racial differences of (these) women are there for com-mercial consumption.

Mainstream network news is also following suit by employing a growing number of hosts and news anchors who—phenotypically speaking—defy unequivocal racial categorization. These new faces respond to the growing demand for multicultural transnationality in visual mediascapes. Talented women like Soledad O'Brien, the Cuban Australian *American Morning* host; ABC anchor Liz Cho, who is of Korean and Jewish descent; White House correspondent Suzanne Malveaux; MSNBC's anchor Alison Stewart; CNN anchor Adaora Udoji; and *Good Morning America* anchor Marysol Castro exemplify this point. These women typify mainstream and corporate media's recognition of demographic shifts and enable broadcast television to present faces reflecting multiethnic creolization.

Halle Berry has succeeded where countless other actresses struggled—in part—because the demographics of the media marketplace are changing society. In seeking to reach ever-larger segments of the commercial market, the film industry is gradually reflecting and incorporating these demographic changes. In the 1950s, Dorothy Dandridge was a "representative character"[33] because she embodied African American beauty, femininity, and glamour at a moment when these concepts could be marketed to a burgeoning black middle class. Halle Berry is a representative character because—for her generation—she epitomizes the gradual recalibration of dominant beauty standards, a shift in the dominant *norms of attractiveness,* which are beginning to encompass the growing body of Afro-Hispanic and racially mixed media consumers.

Berry is the beneficiary of the longstanding—but recently acknowledged—fascination with racially mixed women whose phenotype appears Brazil-ian, Colombian, Cuban, Dominican, and Puerto Rican rather than Anglo or African American. Her stardom exemplifies what Robert Stam and Ella Shohat have termed "the Brazilianization of American beauty standards." Their phrase describes what journalists and social scientists have described as "the browning of America."[34] Author Richard Rodriguez uses the color brown as a metaphor for interstitial or in-between states of racial identification. Rodriguez's intellectual project—like that of colleagues Marta Tienda and Faith Mitchell—is to deconstruct the essentialism of Hispanic and Latino identity and propose a radical rethinking of Hispanicity that incorporates the ethnic diversity, cultural syncretism, and physical phenotypes thusly labeled. He writes: "my . . . eye sees only diversity among the millions of people who call themselves Hispanic." Brazilians, for example, do not consider themselves Hispanic, since they speak Portuguese rather than Spanish, a characteristic that many consider the quintessence of Hispanicity. But in the U.S. context—whether erroneously or not—they are considered Hispanic. It's Latin America, according to Rodriguez, that's giving the United States a more playful notion of race, as the bloodlines become diluted and even the markers of race begin to blur.[35]

Nowhere is the playfulness around the race more comically displayed than in Tony Scott's film *Domino* (2005), when Mo'Nique's character Lateesha Rodriguez introduces the new identity categories "Blactino," "Hispasian," "Koreapanic," and "Chinegro" as part of her "Mixed Race Category Flow Chart" on the *Jerry Springer Show*. *Domino's* short TV sequence demonstrates the absurdity of racial nomenclature and census categories and reveals that the contest for control over the discourse has devolved into fodder for gladiator theatrics in lowbrow talk television.

The "browning of America" is a result of immigration and intermarriage. Trends in Massachusetts demonstrate that this demographic sea change is not solely a West Coast or border-state phenomenon and provide one example. Brazilians made up the single largest group of immigrants to Massachusetts from 2000 to 2003, accounting for one out of five newcomers, according to a report released in 2005 by Mass Inc, a nonprofit public-policy think tank. Brazilians overall made up 19 percent of the 115,482 new immigrants to Massachusetts during that period. These numbers are not surprising given the poor economic conditions in Brazil, South America's largest and most populated country with nearly 186 million people—many of African descent.[36] In Midwestern states like Tennessee the trend is similar. "The country-music capital has rapidly morphed into what one *Nation* journalist dubbed 'a new Ellis Island,' the unlikely symbol of America's biggest refugee and immigrant resettlement since the Industrial Revolution." For more than a decade, most immigrants have been bypassing traditional urban destinations in favor of Middle American towns and cities, where jobs are available and unemployment is scant.[37]

The National Latino Media Coalition's 2004 "Latino Television Study" stated the U.S. Latino presence at 39 million, with an estimated buying power of $653 billion. If statistics are useful indicators, then the burgeoning youth-dominant Latino demographic is underserved and underrepresented in television and cinema despite strides made by networks in the last five years. The Latino/Hispanic overall role share in 2004 inched up to 5.5 percent, scraping close to the historic high of 6 percent in 2002. Given that the current U.S. Latino population represents 14 percent of the country, domestic film and TV have some ways to go before they accurately reflect demographic reality in the United States.[38] This is not to propose that Latin American countries have achieved proportional representation. Nor is it to suggest that Latin America is free of discrimination. Brazil, for example, has the largest proportion by population of people of African descent outside of Africa, but African Brazilians are underrepresented on Brazilian TV and film, with black actors mostly limited to rare supporting roles.[39]

Even Brazilian Jim Crowism periodically raises its ugly head high enough to register on the international radar screen. Brazil's Rio de Janeiro was recently the subject of an article addressing de facto color discrimination on the country's legendary beaches. In the Brazilian imagination, the beach has traditionally been regarded as the great leveler, the place where the general, the teacher, the politician, the millionaire, and the poor student were all equal, says Roberto da Matta, an anthropologist and newspaper columnist. But in Brazil's postcard city, according to Larry Rohter, "the hierarchy in which both class and skin color play a part is clear to all." The beaches facing the ocean in elite neighborhoods on the south side and those who frequent them rank higher than those on the north side, fronting the polluted Guanabara Bay.[40] Rohter's discussion is a reminder that issues of race, class, color, economic opportunity, and de facto segregation are present in Latin American countries, as well. In both Brazil and the United States there is an ongoing struggle for inclusion.

The question behind the U.S. numbers is whether the numerical ascendance of one group necessarily means the decline of the other—whether there is as much natural competition as grounds for alliance. Hispanics generally favor fewer restrictions on immigration. Some African Americans are concerned that more immigrants will compete for the same jobs.[41] Conversely, many African Americans support immigrant rights, and some Hispanics favor stricter regulations. In commercial cinema there is evidence that some competition exists between Blacks and Latinos, but the ramifications are unclear.

In a *Newsweek* article titled "Why Can't a Black Actress Play the Girlfriend?" Allison Samuels noted examples of Hispanic American actresses eclipsing their African American sisters. Samuels claimed that Hollywood's multicultural casting broadens the appeal of its pictures and is meant to reflect—even flatter—a society that increasingly sees itself as multicultural and racially mixed. But she questions whether this reflects reality. "No right-minded person wants to see Hollywood re-segregated," writes Samuels. "On the other hand, there's something strange going on in such films as the Will Smith blockbuster *Hitch*. These days African American leading men tend to be cast opposite Latinas instead of black actresses. In Smith's case, it's Cuban-American Eva Mendes; in *Drumline* (2002) it was Dominican beauty Zoë Saldaña, and in *Honey* (2003) it was the Mexican-French-Dane ingénue Jessica Alba."[42]

To Samuels' list I would add Eva Mendes in *Training Day* (2001) as Denzel Washington's "baby mama"; Rosario Dawson opposite Will Smith in *Men in Black II* (2002); Dominican Dania Ramirez as a sweet teen in *Fat Albert* (2004); Portuguese beauty Lisa Marcos as the fertile other woman in *Diary of a Mad Black Woman* (2005); Italian American Jennifer Esposito playing Don Cheadle's "partner" in *Crash* (2005); Colombian beauty Sofia Vergara as Tyrese's lady love in John Singleton's *Four Brothers* (2005); the two female leads in *I Am Legend* (2007), Brazilian beauty Alice Braga and Cherokee–Italian–African American actress Salli Richardson; and Dawson in *Seven Pounds* (2008), again, opposite Smith.

There is certainly nothing wrong with Latinas, biracial women, or white actresses playing the love interests of African American characters. In point of fact, such couplings reflect the changing demographics and configuration of American relationships as they become increasingly interracial, international, and crosscultural. These screen couplings reveal concomitant shifts in the marriage marketplace. Women of color are also marrying and mating outside their race in increasing numbers. However, these casting choices raise questions of access to acting opportunities for African American actresses, particularly those who have overcome the stereotypes of black women as domineering, hostile, unfeminine, and undesirable mates.

To his credit, Spike Lee has cultivated African American talent and launched the careers of Hispanic American actors and actresses in the process. He featured Rosie Perez in *Do the Right Thing* and Rosario Dawson[43] in *He Got Game* and *25th Hour*. Ever since the release of *Do the Right Thing*, the trend of interracial relationship casting has gained momentum, but almost exclusively within ethnic communities. As Allison Samuels notes, this is not true of ethnic-white interracial couplings in Hollywood features:

Apparently Hollywood doesn't think America is ready for Mos Def and Kate Hudson heating up the screen. But out in the real America, more black men are married to white women than to Latinas and the conventional wisdom is, as actress Nia Long puts it, "two black characters equals a black film and not just a movie about two people." Hispanics are now the largest American minority group: business-wise it's a no-brainer . . . But it's tough on African-American actresses and on Hispanic actors. Nia Long says Smith has called her several times about roles, though not for *Hitch*. "If we can't play the girl-friend, then Hollywood has to figure out what to do with us." Even Mendes herself thinks it's odd. Why is she considered too dark to be paired with a white lead but just right for an African American? "I don't even know what to say about it anymore," Mendes told *Newsweek* in an interview before the movie opened. "Certainly I've benefited, because I've got to work with Ice Cube, Denzel and Will. But it's lame. I wish the mentality wasn't so closed. We don't know what to say either, except that in Hollywood, Hollywood is a work in progress."[44]

Though Eva Mendes did not immediately cross over into mainstream romantic roles, Puerto Rican actresses Rosie Perez (i.e., *White Men Can't Jump*) and Jennifer Lopez did (i.e., *U-Turn*, 1997; *Out of Sight*, 1998; *The Wedding Planner*, 2001; *Maid in Manhattan*, 2002; *Enough*, 2002; *Gigli*, 2003; *Monster-in-Law*, 2005). Lopez and Perez are atypical but share career beginnings as cast members of the TV variety show *In Living Color*. Lopez's precinematic success as a "Fly Girl" dancer on television, and later as a recording artist, facilitated her marketability in mainstream pictures. Rosie Perez was a choreographer before Lee cast her. These women had access to roles typically reserved for white actresses. As Mary Beltrán has aptly observed, scholarship on the dynamics and politics of Latino celebrity reveals the contradictory dynamics and ambivalent role Latinos have historically played in the U.S. racial hierarchy.

However, the ambivalent nature of this role may be changing as the demographic balance shifts. Eva Mendes's observation is correct. This is a moment when the biracial ingénue, the beige or bronzed beauties, and the Latina actresses have increased—albeit uneven—access in Hollywood because they represent a growing segment of the population. Recognizing this gradual but increasing trend contextualizes Halle Berry as a *phenomenon of consumption*. She, like her predecessors and contemporaries, is a commodity to be consumed by the largest reachable market share. Her star appeal to media consumers ought to be understood in terms of her talent and, more pointedly, in terms of the latitude she has in traversing the racial spectrum.

Berry began her public career as a beauty pageant contestant and model, which she has claimed taught her "how to lose without feeling devastated."[45] Her screen debut occurred when she landed a role on the ABC sitcom *Living Dolls*. According to biographer Frank Sanello, she referred to herself as the "token Negro" on a television show with white producers who didn't know how to write dialogue for an African American woman character. But the program enabled her to audition for roles that launched her film career.

Jungle Fever

It is an interesting coincidence that the director responsible for casting Berry in her first major film role also launched the careers of Rosario Dawson and Rosie Perez. Both Berry and Dawson appeared in smaller productions (Dawson in Larry Clark's *kids,* Berry on TV in *Living Dolls*) before Spike Lee cast them in his pictures, but the filmgoing public knew neither well before they landed their first major roles in the 40 Acres and a Mule's productions *Jungle Fever* and *He Got Game,* respectively. Despite initial concern that she was "too beautiful for the role," Lee cast Halle Berry as Vivian, the crack-addicted girlfriend of Samuel L. Jackson's character Gator Purify, brother of protagonist Flipper Purify. This role, writes biographer Sanello, "provided an entrée to the film industry, allowing her to shed her physical self and play a serious character."

The events of Yusef Hawkins's murder inspired Spike Lee to write *Jungle Fever*.[46] The film is about an interracial affair between the upper-middle-class brownstone-dwelling architect Flipper Purify (Wesley Snipes) and his working-class Italian American secretary, Angela Tucci (Annabella Sciorra). These unlikely lovers meet when Angela shows up for temporary employment at the architectural firm where Flipper expects to make partner. Initially, this self-conscious "race man" refuses to work with Angie, having requested an African American secretary. But he reluctantly agrees, and eventually a friendship develops. Working late nights together, Angie and Flipper become closer. One night, when the conversation turns to sex, a passionate affair erupts. Before long, Flipper's fair-skinned African American wife, Drew (Lonette McKee)—who is grappling with her own color issues—learns of the affair, kicks him out, and sinks into her own identity crisis.

Jungle Fever's subplot, involving Gator's and Vivian's drug addiction, presents a critique of the devastating effects of crack cocaine on African American families. The film effectively communicates this message because the performances are so strong. Christopher Farley accurately describes how well Berry performed her role as Vivian. When she first appears, she is seen at Gator's side on an outdoor basketball court late at night. Her eyes are wide, as if she's permanently startled; her movements are quick and jerky, as if she expects attackers to leap out from the shadows. Vivian and Gator launch into an obscenity-laced, drug-fueled argument that proceeds quickly and inaudibly. The indecipherability of their words suggests that they are a pair of doomed souls. *Jungle Fever* is as much about exploring the myths of interracial sex as it is about misdirection. The film seems to be saying that it's absurd for people to be obsessed with interracial sex when real, material problems (i.e., racism, drug addiction, domestic violence, and prostitution) need attention in African American communities.[47]

The portrayal of Vivian remains one of Halle Berry's strongest performances because of the intensity she brought to the character. It marks a moment in her career when the performance was so strong that spectators could suspend disbelief, seeing only Vivian rather than Halle Berry playing a character. The performance was certainly aided by her work with veteran thespian Samuel L. Jackson, who gave the actress a strong character to play off and who reportedly accompanied Berry around New York City to various drug-infested neighborhoods so they could get a feel for the kinds of places their characters were living in.[48]

Released on June 7, 1991, *Jungle Fever* was a modest commercial success by blockbuster standards, grossing $31.7 million in the United States. Since it only cost $14 million to make, it is considered a financial success. Unfortunately, the success of the film was marred by personal tragedy. As Berry biographers Frank Sanello and Christopher Farley noted, a man Berry was dating (and whom she still refuses to identify) injured her, causing 80 percent hearing loss in one ear. Fortunately, she moved on personally and professionally and appeared in two films that year, the romantic comedy *Strictly Business* and a buddy movie titled *The Last Boy Scout.*

In Kevin Hooks's *Strictly Business,* Halle was cast as Natalie, the love interest of Waymon Tinsdale III, an upwardly mobile African American business executive played by handsome heartthrob Joseph C. Phillips. Shot in Manhattan's Harlem neighborhood, it was released on November 8, 1991, to mixed and negative reviews, and it earned only $7.6 million on a budget of $4 million. Not exactly a commercial success, *Strictly Business* was less well received than its predecessor *Coming to America* (John Landis, 1988), which demonstrated the existence of a mass audience for black romantic comedies. However, Landis's 1988 collaboration with Murphy benefited from Murphy's charismatic persona, at its height after *Trading Places* (John Landis, 1983), *Beverly Hills Cop* (Martin Brest, 1984), and *Beverly Hills Cop II* (Tony Scott, 1987).

Berry's next film project—a role in Tony Scott's *The Last Boy Scout*—was also a commercial failure, but for reasons beyond her input or control. *Boy Scout's* story is about burned-out detective Joe Hallenbeck (Bruce Willis) and his partnership with ex–LA Stallions player Jimmy Dix (Damon Wayans). Hallenbeck is hired to protect a stripper named Cory (Halle Berry), who is also Dix's girlfriend. But things go terribly wrong when Cory is executed during a drive-by shooting. Together Hallenbeck and Dix attempt to solve the case. What they discover is deep-seated corruption between a crooked politician and the owner of a pro football team.

The Last Boy Scout was scripted in the tradition of successful interracial buddy films like the *Beverly Hills Cop* movies and the first two *Lethal Weapon* pictures (1987, 1989). But by the time it was released on December 13, 1991, the formula was well worn, and *Boy Scout* did little to improve the existing narrative template. The previous vehicles were successful because the comic banter between male leads (Eddie Murphy and Judge Reinhold in *Beverly Hills Cop,* and Mel Gibson and Danny Glover in *Lethal Weapon*) was biting, if not razor-sharp. The more sensible, levelheaded Reinhold and Glover characters tempered the instability, trickery, and insanity of Murphy and Gibson. But this dynamic was missing from *The Last Boy Scout*. A substantive or memorable role for Halle Berry was also absent. *Boy Scout* earned only $59.5 million on a budget of $70 million, proving a commercial and critical flop. Neither *Strictly Business* nor *The Last Boy Scout* provided much substance for Berry, but her next role would prove an important outing and reinvigorate her career.

Boomerang

The role of Angela Lewis in Paramount's black romantic comedy *Boomerang* was Berry's next major part. This film marks the first time she appeared on the radar screen for many viewers, who would see her as the beautiful newcomer to big-budget, all-black-cast films. A beautiful ingénue, Berry would play opposite one of the most charismatic male stars. Scripted by Barry Blaustein and David Sheffield, *Boomerang* was directed by Reginald Hudlin and produced by Warrington Hudlin. Tall, handsome, and Ivy League educated, the Hudlin Brothers were known as the fraternal team responsible for the enormously popular teen comedy *House Party* (1990). Giving top billing to charismatic Eddie Murphy and sultry Robin Givens, *Boomerang* featured a cornucopia of black talent. The cast included Martin Lawrence, Grace Jones, Geoffrey Holder, Eartha Kitt, Tisha Campbell, and Lela Rochon. According to Warrington Hudlin, Berry was the first to audition for the role of Angela. She gave such a strong reading for the part that Murphy hired her immediately, refusing even to screen other actresses waiting to audition.[49]

Boomerang begins as a story about a player who's about to be played. It opens with the romantic exploits of Marcus Graham (Murphy), a womanizing ad executive employed at the African American advertising firm Chantress. Infamous for breaking women's hearts, Marcus finally meets his match in the ravishing Jacqueline Broyer (Givens), a man-eating cosmetics executive hired as his direct boss after a company merger. A beautiful, bold bombshell, she's got the goods to outdo Marcus in every way. By trampling Marcus's overgrown ego, Jacqueline erodes his confidence until he's so insecure that everything—including his performance at work—begins to suffer. In response, Marcus starts dating Jacqueline's sweet, down-to-earth assistant, Angela Lewis (Berry). Angela's quiet dignity, self-respect, and caring demeanor ultimately disarm Marcus and enable him to see the error of his womanizing ways. When she discovers he's two-timing her with Jacqueline, Angela explodes, calling him a dog and providing a few needed lessons in house training. Eventually, Marcus wants to reconcile and realizes he has to change his ways to win her back.

Throughout the film, Berry is convincing as the kinder, gentler girl next door. In fact, her character Angela is one reason the film's narrative coheres. *Boomerang*'s conventional narrative resolution in the form of heterosexual union hinges on Angela's ability to make you believe the happily-ever-after fairy tale: that a lothario like Marcus would prefer nesting with Angela to casual sex with Jacqueline. Halle Berry's status as a relatively unknown entity helped her credibility in portraying the angelic Angela, an innocent young woman whose very name implies virtue, purity, and wholesomeness. These characteristics enabled her to function as a narrative foil for the sexual cynicism provided by Givens's Jacqueline. After all, Givens's extradiegetic persona included her aura as Mike Tyson's ex-wife. This real-life extracinematic fact gave Givens's Jacqueline a reel-life tough-girl exterior that *Ebony*- and *Jet*-reading spectators would likely take to the cinema with them. Ultimately, *Boomerang* reproduces a conservative narrative of heterosexual union: handsome, eligible bachelors relinquish their playboy freedom only for the sexually guileless and pure at heart.

Ironically, the entertainment value of *Boomerang* derives less from romantic entanglements than from the supporting cast. Chief among them is Eartha Kitt playing Lady Eloise, a sixty-something, sex-starved company figurehead who seduces Murphy's Marcus under the guise of promoting him. Second is Tisha Campbell as Marcus's jilted motor-mouth neighbor who crazily tries to warn women not to sleep with this Don Juan. A young Chris Rock dressed in rainbow colors (resembling TV's Urkel) plays skinny mailroom peon Bony T. Singer. Grace Jones has a role playing herself: an over-the-top diva appropriately named Helen Strangé (read: strange). And there's Martin Lawrence's racial conspiracy theorist, Tyler. One of Marcus's best friends, Tyler finds racism in the most mundane events, including when a Caucasian waitress offers them asparagus "spears" instead of asparagus "tips" as the vegetable du jour. Tyler's explanation of the racist meaning behind billiards is also not to be missed ("It's about the White man's fear of the sexual potency of black balls!").

Eddie Murphy viewed *Boomerang* as a political film. He told the *Los Angeles Times* in 1992 that *Boomerang* is political because it features a black cast yet it's not necessarily about being black, and it cost $40 million.[50] His statement reflects the challenges of producing African American–oriented films that naturalize rather than pathologize black experience like so many 'hood films. Murphy said investors are willing to underwrite ghetto films but reluctant to subsidize projects normalizing black life. Unlike the fantasy feature *Coming to America* (1988)—also scripted by Blaustein and Sheffield—or the quotidian *Strictly Business,* the glittery, retro world of *Boomerang* is populated with black urban professional people as young adults (aka the BUPPY phenomenon). The presentation of upwardly mobile African Americans in mainstream cinema was, and still is, political—or so Murphy maintains.

Released July 1, 1992, the film grossed $70 million domestically and $131 million worldwide. Critically speaking, it was unevenly received. *New York Magazine*'s David Denby said the "situations were so crassly obvious and moralistic that the actors all seem like kids playing at being grown-ups," and he called Hudlin's direction "amateurish."[51] Similarly, *Los Angeles Times* critic Kenneth Turan criticized the film's affirmative-action approach to casting. Ironically, these reviews underscore Eddie Murphy's point: the social sphere of upper-middle-class blacks—albeit humorously depicted in *Boomerang*—is a world unknown to most white critics, who have difficulty believing these enclaves exist. Reviews notwithstanding, the film was a giant step in the right direction for Halle Berry, since it enabled her to shift gears away from the crack addict she had played earlier and expand her screen persona beyond smaller roles in pictures like *The Last Boy Scout.*

More than a success for Berry, *Boomerang* is a Black Entertainment Television (BET) cult classic. A companion picture or semi-sequel to *Coming to America,* it is the pivotal picture that again proved the existence of a market for black romantic comedies, thereby paving the way for *The Inkwell* (1994),

Booty Call (1997), *Love Jones* (1997), *How Stella Got Her Groove Back* (1998), *Woo* (1998), *The Wood* (1999), *The Best Man* (1999), *Love and Basketball* (2000), *Brown Sugar* (2002), and *Deliver Us from Eva* (2003), and nonromantic ensemble comedies like *Friday* (1995), *Next Friday* (2000), *Friday After Next* (2002), *Barbershop* (2002), *Barbershop 2: Back in Business* (2004), *Diary of a Mad Black Woman* (2005), and *Madea's Family Reunion* (2006).

Halle Berry's next role was in not a theatrically released film but in the made-for-TV miniseries *Queen* (John Erman, 1993), a grueling sequel to Alex Haley's *Roots* (Marvin Chomsky and John Erman, 1977) that required her to age several decades and endure months of long days shooting on location. After making *Queen* she would appear in *Father Hood* (Darrell Roodt, 1993) as reporter Kathleen Mercer, in *The Program* (David S. Ward, 1993) as Autumn Haley, in *The Flintstones* (Brian Levant, 1994) as Rosetta Stone, and in the TV movie *Solomon and Sheba* (Robert M. Young, 1995) as Queen Sheba before landing *Losing Isaiah* (1995), a serious, theatrically released drama and a pivotal picture in her catalogue.

Losing Isaiah

Directed by Stephen Gyllenhaal, *Losing Isaiah* struggles to be a complex portrait of the issues involved in transracial adoption. Squeezing crack addiction, prostitution, homelessness, adoption, marital infidelity, twelve-step recovery, and a custody battle into one 111–minute movie would be a challenge for any motion picture. Nonetheless, it marks another one of Berry's stronger, more evenhanded performances and a step away from comedies and toward serious social-problem pictures. Throughout the film she sustains dramatic shifts, changing emotional registers and believably develops four years of maturation in the central character.

Costarring Jessica Lange and Samuel L. Jackson, *Losing Isaiah* tells the story of the eponymous baby boy born addicted to crack cocaine and thereafter accidentally abandoned by his homeless drug-addict mother Khaila Richards (Berry). Shortly after being admitted to the hospital, Isaiah is adopted by white social worker Margaret Lewin (Jessica Lange) and her husband, Charles (David Strathairn). As a family, the Lewins experience some growing pains but ultimately adjust to Isaiah and his special needs. A few years later, Khaila is released from prison and living in an overcrowded apartment in the projects with another single mother, Marie (Joie Lee). When she discovers the baby she never agreed to put up for adoption is still alive, she fights to regain custody.

Khaila's lawyer, Kadar Lewis (Samuel L. Jackson), is a politically motivated attorney who steadfastly opposes the transracial adoption of black children by whites under any circumstances. Khaila's social worker, played by actress Regina Taylor, displays as much Mother Teresa–like patience in her role as Gussie as she did in the 1950s TV drama *I'll Fly Away*. Gussie gently shepherds a lost and confused Khaila from recovery through court battles for custody. When we learn that Charles Lewin is having an extramarital affair, Margaret's emotional dependence on older daughter Hannah (Daisy Eagan) and her tenacious guardianship of new addition Isaiah (played as a three-year old by Marc John Jeffries) comes into clear focus. Despite Margaret's parental devotion (caring diligently for a child born with birth defects), the court grants biological mother Khaila custody. The Lewins' lawyer—who informs them that ideally, black children belong with black families—foreshadows this turn of narrative events.

Losing Isaiah crosscuts between the lives of its two mothers: Margaret and Khaila. This back-and-forth reinforces the abrupt quality of their days once the battle begins. Like the parallel action between parents, the movie continually shifts spectator sympathies, sometimes siding with recovered Khaila (whose struggle to stay clean is given new meaning when she learns her son's alive). Other times it sympathizes with the dedicated Margaret. *Los Angeles Times* staff writer Peter Rainer agrees with this assessment. "Even though the conflict in *Losing Isaiah* is literally black and white, Gyllenhaal and Foner don't stack the deck for either Margaret or Khaila. They give themselves over to the women's competing claims without preconception; they allow each woman her due."[52] Berry and Lange played these roles with a pitch that's neither too shrill nor too dull. But the emotional roller-coaster effect makes an otherwise interesting story somewhat mawkish and—at times—evocative of *Lifetime* television for women.

Isaiah's emotionalism resembles the tone of other films by director Gyllenhaal. His made-for-TV movies, *A Killing in a Small Town* and *Paris Trout* with Barbara Hershey; *Waterland,* with Sinead Cusack; and *A Dangerous Woman,* featuring Debra Winger, are similarly pitched. *Losing Isaiah* positioned Halle Berry well, enabling her to reunite with *Jungle Fever* costar Sam Jackson and introducing her to Jessica Lange. Lange's beginnings as a fashion model enabled the two former beauty queens to bond. Not a major commercial success (earning only $7.6 million on an investment of $17 million) or a critical sensation (opening to mixed reviews), *Isaiah* nonetheless stands out as a significant part of Berry's career trajectory because it allowed her to prove herself as a dramatic actress.

In *The Rich Man's Wife* (1996), playing housewife Josie Potenza, Berry had the rare opportunity to work with female director Amy Holden Jones. Having written screenplays for *Indecent Proposal* and *Mystic Pizza,* Jones was an established screenwriter. The casting decision came easily to Jones, who, according to biographer Frank Sanello, is good friends with Stephen Gyllenhaal. Jones screened *Losing Isaiah* and believed Berry could carry a neo-noir like *The Rich Man's Wife*. Narratively, the film combines the plot of Alfred Hitchcock's *Strangers on a Train* (1953) with a Cinderella story. Halle's Josie is a destitute seventeen-year-old convenience-store clerk. She meets a wealthy older TV executive named Tony Potenza (Christopher McDonald) who sweeps her off her feet.

Seven years later, this Prince Charming has turned into a nasty, abusive drunk who had the foresight to have his young bride sign a prenuptial agreement that leaves her penniless if she divorces him. Having grown accustomed to wealth, and her new boyfriend Jake Golden (Clive Owen), she is not willing to walk away penniless. Over drinks with swarthy stranger Cole Wilson (Peter Greene), Josie reveals her homicidal fantasy about her husband's death, which would free her from the prenuptial agreement and leave her a wealthy widow. Cole agrees to commit the crime, but Josie double-crosses him into also doing the time.

A commercial and critical failure, earning only $8.5 million in the United States, *The Rich Man's Wife* is a noteworthy part of Berry's oeuvre because it is one of the few pictures in which an African American actress plays a "race-neutral" role. In the film, Josie's husband, Tony, is white. Her lover, Jake, is also white. And Cole, the murderer she dupes into killing her husband, is white. Oddly, the narrative makes no mention of Berry's race or of the racial identity of any of its characters. It's not the typical ill-fated interracial love story like *Jungle Fever* (1991), *Zebrahead* (1992), *One False Move* (1992), or *The Bodyguard* (1992), which sought to expose and exploit sexual stereotypes. Nor does it link criminal intentions to any racial signifiers. Instead, it's the kind of race-neutral role ordinarily played by a white actress whose a priori humanity—rather than ethnic identity—has been naturalized by dominant discourses upholding whiteness as normative. Problematically, however, the film's colorblindness actually naturalizes whiteness and the white male gaze by making white people and Berry's ability to blend *the* condition for neutrality.

Given the industry, it is understandable that Berry gleefully told the media, "I got to be colorless for three months and feel what white leading ladies feel every time out." According to biographer Frank Sanello, "Appearing in a colorblind movie may not seem like that big a deal until you learn how sensitized

Halle had become to being rejected for so many jobs just because of the color of her skin." Though Berry is biracial, and thus relatively privileged, she has experienced the insidiousness of a milieu in which the erasure of one's ethnicity is considered a professional perk. The racial politics of *The Rich Man's Wife* would be less skewed if there were a context in which the racial roles could be reversed: where a white woman could be surrounded by black male characters without semiotic hint of their race. Just imagine Julia Roberts or Cameron Diaz saying, "I got to experience what black actresses feel every time out."

In 1997, Halle Berry appeared in Robert Townsend's divas-in-the-hood comedy *B.A.P.S.*, which grossed only $7.2 million domestically. She also appeared in the Charles Burnett–directed "Oprah Winfrey Presents" made-for-TV movie *The Wedding* (1998), based on Dorothy West's renowned novel. *The Wedding* aired February 22 and 23 on ABC. However different *The Wedding* (a prestigious literary adaptation for television) and *B.A.P.S.* (a theatrically released comedy) were, both met with significant criticism. *The Wedding* was criticized for its departure from source material and for not casting an actress who can "pass" for white, since protagonist Shelby Coles does so in the original story. *B.A.P.S.* was widely regarded as shallow, lowbrow comedy that Berry herself disavows. On one occasion she told Roger Ebert she appeared in *B.A.P.S.* because it diverted her attention from the depression over her divorce from David Justice. In another context she described working on the picture as a symptom of her workaholic addiction. Fortunately, Berry would soon appear in a political satire that would have prominent African American authors, literary scholars, and political analysts buzzing.

Bulworth

Released in 1998, *Bulworth* was written, directed, and produced by Oscar-winner and director Warren Beatty. Set in 1996, it stars Beatty as the chronically depressed Senator Jay Billington Bulworth, a liberal California senator forced to adapt to the right-wing politics of the day to retain his Senate seat. Bulworth's true political leanings are disclosed during the film's opening credit sequence, which rolls over photographs of Martin Luther King Jr., Bobby Kennedy, Rosa Parks, and Thurgood Marshall hanging in the senator's office). Depressed by the state of the union, Bulworth puts out a $10 million contract on his own life. In the meantime, he publicizes the ugly backdoor deals struck by fellow politicians. But his fatal plan is complicated when he meets and falls for Nina (Halle Berry), a stunning biracial beauty and lollipop-sucking fly girl from South Central LA.

With a new lease on life, Bulworth leaves political decorum aside and turns his campaign into a rapper's Rabelaisian carnival. Donning a black Kangol and tellin' it like it is, Bulworth transforms himself into a rhyming political pundit whose shtick can only be compared to the antics of comedian Sacha Baron Cohen playing Ali G Indahouse.[53] Bulworth snubs fellow politicians, flouts legal authorities, and overturns established hierarchies, all while eating and drinking insatiably. First he offends the African American congregation of a prominent South Central church by openly admitting that the Democratic Party ignores black voters. "Come on!" he exclaims from the pulpit. "If you don't put down the malt liquor and chicken wings and get behind somebody other than a runningback who stabbed his wife, you're never going to get rid of someone like me!" At his second stop, he casually insults a group of wealthy Jewish Hollywood executives. Along this campaign trail he meets Nina (Halle Berry) and follows her to a nightclub, where he smokes marijuana, fumbles through black vernacular, dances badly, and tries to rap, all in an attempt to impress her. Eventually, it seems to work. He follows her to the dance floor, where a mobile camera encircles Nina and Bulworth as they find their groove. It isn't until later that we learn she's got an ulterior motive for keeping him nearby.

What begins as pithy political satire deflates into a trite, racially essentialist fantasy about the liberating effects of hip-hop on stereotypically uptight white folks. Newly minted rap lyrics are the wrecking ball Bulworth takes to a posh campaign benefit at the Beverly Wilshire Hotel, where he uses rap to riff on the state of the union instead of delivering his scriptwriter's speech. At the podium he rhymes his critique of campaign finance reform, oil-driven Middle East policy, mushrooming health-care costs, and the mistreatment of women. But the rhymes ring hollow, sounding corny rather than catchy, more like mockery and minstrelsy than hip-hop music. At times, *Bulworth* seems embarrassingly puerile, reminiscent of teen pics like *Zebrahead* (Anthony Drazen, 1992), *kids* (Larry Clark, 1995), or *Thirteen* (Catherine Hardwicke, 2003) and foreshadowing the wiggers-gone-wild movies *Black and White* (James Toback, 1999) and *Whiteboyz* (Marc Levin, 1999),[54] all of which tackled white adolescent appropriation of hip-hop culture.

Worse yet, Beatty's Bulworth evokes (whites-in-blackface) minstrelsy. One hallmark of whites performing in blackface was that Caucasian performers could suddenly behave more candidly, acting uninhibited, natural, unreserved, and even sexually liberated. The minstrel overtones present in *Bulworth* might have been mitigated by Beatty's genuine directorial attempts at progressive political commentary. After all, he sprinkled civil-rights leaders throughout the mise-en-scène of the film. Activist and poet laureate Amiri Baraka (aka Leroi Jones) plays a clairvoyant vagabond who utters a near-undecipherable analysis of the political climate. But Baraka's small role in the film (as a soothsayer who encourages Bulworth) adds little depth, dimension, or clarity. His screen time is so limited as to have little or no impact when compared with the narrative and screen time devoted to Bulworth's interracial antics. Apparently, this production hitch was obvious to some of its collaborators. Contributing screenwriter Aaron Sorkin expressed concerned the film would go this route, seeming like a trivialization of rap by a middle-aged white man.[55]

However, there are moments when the film succeeds with a sincere political critique. Berry's Nina delivers a monologue with genuine political content. Sitting in the back seat of a limousine next to Bulworth, she offers the movie's only half-substantive critique of African American disenfranchisement. The senator asks Nina why there are no more black leaders. In a whisper that suggests her intellectualism is also seductive foreplay, she says:

> I think it has more to do with the decimation of the manufacturing base in the urban centers . . . an optimistic energized population throws up optimistic energized leaders. When you shift manufacturing to the Sun Belt and Third World you destroy the blue-collar core of the black activist population. Some people would say the problem is purely cultural. The power of the media is continually controlled by fewer and fewer people. Add to that monopoly a consumer culture based on self-gratification and you're not likely to have a population that wants leadership that calls for self-sacrifice. I'm a materialist at heart. Look at the economic base. High domestic employment means jobs for African Americans. World War II meant *lots* of jobs for black folks. That is what energized the community for the Civil Rights Movement of the 50s and 60s. An energized, hopeful community will not only produce leaders, but—more importantly—it will produce leaders they'll respond to.

Berry's well-scripted monologue is provocatively delivered, making Nina the linchpin holding disparate narrative threads. Addressing urban blight, labor outsourcing, economic reform, and women's liberation, she mesmerizes Bulworth, who has clearly fallen in love. Staying close, Bulworth hides at her family's home from the killer he's contracted. Unbeknownst to him, she's the link in the hit he placed on himself. But this is where the narrative of *Bulworth* derails. Nina's never given any motivation to transition from assassination bait to trigger puller, and then from killer to caregiver. Her changing identities are so confusingly intertwined that audiences never know who Nina is or—barring the moment she witnesses him rescue neighborhood kids from racist white cops—why she falls in love with Bulworth. Moreover, the Berry-Beatty/Nina-Bulworth relationship is implausible at best. They are given too little time to develop a love connection or overcome what would be the experiential gulf between them.

The facile way Nina and Jay Bulworth connect lends credence to the argument that Halle Berry is often cast as the easily acquired sexual object of older white men (i.e., the hardboiled characters of *The Rich Man's Wife*, *Bulworth*, *Swordfish*, and *Monster's Ball*). Some of her African American critics have even called for a boycott of Berry's films, finding them profoundly racially offensive.[56] *Bulworth* could be interpreted as confirming these interpretations, particularly at the moment its genuine political commentary turns farcical. During an on-camera interview, Senator Bulworth proposes interracial sex as the umbrella solution to structured inequality. The answer to inequality, he tells one woman interviewer, is "a voluntary, free-spirited, open-ended program of procreative racial deconstruction . . . everybody needs to fuck everybody else."

Herein is *Bulworth*'s Rabelaisian burlesque of demographic trends. The notion of the "browning of America" emerges once again. According to *Bulworth* screenwriter Aaron Sorkin, "Warren spent many, many hours trying to convince [him] that that's what was actually happening, and even showing [Sorkin] census data about it."[57] In real life, there is more intermarriage. But by making Senator Bulworth's minstrel moment the megaphone through which this message is delivered in the film, the movie trivializes the discourse around economic inequality and inadvertently offends its otherwise progressive audience. Demographic changes may engender cultural changes in representation and alter corporate sponsorship, but there is insufficient evidence these shifts effect government spending on domestic infrastructure.

The disjuncture between nation and cinematic narration is what led Henry Louis Gates Jr. to ask whether *Bulworth* is "a Hollywood film about politics or a political film about Hollywood?" Politicians who pander are—in Beatty's words—"selling tickets." His disenchantment with the Democratic Party mirrors his disenchantment with Hollywood. Beatty was clear about his relationship to the material. "I finally realized," he told Gates, "that if I made a film it was going to be from the point of view of what I am: a depressed Kennedy liberal . . . and a white man." It seems conceivable Warren Beatty intended *Bulworth* as a critique of Clinton's second-term prioritization of popularity (particularly in the black community) over public policy. After all, Clinton was *beloved* enough for literary giant Toni Morrison to dub "Clinton as the

First Black President" in the pages of *The New Yorker* only a few months after Gates's May 11 review of *Bulworth* in the same publication.[58]

Political manifestos and Hollywood metaphors aside, the casting of Halle Berry as Nina articulates the thesis of this chapter. Her extradiegetic iconicity as a biracial woman who identifies as African American enables the diegetic character to function as a polysemic sign. If polysemy is the capacity for every sign to have multiple meanings, then the range of meanings is narrowed down by the context. In the context of *Bulworth,* Berry's Nina is a multilayered signifier. She is a black political activist (she tells Bulworth, "Huey Newton fed the kids on my block!"). She is a biracial woman (Uncle Tyrone reminds Nina about her mother's perilous involvement with white men). She is a bridge between racially polarized constituencies represented by the white political world of Bulworth and the black community of South Central. She becomes the voice of black authenticity (hence her declaration of affection for Bulworth—"You know you my *nigga*").[59] And she is the sexual object and femme-fatale subject (Bulworth's would-be assassin and girlfriend) in a political satire turned inner-city noir. Unfortunately for *Bulworth* as a film, no individual character can credibly shoulder this much narrative responsibility. Warren Beatty's Jay Bulworth may walk off as Nina's "nigga" (or "wigga," for that matter) by the denouement, but her statement is not enough to make Bulworth's black identification credible to movie audiences.

As with other 1990s political satires—the comedy *Bob Roberts* (Tim Robbins, 1992), the fake war film *Wag the Dog* (Barry Levinson, 1997), the real-life parallel *Primary Colors* (Mike Nichols, 1998), the campaign-trail documentary *The War Room* (D. A. Pennabaker, 1993), and even the actual presidential campaigns of Ross Perot (1992, 1996)—there are narrative fissures amid playful parody. Critically, *Bulworth* met with success, scoring high marks with the likes of Stuart Klawans at *The Nation* and Henry Louis Gates at *The New Yorker.* Yet these reviews did little to bolster its box-office performance. *Bulworth* returned a paltry $26 million on a budget of $30 million domestically. Unfortunately, the progressive political intentions of its director required more nuance and sophistication than Warren Beatty anticipated.

For Halle Berry, the quiet dignity of *Introducing Dorothy Dandridge* (1999) and the pyrotechnics of *Swordfish* (Dominic Sena, 2001) would soon follow. With its *Gone in 60 Seconds* director, an $80 million budget, a seasoned cast (including John Travolta, Don Cheadle, Sam Shepard, and Drea de Matteo), and the commercial viability of a techno-thriller bank-heist plot, the film was a recipe for box-office success. Earning only $69 million in theaters, however, *Swordfish* turned out to be a financial failure. Perhaps this failure proves that all the tricks of the trade (i.e., cinematic reflexivity, over-the-top explosives, a flying bus full of hostages, and even a topless Halle Berry) do not a successful movie make if—as one critic riffed—it is "a hodge-podge of mixed parts . . . assembled with no real regard for emotional acuity, focusing instead on maximum sensory impact."[60]

Swordfish

"You know what the problem with Hollywood is?" asks John Travolta's character Gabriel in *Swordfish*'s self-reflexive opening scene. "They make shit." Thus begins the film shot in moody close-up with shifting rack focus. Continuing, Gabriel delivers a derisive monologue on the state of modern movies, culminating in a critique of *Dog Day Afternoon* and Al Pacino's performance. He then steps back into his own hostage drama. Gabriel Shear is not merely an espresso-drinking, Versace-wearing cinephile. He is a maniacal counter-terrorist in the middle of an elaborate bank robbery and hostage crisis. He's holding thirty hostages in a Los Angeles bank, each wrapped with plastic explosives, ball bearings, and electronic detonator collars. When a trigger-happy cop shoots one of the bad guys, a female hostage gets loose and is blown to kingdom come. Filmed in super slow motion—what the makers of *The Matrix* dubbed "bullet time," capable of capturing a bullet in flight—the explosion is stretched over forty-two seconds on screen. We see it as an unbroken panorama of cars and bodies flying through the air, a storm of ball bearings and shattering glass—as if the camera were moving through the explosion, surfing the shock wave.

The footage serving as raw material for the explosion was shot in California over a period of three days, with multiple arrays of more than 180 still cameras firing in programmed sequences. But the task of plotting the sequences, and weaving the bits and pieces into a computer simulated whole, was done by a small Winnipeg-based visual effects company, Frantic Films. Fifteen employees took eight months to compose the shot for Warner Brothers, which spent almost $5 million on the explosion.[61] After opening with a bang, the film then cuts to a flashback occurring four days earlier to establish its narrative and characters.

One of the first characters we meet in *Swordfish* is Halle Berry's Ginger Knowles, Gabriel's seductive and duplicitous girlfriend. Together Ginger and Gabriel have learned that the DEA shut down its network of dummy corporations for laundering drug money code-named Swordfish. In 1986, when Operation Swordfish was terminated, these corporations had generated

$400 million. After fifteen years of compound interest the money swelled to $9.5 billion. To access the money, Gabriel has organized under a covert counterterrorist unit called Black Cell. But the money is locked away behind super-encryption. Gabriel dispatches Ginger to Texas to persuade one of the world's leading computer hackers, Stanley Jobson (Hugh Jackman), to slice into the government mainframes and access the money. Down on his luck, Stanley's motivation is also financial. He cannot afford the legal fees necessary to regain custody of his preteen daughter Holly (Camryn Grimes), currently living with her porn-star mother (Drea de Matteo).

From the outset, there's sexual tension between Halle Berry's Ginger and Hugh Jackman's Stanley. Outfitted in a short, tight red dress, she slinks into his rundown trailer with ten thousand dollars of Gabriel's money, requesting a meeting. In the back room of a trendy nightclub, Stanley meets Gabriel, who stands flanked by hired guns and beautiful women. Testing Stanley's concentration, Gabriel orders Stanley to break the encrypted code. Stanley gains access, proving his intellectual phallus supersedes both sexual arousal and physical fear, and prompting Gabriel to make him an offer he can't refuse. Once in residence at Gabriel's Beverly Hills estate, Stanley learns that Ginger's the ultimate spice girl when she bares her breasts while tanning topless. The exposure takes spectators by surprise, seeming somewhat unmotivated by the narrative.

Berry's topless scene was dubbed "mundane" by critic Mark Olson, who read it as "emblematic of the film's conflicted nature," since it took place "not as part of a steamy love scene but when Stanley asks to borrow Ginger's car keys."[62] Conversely, *Variety*'s Todd McCarthy failed to mention the nudity, probably because toplessness is commonplace in big-budget action features. *McClean's* Brian Johnson remarked on the scene, but only to say that Berry *and* Hugh Jackman looked good with their shirts off. Berry's topless view was marketed as a selling point for the film through "leaked" rumors that she was paid an extra $500,000 for the scene. As far as her critics are concerned, the scene—along with her *Monster's Ball* role—is yet another example of Berry's complicity with the oversexualization of black woman in popular culture. While unmotivated, the scene hardly seems offensive, since it constitutes less exposure than Sharon Stone gave viewers in *Basic Instinct* (Paul Verhoeven, 1992) and less disclosure than myriad celebrities' nude scenes (i.e., Juliette Binoche in *Rendez-vous*, 1985; Uma Thurman in *Dangerous Liaisons*, 1988; Julianne Moore in *Shortcuts*, 1993; Inés Sastre in *Beyond the Clouds*, 1995; Patricia Arquette in *Lost Highway*, 1997; Jennifer Lopez in *U Turn*, 1997; Gwyneth Paltrow in *Shakespeare in Love*, 1998; Angelina Jolie in *Gia*, 1998; Nicole Kidman in *Eyes Wide Shut*, 1999; Katie Holmes in *The*

Gift, 2000; Audrey Tautou in *Le libertin,* 2000; Peta Wilson in *Mercy,* 2000; Monica Bellucci in *Brotherhood of the Wolf,* 2001; Kate Winslet in *Iris,* 2001; Naomi Watts in *Mulholland Drive,* 2001; Maggie Gyllenhaal in *Secretary,* 2002; Frances McDormand in *Laurel Canyon,* 2002; Rosario Dawson in *Alexander,* 2004; Anne Hathaway in *Havoc,* 2005; or Pam Grier in many sexploitation and Blaxploitation films). Unfortunately, it has become commonplace for actresses to comply with the sexist conventions of Hollywood, showing skin as a means of climbing the ladder or staying on top. It may not be admirable, but it comes as no surprise. Berry's complicity with industry expectations may not be commendable, but it is understandable in an industrywide context.

Stanley and Ginger are given another intimate scene, but the second is not as friendly as the first. Returning her car keys, he sneaks into her bedroom, where he catches her off guard and quickly undressing. As she is stripped down to her bra and panties, he notices she is wearing a wire. He asks, "Why are you wearing a wire? Who are you, Ginger?" Under duress she confesses— whether truthfully or not—to being a DEA agent planted to spy on Gabriel, who, at that very moment, walks in on them. He carts Stanley away, taking him off Ginger's hands and into his confidence. In disclosing more about Swordfish to Stanley, we learn of Gabriel's ties to the U.S. government. He's working for Virginia state senator Reisman (Sam Shepard), who, having been contacted by the FBI, wants to terminate their relationship and operation. As chairman of the Joint Subcommittee on Crime, a good old boy like Reisman cannot afford exposure. Defiantly, Gabriel informs the senator he's moving forward with or without him. He proceeds to execute his fascist plan to make the world safe for democracy, bringing spectators to the film's denouement. Jokingly called a "Scientological superman" and a "high-tech Houdini" by critics, John Travolta's Gabriel is hard to take seriously. The role pushes the limits of believability, but he also fails to regain the relaxed performance he delivered in comeback pictures *Pulp Fiction* (1994) and *Face/Off* (1997).

More offensive than the gratuitous nudity is the high-tech lynching of Berry's Ginger near the end of the film. When Stanley double-crosses Gabriel, he strong-arms him by stringing her up by the neck. It is remarkable so few critics commented on this element of the film, mentioning the nudity instead. Perhaps the filmmakers erroneously felt no harm was done in alluding to the history of racist violence. It is the only scene that provides any indirect or visual reference to her racial otherness. For black spectators, this scene—more than any other—requires resistance rather than identification.[63] In a final twist, Gabriel and Ginger are seen together in Monte Carlo, collecting the proceeds from their cyber-heist. Like Pam Grier before her, Berry is playing the phallic femme who walks away with the money and the (maniacal) man in the final reel.

Monster's Ball

Monster's Ball was a critical and commercial success. The film grossed $38 million worldwide on a production budget of $4 million and a print advertising budget of $8 million, tripling its overall budget. However, the film left many members of the African American community—particularly black women—disturbed by its highly implausible message: that an African American woman living in the South could fall in love with the white racist prison guard who supervised her husband's execution.

When *Monster's Ball* begins, we are introduced to the restless Hank Grotowski. A middle-aged widower, he suffers from chronic insomnia, a conditioned response to his duties as an emotionless supervisor of death row detail in a Georgia penitentiary. Unable to sleep but emotionally numb, Hank indulges in his nightly ritual: he settles his upset stomach by driving to the local twenty-four-hour diner, where, greeted by his regular waitress, Lucille (Taylor Simpson), he orders his usual meal of chocolate ice cream and black coffee. Making polite conversation, Lucille asks about Sonny, for whom Hank shows more apathy than concern. The tragedy of their father-son relationship is that despite mutually felt alienation and melancholy, neither can bridge the gulf between them.

The discrepancy between Hank's perception (that Sonny's okay) and the actual pathos of Sonny's life is demonstrated in the next scene, during which Sonny meets the town prostitute, Vera (Amber Rules), in a cheap motel. Waiting for her to arrive, he examines his face in the motel's magnifying mirror. His distorted countenance fills the mise-en-scène as he pauses in forlorn self-reflection. Immediately following their sexual transaction, Sonny's despondent expression returns. He sinks back into his chair, provoking Vera to ask: "What's wrong, hon—you look so sad." Sonny's sadness is one of many ironies in *Monster's Ball,* and his moment of mirrored self-examination establishes reflection and introspection as motifs in the film. It is not simply that characters (mis)recognize themselves in the mirror, seeing an alienated self marked by a Lacanian lack. They are struggling with depression induced by the difference between who they are and who they want to be. In this reflection of a fragmented self, the very notion of a unified, unambiguously gendered subject (i.e., a white heterosexual male) is rendered dubious. Both

Berry's controversial role in the volatile *Monster's Ball* (Marc Forester, 2001) ignited debate over racial stereotypes of black sexuality. The film is the most risqué of her career.

father and son are depicted as brooding, contemplative men for whom the daily performance of masculinity has itself become burdensome.

Sonny's inability to express emotion reveals itself as a patrilineal family trait—a trait linked to their personal brand of masculinity and their professional (multigenerational) commitment to vocation as correction officers. Hank's stoic conduct as an unfeeling executioner mirrors his fatherly demeanor as an indifferent parent. As Sonny's boss *and* father, Hank has made the judicial machinations of the state indistinguishable from Grotowski family tradition (as evidenced by the scrapbook Sonny's grandfather, Buck, keeps). From Sonny, Hank expects flawless performance as an executioner, a sign of Grotowski manhood, and from his friendships, Hank demands racial segregation, since loyalty to family depends upon enforcing the color line. Literally and figuratively, personally and professionally, Sonny—like Hank before him—is gradually being conditioned to the patriarchal Law of the white Southern Father.

Within psychoanalytic discourse, masculinity is irrevocably tied to sexuality. Because the father is an obstacle in the boy's Oedipal desire for the mother, a boy's first emotional experience—following his experience of desire—is fear of the bigger, stronger, more sexually potent father. According to the cultural logic of this model, Sonny's sexuality would resemble his father's. In *Monster's Ball*, Sonny's sexuality does in fact resemble Hank's. Both men have sex with the same prostitute, in the same position, in what appears to be the same motel room. Despite his Oedipal trajectory, Sonny resists identification with his oppressive father. The distorted image of masculine self that Sonny sees in the mirror is, perhaps, cinematically coded in the film script as patrilineal. For instance, the family name Grotowski is doubly endowed with meaning. First, the character name Grotowski—in its homonymic resonance with grotesqueries—indirectly but semiotically suggests that a distorted sense of masculinity is a familial characteristic. Second, the name evokes the legacy of theater director Jerzy Grotowski (a master of modern theater along with Stanislavski, Meyerhold, Artaud, and Brecht), who, in addition to establishing the Polish Laboratory Theater, cultivated a "poor theatre," which eliminated all nonessentials like costumes, sound effects, makeup, sets, and lighting and strictly defined the playing area in an effort to redefine the relation between actors and audience to underscore "self-discovery."

The ultimate indictment of Sonny's splintered manhood comes from Hank, who declares that Sonny is "weak" like his mother (who committed suicide years earlier). This association with the mother emasculates Sonny, because it links him to her maternal hysteria. Hank's accusation unmasks Sonny as a fraud, indicting him for being a man who has not completely separated from the things mothers represent: humiliation, infancy, helplessness, and dependency.[64] This indictment triggers an emotional reaction from the character and cultural associations for the spectator. In traditional Freudian thought, the mother, the womb, and hysteria are inextricably linked. Freud's teacher, the French neurologist Jean Martin Charcot (1824–1893), claimed hysteria was a heredity disposition. In *Monster's Ball*, mother and son ultimately reject the repressive Grotowski family tradition, a rejection that is psychological and physiological (i.e., Sonny involuntarily rejects the authoritarian masculine code of withholding emotion, a code of behavior often endemic to prison culture).

If the penitentiary in the United States was from the onset a system of class control, it was also from the beginning a system of racial control.[65] That the Grotowski family has a history of working as correction officers in Georgia is an important signifier of race and class stratification in *Monster's Ball*. This history is the backdrop informing Buck and Hank's racism, as well as Sonny's rejection of his father's bigotry. The southern postbellum penal system (from which the present-day prison industrial complex derives) cannot be understood without reference to the end of slavery and the transition to free labor. Economic modernization in the New South relied upon penal slavery. For the transitional period from Reconstruction through the 1930s, hybrid forms of capitalist relations made up of relics of slavery were grafted onto developing labor relations. The penal system of convict leasing in the New South was not just a corrupt system of labor recruitment, control, and exploitation; it was also suited to the political economy of a postemancipation society. "From a purely penological point of view," writes Alex Lichtenstein, "the convict lease was a fiscally conservative means of coping with a new burden: ex-slaves were emancipated from the dominion of the slaveholder only to be subject to the authority of the state." Lichtenstein's argument echoes Angela Davis's work on the prison industrial complex.[66] And Davis's work echoes W. E. B. Du Bois's *Black Reconstruction,* in which he condemned the conscious "traffic in crime for deliberate social degradation and private profit in the South." The current rates of racial disproportionality in U.S. imprisonment—and the critical role of the PIC (prison-industrial complex) in sustaining the new global economy[67]—can be understood only against the backdrop of the full historical trajectory of racial domination in the United States.

The impact of massive downsizing in the United States on urban African American and Latino communities was catastrophic in northern cities. Redlining and racist violence kept African Americans, Native Americans, and Latinos out of the 1950s suburbanization drive that allowed many working-class white families to move out of the inner cities, restricting the former to urban ghettos, where they were warehoused with few opportunities for mobility. As job cuts hit these communities, they were devastated by pandemic rates of unemployment, a declining tax base, and resultant cuts in social welfare, education, and medical provision. The result: spiraling rates of poverty, drug addiction, violence, and social dislocation. The scene had therefore been set for the mass criminalization of African Americans, Native Americans, and Latinos.[68]

One political corollary of the convict labor system in the South (and the new criminal-justice system in relation to capital) was the preservation of white supremacy.[69] Whether Swiss film director Marc Forster intended it or not, it is incumbent upon progressive spectators to place the racism and sexism displayed by Hank and Buck (Peter Boyle) into this larger socioeconomic, historical context. The political economy of the South has historically conditioned white men to traffic black bodies through a penal system, thereby creating jobs and stimulating a flailing economy. Signs of this depressed economy are everywhere visualized in the film, including the presence of one homeless demonstrator holding a plaque that reads: "It Must Be Somebody's Fault." And signs of the racially disproportionate rate of the death sentence are in evidence, as well. During a dry run for the execution, a black police officer is obliged to stand in for the prisoner, a morosely ironic plot point that doesn't strike any of the characters as telling[70] but that shouldn't be missed by politically conscious spectators.

The southern political economy, its patriarchal laws, and its concomitant code of racial ethics are evident in the relationship Hank and Sonny establish with inmate Lawrence Musgrove (Sean Puffy Combs), the death row prisoner to whom Leticia is married. Ultimately, the dissimilar ways Hank and Sonny react to Lawrence's sentence reflect the extent to which each man has become inured to the racial and economic order as well as the brutality of capital punishment. Whereas Hank maintains his equanimity, Sonny loses his composure. Oddly enough, Hank is not the only character to withhold emotion with respect to Lawrence's impending sentence. Leticia also appears to negate the finality of the circumstances.

Spectators first meet Leticia (and her son, Tyrell) en route to visit Lawrence hours before his electrocution. For Leticia, visiting the state penitentiary has become another burden, one indistinguishable from her financial and provisional needs. A leaking car radiator, an unaffordable mortgage, and her depressed son reflect Lawrence's inability to be provider, partner, or father. Leticia's despair results from the financial and personal ramifications of her broken relationship with Lawrence. For some black spectators—particularly hip-hop generationers in their twenties and early thirties—Leticia's movement from Lawrence to Hank (chiefly her explicit sexual relations with the older white man) is deeply problematic, primarily because the film too easily forgives his racism, but secondarily because *Monster's Ball* exploits (without contextualizing) the growing gender divide between black men and women.

Author Bakari Kitwana discusses the gender divide among African American hip-hop generationers. The growing gender split is attributable to the increased sexism, misogyny, and patriarchy of rap lyrics; the way some male hip-hop devotees have adopted anti–black woman attitudes espoused on countless rap songs; the unrealistic material expectations of black women; and higher rates of black incarceration and socioeconomic antagonisms, which lead to higher rates of divorce for blacks than whites.[71] This is not to mention that black women have watched successful black men (i.e., athletes, movie stars, entertainers) choose white women as sexual partners, lovers, or trophy wives for decades.[72] Though set in the rural South and removed from urban hip-hop culture, *Monster's Ball* invokes the social dynamic Kitwana identifies through the extracinematic celebrity personae of rap artist and clothing mogul Sean P. Combs, as well as Mos Def. Combs and Def bring the extrafilmic reality of their hip-hop stardom to the screen the same way Berry brings her extratextual status as a former beauty queen. Neither fact has any direct bearing on *Monster's* story, but both impact spectators' decision to see the film. The movie frames the breakdown in Leticia and Lawrence's relationship as a gender divide ("I'm sorry for every time I hurt you," he tells Leticia); it's part of the precondition for Leticia's receptiveness to Hank's advances.

During the family's last visit, Lawrence renounces his criminal legacy and his relationship with Tyrell, telling him: "Remember, you ain't me. You're everything that's good about me. You're the best of who I am." Lawrence's compassionate disavowal of paternal influence inversely reflects Hank's brutal negation of Sonny later in the film when the Grotowski men brawl over Sonny's breakdown at Lawrence's execution. Whereas Lawrence wants Tyrell to escape his legacy of criminality, Hank demands that Sonny conform to an inheritance of disciplinarity.

Guarding Lawrence before the sentence, Sonny sits calmly as the inmate sketches his portrait. During the quietude of this brief exchange, the surveilling gaze is momentarily reversed: Lawrence observes Sonny, capturing his countenance on paper with the steady dexterity of a forensic detective. They view each other not as inmate and guard, guilty versus innocent, black or white, but as individuals. This scene encompasses the neoliberal, nonconformist optimism of *Monster's Ball*. It prefigures the film's naive ethos of "colorblind" interracial relationships that miraculously transcend history without any on-screen discussion or negotiation of race relations. It also prefigures the relationship between Hank and Leticia that will become the center of the film. What makes the exchange between Sonny and Lawrence more credible than the relationship between Hank and Leticia is that the two men are of the same generation—a post–civil rights demographic less emotionally encumbered by the legacy of segregation.

The fleeting exchange between Sonny and Lawrence contributes to Sonny's malaise, preventing him from stoically performing duties at Lawrence's execution. The film's narrative implies that Sonny's compassion for Lawrence is related to his general attitude toward blacks. Unlike his father, Sonny is not overtly racist. After all, Sonny's only friends, Willie and Darryl (actors Charles Cowan and Taylor LaGrange), are the two young sons of a black neighbor. But the kids are frightened off Grotowski land shotgun style when Hank executes Buck's orders to get those "porch monkeys" off his property. This crucial scene establishes the way borders and boundaries are an essential part of maintaining the fixity of identity—in this case white masculinity. As Abby Ferber notes, "the re-establishment of racial boundaries" (in this case the boundaries of the Grotowski homestead) "and the reassertion of a white identity also require the reestablishment of gender boundaries and the reassertion of traditional gender identities."[73] Here, the assertion of white manhood is positioned in opposition to black boyhood, as male identity is made the central project of white supremacist behavior. Mixing with these racial "others" calls Sonny's allegiance to white masculinity into question much like his involuntary reaction to Lawrence's execution.

Walking Lawrence to the electric chair, Sonny buckles and vomits, disrupting Lawrence's last walk and embarrassing his supervisor-father. This loss of self-control is another moment when Sonny fails to maintain physical and personal boundaries. If masculinity depends upon remaining calm and reliable in a crisis (i.e., withholding emotions), then proving you're a man means never revealing involuntary emotions. The inability to maintain a facade and safeguard these boundaries is taken as weakness. Hank knows Sonny is under the scrutiny of other men. In society at large, but in prison culture specifically, a particular brand of masculinity must be performed. In his research on masculinity, Michael Kimmel has argued that "manhood is demonstrated for other men's approval" and that "masculinity is a *homosocial* enactment." He writes: "We test ourselves, perform heroic feats, take enormous risks, all because we want other men to grant us our manhood."[74] Reading the narrative of *Monster's Ball* in light of the literature on the social construction of masculinity (Lehman, 1993 and 2001; Cohan and Hark, 1993; Cohan 1997; Harper, 1998; Bordo, 2000; Deangelis, 2001) enables viewers to access both the text and subtext of the film. Embedded in the subtext of the story is a somber meditation on the relationship between whiteness and heterosexual masculinity. This meditative state is given temporal expression in film's slow pacing and physical manifestation in the character Hank.

Given this cultural context, Sonny's loss of control reflects negatively on Hank. Sonny's sickness creates an unbridgeable rift between father and son: it provokes a fistfight and ultimately fuels Sonny's retaliatory suicide. His suicide has multiple meanings: first, it once again links Sonny to feminine hysteria; second, it evinces the depth of his alienation; third, it indicts Hank's neglectful parenting as unrequited parent-child love; and finally, it serves as a full-force rejection of Hank's unjust justice system and accompanying values.

If *Monster's Ball* parallels the two failed father-and-son relationships (Lawrence and Tyrell with Hank and Sonny), then it also parallels the sudden death of two sons. Late one rainy night, a car hits Tyrell as he walks home with Leticia. When the coroner pronounces the boy dead, Leticia is inconsolable. In the absence of any family, friends, or companions, she is comforted by Hank, who drove by minutes after the accident and took them to the hospital. Having recently lost Sonny, Hank provides the emotional support Leticia needs.

On another evening, he drives her home from waitressing. Before dropping her off, Hank explains why he helped her the night Tyrell died. Touched by his honesty and identifying with his admission that he never was a very good parent, Leticia invites Hank inside. They drink Jack Daniels as she slowly unleashes her grief. Mourning while intoxicated, she talks about Lawrence, Tyrell, and motherhood. Lamenting Tyrell's obesity, she says, "He was a good kid . . . but he was so *fat!* I didn't want my baby to be like that. As a black man in America you can't be like that." This scene is one in which race and class are identified as mutually entangled. Here, Leticia expresses anxiety over the socially constructed stigmas attached to race and obesity. In American culture, it is unacceptable to be overweight, since obesity is considered a deviation from the norm. It is even more unacceptable to be heavy *and* black in a society that constructs blackness and fatness as ugly, offensive, and abject.

In her research on obesity and race, Margaret Bass claims: "The nation and the medical profession have determined that what many black folks and poor folks and southerners eat is unhealthy food, food that no one should eat."[75] While Leticia is not fat, spectators understand that her household relies on the kind of unhealthy diet of which Bass speaks. Leticia inadvertently admits as much when she tells Hank that Tyrell would "eat up all the Popeye's chicken before I could get a chance to eat." Tyrell's obesity is a result of his childhood depression and Leticia's incessant verbal abuse, and also a consequence of their socioeconomic status. Similarly, Leticia's alcoholism is a manifestation of her depression. Her child, however, is not only an extension of her body; he is a reflection of her educational background and mothering skills. Just as Sonny's work performance was a reflection on Hank, so Tyrell's fatness was a reflection on Leticia. Hank's nonjudgmental response to Tyrell's obesity (and Leticia's drinking) is tantamount to an acceptance of her failings and foibles, as well as a reminder of his own neglectful parenting.

A precoitus confession turns into a gritty sexual come-on, as an intoxicated Leticia repeatedly groans, "I want you to make me feel *good.*" Images of their frenetic, desperate lovemaking are intercut with images of Leticia's hands reaching to free a caged bird. This use of parallel editing creates a visual metaphor for release from sexual confinement. That Hank is the man who unleashes "Leticia" proves doubly ironic given his former status as a prison guard on "The Row" and, secondly, his own emotional caginess. The film's avian metaphor for freedom resonates with other characters in the film, struggling to escape the personal prisons in which they find themselves. For instance, Sonny lived in the prison of his father's house and the patriarchal legacy of white supremacy maintained by his grandfather. Lawrence lived in the literal prison house of a racist state. Until meeting Leticia, Hank lived inside the shell of his emotional alienation. And Leticia escapes economic entrapment through Hank's goodwill.

Throughout the mise-en-scène of *Monster's Ball* there is ironic play with visual metaphors for freedom and for captivity. At one point, the director brings these contrasting images into dialectical relationship. After visiting Lawrence at the penitentiary, Leticia and Tyrell go home and watch television. They sit quietly watching as a young white woman (with valley-girl cadence) enthusiastically describes sky surfing. "Sky surfing . . . is when you skydive with a board attached to your feet . . . and try to do different maneuvers. A camera flyer flies with a camera on top of their helmet filming the sky surfer . . . and flies interactively with the sky surfer capturing the moves. My camera flyer is my husband: Craig O'Brien. Freefall is usually around 50 seconds. The altitude that we jump from is 12,500 feet."

Following the grainy image of a happy white couple kissing, the film cuts to an image of Lawrence sitting in his cell. As if employing thesis-antithesis dialectical montage, *Monster's Ball* suggests something specific in the juxtaposition of the happily married white sky surfers and the lonely black prison inmate, separated from his family. Whereas Lawrence is captive, motionless and caged, they are flying freely, sailing against the wind current. This disparity expresses the melodrama of subjectivity, marks the privileges of the leisure class, and visualizes the extravagant recreational activities that fill their immense free time. Here the claustrophobic space of the prison is played against the immensity of flying or sky surfing. As the film continues to crosscut between Lawrence being handcuffed and the sky surfers diving, spectators can hear the sound of wind blowing on the television. Director Marc Forster uses the television to issue ironic comment. The commercial for the RE/MAX Real Estate agency encourages TV viewers to sell their homes. This message functions to remind the film's spectators that Leticia is not only incapable of selling her residence, she's losing her home to creditors.

The closest we see Leticia come to the freeing sensations presented by the sky surfers is the liberation she feels in her sexual relationship with Hank. As cathartic as the narrative renders it, their sexual relationship still stands out as a contrived plot point and one of the most implausible aspects of *Monster's Ball*. The notion that a black woman living in the Deep South would have no extended family, community, or network upon which to rely for support is implausible. Even more improbable is the notion that in the absence of such a network she would find solace in the arms of an older white man whose paternal guilt has expediently overturned his racist conditioning. Many black spectators were appalled by this portrayal of black sexuality.

If Leticia is a problematic cinematic character, it is not only because of her facile intimacy with the bigoted Hank. Rather, it is because the narrative of *Monster's Ball* places Leticia (and her son Tyrell) in a socioeconomic vacuum. They exist outside the context of any black institutions: churches, schools, civic groups, or extended family network. This storyline provides no framework for the financial conditions of black underclass life and/or the racial division of labor. It consequently fails to explicate the economic structure of racism and the relationship between slavery and mass incarceration. In the absence of such an explanation, it inadvertently reinforces the stereotype of pathological blackness. Even a conservative sociologist like William Julius Wilson would argue that "when figures of black crime, teenage pregnancy, female-headed families and welfare dependency are released to the public without sufficient explanation, racial stereotypes are reinforced."[76] And, as Wahneema Lubiano suggests, such images surface as manifestations of narrative ideological battle. They present, she writes, "a particular nuanced 'blackness' constructed and strengthened by narratives preexisting in the national historical memory around the 'black lady' and the 'welfare mother.'"[77]

That the film relies on these racial stereotypes is ironic because—to its credit—*Monster's Ball* reveals the relationship between race, gender, and class. The overdetermining economic forces bringing Hank and Leticia into a relationship reveal the narrative link between this triumvirate of identity categories. Even the sex scenes between Hank and Leticia cannot be extricated from the historic and economic conditions that make the relationship possible in the first place. For instance, the narrative literally and figuratively links financial security with sexual activity. After Leticia moves in with Hank, the couple decides to share the same bedroom. During foreplay, Hank tells Leticia, "I wanna take care of you."

"Good," she replies, " . . . because I really need to be taken care of."

This conversation occurs immediately before Hank performs oral sex on Leticia. The double entendre couldn't be clearer. He's taking care of *all* her needs.

In *Monster's Ball* Leticia is not only sexually reckless, she is also economically dependent. Hank's desire for Leticia manifests as economic paternalism. He gives her Sonny's car, moves her when she's evicted, invites her to live with him, and names his newly purchased gas station after her. Because she's in no financial position to refuse Hank's generosity, her (sexual) desire to reciprocate his caretaking is inextricably linked to her monetary needs. Leticia has no choice but to accept the comfort of her chocolate-ice-cream-eating sugar daddy. The consumption of which is itself symbolic for Leticia. She responds in kind, selling her wedding ring to purchase a white Stetson for her chivalrous cowboy. *Monster's Ball* makes an insidious ideological maneuver by allowing its protagonist to atone for his racism (and parental neglect) through the charitable assistance he gives his black girlfriend. The film neatly absolves Hank of his racism, thereby allowing the white theater audience to feel resolution with the denouement. But it's a resolution that's more difficult—perhaps impossible—for black audiences.

Although this movie problematically links Leticia's lustful cravings to her financial circumstances, it salvages her moral fiber by presenting her as a sexually respectable woman. Her brand of womanhood stands in opposition to that of the only other sexually viable woman in the film, Vera. In juxtaposing the white prostitute and black waitress, the film calls attention to the paucity of employment choices/opportunities available to low-skilled women. Clearly, the narrative more readily dismisses Vera's brand of working-poor womanhood, since it is through this black/white contrast that her livelihood seems a preference rather than a consequence of economic opportunity.

As the response to the film demonstrates, multiple and competing readings arise from *Monster's Ball*. Many of these readings are valid given the film's narrative. While I read the text as grappling with gender, race, and class, I view it as ultimately redeeming southern white masculinity through the symbolic reparations Hank makes in Leticia's name (i.e., the gas station). This superficial redemption (which makes sexual partnership its reward) is what angered so many African American viewers. The tumultuous events preceding and following the Academy Awards made the polemics of the film evident.[78]

After *Monster's Ball,* Berry became the first woman to secure successive contracts to play a Bond girl after *Die Another Day* (Lee Tamahori, 2002). She also starred in the gothic ghost story *Gothika* (2003). She has appeared in campy comic book features like *Catwoman* (Mathieu Kassovitz and Thom Oliphant, 2004), for which she received a Razzie (a worst actress prize) at the Golden Raspberry Awards. Since then, she has pursued various films. Despite working in mainstream features, she continues to support smaller TV productions like the African American–directed *Their Eyes Were Watching God* (Darnell Martin, 2005). While a reading of all these films is beyond the scope of this chapter, they all constitute part of her post-Oscar celebrity. Halle Berry is a diva of the silver screen because she successfully negotiates the minefield of an industry that has historically closed its doors to people of color. In the multicultural new millennium, she is a celebrity for a multiracial era.

Notes

Introduction

1. James Baldwin, *The Devil Finds Work* (London: Pan Michael Joseph, 1976).

2. Elaine K. Ginsberg, *Passing and the Fictions of Identity* (Durham, N.C.: Duke University Press, 1996).

3. James Goodwin, *Akira Kurosawa and Intertextual Cinema* (Baltimore, Md.: Johns Hopkins University Press, 1994).

4. The term *culture industry* was coined by Theodor Adorno (1903–69) and Max Horkheimer (1895–1973). They argued that popular culture is like a factory producing standardized cultural goods to manipulate the masses into passivity; the easy pleasures available through consumption of popular culture make people docile and content, no matter how difficult their economic circumstances. Adorno and Horkheimer saw this mass-produced culture as a danger to the more difficult high arts. Culture industries cultivate false needs—that is, needs created and satisfied by capitalism. True needs, in contrast, are freedom, creativity, or genuine happiness. Marcuse was the first to demarcate true needs from false needs.

5. Christopher Lasch, *The Culture of Narcissism: American Life in an Age of Diminishing Expectations* (London: Norton, 1979), 218–21. He writes, "Although it continues to administer American institutions in the interests of private property (corporate property as opposed to entrepreneurial property), it has replaced character building with permissiveness, the cure of souls with the cure of the psyche, blind justice with therapeutic justice."

6. In *The Theory of the Leisure Class* (1899), Veblen asserted that "the upper classes are by custom exempt or excluded from industrial occupations and are reserved for certain employments to which a degree of honor attaches."

7. The ironies of this commercial were reiterated in Kissling's essay. See Elizabeth

Arveda Kissling, "I Don't Have a Great Body, but I Play One on TV: The Celebrity Guide to Fitness and Weight Loss in the United States," *Women's Studies in Communication* 18, no. 2 (Fall 1995): 209–16.

8. Other examples include *Deal or No Deal, The Amazing Race, Eco-Challenge, Pussycat Dolls: The Search, Top Model, Little People, Big World,* and *Are You Smarter Than a 5th Grader?*

9. Examples include Ronald Reagan, Arnold Schwarzenegger, Jesse "The Body" Ventura, Clint Eastwood.

10. Lance Armstrong, David Beckham, Larry Bird, Mia Hamm, Anna Kournikova, Yao Ming, Wayne Gretzky, Michael Jordan, Pelé, Tiger Woods, the Williams sisters.

11. Marilyn Monroe, Elvis, Billie Holliday, John Lennon, Princess Diana, Aaliyah, Kurt Cobain, Michael Jackson, and Anna Nicole Smith are examples.

12. In this case the following programs come to mind: *The Osbournes, Growing Up Gotti, Sons of Hollywood, Gene Simmons Family Jewels, Driving Force, The Real Housewives of Orange County, Playboy's Girls Next Door.*

13. These are the perpetrators of the Long Island Railroad Massacre (1993), the Columbine High School massacre (1999), and the Virginia Tech massacre (2007).

14. Timothy Lenoir, "All But War Is Simulation: The Military-Entertainment Complex," *Configurations* 8, no. 3 (Fall 2000): 289–335. In the 1990s, with the end of the Cold War, came an emphasis on a fiscally efficient military built on sound business practices, with military procurement interfacing seamlessly with industrial manufacturing processes.

15. Tim Lenoir and Henry Lowood's *Theaters of War: The Military-Entertainment Complex* (2002), http://www.stanford.edu/class/sts145/Library/Lenoir-Lowood_ TheatersOfWar.pdf.

16. Karen Grigsby Bates, "Angela Bassett Is *NOT* a Diva," *Essence* 26, no. 8 (December 1995): 78.

17. Hilton Als, "A Crossover Star," *The New Yorker* (April 29, 1996): 132–36.

18. Ibid., 132.

19. Manthia Diawara, "Black Spectatorship: Problems of Identification and Resistance," reprinted in Leo Braudy and Marshall Cohen, eds., *Film Theory and Criticism* (New York: Oxford University Press, 2004), 892–900.

20. For example, there are three full-blown biographies of Dandridge (Earl Mills's *Dorothy Dandridge,* Dandridge's autobiography *Everything and Nothing,* and Donald Bogle's previously mentioned tome).

Chapter 1: Dorothy Dandridge's Erotic Charisma

1. Dwight Ernest Brooks, *Consumer Markets and Consumer Magazines: Black America and the Culture of Consumption, 1920–1960,* PhD dissertation, University of Iowa, 1991.

2. Douglas Miller and Marion Nowak, *The Fifties: The Way We Really Were* (New York: Doubleday, 1977), 7.

3. John D'Emilio and Estelle B. Freedman, *Intimate Matters: A History of Sexuality in America* (New York: Harper and Row, 1988), 309.

4. Ibid., 151. "If there was unhappiness and uncertainty in modern life, wrote Farnham and Lundberg [in *Modern Woman*], it had a sexual reason: modern woman had denied her femininity and her womanly role. Only by accepting her place as wife, mother, homemaker and by erasing her 'masculine-aggressive' outside interests could woman be content."

5. Carroll Parrott Blue, *The Dawn at My Back: Memoir of a Black Texas Upbringing* (Austin: University of Texas Press, 2003), 52.

6. Marjorie Rosen, "Popcorn Venus or How the Movies Have Made Women Smaller than Life," in Patricia Erens, ed., *Sexual Stratagems: The World of Women in Film* (New York: Horizon Press), 26.

7. See Robert Sklar's *Movie-Made America: A Cultural History of American Movies* (New York: Vintage Books, 1975), 269–85. He is among many scholars who've discussed the impact of television and radio on the film industry. He writes: "By 1946, the movie industry had had two decades to worry about the possible effect of competition from commercial home television (the picture tube had been invented in the 1920s)."

8. Rosen writes: "A good many fifties' notions about little girls and burgeoning sexuality were embodied on screen by Sandra Dee. While Dee presented the most passive fluttery pink-and-white-ribbons perfection, her ample mouth recalled the petulance of an adolescent Bardot. By scaling down this image of feline sexuality for the high school set, Dee wove the transition between the fifties' naiveté and the sixties nymphet, exhibiting a provocative self-awareness, almost a fear of her own sexuality."

9. Steven Cohan, *Masked Men: Masculinity and the Movies in the Fifties* (Bloomington: Indiana University Press, 1997), 266.

10. Jackie Stacey, *Star Gazing: Hollywood Cinema and Female Spectatorship* (New York: Routledge, 1994), 205.

11. Interestingly, this is exactly how the *Oprah Winfrey Show* functions fifty years later, as a vehicle through which women are sold various technologies of self-improvement.

12. Adrienne L. McLean, *Being Rita Hayworth: Labor, Identity, and Hollywood Stardom* (New Brunswick, N.J.: Rutgers University Press, 2004), 31–65.

13. This assertion is predicated on Richard Dyer's discussion of Marilyn Monroe in *Heavenly Bodies: Film Stars and Society.* See also Norman Mailer's *Marilyn* (New York: Grosset and Dunlap, 1973); Anthony Summers' *Goddess: The Secret Lives of Marilyn Monroe* (New York: Macmillian, 1985); Robert Slatzer's books *The Life and Curious Death of Marilyn Monroe* (Los Angles: Pinnacle Books, 1974) and *The Marilyn Files* (New York: S.P.I. Books, 1992); Milo Speriglio and Adela Gregory's *Crypt 33: The Saga of Marilyn Monroe: The Final Word* (New York: Birch Lane, 1993); Lenore Canevari, Jeannette Van Wyhe, Christian Dimas, and Rachel Dimas's *The Murder of Marilyn*

Monroe (New York: Carroll and Graf, 1992); and S. Paige Baty's *American Monroe: The Making of the Body Politic* (Berkeley: University of California Press, 1995).

14. A. S. "Doc" Young, "The Life and Death of Dorothy Dandridge," *Sepia* (December 1965): 8–12.

15. Ibid., 8–10.

16. Robert Lightning, "Dorothy Dandridge: Ruminations on Black Stardom," *Cine-ACTION* 44 (July 1997): 32–39.

17. Elizabeth Hadley-Freydberg, "Prostitutes, Concubines, Whores and Bitches: Black and Hispanic Women in Contemporary American Film," in Audrey McCluskey, ed., *Women of Color: Perspectives on Feminism and Identity* (Bloomington: Indiana University Women's Studies Program, 1985), 46–65.

18. This comment comes from one of many interviews I conducted with the spectators who saw Dandridge's movies theaters during the 1950s.

19. Ibid.

20. Joan Nestle, "I Lift My Eyes to the Hill: The Life of Mabel Hampton as Told by a White Woman," in Martin Duberman, ed., *Queer Representations: Reading Lives, Reading Cultures* (New York: New York University Press, 1997), 258–75.

21. Manthia Diawara, "Black Spectatorship: Problems of Identification and Resistance," in *Black American Cinema* (New York: Routledge, 1993), 211.

22. Bogle, *Introducing Dorothy Dandridge,* 288.

23. E. Franklin Frazier, *Black Bourgeoisie* (New York: Simon and Schuster, 1957), 51–54. These figures are based on U.S. Bureau of the Census, 1950, Volume IV. Special Reports, Part 3, Chapter B, Non-white Population by Race. Government printing office, Washington, D.C., 1953, Table 9.

24. Bart Landry, *The New Black Middle Class* (Berkeley: University of California Press, 1987), 79.

25. James Baldwin, *The Devil Finds Work* (New York: Dial Press, 1976).

26. James Baldwin, "*Carmen Jones:* The Dark Is Light Enough," in Lindsay Patterson, ed., *Black Films and Filmmakers: A Comprehensive Anthology from Stereotype to Superhero* (New York: Dodd, Mead, 1975), 93.

27. Baldwin, *The Devil Finds Work,* 100–102.

28. Marguerite H. Rippy, "Commodity, Tragedy, Desire: Female Sexuality and Blackness in the Iconography of Dorothy Dandridge," in Daniel Bernardi, ed., *Classic Hollywood, Classic Whiteness* (Minneapolis: University of Minnesota Press, 2001), 179.

29. My use of this term is informed by Barry King's widely anthologized essay "Articulating Stardom." King discusses the way a star's persona is in and of itself a character, one that transcends placement or containment in a particular narrative. He writes: "The persona, buttressed by discursive practices of publicity, hagiography and by regimes of cosmetic alteration and treatment, is relatively durable and if sedimented in public awareness will tend to survive discrepant casting and performance."

30. Arthur Schweitzer, *The Age of Charisma* (Chicago: Nelson-Hall Press, 1984), 392.

31. Baty's concept of representative characters is derived from a seminal study of American culture by Robert Bellah, Richard Madsen, William Sullivan, Ann Swindler, and Steven Tipton, *Habits of the Heart: Individualism and Commitment in American Life* (Berkeley: University of California Press, 1996), 40.

32. Donald Bogle, *Dorothy Dandridge: A Biography* (New York: Amistad, 1997). His monumental biographical study of Dandridge, to which my work is indebted, makes a persuasive argument for her as the first black movie star.

33. Richard Dyer, *Stars* (London: British Film Institute, 1979), 16.

34. Baty, *American Monroe,* 12.

35. Stacey, *Star Gazing,* 197.

36. "Who Should Play the Tragic Star?" *Ebony* (August 1997): 66–67.

37. See Weber's *Economy and Society* on "The Routinization of Charisma" and Eisenstadt's introduction to *On Charisma and Institution Building.* Eisenstadt summarizes: "The charismatic quality of an individual as perceived by others, or himself, lies in what is thought to be his connection with (including possession by or embedment of) some *very central* feature of man's existence and the cosmos in which he lives. The centrality, coupled with intensity, makes it extraordinary. The centrality is constituted by its formative power in initiating, creating, governing, transforming, maintaining, or destroying what is vital in man's life. That central power has often, in the course of man's existence, been conceived of as God, the ruling power or creator of the universe, or some divine or other transcendent power controlling or markedly influencing human life and the cosmos within which it exists."

38. See the 1950s *Ebony* article "Why Negroes Don't Like Eartha Kitt: Singing Star Has Much-Misunderstood Personality That Irritates Many Fans," *Ebony* (December 1955). In a series of articles in this issue, the unknown authors discuss the fact that Kitt erupted when told she "ought to be more social with other Negroes," and they state that "in many ways, the trouble with Eartha Kitt where Negroes are concerned is simply that she has been a victim of her own indefinitive personality . . . The only unfortunate part about it is that too many Negroes have happened to catch her 'between acts' when her shrewish character is at its ill-mannered best." See also the *Our World* cover story titled "How Evil Is Eartha Kitt?" in which writer David Hepburn defends Kitt and explains her misunderstood and maligned star persona.

39. Donald Bogle, *Dorothy Dandridge: A Biography* (New York: Amistad, 1997), 70. This story was also recounted in the other Dandridge biographies. Earl Mills recounts similarly abusive incidents during which Williams physically abused young Dorothy.

40. This is corroborated in much of the literature on film stars. While no one would make the universal claim that *all* film stars have had traumatic childhoods, there is considerable evidence to suggest that a pattern exists among those who seek and achieve celebrity stardom. For example, see Jib Fowles's *Star Struck: Celebrity*

Performers and the American Public (Washington, D.C.: Smithsonian Institution Press, 1992).

41. The root of the word, *mulatto,* is Spanish, according to Webster, from *mulo,* a mule. The word refers to (1) a person, one of whose parents are Negro and the other Caucasian, or white; and (2) popularly, any person with mixed Negro and Caucasian ancestry. A mule is defined as the offspring of a donkey and a horse, especially the offspring of a jackass and a mare—*mules are usually sterile.* And in biology they are defined as hybrid, especially a sterile hybrid. Given its racist etymology, *mulatto* is construed here as a pejorative term with various literary and cultural association in American society. It has positive connotations in Latin American cultures due to its linguistic relationship to the word *mestizo,* meaning a person of European and American Indian ancestry.

42. Don De Leighbur, "Stardom for Negroes Only," *Philadelphia Tribune,* September 16, 1944. Note: Don De Leighbur was the pseudonym for Dan Burley, managing editor of the *New York Amsterdam News* and widely known as the father of jive talk. He was also an accomplished boogie-woogie pianist.

43. Kathy Russell, Midge Wilson, and Ronald Hall, *The Color Complex: The Politics of Skin Color among African Americans* (New York: Doubleday, 1992), 2, 24–40.

44. James Weldon Johnson, *The Autobiography of an Ex-Colored Man* (New York: Knopf, 1927). He writes that "among Negroes themselves there is the inconsistency of a color question. It existence is rarely admitted and hardly ever mentioned; it may not be too strong a statement to say that the greater portion of the race is unconscious of its influence; yet this influence, though silent, is constant. It is evident most plainly in marriage selection; thus black men generally marry fairer than themselves; while the dark women of stronger mental endowment are often married to light-complexioned men; the effect is a tendency toward lighter complexions . . . Some might claim that this is a tacit admission of colored people among themselves of their own inferiority judged by the color line. I do not think so. What I have termed an inconsistency is, after all, most natural; it is, in fact, a tendency in accordance with what might be called economic necessity. So far as racial differences go, the United States puts a greater premium on color, or better, lack of color, than upon anything else in the world. To paraphrase, 'Have a white skin, and all things else may be added unto you.' I have seen advertisements in newspapers for waiters, bellboys or elevator men, which read, 'Light colored man wanted.' It is this tremendous pressure which the sentiment of the country exerts that is operating on the race. There is involved not only the question of higher opportunity, but often of earning a livelihood; and so I say it is not strange, but a natural tendency. Nor is it any more a sacrifice of self-respect that a black man should give to his children every advantage he can which complexion of the skin carries than that the new or vulgar rich should purchase for their children the advantages which ancestry, aristocracy and social position carry."

45. Bogle, *Introducing Dorothy Dandridge,* 18.

46. Ibid., 415.

47. David Theo Goldberg, *Racist Culture: Philosophy and the Politics of Meaning* (Oxford, UK: Blackwell, 1993). Goldberg's discussion of race and modernity put into perspective the vast philosophical, aesthetic, and cultural depths of racist domination. His discussion offers an explanation of racist ideology informing the philosophical discourses of the Enlightenment. I am not implying Goldberg is first, or chief, among such critical scholars. His predecessors include W. E. B. Du Bois, Aimé Césaire, Albert Memmi, and Frantz Fanon, to name a few.

48. Frantz Fanon was one of the first psychiatrists to articulate a theory (albeit flawed) for the internalization of white beauty standards as a "corporeal schema" among persons of color. See his chapter titled "The Fact of Blackness." He discusses how blacks develop an awareness of the body. He describes black consciousness of the self and body as a negating activity.

49. Russell, Wilson, and Hall, *The Color Complex,* 41.

50. Ella Shohat and Robert Stam, *Unthinking Eurocentrism: Multiculturalism and the New World Border* (New York: Routledge, 1994), 322.

51. Ibid.

52. "Can Dandridge Outshine Lena Horne?" *Our World* (June 1952): 28–32.

53. Robyn Wiegman, "Black Bodies/American Commodities: Gender, Race and the Bourgeois Ideal in Contemporary Film," in Lester Friedman, ed., *Unspeakable Images: Ethnicity and the American Cinema* (Chicago: University of Illinois Press, 1991), 311.

54. Evelyn Higginbotham's "The Politics of Respectability," in *Righteous Discontent: The Women's Movement in the Black Baptist Church, 1880–1920* (Cambridge, Mass.: Harvard University Press, 1994). "The black Baptist women condemned what they perceived to be negative practices and attitudes among their own people. Their assimilationist leanings led to their insistence upon blacks' conformity to the dominant society's norms of manners and morals. Thus, the discourse of respectability disclosed class and status differentiation. The Woman's Convention identified with the black working poor and opposed lower-class idleness and vice on the one hand and opposed high society's hedonism and materialism on the other."

55. Robert Lightning writes: "The political dilemma of the black star acquires a specifically sexual aspect for the female star, the problem being how to remain a viable Hollywood commodity while not reinforcing dominant cultural sexual myths (i.e., the moral laxity and sexual availability of non-white women). The star's commodity status as sex goddess multiplies the opportunity not only for criticism from the various interest groups she serves but potentially provides a unique personal crisis, for she is just as likely to be burdened not only with her own sense of political responsibility and deeply ingrained sense of bourgeois propriety but a specifically *black* bourgeois ideology which dictates its own proprieties for the sexual behavior of black women, particularly in relation to non-black men," p. 35.

56. Arthur Marwick, *Beauty in History: Society, Politics and Personal Appearance: 1500 to the Present* (New York: Thames and Hudson, 1988), 349–50.

57. Dwight Ernest Brooks, *Consumer Markets and Consumer Magazines: Black America and the Culture of Consumption, 1920–1960,* PhD dissertation, University of Iowa, 1991.

58. Marwick, *Beauty in History,* 360–61. Marwick is quoting from *Ebony,* July 1956 and November 1965.

59. Christopher Lasch, *The Culture of Narcissism: American Life in an Age of Diminishing Expectations* (New York: Norton), 72.

60. *Ebony* (September 1954): 100.

61. *Ebony* (December 1955): 24.

62. Louie Robinson, "The Private World of Dorothy Dandridge," *Ebony* (June 1962): 116–21.

63. John Ellis, "Stars as Cinematic Phenomenon," in *Visible Fictions: Cinema, Television, Video* (Boston: Routledge and Kegan Paul, 1982).

64. David Evans, *Sexual Citizenship: The Material Construction of Sexualities* (London: Routledge, 1993), 40.

65. "Negro Market Is Too Large to Offend, Says Columnist," *Ebony* (December 1955), 29. Louella Parsons, by the way, was a journalist who wrote an article on Dandridge for *Cosmopolitan* in December 1954.

66. Frantz Fanon, *Black Skin, White Masks,* 111.

67. Stacey, *Star Gazing,* 206–7. Stacey writes, "The transformation of the body, through consumption, emerged as one of the key consumption practices that connected spectators with their favorite stars. Respondents recognized or desired a particular look or style in their favorite star which they sought to replicate in their own self-image by purchasing certain commodities . . . The whole body of the female star is a commodity, but the parts of her body (hair, legs, face) and the parts of her face (eyes, nose, mouth) and the parts of her eyes (color, lashes, eyebrows) are also commodified. The female star's body is thus infinitely commodifiable, and . . . spectators attached immense significance to particular body parts of Hollywood stars." One of the problems I have with Donald Bogle's careful biography of Dandridge is that he merely reproduces the aura around Dandridge's complexion. He does nothing to deconstruct the fetish of light skin. Light skin is still a highly prized commodity in black communities. This issue is one of the major themes of Spike Lee's film *School Daze.*

68. Stacey also connects Bourdieu's work to the study of spectator consumption. She explains that his notion of "cultural capital" extends beyond the purely economic to include the symbolic meaning of commodities in people's lives. Distinctions in aesthetic tastes define different groups' relationships to cultural commodities.

69. "Can Dandridge Outshine Lena Horne?" *Our World* (June 1952): 28–32.

70. Max Weber, "The Routinization of Charisma," in *Economy and Society,* 246.

71. Kathleen Rowe, *The Unruly Woman: Gender and the Genres of Laughter* (Austin: University of Texas Press, 1995), 8. See also Victor Turner's "Frame, Flow and Reflection: Ritual and Drama as Public Liminality," in Michael Benamou and Charles Caramello, eds., *Performance and Postmodern Culture* (Milwaukee: University of Wisconsin–Milwaukee Press, 1977), 33–55.

72. Lightning, "Dorothy Dandridge: Ruminations," 36.

73. He writes: "In a racially hegemonic society (that is, where relations, both so-cial and deriving from capitalist production, are established along racial lines) the mulatto is mythic symbol of the hopeless division of two cultures: The races *must* be essentially incompatible for the underlying economic and social bases of segregation to remain mystified. She is a figure of taboo or tragedy who operates as a symbol of the costs of interracial engagement."

74. First published in 1845, *Carmen* is a novella about Spanish Gypsy life. Don José, a hot-blooded young corporal in the Spanish cavalry, is ordered to arrest Carmen, a young, flirtatious Gypsy woman. Greatly charmed, José allows her to escape. He deserts the army, kills two men on Carmen's account, and takes up a life as a robber and smuggler. José is insanely jealous of Carmen, who is unfaithful to him. When she refuses to change on his behalf, he kills her and surrenders himself to the authorities. Georges Bizet's well-known opera of the same name is based on this story. The film *Carmen Jones* is based on Bizet's opera.

75. Ray Freiman, *The Samuel Goldwyn Motion Picture Production of Porgy and Bess* (New York: Random House, 1959). Based on the DuBose Heyward novel *Porgy*, the stage play was adapted by Heyward and his wife, playwright Dorothy Heyward. George Gershwin, once he read *Porgy* in 1926, never gave up the idea of making it into an American folk opera. His brother, Ira Gershwin, was the American composer who collaborated with Heyward on the lyrics. In 1930, Gershwin received a commission from the Metropolitan Opera to write a grand opera for them. Mr. Goldwyn's first action, after acquiring the motion picture rights, was to engage New York playwright N. Richard Nash for the task of adapting the work to screen. Goldwyn decided to film the picture in the Academy Award–winning Todd-AO process, with six-track stereophonic sound system, thus providing some of the most technologically sophis-ticated filmmaking techniques of the 1950s. The cameraman was Leon Shamroy. The musical director was André Previn.

76. Baldwin, "*Carmen Jones*: The Dark Is Light Enough," 50.

77. James Standifer, "The Complicated Life of *Porgy and Bess*," *We, the People: Hu-manities Magazine*. Online publication at http://www.neh.fed.us/wtp/neh/articles/ porgy.html. In this article Standifer outlines the history of complaint, controversy, and legal squabbles in which the film has been tied up. He also produced the docu-mentary "*Porgy and Bess*: An American Icon," which aired on PBS.

78. Harold Cruse, *The Crisis of the Negro Intellectual: A Historical Analysis of the Failure of Black Leadership* (New York: Quill, 1984), 100–103.

79. Ibid.

80. Ibid, 102–3. He writes: "It must be criticized from the Negro point of view as the most perfect symbol of the Negro creative artist's cultural denial, degradation, exclusion, exploitation and acceptance of white paternalism. *Porgy and Bess* exempli-fies this peculiarly American cultural pathology, most vividly, most historically, and most completely. It combines the problems of Negro theater, music, acting, writing,

and even dancing, all in one artistic package, for the Negro has expressed whatever creative originality he can lay claim to, in each of the aspects of art. However, Negroes had no part in writing, directing, producing, or staging this folk-opera about Negroes . . . As a symbol of that deeply-ingrained, American cultural paternalism practiced on Negroes ever since the first Southern white man blacked his face, the folk-opera *Porgy and Bess* should be forever banned by all Negro performers in the United States. No Negro singer, actor, or performer should ever submit to a role in this vehicle again."

81. Thomas Cripps, *Making Movies Black: The Hollywood Message Movie from World War II to the Civil Rights Era* (New York: Oxford University Press, 1993), 263.

82. Donald Bogle, *Dorothy Dandridge: A Biography*, 381. The film was to be shot mainly in French. To prepare for the role, Dandridge studied French in Los Angeles and worked on the Riviera with French coach Michel Thomas. Her voice was later dubbed.

Chapter 2: Pam Grier

1. Ward Churchill, *The Cointelpro Papers: Documents from the FBI's Secret Wars against Dissent in the United States* (Boston: Turnaround, 2002). See also Nelson Blackstock, *Cointelpro: The FBI's Secret War on Political Freedoms* (New York: Vintage, 1975). Created for the purpose of monitoring communist activity in the United States, COINTELPRO surveillance encompassed suppressing progressive radical groups like the Black Panther Party.

2. The case originated in Texas in March 1970. It started when a pregnant woman named Norma McCorvey, using the pseudonym "Jane Roe," headed a class-action lawsuit against the state of Texas's anti-abortion laws, claiming that the laws were unconstitutionally vague and abridged her rights under the First, Fourth, Fifth, Ninth, and Fourteenth Amendments to the United States Constitution. Dallas district attorney Henry Wade was the defendant in the case. The trial court denied "Jane Roe" relief, but on appeal the lower court's decision was overturned, and finally it was argued in the Supreme Court on December 13, 1971, and then reargued on October 11, 1972. The court issued its opinion, backed by a 7–2 majority on January 22, 1973, with Justices White and Rehnquist dissenting. On the same day, the same 7–2 majority issued a similar ruling in the lesser-known case of *Doe v. Bolton*, 410 U.S. 179 (1973), involving Georgia's abortion laws.

3. Mark Barringer, "The Anti-War Movement in the United States," *Modern American Poetry* (see Web site www.english.uiuc.edu/maps/vietnam/antiwar.html).

4. See the IFC documentary *A Decade under the Influence: The 70s Films That Changed Everything,* directed by Richard LaGravenese and Ted Demme, 2003.

5. *Baadass Cinema* interview transcript provided by Isaac Julien.

6. Manthia Diawara, "Afro-Kitsch," in *Black Popular Culture: A Project by Michele Wallace* (Seattle: Bay Press, 1992), 285–91.

7. Yvonne Tasker, *Working Girls: Gender and Sexuality in Popular Cinema* (New York: Routledge, 1998), 91.

8. Eric Schaefer, *Bold! Daring! Shocking! True! A History of Exploitation Films, 1919–1959* (Durham, N.C.: Duke University Press, 1999), 17.

9. Rob Latham, "Art, Trash, and Sexploitation: The Aesthetics of 'Le Bad Cinema,'" *Vanishing Point: Studies in Comparative Literature* 1 (1994): 89–99. Published by graduate students in the Department of Comparative Literature, Stanford University.

10. *Cult film* has been defined in various ways. By *cult* I mean movies that were not part of the mainstream during their initial releases or remained fairly anonymous for a significant period of time. The cult reputation is built by word of mouth, enabling the picture to enter popular culture. They are often genre pictures that are too dark, too sexually explicit, or too bizarre for mainstream consumption. Many works gain a cult aura because of anticanonical and extra-industrial forces.

11. In 1971 he took up a position as the first professor of semiotics at Europe's oldest university, the University of Bologna. Here, his theories would really begin to fall in place, and throughout the 1970s he published several books on semiotics. In 1974, Eco organized the first congress of the International Association for Semiotic Studies, and during the closing speech, he summarized the field with the now famous statement that semiotics is "a *scientific attitude,* a critical way of looking at the objects of other sciences." In 1979 Eco edited *A Semiotic Landscape,* a collection of essays that had their origins in the conference. See http://www.themodernword.com/eco/eco_biography.html for additional information.

12. Umberto Eco, "*Casablanca:* Cult Movies and Intertextual Collage," *Substance* 47 (1985): 11.

13. J. P. Telotte, "Beyond All Reason: The Nature of the Cult," in *The Cult Film Experience: Beyond All Reason* (Austin: University of Texas Press, 1991), 9.

14. Pam Cook writes: "The positive-heroine figure as developed here is based on the idea of putting the woman in the man's place. The woman takes on male characteristics, uses male language, male weapons. In their film *Penthesilea* (1974), Laura Mulvey and Peter Wollen show how this image rests on the age-old myth of woman as Amazon queen, a warlike and destructive figure created in man's image, set apart from ordinary women and desirable only in death. Penthesilea's death symbolizes the suppression of female desires at the moment of the institution of patriarchy: the erotic force of the image lies in the threat inherent in it; that those desires will once again rise to the surface, and the female will take the place of the male. Thus while the positive-heroine stereotype rests on the possibility of woman becoming the subject rather than the object of desire, that desire is totally in terms of male phantasies and obsessions."

15. Susan Sontag, "Notes on 'Camp,'" *Partisan Review* 31, no, 4 (Fall 1964): 515–30. Reprinted in Fabio Cleto, ed., *Camp: Queer Aesthetics and the Performing Subject: A Reader* (Ann Arbor: University of Michigan Press, 1999).

16. One way of reading her biographical anecdotes is to view them as part of the manufactured discourse of the celebrity's ordinariness. They align the celebrity with the average citizenry, convincing spectators s/he's a person with whom most Americans can identify. A second way of reading the orchestrated release of these personal stories is as a continual retelling of the "rags-to-riches" Horatio Alger success narrative. Here Grier's anecdote—whether true or not—literally and figuratively narrates her shift from a modest childhood spent in used clothing (read: rags) to a moment of material comfort in adulthood (read: riches) in which she's capable of reflecting on her "modest" beginnings from the vantage point of fairy-tale-like success.

17. "Pam Grier Biography," www.inetworld.net-piranha.bio-hio, accessed May 31, 2000.

18. Production notes and press kit information obtained at the Schomburg Center for Research in Black Culture.

19. Roger Corman was known for his low-budget, highly profitably films, but also for having trained many young filmmakers. In 1955 he made his directorial debut. The formula was simple: quirky characters; offbeat plots; slight social commentary; clever but inexpensive special effects, sets, and cinematography; hungry talent; very small budgets; and breakneck shooting schedules. Once dissatisfied with increasing studio interference in both the content and budgets of his films, Corman decided to start his own company in order to exert total control over his product. Corman demonstrated his Midas touch with New World, which became the largest independent production and distribution company in the United States, and in January 1983 he reportedly sold it for $16.5 million. In addition to successful business ventures, Corman sponsored new directorial talent, producing an impressive roster of directors, including Francis Ford Coppola, Peter Bogdanovich, and Martin Scorsese, to name a few.

20. Gary Morris, "An Introduction to New World Pictures," *Bright Lights* 1, no. 1 (Fall 1979): 22.

21. Baadass Cinema interview transcript provided by Isaac Julien.

22. Homi Bhabha, "The Other Question: The Stereotype and Colonial Discourse," *Screen* 24, no. 4 (1983): 30.

23. Kobena Mercer, *Welcome to the Jungle: New Positions in Black Cultural Studies* (New York: Routledge, 1994), 184. See also Lorraine Gamman and Marja Makinen, *Female Fetishism* (New York: New York University Press, 1994), 14–50.

24. J. Laplanche and J.-B. Pontalis, *The Language of Psychoanalysis,* translated by Donald Nicholson-Smith (New York: Norton, 1973), 312–13.

25. bell hooks, *Feminist Theory: From Margin to Center* (Boston: South End Press, second edition, 2000). See also Michele Wallace, *Black Macho and Myth of the Superwoman* (New York: Verso Classics, second edition, 1999) and Patricia Hill Collins, *Black Feminist Thought: Knowledge, Consciousness and the Politics of Empowerment* (New York: Routledge, second edition, 2000).

26. For Michel Foucault, a "discursive formation" is a group of statements belonging to a single system formation. These statements circulate or exist in a system of

dispersion where there is regularity among elements such as objects, types of statement, concepts, or thematic choices.

27. Angela Davis, *Women, Race and Class* (New York: Vintage Books, 1983), 13. See also Linda Williams's essay "Erotic Thrillers and Rude Women," *Sight and Sound* (July 1993): 12–14.

28. Hazel V. Carby, "White Women Listen! Black Feminism and the Boundaries of Sisterhood," in Houston A. Baker Jr., Manthia Diawara, and Ruth H. Lindeborg, eds., *Black British Cultural Studies,* (Chicago: University of Chicago Press, 1996), 64.

29. Patrick Salvo, "Pam Grier: The Movie Super-sex Goddess Who's Fed Up with Sex and Violence," *Sepia* (February, 1976): 56.

30. Sontag, "Notes on 'Camp,'" 62. Sontag distinguished between *naive* and *deliberate* camp. The former is unintentional, serious in its presentation. The latter is intentional, unserious, parodic and may be referred to as "camping."

31. Linda Williams, *Hard Core: Power, Pleasure, and the Frenzy of the Visible* (Berkeley: University of California Press, 1999), 29. The continuum includes traditional romantic images at one end of the cinematic spectrum (i.e., *Love Story,* 1970; *Endless Love,* 1981; *Sex, Lies, and Videotape,* 1989), explicit sexual activity at the midpoint (i.e., *9½ Weeks,* 1986; *Basic Instinct,* 1992; *Lost Highway,* 1997), and hardcore pornography (i.e., *Deep Throat,* 1972; *Debbie Does Dallas,* 1978; the Afrocentric *Baby Got Back* porn series) at the other end.

32. Suzanna Danuta Walters, "Caged Heat: The (R)evolution of Women-in-Prison Films," in Martha McCaughey and Neal King, eds., *Reel Knockouts: Violent Women in the Movies* (Austin: University of Texas Press, 2001), 106.

33. Ibid., 108.

34. Mary Anne Doane, *Femme Fatales: Feminism, Film Theory and Psychoanalysis* (New York: Routledge, 1991), 1–17.

35. Pamela Robertson, *Guilty Pleasures: Feminist Camp from Mae West to Madonna* (Durham, N.C.: Duke University Press, 1996), 57–84.

36. In an interview Bram Dijkstra said: "In the earlier book, I dealt with the academic art of the late nineteenth century, what was considered high art before the arrival of modernism, and I showed how an increasingly anti-feminine concept of women became popular after the introduction of theories of evolution, and created what I called an 'iconography of misogyny.' That iconography became the basis for a lot of the twentieth century's popular culture."

37. Elaine Shefer, *Birds, Cages and Women in Victorian and Pre-Raphaelite Art* (New York: Peter Lang, 1990), xxiii.

The term *pre-Raphaelite,* which refers to both art and literature, is confusing because there were essentially two different and almost opposed movements, the second of which grew out of the first. The term itself originated in relation to the Pre-Raphaelite Brotherhood, an influential group of mid-nineteenth-century avant-garde painters associated with Ruskin who had great effect upon British, American, and

European art. Those poets who had some connection with these artists and whose work presumably shares the characteristics of their art include Dante Gabriel Rossetti, Christina Rossetti, George Meredith, William Morris, and Algernon Charles Swinburne.

38. Bram Dijkstra, *Idols of Perversity: Fantasies of Feminine Evil in Fin-de-Siècle Culture* (New York: Oxford University Press, 1986), 65–67.

39. For example, Mount Holyoke was founded in 1837; Columbia College was founded in 1854; Vassar College in 1861; Wilson College in 1869; Wellesley College in 1870; Smith College in 1871; Spelman College in 1881; Bryn Mawr College in 1885; and Barnard College in 1889. By 1870, an estimated one-fifth of resident college and university students were women. By 1900, the proportion had increased to more than one-third.

40. Dijkstra, *Idols of Perversity,* 65–67.

41. Ibid., 100–101.

42. See press kit for *The Big Bird Cage,* courtesy of the Schomburg Center for Research in Black Culture.

43. Governor George Wallace's first administration was marked by social tension. Among the major incidents of the administration were racial demonstrations in Birmingham and Montgomery, desegregation of schools in Macon County, his dramatic "stand in the school house door," and the nationally publicized fire hose and police dog incidents of Birmingham.

44. Andrew Ross, *No Respect: Intellectuals and Popular Culture* (New York: Routledge, 1989). Reprinted in Fabio Cleto, ed., *Camp: Queer Aesthetics and the Performing Subject, a Reader* (Ann Arbor: University of Michigan Press, 1999), 324.

45. In the 1920s, films about women in prison began to emerge. The earliest film in this subgenre came in 1922 with *Manslaughter* (Cecil B. DeMille), which looked at the reformation while in prison of a "society-girl thrill-seeker."

46. See press kit courtesy of the Schomburg Center for Research in Black Culture for additional cast and crew information.

47. Carol Clover, *Men, Women and Chainsaws: Gender in the Modern Horror Film* (Princeton, N.J.: Princeton University Press, 1992), 12.

48. Suzanne Pharr, *Homophobia: A Weapon of Sexism* (Inverness, Calif.: Chardon Press, 1988), 27–43.

49. Pam Cook, "'Exploitation' Films and Feminism," *Screen* 17, no. 2 (1976): 124.

50. See the press kit for *Black Mama, White Mama,* courtesy of the Schomburg Center for Research in Black Culture.

51. Jeanine Basinger, *The World War II Combat Film: Anatomy of a Genre* (New York: Columbia University Press, 1986), 57, 160.

52. Clover, *Men, Women and Chainsaws,* 49. Clover writes: "But the 'certain link' that put killer and Final Girl on terms . . . is more than 'sexual repression.' It is also a shared masculinity, materialized in 'all those phallic symbols'—and it is also a shared femininity materialized in what comes next (and what Carpenter, perhaps

significantly, fails to mention): the castration, literal or symbolic, of the killer at her hands. The Final Girl has not just manned herself; she specifically unmans an oppressor whose masculinity was in question to begin with."

53. In 1966, movie theater teasers heralded the release of the bizarrely titled *Faster, Pussycat! Kill! Kill!* It was a black-and-white independent picture that proved to be one of the most popular sexploitation B-films in history, largely due to the memorable character of Varla, the trash classic's reckless lady of sexual abandonment played by stripper Tura Satana. Her character Varla had a pale "Oriental" face and a revved-up engine, and she steamed the scorching California landscape with her uncontrolled antics. Her look was combination of voluptuous boobs and hardbody sinews encased in tight black jeans, a tight black top, black boots, and black racing gloves, and the psychotic murderess's all-consuming passions embroiled her in a win-or-nothing struggle with life. Like Grier after her, she was considered "the baddest bitch of all time!" The Varla who chewed up men for breakfast was not far removed from the Amazonian actress who portrayed her. Tura, her name derived from the Indian word meaning "white flower," was born of Japanese, Filipino, American Indian, and Scots-Irish blood, the second child in a family of one son and four daughters. Growing up in 1940s Chicago, she learned how to deal with bullies in school skirmishes. Tura's father taught her martial arts techniques such as karate and aikido.

54. James Robert Parish and George Hill, *Black Action Films: Plots, Critiques, Casts and Credits for 235 Theatrical and Made-for-Television Releases* (Jefferson, N.C.: McFarland, 1989), 15.

55. See the press kit for *The Arena*, courtesy of the Schomburg Center for Research in Black Culture.

56. See the press kit for *Coffy*, courtesy of the Schomburg Center for Research in Black Culture.

57. Salvo, "Pam Grier," 48–56.

58. Ibid., 52.

59. William L. Van Deburg, *Black Camelot: African-American Culture Heroes in Their Times, 1960–1980* (Chicago: University of Chicago Press, 1997), 135.

60. Paul Kerr, "Out of What Past? Notes on the B Film Noir," *Screen Education* 32–33 (Autumn/Winter 1979). See also Linda Williams, "Erotic Thrillers and Rude Women," *Sight and Sound* (July 1993): 12–14; and Yvonne Tasker, *Working Girls: Gender and Sexuality in Popular Cinema* (London: Routledge, 1998).

61. Clover, *Men, Women, and Chainsaws,"* 20.

62. Fred Botting and Scott Wilson, *The Tarantinian Ethics* (Thousand Oaks, Calif.: Sage, 2001), 154.

63. Benedict Anderson, *Imagined Communities: Reflections on the Origin and Spread of Nationalism* (London: Verso, 1983). See also Homi Bhabha, *Nation and Narration* (London: Routledge, 1990), and Fredric Jameson, "Third-World Literature in the Era of Multinational Capitalism," *Social Text* 15 (Fall 1986): 65–88.

64. *Baadass Cinema* interview transcript provided by Issac Julien.

65. *Black pride* refers to feelings among African Americans toward their African heritage, accomplishments, culture, and contributions as Americans. *Black Power* as a slogan and philosophy grew out of the U.S. civil rights movement. Made famous by Stokely Carmichael (Kwame Toure) in 1966, it was employed by various groups who attached different meanings, ranging from violent revolution and black separatism to maximization of independent political and economic power for black Americans within a community. Black nationalist theory holds that blacks must unite, gain power, and liberate themselves from an oppressive white supremacist society.

66. Manifestations of the *esthétique du cool* in *Coffy* and *Shaft* were a result of a larger cultural movement, which took flight in the 1960s and gained expression in literature, theater, cinema, and fashion. This movement gained formal expression in the notion of a black aesthetic. The black aesthetic, as a central component of black political and cultural empowerment, emerged in the 1960s as the Black Arts Movement came to prominence. Everywhere, throughout the 1960s and 1970s, racial and ethnic communities were in revolt against old authorities and staid conventions. This revolt included jettisoning European beauty conventions. African hairstyles, kente cloth, dashikis, and black vernacular were concomitants of the broader countercultural movement proclaiming Black is Beautiful! The black aesthetic is a way of perceiving the world through the unique experiences of a self-aware African American. It is a way of perceiving form as more than aesthetic beauty. It is also a set of criteria by which readers judge whether a particular work or art is truly "black." According to Hoyt Fuller, the black aesthetic is the realization that after hundreds of years of being told they are not beautiful, black Americans reclaimed their beauty through art. See Addison Gayle's *The Black Aesthetic* (Garden City, N.Y.: Doubleday, 1971). Film scholars Thomas Cripps, Ed Guerrero, Manthia Diawara, and William Van Deburg observed the *esthétique* in Blaxploitation films.

Arthur Marwick, *Beauty in History: Society, Politics, and Personal Appearance, 1500 to the Present* (New York: Thames and Hudson, 1988), 349–50.

67. *Baadass Cinema* interview transcript provided by Issac Julien.

68. Clint Eastwood in *High Plains Drifter* (1973), *Magnum Force* (1973), *Dirty Harry* (1971), *Play Misty for Me* (1971), *Where Eagles Dare* (1969), *Coogan's Bluff* (1968), *Hang 'Em High* (1968), *The Good, the Bad, and the Ugly* (1967), *For a Few Dollars More* (1965), and *A Fistful of Dollars* (1964). Charles Bronson in *Death Wish* (1974) and its sequels. Chuck Norris in *Enter the Dragon* (1973), *Slaughter in San Francisco* (1974), *Breaker! Breaker!* (1977), and *Game of Death* (1978).

69. Umberto Eco, "*Casablanca*: Cult Movies and Intertextual Collage," *Substance* 47 (1985): 5. This is the argument Eco makes for *Casablanca*.

70. Peter Brown was well known as Dr. Greg Peter in the NBC-TV daytime series *Days of Our Lives*. Earlier in his career he also starred in the *Lawman* and *Laredo* television series.

71. Ed Guerrero, *Framing Blackness: The African American Image in Film* (Philadelphia: Temple University Press, 1993), 98–99.

72. The basic story is as follows: Jenny, a New Yorker who goes to a secluded country retreat to finish work on her novel, is one day assaulted, raped, and left for dead by four men. But she survives to take revenge. She seduces each of her rapists separately and she personally performs their painful executions.

73. Parish and Hill, *Black Action Films,* 259.

74. "I'd been jogging that morning and I was almost to the driveway of my house when a couple of cops stopped me and started harassing me. They wondered what a black person was doing in that neighborhood, claiming that I fit the description of someone who'd been reported to be prowling in the area, and nothing I could say would make them believe that this was my house, that I lived here," remembers Pam. "I'd never felt so threatened in my life. They had me put my hands on the garage door and told me to spread my legs, and I'll never forget the sensation of this little bead of sweat rolling down the middle of my back, and how petrified I was that, if I moved or tried to wipe it away with my hand, they'd probably have shot me right then and there. It was only when a neighbor came out to vouch for me that they finally decided to leave me alone. They never apologized for their behavior, though, and the whole experience was enough to open my eyes to the fact that I really didn't want to be there anymore."

75. Brian Lowry, "Showtime Skeds Sex in the Company of Women," *Variety* (January 12–18, 2004): 52.

Chapter 3: Goldberg's Variations on Comedic Charisma

1. Bebe Moore Campbell, "Whoopi Talks B(lack)," *Essence* (January 1997). In this article Campbell quipped that Goldberg was too everything to make it to the Big Time: too dark with hair too nappy, and looks too unconventional.

2. Donald Bogle, *Toms, Coons, Mulattoes, Mammies, and Bucks: An Interpretive History of Blacks in American Films* (New York: Continuum, 2003), 7–9. Historically, "pickaninnies" were called by various names. For example, in the 1920s and the 1930s, child actors Sunshine Sammy, Farina, Stymie, and Buckwheat emerged as variations on the pickaninny theme. In versions of Harriet Beecher Stowe's *Uncle Tom's Cabin,* the slave-child Topsy was presented as a lively pickaninny, used for comic relief. Topsy was clownish and droll yet became such a favorite figure of literature that she starred in *Topsy and Eva* (1927), in which her far-fetched meanderings and her pickaninnying won mass audience approval. See also Cripps, 1976, 1993; Gaines, 1990; Snead, 1994; Taylor 1996.

3. Karen Alexander, "Fatal Beauties," in Christine Gledhill, ed., *Stardom: Industry of Desire* (London: Routledge, 1991), 53.

4. Yvonne Takser, *Spectacular Bodies: Gender, Genre, and the Action Cinema* (London: Routledge, 1993), 33.

5. James Robert Parish, *Whoopi Goldberg: Her Journey from Poverty to Megastardom* (New York: Birch Lane Press, 1997), 66.

6. Lisa Merrill, "Feminist Humor: Rebellious and Self-Affirming," *Women Studies* 15 (1988): 272.

7. Maurice Charney, *Comedy High and Low: An Introduction to the Experience of Comedy* (New York: Oxford University Press, 1978), 69.

8. James Naremore, *Acting in the Cinema* (Berkeley: University of California Press, 1988), 64–65.

9. Martin Grotjahn, *Beyond Laughter: Humor and the Subconscious* (New York: Blakiston Division, McGraw-Hill, 1957), 33.

10. Kathleen Rowe, *The Unruly Woman: Gender and the Genres of Laughter* (Austin: University of Texas Press, 1995).

11. Frantz Fanon, *Black Skin, White Masks* (New York: Grove Press, 1952), 110.

12. Judith Butler, *Bodies That Matter: On the Discursive Limits of "Sex"* (New York: Routledge, 1993), 231.

13. Richard Dyer, *White* (London: Routledge, 1999). See his chapter on the use of cinematography to construct the beauty of white womanhood.

14. Lea DeLaria, "Exclusive Interview: Whoopi Goldberg," *The Advocate*, February 7, 1995.

15. Kim Chernin, *The Obsession: Reflections on the Tyranny of Slenderness* (New York: Harper and Row, 1981). See also Susan Bordo's *Unbearable Weight: Feminism, Western Culture, and the Body* (Berkeley: University of California Press, 1993).

16. Charles Herbert Stember, *Sexual Racism: The Emotional Barrier to an Integrated Society* (New York: Elsevier Scientific, 1976), 121–43.

17. Andrew Horton, ed., *Comedy/Cinema/Theory* (Berkeley: University of California Press, 1991), 12–13.

18. Robert Stam, *Subversive Pleasures: Bakhtin, Cultural Criticism, and Film* (Baltimore, Md.: Johns Hopkins University Press, 1989), 87.

19. Horton, ed., *Comedy/Cinema/Theory,* 10. Horton discusses pre-Oedipal comedy as wish fulfillment, dreams-oriented comedy. When children are in the pre-Oedipal phase they have not yet confronted or resolved their Oedipal conflicts. They have not yet integrated a sense of self with the needs of socialization with others. Pre-Oedipal comedy, which he defines as Aristophanic, is the only pure example of a form of comedy in which wish fulfillment without parental or social hindrance is clearly seen. In most of Aristophanes' surviving comedies, a middle-aged adult goes through three stages: he or she is dissatisfied, dreams up a plans to cure that dissatisfaction, and then carries out that plan to a successful resolution. The final phase is a glorious celebration of the character's success. Horton acknowledges that most screen comedy concerns romance and is therefore Oedipal. Commitment to heterosexual partnerships ultimately means that some Oedipal resolution must emerge.

20. Rowe, *The Unruly Woman,* 43.

21. Ibid., 8. See also Victor Turner's "Frame, Flow, and Reflection: Ritual and Drama as Public Liminality," in Michael Benamou and Charles Caramello, eds., *Performance and Postmodern Culture* (Milwaukee: University of Wisconsin-Milwaukee Press, 1977), 33–55.

22. Rowe, *The Unruly Woman*, 11.

23. Peter Stallybrass and Allon White, *The Politics and Poetics of Transgression* (Ithaca, N.Y.: Cornell University Press, 1986), 8–9.

24. Michael Rogin, *Blackface, White Noise: Jewish Immigrants in the Hollywood Melting Pot* (Berkeley: University of California Press, 1996). See also David Roediger's *The Wages of Whiteness: Race in the Making of the American Working Class* (London: Verso, 1991). Roediger, five years before Rogin, made a persuasive case for the "psychological wage" of whiteness for working-class ethnic immigrants eager to assimilate to white society and distance themselves from African Americans. According to native wisdom, both Jews and the Irish were considered low-browed, savage, bestial, lazy, and simian and were often referred to as "nigger." These are many of the pejorative epithets used against blacks. One of the ways ethnic immigrants distinguished themselves from slaves (and from a black working class) was through minstrelsy. Roediger writes: "In creating a new sense of whiteness by creating a new sense of blackness, minstrel entertainers fashioned a theater in which the rough, the respectable and the rebellious among craft workers could together find solace and even joy. By doing so, the minstrel stage became a truly popular form of entertainment able to attract the immigrants and unskilled of the city while also making special appeals to those in the West and some in the respectable middle classes and above . . . The blackface whiteness that delighted and unified the increasingly wage-earning urban masses was empty of positive content."

25. James Robert Parish, *Whoopi Goldberg: Her Journey from Poverty to Mega-Stardom* (Secaucus, N.J.: Birch Lane Press, 1997), 108. Parish writes: "As Whoopi prepared for her Broadway debut, Mike Nichols and the other backers decided not to call it *The Spook Show*. At first, the producers titled it *Whoopi Goldberg Variations*, then simply *Whoopi Goldberg*, thus avoiding the problem of reviewers and potential patrons dealing with the multilayered meaning of the word 'spook,' which might refer to ghosts, as Goldberg insisted, or to a demeaning slang term referring to African Americans, as others contended. Calling the show *Whoopi Goldberg* would produce a surprise in many less-informed playgoers who thought the show was headlining a white, Jewish comedian in stand-up routines revolving around extremely serious issues. (Ironically, many potential black patrons were still unaware that this strangely named woman was actually a 'sister' and only belatedly became members of her audience.)"

26. Ibid., 168.

27. Christy L. Burns, "Parody and Postmodern Sex: Humor in Thomas Pynchon and Tama Jonowitz," in Shannon Hengen, ed., *Performing Gender and Comedy: Theories, Texts and Contexts* (Amsterdam: Gordon and Breach, 1998), 150.

28. Marianna Torgovnick, *Gone Primitive: Savage Intellects, Modern Lives* (Chicago: University of Chicago Press, 1990), 8.

29. Guy Debord, *Society of the Spectacle* (Paris: Buchet-Chastel, 1967).

30. This is a process by which parts of the middle class become effectively absorbed into the working class. Proletarianization of action must be distinguished

by proletarianization of condition. The latter is determined by market, work, and status considerations. The more closely white-collar workers' pay, holidays, chances of promotion, benefits, and autonomy approach that of manual workers, the more proletarianized they have become.

31. Michele Wallace, *Invisibility Blues: From Pop to Theory* (New York: Verso, 1990), 5.

32. Henry Louis Gates Jr., *The Signifying Monkey: A Theory of African American Literary Criticism* (New York: Oxford University Press, 1988), 78.

33. Parish, *Whoopi Goldberg,* 243.

34. Jerry Palmer, *The Logic of the Absurd: On Film and Television Comedy* (London: British Film Comedy, 1987), 39. In classical aesthetics the *peripeteia* is the moment when the fortunes of the principal character are reversed. The example Aristotle gives is that of Oedipus in Sophocles' eponymous tragedy: Oedipus is eventually forced to recognize that Tiresias has seen the situation correctly and that he himself has in fact murdered his father and married his mother in exactly the way the prophecy foretold. Palmer uses the term *peripetieia* on the grounds that this form of surprise is constructed in the film narrative and is thus a specifically aesthetic form of surprise. I use it here to mean both the form of comic surprise and the reversal of fortune for the protagonist.

35. Dyer, *White,* 17.

36. Horace Clarence Boyer, "Contemporary Gospel Music: Sacred or Secular?" *The Black Perspective in Music* 1, no. 7 (Spring 1979): 5–35.

37. Stam, *Subversive Pleasures,* 99. I am paraphrasing Stam's discussion of marginal art and its relationship to dominant culture.

38. Peter Stallybrass and Allon White, *The Politics and Poetics of Transgression* (Ithaca, N.Y.: Cornell University Press, 1986), 8, 58.

39. Stam, *Subversive Pleasures,* 89. Nietzsche as quoted by Stam.

40. Richard Dyer, "Entertainment and Utopia," *Movie* 24 (Spring 1977). Reprinted in Bill Nichols, ed., *Movies and Methods: Volume II* (Berkeley: University of California Press, 1985).

41. Gates Jr., *The Signifying Monkey,* 99.

42. Parish, *Whoopi Goldberg,* 230.

43. In focusing on these films I have bypassed Herbert Ross's *Boys on the Side* (1995), in which Goldberg plays Jane, a Greenwich Village–based lesbian and musician who is in love with a white woman dying of AIDS. And I bypass Steve Rash's *Eddie* (1996), in which she portrays the professional sportscaster turned NBA coach. Yet even the movies *Boys on the Side* and *Eddie* reveal Goldberg's carnivalesque rebellion against traditional authority as unruly womanhood, since they assign her nontraditional identities (i.e., lesbian, NBA coach).

44. Chris Straayer, *Deviant Eyes, Deviant Bodies: Sexual Re-Orientation in Film and Video* (New York: Columbia University Press, 1996), 47.

45. Ibid.

46. Gaylyn Studlar, "Masochism, Masquerade and the Erotic Spectacle," in Jane Gaines, ed., *Fabrications: Costume and the Female Body* (New York: Routledge, 1990), 230.

47. Eugene D. Genovese, *The Political Economy of Slavery: Studies in the Economy and Society of the Slave South* (New York, Pantheon Books, 1965). See also Hugh Honour, *The Image of the Black in Western Art, vol. 4: From the American Revolution to World War I* (Cambridge, Mass: Harvard University Press, 1989), 54.

48. Michael Rogin, *Blackface, White Noise: Jewish Immigrants in the Hollywood Melting Pot* (Berkeley: University of California Press, 1996), 38–39. See also Marjorie Garber, *Vested Interests: Cross Dressing and Cultural Anxiety* (New York: Routledge, 1992).

49. Linda Williams, "Something Else Besides a Mother," in Christine Gledhill, ed., *Home Is Where the Heart Is* (London: British Film Institute, 1987), 311.

50. Gaylyn Studlar, "Midnight S/excess: Cult Configurations of 'Femininity' and the Perverse," *Journal of Popular Film & Television* 17, no. 1 (Spring 1989): 6.

Chapter 4: Oprah Winfrey

1. Genevieve Wilkinson, "Talk-Show Host Oprah Winfrey," *Investor's Business Daily,* June 1, 1998.

2. John Young, "Toni Morrison, Oprah Winfrey, and Postmodern Popular Audiences" *African American Review* 35, no. 2 (2001): 181.

3. Oprah's media empire grew steadily in 2002 and she made the *Forbes* list of billionaires in 2003 with a net worth of $1 billion. Oprah is the third self-made woman to ever make the list. Her debut comes just two years after Black Entertainment Television founder Robert Johnson became the first black billionaire. Also see an article by Richard Thomas, titled "Queen of the Dream," *The Guardian* (London), May 19, 1997.

4. K. Sue Jewell, *From Mammy to Miss American and Beyond: Cultural Images and the Shaping of US Social Policy* (New York: Routledge, 1993), 184–85.

5. Doris Witt, "What (N)ever Happened to Aunt Jemima: Eating Disorders, Fetal Rights, and Black Female Appetite in Contemporary Culture," *Discourse: Journal for Theoretical Studies in Media and Culture* 17, no. 2 (1994–95): 99.

6. Review transcripts from *The Oprah Winfrey Show,* July 9, 1998. The show was titled "John Gray on Loving Again," and my transcript was produced by *Burrelle's Information Services.*

7. Donald Bogle is among the African American film scholars who have developed a typology of black stereotypes in film. According to Bogle, the mammy made her debut in 1914 when audiences were treated to a blackface version of *Lysistrata.* Hazel Carby, 1987; bell hooks, 1981; Patricia Collins, 1990; K. Sue Jewell, 1993, Jacqueline Bobo, 1995; and Lisa Anderson, 1997, are foremost among the feminist cultural critics who have written about the image of the mammy figure in literature, theater, film, and folklore.

8. My use of this term is informed by Barry King's widely anthologized essay "Articulating Stardom." King discusses the way a star's "persona" is in itself a character, one that transcends placement or containment in a particular narrative. He writes: "The persona, buttressed by discursive practices of publicity, hagiography and by regimes of cosmetic alteration and treatment, is relatively durable and if sedimented in public awareness will tend to survive discrepant casting and performance."

9. Gloria-Jean Masciarotte, "C'mon, Girl: Oprah Winfrey and the Discourse of Feminine Talk," *Genders* 11 (Fall 1991): 100. Masciarotte quotes Henry Louis Gates Jr.'s application of Bakhtin's double voice.

10. Ibid. Masciarotte acknowledges this as an application of Julia Kristeva's notion of abjection as explained in *Powers of Horror: An Essay on Abjection.* Kristeva acknowledged her theoretic debt to Mary Douglas's *Purity and Danger: An Analysis of the Concepts of Pollution and Taboo.* Masciarotte maintains that "Oprah Winfrey produces the spectacle of abjection by refusing the essentialist algebra of hegemonic acceptance: black + woman = Mammy = M(o)ther = the absolutely Othered = the Other of us all . . . [ ] . . . one can see Oprah Winfrey's double-voiced sign in that while she does not fulfill the hegemonic sign of the 'mammy' in that she is silent mirror of the dominant order, she fills hegemonic sign of the 'mammy' by exposing the labor of M/Othering that upholds the economic, racial, and gender oppression."

11. Ibid.

12. Used here, this term refers to the explanation of declining working-class support for radical political movements, as the result of increased affluence. This increased affluence causes workers to adopt middle-class (bourgeois) values and lifestyles. Embourgeoisement was a popular argument in Britain in the 1950s and 1960s. It was criticized in the *Affluent Worker: Political Attitudes and Behavior* research. The notion of proletarianization holds, conversely, that some of the middle class are becoming like the working class.

13. See Jane Shattuc's *The Talking Cure: TV Talk Shows and Women* (New York: Routledge, 1997) for an explanation of how talk shows have appropriated therapeutic discourse.

14. According to the *New York Times,* the Disney Company is estimated to have spent as much as $75 to $80 million to produce and market the film. See Bernard Weinraub's article "Despite Hope, 'Beloved' Generates Little Heat among Moviegoers," in the *New York Times,* Monday 9, 1998.

15. Pearl Cleage, "The courage to Dream," *Essence* (December 1998): 80–81, 145, 149.

16. Jeff MacGregor, "Inner Peace, Empowerment and Host Worship," *New York Times,* Sunday, October 25, 1998.

17. Ibid.

18. There are several clear signs of America's heightened concern with its moral character. The Clinton-Lewinsky sex scandal, controversy over the Microsort method of genetically engineered procreation, the violent assaults on abortion providers, the

RU-486 pill debate, the rise of New Age religion are all indicators of the rising tide of concern with our national moral character.

19. Dana Cloud, *Control and Consolation in American Culture and Politics, Rhetoric and Therapy* (Thousand Oaks, Calif.: Sage, 1998), 26.

20. Michel Foucault, "Technologies of the Self," in Luther H. Martin, Huck Gutman, and Patrick H. Hutton, eds., *Technologies of the Self: A Seminar with Michel Foucault* (Amherst: University of Massachusetts Press, 1988). Technologies of the self are specific techniques or practices through which subject positions are inhabited by individuals. Foucault, in his comments on these techniques, emphasized his interest in forms of writing such as private diaries or other "narratives of the self." These represented, for him, characteristically modern forms of "practices of the self." Coincidentally, Winfrey advocates that her viewers follow her lead by writing diary entries in a "gratitude journal." This is a daily practice whereby one records all the events, persons, achievements, and objects for which the subject is grateful.

21. T. Jackson Lears, "From Salvation to Self-Realization: Advertising and the Therapeutic Roots of the Consumer Culture, 1880-1930," in R. W. Fox and T. J. Lears, eds., *The Culture of Consumption: Critical Essays in American History, 1880-1980* (New York: Pantheon, 1983), 28.

22. George Mair, *Oprah Winfrey: The Real Story* (New York: Birch Lane Press, 1994), 2-15.

23. David Aberbach, *Charisma in Politics, Religion, and the Media: Private Trauma, Public Ideals* (New York: New York University Press, 1996), 87-88. Aberbach asserts that the entertainment-charismatic (Monroe, Presley, Lennon) retains "more than a veneer of religion" in the celebrity sign. Even the "language" of religion is used to describe these figures. Also see Jib Fowles's *Star Struck: Celebrity Performers and the American Public* (Washington, D.C.: Smithsonian Institution Press, 1992).

24. Richard Dyer, *Stars* (London: British Film Institute, 1979), 34-35.

25. P. David Marshall, *Celebrity and Power: Fame in Contemporary Culture* (Minneapolis: University of Minnesota Press, 1997).

26. Janice Peck, "Talk about Racism: Framing a Popular Discourse of Race on *Oprah Winfrey*," *Cultural Critique* (Spring 1994). The show often provides a format for discussing social and political issues. Also see Dana Cloud's account of the therapeutic in history. She discusses the way therapeutic discourse has been employed to elide the political and the social throughout history.

27. See also Rosario Champagne's essay titled "Oprah Winfrey's *Sacred Silent* and the Spectatorship of Incest," *Discourse* 17, no. 2 (Winter 1994-95): 123-38, and Doris Witt's "What (N)ever Happened to Aunt Jemima: Eating Disorders, Fetal Rights, and Black Female Appetite in Contemporary American Culture," *Discourse: Journal for Theoretical Studies in Media and Culture* 17, no. 2 (Winter 1994-95): 98-122.

28. Arthur Schweitzer, *The Age of Charisma* (Chicago: Nelson-Hall, 1984). This term is borrowed from Schweitzer and is understood here as mass enthusiasm for an individual that tends toward their glorification and generates a sense of loyalty and

readiness to follow the leader in her cause. In Winfrey's case, "the cause" is usually whatever popular self-help technique she's promoting or whatever media attention she brings to a social issue, be it rape, incest, eating disorders, racism, sexism, homophobia, or body image.

29. John Langer, "Television's Personality System," *Media, Culture and Society* 4 (1981): 351–65.

30. Ibid.

31. John Ellis, "Stars as Cinematic Phenomenon," *Visible Fiction: Cinema, Television, Video* (London: Routledge and Kegan Paul, 1982), 93. Ellis has written one of the seminal essays on the incomplete and paradoxical nature of the star phenomenon.

32. Susan Bordo, *Unbearable Weight: Feminism, Western Culture, and the Body* (Berkeley: University of California Press, 1995), 166.

33. Susan Bordo, *The Male Body: A New Look at Men in Public and Private* (New York: Farrar, Strauss, and Giroux, 2000).

34. Cornel West, "Nihilism in Black America," in Gina Dent, ed., *Black Popular Culture* (Seattle: Bay Press, 1992), 42.

35. Christopher Lasch, *The Culture of Narcissism: American Life in an Age of Diminishing Expectations* (New York: Norton, 1979), 50. Elsewhere Lasch writes: "After the political turmoil of the sixties, Americans have retreated to purely personal preoccupations. Having no hope of improving their lives in ways that matter, people have convinced themselves that what matters is psychic self-improvement: getting in touch with their feelings, eating health food, taking lessons in ballet or belly-dancing, immersing themselves in the wisdom of the East, jogging, learning how to 'relate,' overcoming the 'fear of pleasure.' Harmless in themselves, these pursuits . . . signify a retreat from politics and a repudiation of the recent past. . . . Contemporary man, tortured by self-consciousness, turns to new cults and therapies not to free himself from obsession but to find meaning and purpose in life, to find something to live for, precisely to embrace an obsession, if only the *passion maîtresse* of therapy itself."

36. Review transcripts from *The Oprah Winfrey Show,* January 11, 1999. The episode was titled "Suze Orman." My transcript was produced by *Burrelle's Information Services.* I have edited together three statements made by Orman throughout the program.

37. According to Laplanche and Pontalis, the cathartic method is a mode of psychotherapy in which the therapeutic effect sought is "purgative": an adequate discharge of pathogenic affects. The treatment allows the patient to evoke and even relive the traumatic events to which these affects are bound. *Cathexis* refers to the fact that a certain amount of psychical energy is attached to an idea, or to a group of ideas, to a part of the body, to an object. The word *cathect,* a derivative of *cathetic* and *cathexis,* is a transitive verb that means "to invest with mental energy or emotional energy." I use the phrase "cathartic cathexis" ironically.

38. Stewart M. Hoover's *Mass Media Religion: The Social Sources of the Electronic Church* (Newbury Park, Calif.: Sage, 1988), 19. Hoover provides one of many histori-

cal narratives of the rise of neo-evangelicalism and resurgent fundamentalism in the wake of the 1960s.

39. T. J. Lears, "From Salvation to Self-Realization: Advertising and the Therapeutic Roots of Consumer Culture, 1880–1930," in Fox and Lears, *Culture of Consumption,* 1–38. Quoting another of his writings, Lears says, "Nervous prostration or neurasthenia were shorthand terms for the immobilizing depressions that plagued many among the urban bourgeoisie during the late nineteenth century and after." Also see Barbara Ehrenreich and Deirdre English's *For Her Own Good,* detailing the sexual politics of sickness among bourgeois women of the late nineteenth century.

40. Ibid. Lears is quoting Reisman's *The Lonely Crowd: A Study of the Changing American Character,* third revised ed. (New Haven, Conn.: Yale University Press, 1969), 22, 25, 127, 149, 157.

41. Lears, "From Salvation to Self-Realization," in *The Culture of Consumption,* 1–38. Also see Peter Berger's essay in Mary Douglas and Steven M. Tipton, eds., *Religion and America: Spiritual Life in a Secular Age* (Boston: Beacon Press, 1983). Berger underscores Lears's argument. Berger writes: "While modernization brings promises and tangible benefits, it also produces tensions and discontents both institutionally and psychologically. In addition to the external institutional dislocations resulting from changes in the economic and political structures, there is massive alienation as a result of the loss of community and the turbulent upheavals caused by social mobility, urbanization and the technological transformations of everyday life."

42. See Daniel Bell's work, which dovetails with Lears's. Bell has suggested the crisis in self-consciousness arose from the loss of religious certitude, of belief in an afterlife. "Traditional modernism as a movement sought to substitute for religion or morality an aesthetic justification of life; to create a work of art, to be a work of art—this alone provided meaning in man's effort to transcend himself. But in going back to art, as is evident in Nietzsche, the very search for the roots of self moves the quest of modernism from art to psychology: from the product to the producer, from the object to the psyche."

43. This list could also include Robert Abelman and Stewart M. Hoover's *Religious Television: Controversies and Conclusions* (Norwood, N.J.: Ablex, 1990). Their book was a resource but did not directly influence my writing.

44. Hoover, *Mass Media Religion,* 24.

45. Quentin J. Schultze, *Televangelism and American Culture* (Grand Rapids, Mich.: Baker Book House, 1991), 95.

46. Ibid., 70.

47. Nicole Woolsey Biggart, *Charismatic Capitalism: Direct Selling Organizations in America* (Chicago: University of Chicago Press, 1989). Members of the direct selling industry, such as Amway Corporation, Tupperware, and Mary Kay Cosmetics, have stopped trying to fine-tune bureaucracy in the search for productivity. Instead, they have adopted a form of organization that dates from this nation's colonial past and shaped it to fit aspirations of contemporary Americans. Biggart demonstrates

that direct-selling organizations (DSOs) have been amazingly successful. In 1984 DSOs sold $8.6 billion in goods and services. More surprising, perhaps, 5.8 million Americans, 5 percent of the labor force, were members of DSOs in 1984.

48. Schultze, *Televangelism*, 160–62.

49. Jeffrey Louis Decker, *Made in America: Self-Styled Success from Horatio Alger to Oprah Winfrey* (Minneapolis: University of Minnesota Press, 1997), 113. See Decker's tome. He writes: "Media culture, in its capacity to collapse the distinctions between the private and public spheres and the inner and outer selves, also flattens the distinction between actors, entrepreneurs, and presidents. Other female stars have paralleled their entrepreneurial spirit with physical self-reinvention. Today's enterprising women have been most successful in exploiting consumer societies' desire to adorn the female form. Business pioneers such as Harriet Ayer and Madam C. J. Walker marketed fashion trends as a means of personal autonomy outside their marriages. Today's enterprising woman sells her media-manufactured image—including her story of self-making—as the product of entrepreneurial triumph . . . The media-manufactured woman is neither wholly objectified nor simply empowered: as narratives of the female celebrity suggest, she is both simultaneously. Even as the women provide their fans with models for self-improvement and uplift, they belong to the multimillion-dollar-a-year diet, fitness and medical establishment, which targets female consumers by promoting nearly impossible (if not unhealthy) standards of beauty. . . . Whereas the traditional self-made man sold his story as an afterthought to the accumulation of riches, the female celebrity's primary source of income is her story."

50. In his *Village Voice* film review of *Beloved,* Jim Hoberman made an observation about the film as a platform for the issues Winfrey pursues in her show: "*Beloved* is less Oprah's vehicle than her time machine. Even more than Morrison, Winfrey—who sees herself as a medium for the spirits of specific Negro slaves—has assumed the role of a tribune. *Beloved*'s oscillating tone and close-up driven absence of perspective become more coherent once the movie is understood as an epic version of *Oprah!*—a show in which the star naturally shifts between autobiographical confession and maternal advice, reliving personal adversity and offering the model of her own empowerment as New Age therapy."

51. Alex Kuczynski, "Trading on Hollywood Magic: Celebrities Push Models off Women's Magazine Covers," *New York Times*, Saturday, January 30, 1999.

52. Franz Roh, a German art critic, first used the term *magical realism*. To him it was a way of representing and responding to reality depicted in the post-expressionist art of the 1920s. Introduction of Roh's magical realism to Latin America occurred through the Spanish translation of his book by the *Revista de Occidente* in 1927. Within a year, magical realism was being applied to the prose of European authors in the literary circles of Buenos Aires. The cultural migration from Europe to the Americas in the 1930s and 1940s probably played a role in disseminating the term. Various scholars have speculated as much. See P. Gabrielle Foreman's essay "Past-On

Stories: History and the Magically Real, Morrison and Allende on Call," and Irene Guenther's essay "Magic Realism, New Objectivity, and the Arts during the Weimar Republic," both in *Magical Realism: Theory, History, Community.*

53. Brian Finney, "Temporal Defamiliarization in Toni Morrison's *Beloved,*" in Barbara Solomon, ed., *Critical Essays on Toni Morrison's* Beloved (New York: G. K. Hall, 1998). Finney writes: "The novel was received with adulation (it topped the best-seller lists and was awarded the 1988 Pulitzer Prize) and reserve (she was passed over for both the National Book Award and the National Book Critics Circle Award, leading to a protest in the *New York Times Book Review* by forty-eight Black writers)."

54. Lois Parkinson Zamora and Wendy B. Faris, eds. *Magical Realism: Theory, History, Community* (Durham, N.C.: Duke University Press, 1995), 9.

55. David Danow's *The Spirit of Carnival: Magical Realism and the Grotesque* (Lexington: University Press of Kentucky, 1995), 64 . Danow traverses from the carnivalesque to the grotesque, defining the latter as a contradiction in terms that suggests a range of ideas in expression. It is an irresolvable paradox that is universal and archetypal, that subverts an established value system in order to institute one of its own. It creates language and behavior codes in the work of creating new ones and superimposes one paradox upon another.

56. See *Variety* data, March 1, 1999. Also, according to the *New York Times,* the Disney Company is estimated to have spent as much as $75 to $80 million to produce and market the film. See Bernard Weinraub's "Despite Hope, 'Beloved' Generates Little Heat among Moviegoers," *New York Times,* Monday November 9, 1998.

57. George Bluestone, *Novels into Films: The Metamorphosis of Fiction into Cinema* (Berkeley: University of California Press, 1957), 34.

58. Max Horkheimer and Theodor W. Adorno, *Dialectic of Enlightenment,* translated by John Cumming (New York: Continuum, 1991). One of the most celebrated texts of the Frankfurt School, this text endeavors to answer why modernity, instead of fulfilling the promises of the Enlightenment has sunk into a new barbarism. Drawing on their work on the "culture industry," as well as the ideas of key thinkers of the Enlightenment project (Descartes, Newton, Kant) Horkheimer and Adorno explain how the Enlightenment's orientation toward rational calculability and man's domination of a disenchanted nature evinces a reversion to myth and is responsible for the reified structures of modern administered society, which has grown to resemble a new enslavement.

59. D. N. Rodowick, *The Crisis of Political Modernism: Criticism and Ideology in Contemporary Film Theory* (Berkeley: University of California Press, 1988).

60. Manthia Diawara, *Black American Cinema* (New York: Routledge, 1993).

61. Natalie Zemon Davis, *Slaves on Screen: Film and Historical Vision* (Cambridge, Mass.: Harvard University Press, 2000), 108.

62. Robert Stam, "Beyond Fidelity: The Dialogics of Adaptation," in James Naremore, ed., *Film Adaptation* (New Brunswick, N.J.: Rutgers University Press, 2000), 54–76.

63. Ibid., 64.

64. Bernard W. Bell, "*Beloved:* A Womanist Neo-Slave Narrative; or Multivocal Remembrances of Things Past," in Barbara Solomon, ed., *Critical Essays on Toni Morrison's Beloved* (New York: G. K. Hall, 1998), 173.

65. Henry Louis Gates Jr. and Nellie Y. McKay, *The Norton Anthology of African American Literature* (New York: Norton, 1997), 2097.

66. Davis, *Slaves on Screen,* 95.

67. Hayden White, *Tropics of Discourse: Essays in Cultural Criticism* (Baltimore, Md.: Johns Hopkins University Press, 1985), 53.

68. Toni Morrison, *Playing in the Dark: Whiteness and the literary Imagination* (New York: Vintage Books, Random House, 1992), 9.

69. Marc C. Conner, "From the Sublime to the Beautiful: The Aesthetic Progression of Toni Morrison," in Marc Conner, ed., *The Aesthetics of Toni Morrison: Speaking the Unspeakable* (Jackson: University Press of Mississippi, 2000), 64.

70. Ibid.

71. For instance, this is allegedly why Alfred Hitchcock avoided using an actress's image for the eponymous character of *Rebecca* (1940). Hitchcock surmised each spectator would visualize (in his/her mind's eye) a more enigmatically beautiful woman than any real actress could render.

72. Lois Parkinson Zamora and Wendy B. Faris, eds., *Magical Realism: Theory, History, Community* (Durham, N.C.: Duke University Press, 1995), 3.

73. Deborah Horvitz, "Nameless Ghosts: Possession and Dispossession in *Beloved*," in Barbara Solomon, ed., *Critical Essays on Toni Morrison's* Beloved (New York: G. K. Hall, 1998), 93.

74. Mikhail Bakhtin, *Rabelais and His World,* translated by Helene Iswolsky (Bloomington: Indiana University Press, 1984), 21–27.

75. Robert Stam, *Subversive Pleasures: Bakhtin, Cultural Criticism, and Film* (Baltimore, Md.: Johns Hopkins University Press, 1989), 160.

76. Saidiya Hartman, *Scenes of Subjection: Terror, Slavery, and Self-Making in Nineteenth-Century America* (New York: Oxford University Press, 1997), 23. See also David Danow's *The Spirit of Carnival: Magical Realism and the Grotesque* (Lexington: University Press of Kentucky, 1995), 50.

77. E. Ann Kaplan, *Motherhood and Representation: The Mother in Popular Culture and Melodrama* (London: Routledge, 1992), 66. Kaplan also cites Janet Staiger's essay "Mass-Produced Photoplays: Economic and Signifying Practices in the First Years of Hollywood," *Wide Angle* 4 (3): 12–27.

78. Stam, "Beyond Fidelity: The Dialogics of Adaptation," 61.

79. Alex Lichtenstein, *Twice the Work of Free Labor: The Political Economy of Convict Labor in the New South* (London: Verso: 1996), 1–17.

80. Ibid., 3.

81. Loïc Wacquant, "From Slavery to Mass Incarceration: Rethinking the 'Race Question' in the US," *New Left Review* 13 (January–February 2002): 41–60.

82. Hayden White, "The Value of Narrativity in the Representation of Reality," *Critical Inquiry* (Autumn 1980), 17. See also Brenda Cooper's discussion of White's work in *Magical Realism in West African Fiction: Seeing with a Third Eye* (New York: Routledge, 1998).

83. Rafael Perez Torres, "Knitting and Knotting the Narrative Thread: *Beloved* as Postmodern Novel," in Nancy Peterson, ed., *Toni Morrison: Critical and Theoretical Approaches* (Baltimore, Md.: Johns Hopkins University Press, 1993), 105.

84. Brian Finney, "Temporal Defamiliarization in Toni Morrison's *Beloved*," in Barbara Solomon, ed., *Critical Essays on Toni Morrison's* Beloved (New York: G. K. Hall, 1998), 104.

85. Torres, "Knitting and Knotting the Narrative Thread," 94.

86. Stam, "Beyond Fidelity: The Dialogics of Adapation," 62.

87. See the NAACP Image Awards Web site and the *New York Amsterdam News* arts and entertainment section December 31, 1998. Three hundred industry professionals and NAACP leaders decide the forty-one categories.

88. Ron Stodghill, "Daring to Go There," *Time* (October 5, 1998).

89. I'm not suggesting black audiences don't support black film. *Blade, How Stella Got Her Groove Back,* and *Dr. Dolittle* were tremendous commercial successes in part because of black audience support.

90. Armond White, "*Beloved:* Directed by Jonathan Demme," *New York Press* (October 21, 1998).

91. David Denby, "Haunted by the Past," *The New Yorker* (October 26, 1998).

92. Talise D. Moorer, "Oprah's *Beloved* personalizes impact of slavery," *New York Amsterdam News* (October 15, 1998): 24.

93. Laura B. Randolph, "Sizzle: In Her First Love Scenes in the Powerful Film *Beloved*," *Ebony* (November 1998): 36–42.

94. Ashraf Rushdy, "Daughters Signifyin(g) History: The Example of Toni Morrison's *Beloved*," in Linden Peach, ed., *Toni Morrison Contemporary Critical Essays* (New York: St. Martin's Press, 1998), 140–53.

Chapter 5: Halle Berry

1. Hamid Naficy, "Phobic Spaces and Liminal Panics: Independent Transnational Film Genre," in Rob Wilson and Wimal Dissanayake, eds., *Global/Local: Cultural Production and the Transnational Imaginary* (Durham, N.C.: Duke University Press, 1996), 121.

2. Peter Bart, "Greats under Pressure: The Oscar Curse," *Variety* (March 12, 2006).

3. Christopher John Farley, *Introducing Halle Berry* (New York: Simon and Schuster, 2002), 167.

4. Walter Leavy, "Denzel, Halle & Jamie," *Ebony* (November 2005): 90.

5. Hollywood celebrity is, in some ways, an American corollary to European mon-

archy. We have long felt affection for—and had a fascination with—a range of celebrity families whom we honor and display much like royalty. This illusion or fantasy of compatibility between monarchy and celebrity achieved its fullest expression in the fairytale marriage of Grace Kelly to Prince Rainier of Monaco. In the United States we have constructed aura around the Baldwins, the Barrymores, the Cassidys, the Coppolas, the Fondas, the Hudlin Brothers, the Hughes Brothers, the Hustons, the Jacksons, the Kennedys, the Marshalls, the Osmonds, the Rockefellers, the Rossellinis, the Sheens/Estevezes, the Sutherlands, the Vanderbilts, the Wayans, and the Winans, to name but a few. This is not to mention those families in professional sports. The widely held belief is that talent "runs in the family," thereby bestowing the aura of charisma upon members of a given tribe or clan.

6. Examples include Katherine Hepburn in *Mary of Scotland* (1936), Henry Fonda in *Young Mr. Lincoln* (1939), Orson Welles in *Citizen Kane* (1941), Marlon Brando in *Julius Caesar* (1953), Richard Burton in *Alexander the Great* (1956), Bette Davis in *The Virgin Queen* (1955), Charlton Heston in *The Ten Commandments* (1956), and Peter O'Toole in *Lawrence of Arabia* (1962).

7. Pamela Lambert, "Hollywood Blackout: The Film Industry Says All the Right Things but Its Continued Exclusion of African Americans Is a National Disgrace," *People* (March 18, 1996).

8. Reverend Jesse L. Jackson, "From Selma, Alabama, to Hollywood, California: A Thirty-One Year Struggle for Fairness and Inclusion in the American Dream," *Motion Magazine* (April 10, 1996).

9. "Movie Box Office Data, Film Stars, Idle Speculation," retrieved from http://www.the-numbers.com/index.php, March 7, 2006. See also the site Box Office Mojo," at http://www.boxofficemojo.com/, accessed March 24–26, 2006.

10. Richard Dyer, *Only Entertainment* (London: Routledge: 1992, 2002), 2.

11. Ramón Grosfoguel, "Cultural Racism and Colonial Caribbean Migrants in Core Zones of the Capitalist World Economy," *Review Binghampton* 22 (Part 4, 1999): 409–34.

12. Elizabeth Guider, "White Bread," *Variety* (April 17–23): 1. President Jacques Chirac convened broadcasters in March 2006 and instructed them to put more black faces on the box. Two weeks later, TF1 unveiled a lead role for a North African in an upcoming primetime cop show.

13. The root of the word *mulatto* is Spanish according to Webster's English Dictionary, from *mulo,* a mule. The word refers to (1) a person, one of whose parents are Negro and the other Caucasian, or white; and (2) popularly, any person with mixed Negro and Caucasian ancestry. A mule is defined as (1) the offspring of a donkey and a horse, especially the offspring of a jackass and a mare—*mules are usually sterile.* And in biology mules are defined as hybrid, especially a sterile hybrid. Given its racist etymology, *mulatto* is construed here as a pejorative, offensive term with various literary and cultural associations in American society. It has positive connotations in Latin American cultures due to its linguistic relationship to the word *mestizo,* meaning a person of European and American Indian ancestry.

14. Ira Robbins, "Basic Berry," *New York Newsday* (March 15, 1995).

15. Mary Turner, ed. *From Chattel Slaves to Wage Slaves: The Dynamics of Labour Bargaining in the Americas* (London: James Carrey, 1995). See also Pierre Bourdieu, *Distinction: A Social Critique of the Judgment of Taste* (Cambridge, Mass.: Harvard University Press, 1987), and Marcel Mauss, "Techniques of the Body," translated Ben Brewster, *Economy and Society* 2(1): 70–88, originally published in *Journal de psychologie normal et pathologique* (Paris: Année, 1935): 271–93.

16. Pierre Bourdieu, "The Forms of Capital," in John Richardson, ed., *Handbook of Theory and Research for the Sociology of Education* (New York: Greenwood Press, 1986), 241–58.

17. Jennifer González, "Morphologies: Race as a Visual Technology," Coco Fusco and Brian Wallis, eds., *Only Skin Deep: Changing Visions of the American Self* (New York: Harry N. Abrams, 2003), 380.

18. Colorism is a global form of discrimination and occurs where lighter skin tones are preferred and darker skin tones are considered to be less desirable. There seems to be an implicit calculus behind this belief that makes the goodness of the individual inversely related to the darkness (or sometimes lightness) of his/her skin. An example of this occurs in African American communities and throughout India as a result of the caste system. In American society, lighter, whiter complexions have historically been associated with the bourgeoisie, colonial authority, domesticity, wealth, ownership, education, and leisure. Brown bodies and complexions signify proletarianization, colonial dependency, externality, poverty, slavery, illiteracy, and labor.

19. Adrienne L. McLean, *Being Rita Hayworth: Labor, Identity, and Hollywood Stardom* (New Brunswick, N.J.: Rutgers University Press, 2004).

20. See *The Bronze Screen: 100 Years of the Latino Image in American Cinema* (2002), directed by Nancy De Los Santos and Albert Domínguez.

21. Merry Elkins, "The Westmores: Sculpting the Faces of the World," *American Cinematographer* 65 (July 1984): 34–40.

22. Richard Dyer, *White* (London: Routledge, 1997), 127.

23. Catherine A. Lutz and Jane L. Collins, "The Color of Sex: Postwar Photographic Histories of Race and Gender," in *Reading National Geographic* (Chicago: University of Chicago Press, 1993): 155–85.

24. Mary C. Beltrán, "The Hollywood Latina Body as Site of Social Struggle: Media Constructions of Stardom and Jennifer Lopez's 'Cross-Over Butt,'" *Quarterly Review of Film and Video* 19: 71–86, 2002.

25. James Naremore, *Acting in the Cinema* (Berkeley: University of California Press, 1990).

26. P. David Marshall, *Celebrity and Power: Fame in Contemporary Culture* (Minneapolis: University of Minnesota Press, 1997), 65.

27. Mary Beltrán, "The New Hollywood Racelessness: Only the Fast, Furious (and Multiracial) Will Survive," *Cinema Journal* 44, no. 2 (Winter 2005): 50–67.

28. Ordinarily, the term *Creole* means (1) a person of European descent born in the

West Indies or Spanish America; (2) a person descended from, or culturally related to, the original French settlers of the southern United States, especially Louisiana; (3) the French dialect spoken by the people; (4) a person descended from, or culturally related to, the Spanish and Portuguese settlers of the Gulf states; (5) a person of mixed black and European ancestry who speaks a creolized language, especially one based on French or Spanish; (6) a black slave born in the Americas as opposed to one brought from Africa. The term is also commonly applied to things native to the New World.

29. Mary-Frances Winters, "Majority Shifts, Problems Remain," *USA Today*, August 10, 2001.

30. Clarence Page, "Unspoken Conflicts: America's Blacks and Latinos Are Struggling with a New Racial Paradigm for the New Century," *Chicago Tribune*, February 8, 2004.

31. Noy Thrupkaew, "The Multicultural Mysteries of Vin Diesel," retrieved August 16, 2002, from Alter Net, at www.alternet.org/story/13863/.

32. The Pussycat Dolls, for example, are also known for their range of ethnic backgrounds, which include Filipino, Hawaiian, African American, Mexican, English, French, Chinese, Israeli, Indonesian, Dutch, Russian, Polish, Japanese, and Irish heritages.

33. These are figures through which people in a given social environment organize and give meaning and direction to their lives. Representative characters are not only icons or symbols, they can be products or commodities that consumers purchase when they buy a magazine, watch a movie, or listen to music.

34. Jack E. White, "I'm Just Who I Am," *Time* 149, no. 18 (May 5, 1997): 32–36.

35. Richard Rodriguez, *Brown: The Last Discovery of America* (New York: Penguin, 2003), 130. See also *Multiple Origins, Uncertain Destinies: Hispanics and the American Future* (Washington, D.C.: National Academies Press, 2006).

36. Kathy McCabe, "Brazilians Add a Touch of Home," *Boston Globe*, January 5, 2006.

37. Bob Moser, "White Heat," *The Nation* (August 28, 2006): 11.

38. Anna Marie De La Fuente, "Truth and Consequences: As NALIP Confabs, Latinos' Struggle for Representation Continues," *Daily Variety*, Thursday, March 9, 2006.

39. Marcel Cajueiro, "Brazil Begins to Break Down TV Color Bar," *Variety* (February 20–26, 2006): 22. This is one reason Brazil serves as an appropriate point of comparison. When the Portuguese invaded Brazil in the sixteenth century, they established a color hierarchy remarkably similar to our own. Lighter-skinned Portuguese subdued the brown-skinned Indian natives and the Africans imported as slaves. Today, while the vast majority of Brazilians (80 percent) are of African or Indian descent, Brazil remains predominantly controlled by whites. Despite centuries of racial mixing in both countries, there's still a demand for greater inclusion in commercial cinema and television.

40. Larry Rohter, "Drawing Lines Across the Sand, Between Classes," *New York Times*, February 6, 2007.

41. Sam Roberts, *Who We Are Now: The Changing Face of America in the Twenty-first Century* (New York: Times Books 2004), 158. Sam Roberts noted that Michael Lind revised Rodriguez's thesis. In *New York Times Magazine,* Lind wrote, "There is not going to be a non-white [brown] majority in the 21st century. Rather, there is going to be a mostly white mixed-raced majority. We are more likely to see something more complicated: a white-Asian-Hispanic melting pot majority—a hard to differentiate group of beige Americans—offset by a minority consisting of blacks who have been left out of the melting pot once again." Michael Lind, "The Beige and the Black," *New York Times Magazine,* August 16, 1998.

42. Allison Samuels, "Why Can't a Black Actress Play the Girlfriend?" *Newsweek* (March 14, 2005): 52.

43. Rosario Dawson is of Puerto Rican, Cuban, African American, Irish, and Native American descent.

44. Samuels, "Why Can't a Black Actress Play the Girlfriend?" 52.

45. Frank Sanello, *Halle Berry: A Stormy Life: The Unauthorized Biography* (London: Virgin Books, 2003), 19.

46. On August 23, 1989, Yusef Hawkins, who was sixteen at the time, went to look for a used car in Bensonhurst with three of his friends. A mob of about thirty white youths soon approached them. Most of them were carrying bats; however, one was carrying a gun. This mob of mostly white Italians was angry because one of their girlfriends invited a black boy to her eighteenth birthday party. The mob thought that Hawkins and his friends were there for the party, so the mob beat Hawkins and his friends with the bats and shot Hawkins dead.

47. Farley, *Introducing Halle Berry,* 65.

48. Ibid., 62.

49. Sanello, *Halle Berry: A Stormy Life,* 40.

50. Ibid.

51. David Denby, "Bad-News Girls," *New York Magazine* (July 20, 1992): 52.

52. Peter Rainer, "Lange, Berry, Passionately Claim *Isaiah,*" *Los Angeles Times,* March 17, 1995.

53. Cohen's character Ali G made his U.S. television debut one year later in 1999 on *Da Ali G Show.*

54. A wigger (or wigga) is a stereotype of a Caucasian person who emulates phrases, mannerisms, and fashion commonly and stereotypically associated with black, Caribbean, or hip-hop cultures. The stereotype of the wigger usually involves a young Caucasian person who generally knows little about the culture they are appropriating, with the exception of the music, style, and slang associated with that culture. The term is a portmanteau combining the words *white* and *nigger* or *wannabe* and *nigger* and is thus generally considered offensive.

55. Henry Louis Gates, "The White Negro: With *Bulworth* Warren Beatty Puts His Career on the Color Line," *The New Yorker* (May 11, 1998): 63.

56. Tyrone R. Simpson, "Hollywood Bait and Switch: The 2002 Oscars, Black Commodification, and Black Political Silence (Part One)," *Black Camera* 17, no. 2 (Fall/

Winter 2002): 6–11. See also "Hollywood Bait and Switch: The 2002 Oscars, Black Commodification, and Black Political Silence (Part Two)," *Black Camera* 18, no. 1 (Spring/Summer 2003).

57. Gates, "The White Negro," 65.

58. Toni Morrison, "Clinton as the First Black President," *The New Yorker* (October 1998). "Clinton," Morrison wrote in the 1998 *New Yorker* essay, "displays almost every trope of blackness: single-parent household, born poor, working-class, saxophone-playing, McDonald's-and-junk-food-loving boy from Arkansas." See also Suzy Hansen, "Why Blacks Love Bill Clinton," Salon.com, February 20, 2002.

59. "To proclaim oneself a nigger is to identify oneself as real, authentic, uncut, unassimilated and unassimilable—the opposite of someone whose rejection of nigger is seen as part of an effort to blend into the white mainstream." Berry's declaration in this context authenticates Bulworth's black identification. See Randall Kennedy's *Nigger: The Strange Career of a Troublesome Word* (New York: Pantheon Books, 2002).

60. Mark Olsen, "Swordfish," *Sight & Sound* 11, no 9: 54–55.

61. Brian D. Johnson, "Swordfish," *Maclean's*.

62. Olson, "Swordfish," 55.

63. See Manthia Diawara's "Black Spectatorship: Problems of Identification and Resistance," in *Black American Cinema* (New York: Routledge, 1992).

64. Michael Kimmel, "Masculinity as Homophobia: Fear, Shame, and Silence in the Construction of Gender Identity," in Harry Brod and Michael Kaufman, eds., *Theorizing Masculinities* (Thousand Oaks, Calif.: Sage), 127.

65. Paul Sweezy, Harry Magdoff, John B. Foster, and Robert McChesney, "Prisons and Executions—the U.S. Model: A Historical Introduction," *Monthly Review* 53, no. 3 (July–August, 2001): 1–18. There is a long tradition of protest against convict leasing and the evolution of prison culture in the United States. Scholars from Booker T. Washington and W. E. B. Du Bois to Angela Davis have written extensively on the subject.

66. Joy James, ed., "From the Prison of Slavery to the Slavery of Prison: Frederick Douglass and the Convict Lease System," in *The Angela Y. Davis Reader* (Malden, Mass.: Blackwell, 1998), 75.

67. Julia Sudbury, "Celling Black Bodies: Black Women in the Global Prison Industrial Complex," *Feminist Review* 70 (2002): 57–74.

68. Ibid., 60.

69. Alex Lichtenstein, *Twice the Work of Free Labor: The Political Economy of Convict Labor in the New South* (New York: Verso, 1996), 4.

70. Clifford Thompson, "Monster's Ball" in *Cineaste* (Summer 2002).

71. Bakari Kitwana, *The Hip Hop Generation: Young Blacks and the Crisis in African American Culture* (New York: Perseus, 2002), 85–174.

72. Crystal L. Keels, "*Monster's Ball:* Hollywood's Grotesque History and/or Something Else Besides?" *Black Camera* 17, no 2 (Fall/Winter 2002), 4–5.

73. Abby L. Ferber, *White Man Falling: Race, Gender, and White Supremacy* (Lanham, Md.: Rowman and Littlefield), 135.

74. Kimmel, Michael, "Masculinity as Homophobia: Fear, Shame, and Silence in the Construction of Gender Identity," in Harry Brod and Michael Kaufman, eds., *Theorizing Masculinities* (Thousand Oaks, Calif.: Sage, 1994), 128–29.

75. Margaret K. Bass, "On Being a Fat Black Girl in a Fat-Hating Culture," in Michael Bennett and Vanessa Dickerson, eds., *Recovering the Black Female Body: Self-Representations by African American Women* (New Brunswick, N.J.: Rutgers University Press, 2000), 228.

76. William Julius Wilson, *The Truly Disadvantaged: The Inner City, the Underclass and Public Policy* (Chicago: The University of Chicago Press, 1987), 21.

77. Wahneema Lubiano, "Black Ladies, Welfare Queens, and State Minstrels: Ideological War by Narrative Means," in *Race-ing Justice, En-gendering Power: Essays on Anita Hill, Clarence Thomas, and the Construction of Social Reality* (New York: Pantheon, 1992), 330.

78. For a longer discussion of the film, see my article, Mia Mask, "Monster's Ball," *Film Quarterly*, 58, no. 1 (Sept. 2004): 44–55.

Selected Bibliography

Abel, Elizabeth, Barbara Christian, and Helene Moglen, eds. *Female Subjects in Black and White: Race, Psychoanalysis, and Feminism.* Berkeley: University of California Press, 1997.

Abelman, Robert, and Stewart M. Hoover, eds. *Religious Television: Controversies and Conclusions.* Norwood, N.J.: Ablex, 1990.

Aberbach, David. *Charisma in Politics, Religion, and the Media: Private Trauma, Public Ideals.* New York: New York University Press, 1996.

Abt, Vicki, and Leonard Mustazza. *Coming After Oprah: Cultural Fallout in the Age of the TV Talk Show.* Bowling Green, Ohio: Bowling Green State University Popular Press, 1997.

Ackroyd, Peter. *Dressing Up, Transvestism and Drag: The History of an Obsession.* New York: Simon and Schuster, 1979.

Alberoni, Francesco. "The Powerless 'Elite': Theory and Sociological Research on the Phenomenon of the Stars." In *Sociology of Mass Communications,* edited by Denis McQuail. London: Penguin, 1972.

Alexander, Karen. "Fatal Beauties: Black Women in Hollywood." In *Stardom: Industry of Desire,* edited by Christine Gledhill. London: Routledge, 1991.

Allen, Clifford. "The Erotic Meaning of Clothes." *Sexology* 41 (1974): 31–34.

Allen, Robert C., ed. *Channels of Discourse: Television and Contemporary Criticism.* Chapel Hill: University of North Carolina Press, 1987.

Als, Hilton. "A Crossover Star." *The New Yorker* (April 29, 1996): 132–36.

Anderson, Lisa. *Mammies No More: The Changing Image of Black Women on Stage and Screen.* Lanham, Md.: Rowman and Littlefield, 1997.

Apter, Emily, and William Pietz, eds. *Fetishism as Cultural Discourse.* Ithaca, N.Y.: Cornell University Press, 1993.

Archer-Straw, Petrine. *Negrophilia: Avant-Garde Paris and Black Culture in the 1920s.* London: Thames and Hudson, 2000.

Arens, W. *The Man-Eating Myth: Anthropology and Anthropophagy.* New York: Oxford University Press, 1979.

Armstrong, Mark. "Bassett Bashes Berry's *Monster* Role." *E! Online,* June 24, 2002.

Arnold, A. James. *Modernism and Negritude: The Poetry and Poetics of Aimé Césaire.* Cambridge, Mass.: Harvard University Press, 1981.

Ashcroft, Bill, Gareth Griffiths, and Helen Tiffin, eds. *The Empire Writes Back: Theory and Practice in Post-Colonial Literatures.* New York: Routledge, 1989.

Austin, Guy. "Vampirism, Gender Wars and the 'Final Girl': French Fantasy Film in the Early Seventies." *French Cultural Studies* 7, no. 3 (October 1996): 321–31.

Ayer, Deborah. "The Making of a Man: Dialogic Meaning in *Beloved.*" In *Critical Essays on Toni Morrison's Beloved,* edited by Barbara Solomon. New York: G. K. Hall, 1998.

Bak, Robert C. "The Phallic Woman: The Ubiquitous Fantasy in Perversions." *Psychoanalytic Study of the Child* 23 (1968): 15–36.

Baker, Houston A., Manthia Diawara, and Ruth H. Lindeborg, eds. *Black British Cultural Studies: A Reader.* Chicago: University of Chicago Press, 1996.

Baker, Roger. *Drag: A History of Female Impersonations in the Performing Arts.* London: Cassell, 1994.

Bakhtin, Mikhail. *Art and Answerability: Early Philosophical Essays by M. M. Bakhtin.* Translated by Vadim Liapunov. Edited by Michael Holquist and Vadim Liapunov. Austin: University of Texas Press, 1990.

———. *Problems of Dostoevsky's Poetics.* Translated by P. W. Rotsel. Ann Arbor, Mich.: Ardis, 1973.

———. *Rabelais and His World.* Translated by Helene Iswolsky. Cambridge, Mass.: MIT Press, 1968.

———. *Speech Genres and Other Late Essays.* Austin: University of Texas Press, 1986.

Baldwin, James. "Carmen Jones: The Dark Is Light Enough." In *Notes of a Native Son.* Boston: Beacon Press, 1955.

———. *The Devil Finds Work.* New York: Dial Press, 1976.

———. *Nobody Knows My Name: More Notes of a Native Son.* New York: Bantam: Double Day, 1961.

———. *The Price of the Ticket: Collected Nonfiction Essays, 1948–1985.* New York: St. Martin's Press, 1985.

Barthes, Roland. *The Fashion System.* Translated by Matthew Ward and Richard Howard. Berkeley: University of California Press, 1983. Originally published as *Système de la mode* (Paris: Editions de Seuil, 1967).

———. *Image-Music-Text.* Translated by Stephen Heath. New York: Hill and Wang, 1977.

———. *Mythologies.* Translated by Jonathan Cape. New York: Hill and Wang, 1972. Originally published in Paris by Editions du Seuil, 1957.

Bataille, Georges. *Eroticism: Death and Sensuality, A Study of Eroticism.* Translated by Mary Dalwood. New York: Walker, 1962.

Baty, S. Paige. *American Monroe: The Making of a Body Politic.* Berkeley: University of California Press, 1995.

Bell, Bernard W. *"Beloved:* A Womanist Neo-Slave Narrative; or, Multivocal Remembrances of Things Past." In *Critical Essays on Toni Morrison's* Beloved, edited by Barbara Solomon. New York: G. K. Hall, 1998.

Bell, K. Sue. *From Mammy to Miss America and Beyond: Cultural Images and the Shaping of US Social Policy.* New York: Routledge, 1993.

Beltrán, Mary C. "The Hollywood Latina Body as Site of Social Struggle: Media Construction of Stardom and Jennifer Lopez's Cross-Over Butt." *Quarterly Review of Film and Video* 19, no. 1 (2002): 71–86.

Bernardi, Daniel, ed. *The Birth of Whiteness: Race and the Emergence of U.S. Cinema.* New Brunswick, N.J.: Rutgers University Press, 1996.

———, ed. *Classic Hollywood, Classic Whiteness.* Minneapolis: University of Minnesota Press, 2001.

Benjamin, Walter. *Illuminations.* Translated by Harry Zohn. Edited by Hannah Arendt. New York: Schocken Books, 1968.

Bennett, Lerone, Jr. "The Emancipation Orgasm: Sweetback in Wonderland." *Ebony* 26 (September 1971): 106–8.

Bennett, Michael, and Vanessa Dickerson, eds. *Recovering the Black Female Body: Self-Representations by African American Women.* New Brunswick, N.J.: Rutgers University Press, 2001.

Bhabha, Homi. *The Location of Culture.* New York: Routledge, 1994.

———. "Race and the Humanities: The 'Ends' of Modernity?" *Public Culture* 4, no. 2 (Spring 1992): 81–85.

Bianculli, David. *Teleliteracy: Taking Television Seriously.* New York: Continuum, 1992.

Biggart, Nicole Woolsey. *Charismatic Capitalism: Direct Selling Organizations in America.* Chicago: University of Chicago Press, 1989.

Biskind, Peter. *Seeing Is Believing: How Hollywood Taught Us to Stop Worrying and Love the Fifties.* New York: Pantheon Books, 1983.

Bloom, Harold, ed. *Modern Critical Views: Toni Morrison.* New York: Chelsea House, 1990.

Bogle, Donald. *Blacks in American Films and Television: An Encyclopedia.* New York: Garland, 1980.

———. *Bright Boulevards, Bold Dreams: The Story of Black Hollywood.* New York: Ballantine, 2005.

———. *Brown Sugar: Eighty Years of America's Black Female Superstars.* New York: Da Capo Press, 1980.

———. *Dorothy Dandridge: A Biography.* New York: Amistad Press, 1997.

———. *Toms, Coons, Mulattoes, Mammies, and Bucks: An Interpretive History of Blacks in American Films.* New York: Continuum, reprinted in 1995.

Bordo, Susan. *Unbearable Weight: Feminism, Western Culture, and the Body.* Berkeley: University of California Press, 1993.

Botting, Fred, and Scott Wilson, eds. *The Tarantinian Ethics*. Thousand Oaks, Calif.: Sage, 2001.

Bourdieu, Pierre. *Distinction: A Social Critique of the Judgement of Taste*. Translated by Richard Nice. London: Routledge, 1984.

———. "The Forms of Capital." Translated by Richard Nice. In *Handbook of Theory and Research for the Sociology of Education* (pp. 241–58). Edited by John G. Richardson. New York: Greenwood, 1986.

Bradley, Raymond Trevor. *Charisma and Social Structure: A Study of Love and Power, Wholeness and Transformation*. New York: Paragon House, 1987.

Braxton, Greg. "She Back and Badder Than Ever." *Los Angeles Times,* August 27, 1995.

Brode, Douglas. *Money, Women, and Guns: Crime Movies from* Bonnie and Clyde *to the Present*. Secaucus, N.J.: Carol, 1995.

Brooks, Peter. *Body Work: Objects of Desire in Modern Narrative*. Cambridge, Mass.: Harvard University Press, 1993.

Brubach, Holly. "Whose Vision Is It, Anyway?" *New York Times Magazine* (July 17, 1994): 46–49.

Bruno, Giuliana. "Spectatorial Embodiments: Anatomies of the Visible and the Female Bodyscape." *Camera Obscura* 28 (January 1992): 238–61.

Bullough, Vern L., and Bonnie Bullough. *Cross Dressing, Sex, and Gender*. Philadelphia: University of Pennsylvania Press. 1993.

Butler, Jeremy G., ed. *Star Texts: Image and Performance in Film and Television*. Detroit, Mich.: Wayne State University Press, 1991.

Butler, Judith. *Bodies That Matter: On the Discursive Limits of "Sex."* New York: Routledge, 1993.

———. *Gender Trouble: Feminism and the Subversion of Identity*. New York: Routledge, 1990.

Calhoun, Craig, ed. *Habermas and the Public Sphere*. Cambridge, Mass.: MIT Press, 1996.

Carby, Hazel. *Race Men*. Cambridge, Mass: Harvard University Press, 1998.

———. *Reconstructing Womanhood: The Emergence of the Afro-American Woman Novelist*. New York: Oxford University Press, 1987.

Carpignano, Paolo, Robin Anderson, Stanley Aronowitz, and Willian Difazio. "Chatter in the Age of Electronic Reproduction: Talk Television and the 'Public Mind.'" *Social Text* 25–26 (1990): 33–55.

Carrithers, Michael, Steven Collins, and Steven Lukes, eds. *The Category of the Person: Anthropology, Philosophy, History*. Cambridge, UK: Cambridge University Press, 1985.

Carroll, Peter N. *It Seemed Like Nothing Happened: The Tragedy and Promise of America in the 1970s*. New York: Holt, Rinehart, and Winston, 1982.

Carson, L. M. Kit. "It's Here! Hollywood's Ninth Era." *Esquire* 83, no. 2 (February 1975): 65–75.

Carter, Angela. *The Sadeian Woman and the Ideology of Pornography.* New York: Harper Colophon, 1980.

Case, Sue-Ellen. "Toward a Butch–Femme Aesthetic." *Discourse* 11, no. 1 (Fall–Winter 1988–89): 55–73.

Césaire, Aimé. *Discourse on Colonialism.* Translated by Joan Pinkham. New York: Monthly Review Press, 1972. Originally published as *Discourse sur le colonialisme* (Presence Africaine, 1955).

Champagne, Rosario. "Oprah Winfrey's *Sacred Silent* and the Spectatorship of Incest." *Discourse: Journal for Theoretical Studies in Media and Culture* 17, no. 2 (Winter 1994–95): 123–38.

Charney, Maurice. *Comedy High and Low: An Introduction to the Experience of Comedy.* New York: Oxford University Press, 1978.

Chernin, Kim. *The Obsession: Reflections on the Tyranny of Slenderness.* New York: Harper Collins, 1981.

Churchill, Ward. *Fantasies of the Master Race: Literature, Cinema, and the Colonization of American Indians.* Edited by M. Annette Jaimes. Monroe, Me.: Common Courage Press, 1992.

Cleaver, Eldridge. *Soul on Ice.* New York: Bantam–Doubleday–Dell, 1968.

Cleto, Fabio. *Camp: Queer Aesthetics and the Performing Subject: A Reader.* Ann Arbor: University of Michigan Press, 1999.

Cloud, Dana. *Control and Consolation in American Culture and Politics: Rhetoric of Therapy.* Thousand Oaks, Calif.: Sage, 1998.

Cohan, Steven. *Masked Men: Masculinity and the Movies in the Fifties.* Bloomington: Indiana University Press, 1997.

Collins, Patricia H. *Black Feminist Thought: Knowledge, Consciousness and the Politics of Empowerment.* Boston: Unwin Hyman, 1990.

Conner, Marc, ed. *The Aesthetics of Toni Morrison: Speaking the Unspeakable.* Jackson: University Press of Mississippi, 2000.

Cook, David. *Lost Illusion: American Cinema in the Shadow of Watergate and Vietnam, 1970–1979.* Berkeley: University of California Press, 2000.

Cook, Pam. "Exploitation Films and Feminism." *Screen* 17, no. 2 (Summer 1976): 112–27.

Corey, Susan. "Toward the Limits of Mystery: The Grotesque in Toni Morrison's *Beloved.*" In *The Aesthetics of Toni Morrison: Speaking the Unspeakable,* edited by Marc Conner. Jackson: University Press of Mississippi, 2000.

Corliss, Richard. "Bewitching Beloved." *Time* (October 5, 1998): 74–77.

Courtney, Susan. *Hollywood Fantasies of Miscegenation: Spectacular Narratives of Gender and Race, 1903–1967.* Princeton, N.J.: Princeton University Press, 2005.

Crawford, Robert. "A Cultural Account of 'Health': Control, Release, and the Social Body." In *Issues in the Political Economy of Healthcare,* edited by John McKinlay. New York: Tavistock, 1985.

Crenshaw, Kimberlé, Neil Gotanda, Gary Peller, and Kendall Thomas, eds. *Criti-*

cal Race Theory: The Writings That Formed the Movement. New York: The New Press, 1995.

Crowther, Bruce. *Captured on Film: The Prison Movie.* London: B. T. Batsford, 1989.

Cruse, Harold. *The Crisis of the Negro Intellectual: A Historical Analysis of the Failure of Black Leadership.* New York: Quill, 1967.

Curtin, Philip D. *The Image of Africa: British Ideas and Action, 1780–1850.* Madison: University of Wisconsin Press, 1964.

Curtis, Susan. *Passing for Colored: Meanings for Minstrelsy and Ragtime.* New York: Oxford University Press, 1994.

Dahlgren, Peter. *Television and the Public Sphere: Citizenship, Democracy and the Media.* Thousand Oaks, Calif.: Sage, 1992.

DaMatta, Roberto. *Carnivals, Rogues, and Heroes: An Interpretation of the Brazilian Dilemma.* Notre Dame, Ind.: University of Notre Dame Press, 1991.

Dandridge, Dorothy, and Earl Conrad. *Everything and Nothing: The Dorothy Dandridge Tragedy.* New York: Abelard–Schuman, 1970.

Danow, David. *The Spirit of Carnival: Magical Realism and the Grotesque.* Lexington: University Press of Kentucky, 1995.

Davis, Natalie Zemon. *Slaves on Screen: Film and Historical Vision.* Cambridge, Mass.: Harvard University Press, 2000.

Deker, Jeffrey Louis. *Made in America: Self-Styled Success from Horatio Alger to Oprah Winfrey.* Minneapolis: University of Minnesota Press, 1997.

DeKoven, Marianne. "Postmodernism and Post-Utopian Desire in Toni Morrison and E. L. Doctorow." In *Toni Morrison: Critical and Theoretical Approaches,* edited by Nancy Peterson. Baltimore, Md.: Johns Hopkins University Press, 1997.

Deleuze, Gilles, and Félix Guattari. *Anti-Oedipus: Capitalism and Schizophrenia.* Translated by Robert Hurley, M. Seema, and H. R. Lane. New York: Viking Press, 1977.

D'Emilio, John, and Estelle B. Freedman. *Intimate Matters: A History of Sexuality in America.* New York: Harper and Row, 1988.

Dent, Gina, ed. *Black Popular Culture: A Project by Michele Wallace.* Seattle: Bay Press, 1992.

Derwent, George Harcourt. *Prosper Mérimée: A Mask and a Face.* London: Routledge, 1926.

Diawara, Manthia. *African Cinema: Politics and Culture.* Bloomington: Indiana University Press, 1992.

———. *Black American Cinema.* New York: Routledge, 1993.

———. *In Search of Africa.* Cambridge, Mass.: Harvard University Press, 1998.

———. "Noir by Noirs: Toward a New Realism of Black Cinema." In *Shades of Noir,* edited by Joan Copjec. London: Verso, 1993.

Dickens, Homer. *What a Drag: Men as Women and Women as Men in the Movies.* New York: Quill, 1984.

Dickerson, Vanessa. "Summoning Some Body: The Flesh Made Word in Toni Morrison's Fiction." In *Recovering the Black Female Body: Self-Representations by African American Women,* edited by Michael Bennett and Vanessa D. Dickerson. New Brunswick, N.J.: Rutgers University Press, 2001.

Dixon, Kathleen. "The Dialogic Genres of Oprah Winfrey's 'Crying Shame.'" *Journal of Popular Culture* 35, no. 2 (Fall 2001): 171–91.

Doane, Mary Anne. *Femmes Fatales: Feminism, Film Theory, Psychoanalysis.* New York: Routledge, 1991.

Dollimore, Jonathan. *Sexual Dissidence: Augustine to Wilde, Freud to Foucault.* Oxford, UK: Clarendon Press, 1991.

Duberman, Martin, ed. *Queer Representations: Reading Lives, Reading Cultures.* New York: New York University Press, 1997.

Du Bois, W. E. B. *The Souls of Black Folk: Essays and Sketches.* Chicago: A. C. McClurg, 1903.

Dumond, Dwight, L. *Antislavery: The Crusade for Freedom in America.* Ann Arbor: University of Michigan Press, 1961.

Dyer, Richard. *Heavenly Bodies: Film Stars and Society.* New York: St. Martin's Press, 1986.

———. *Stars.* London: British Film Institute, 1979.

———. *White.* London: Routledge, 1997.

Eco, Umberto. "*Casablanca:* Cult Movies and Intertextual Collage." *Sub/stance* 47 (1985): 3–12.

Eddy, John Herbert. "Buffon, Organic Change and the Race of Man." Doctoral dissertation, University of Oklahoma, 1977.

Edwards, Geoffrey. "Carmen's Transfiguration from Mérimée to Bizet: Beyond the Image of the Femme Fatale." *Nottingham: French Studies* 32, no. 2 (Autumn 1993): 48–54.

Ellen, Holly. "Where Are the Films about Real Black Men and Women?" *New York Times,* June 2, 1974.

Ellis, Albert. *The American Sexual Tragedy.* New York: Twayne, 1959.

Evans, David. *Sexual Citizenship: The Material Construction of Sexualities.* New York: Routledge, 1993.

Fanon, Frantz. *Black Skin, White Masks.* Translated by Charles Lam Markmann. New York: Grove Press, 1967.

———. *A Dying Colonialism.* Translated by Haakon Chevalier. New York: Grove Press, 1965.

———. *Toward the African Revolution: Political Essays.* Translated by Haakon Chevalier. New York: Grove Press, 1967.

———. *The Wretched of the Earth.* Translated by Contance Farrington. New York: Grove Press, 1963.

Farley, Christopher John. *Introducing Halle Berry.* New York: Simon and Schuster, 2000.

Farley, John. "Queen of All Media." *Time* (October 5, 1998): 82–84.

Feher, Michael, Ramona Naddaff, and Nadia Tazi. *Fragments for a History of the Human Body.* Three volumes. Cambridge, Mass.: MIT Press, 1989.

Feinberg, Leslie. *Transgender Warriors: Making History from Joan of Arc to Dennis Rodman.* Boston: Beacon Press, 1996.

Finkelman, Paul., ed. *Slavery and Historiography: Articles on American Slavery.* New York: Garland, 1989.

Finney, Gail, ed. *Look Who's Laughing: Gender and Comedy.* Langhorne, Pa.: Gordon and Breach, 1994.

Fisher, Seymour. *Sexual Images of the Self: The Psychology of Erotic Sensations and Illusions.* Hillside, N.J.: L. Erlbaum, 1989.

Fiske, John. "Radical Shopping in Los Angeles: Race, Media and the Sphere of Consumption." *Media, Culture and Society* 16 (1994): 469–86.

Fitzgerald, Jennifer. "Selfhood and Community: Psychoanalysis and Discourse in *Beloved.*" In *Toni Morrison: Contemporary Critical Essays,* edited by Linden Peach. New York: St. Martin's Press, 1998.

Foster, Gwendolyn Audrey. *Performing Whiteness: Postmodern Re/Constructions in the Cinema.* New York: State University of New York Press, 2003.

Foucault, Michel. *The Care of the Self: The History of Sexuality, vol. 3.* Translated by Robert Hurley. New York: Random House, 1986.

——. *Discipline and Punish: The Birth of the Prison.* Translated by Alan Sheridan. New York: Pantheon, 1977.

——. "The Ethic of Care for the Self as a Practice of Freedom: An Interview with Michel Foucault." *Philosophy and Social Criticism* 12 (Summer 1987): 112–31.

——. *Foucault Live (Interviews, 1966–84).* Translated by John Johnston. Edited by Sylvère Lotringer. New York: Semiotext(e), 1989.

——. "Governmentality." Translated by Rosi Braidotti. *I and C* 6 (Autumn 1979). Revised translation by Colin Gordon published in *The Foucault Effect,* edited by Burchell, Gordon, and Miller.

——. *The History of Sexuality, vol. 1: An Introduction.* Translated by Robert Hurley. New York: Pantheon, 1978.

——. "Kant on Enlightenment and Revolution." Translated on Colin Gordon. *Economy and Society* 15, no. 1 (February 1986): 88–96.

——. "The Order of Discourse." Translated by Ian McLeod. In *Untying the Text: A Post-Structuralist Reader,* edited by Robert Young. Boston: Routledge, Kegan Paul, 1981.

——. "Politics and the Study of Discourse." Translation by Anthony M. Nazzaro, revised by Colin Gordon. *Ideology and Consciousness* 3 (Spring 1978): 7–26. Originally published as "Reponse à une question." *Esprit* (1968). Revised translation of "History, Discourse and Discontinuity," *Salmagundi* (Spring 1972).

——. *Power/Knowledge: Selected Interviews and Other Writings, 1972–1977.* Colin Gordon, ed. New York: Pantheon, 1980.

————. *Remarks on Marx: Conversations with Duccio Trombadori.* Translated by R. James Goldstein and James Cascaito. 1981; New York: Semiotext(e), 1991.

————. *This Is Not a Pipe.* Translated and edited by James Harkness. Berkeley: University of California Press, 1981.

————. *The Use of Pleasure: The History of Sexuality, vol. 2.* Translated by Robert Hurley. New York: Random House, 1985.

Foucault, Michel, and James Bernauer. "Is It Useless to Revolt?" *Philosophy and Social Criticism* 8 (Spring 1981): 2–4.

Foucault, Michel, with Richard Sennett. "Sexuality and Solitude." *London Review of Books* (May 21, 1981): 3–7.

Fowles, Jib. *Star Struck: Celebrity Performers and the American Public.* Washington, D.C.: Smithsonian Institution Press, 1992.

Frankl, Razelle. *Televangelism: The Marketing of Popular Religion.* Carbondale: Southern Illinois University Press, 1987.

Fraser, Nancy. *Unruly Practices: Power, Discourse and Gender in Contemporary Social Theory.* Minneapolis: University of Minnesota Press, 1989.

Frazier, E. Franklin. *Black Bourgeoisie.* New York: Simon and Schuster, 1957.

————. *The Negro Family in the United States.* Chicago: University of Chicago Press, 1939.

Fredrickson, George M. *The Black Image in the White Mind: The Debate on Afro-American Character and Destiny, 1817–1914.* Hanover, N.H.: Wesleyan University Press, 1971.

French, Brandon. *On the Verge of Revolt: Women in American Films of the Fifties.* New York: Frederick Ungar, 1978.

Freud, Sigmund. *Jokes and Their Relation to the Unconscious.* Translated and edited by James Strachey. New York: Norton, 1966.

Friedman, Dan, and Gabrielle Kurlander. "Deconstruction and Development of the Opera *Carmen.*" *Modern Drama* 43, no. 2 (Summer 2000): 276–87.

Frum, David. *How We Got Here: The 70s: The Decade That Brought You Modern Life.* New York: Basic Books, 2000.

Fry, Christopher. *The Dark Is Light Enough: A Winter Comedy.* New York: Oxford University Press, 1954.

Frye, Northrop. *Anatomy of Criticism: Four Essays.* Princeton, N.J.: Princeton University Press, 1957.

Furedi, Frank. *Therapy Culture: Cultivating Vulnerability in an Uncertain Age.* London: Routledge, Taylor and Francis, 2004.

Gabbard, Krin. *Black Magic: White Hollywood and African American Culture.* New Brunswick, N.J.: Rutgers University Press, 2004.

Gabler, Neal. *Winchell: Gossip, Power and the Culture of Celebrity.* New York: Vintage Books, 1995.

Gaines, Jane. "Fabricating the Female Body." In *Fabrications: Costume and the Female Body,* edited by Jane Gaines and Charlotte Herzog. New York: Routledge, 1990.

———. "White Privilege and Looking Relations: Race and Gender in Feminist Film Theory." *Screen* 29, no. 4 (Autumn): 12–27.

Gamman, Lorraine, and Merja Makinen. *Female Fetishism.* New York: New York University Press, 1994.

Gamson, Joshua. *Claims to Fame: Celebrity in Contemporary America.* Berkeley: University of California Press, 1994.

———. *Freaks Talk Back: Tabloid Talk Shows and Sexual Nonconformity.* Chicago: University of Chicago Press, 1998.

Garber, Marjorie. *Vested Interests: Cross Dressing and Cultural Anxiety.* New York: Harper Perennial, 1992.

Gates, Henry Louis, Jr. "Must Buppiehood Cost Homeboy His Soul?" *New York Times,* March 1, 1992.

———. *The Signifying Monkey: A Theory of African-American Literary Criticism.* Oxford and New York: Oxford University Press, 1988.

Gates, Henry Louis, Jr., and K. A. Appiah, eds. *Toni Morrison: Critical Perspectives Past and Present.* New York: Amistad, 1993.

Gilman, Sander. *Difference and Pathology: Stereotypes of Sexuality, Race and Madness.* Ithaca, N.Y.: Cornell University Press, 1985.

———. *Disease and Representation: Images of Illness from Madness to AIDS.* Ithaca, N.Y.: Cornell University Press, 1988.

Ginsberg, Elaine K. *Passing and the Fictions of Identity.* Durham, N.C.: Duke University Press, 1996.

Giroux, Henry, and Peter McLaren, eds. *Between Borders: Pedagogy and the Politics of Cultural Studies.* New York: Routledge, 1994.

Glassman, Ronald, and William H. Swatos, Jr., eds. *Charisma, History and Social Structure.* Westport, Conn.: Greenwood Press, 1986.

Gledhill, Christine, ed. *Stardom: Industry of Desire.* New York: Routledge, 1991.

Goldberg, Whoopi. *Whoopi Goldberg Book.* New York: Rob Weisbach Books, 1997.

Gordon, Lewis R., T. Denean Sharpley-Whiting, and Renée T. White, eds. *Fanon: A Critical Reader.* Cambridge, Mass.: Blackwell, 1996.

Gosselin, Chris, and Glenn Wilson. *Sexual Variation: Fetishism, Sadomasochism, and Transvestism.* London: Faber and Faber, 1980.

Gray, Herman. *Watching Race: Television and the Struggle for "Blackness."* Minneapolis: University of Minnesota Press, 1995.

Grayson, Deborah R. "Is It Fake? Black Women's Hair as Spectacle and Spec(tac)ular." *Camera Obscura: Feminism, Culture and Media Studies* 36 (1995): 13–31.

Green, Theophilus. "The Black Man as Movie Hero: New Films Offer a Different Male Image." *Ebony* (August 1972): 144–48.

Grinder, Katrina. "Hair Salons and Racial Stereotypes: The Impermissible Use of Racially Discriminatory Pricing Schemes." *Harvard Women's Law Journal* 12 (1989): 75–113.

Grizzuti-Harrison, Barbara. "The Importance of Being Oprah." *New York Times Magazine.* June 11, 1989.

Grosz, Elizabeth. *Volatile Bodies: Toward a Corporeal Feminism.* Bloomington: Indiana University Press, 1994.

Grotjahn, Martin. *Beyond Laughter.* New York: The Blakiston Division, 1957.

Guerrero, Ed. *Framing Blackness: The African American Image in Film.* Philadelphia: Temple University Press, 1993.

Guthrie, R. Dale. *Body Hot Spots: The Anatomy of Human Social Organs and Behavior.* New York: Van Nostrand Reinhold, 1976.

Habermas, Jürgen. *The Philosophical Discourse of Modernity.* Translated by Frederick G. Lawrence. Cambridge, Mass.: MIT Press, 1995.

Halberstam, David. *The Fifties.* New York: Villard Books, Random House, 1993.

Hall, Stuart. "Culture, the Media and the 'Ideological Effect.'" In *Mass Communication and Society,* edited by James Curran, Michael Gurevich, and Janet Wallacott. London: Edward Arnold, 1977.

———. "The Emergence of Cultural Studies and the Crisis of the Humanities." *October* 53 (1990): 11–23.

———. "Notes on Deconstructing 'The Popular.'" In *People's History and Socialist Theory,* edited by Raphael Samuel. London: Routledge, 1981.

Hall, Stuart, and Bram Gieben, eds. *Formations of Modernity.* Cambridge, UK: Polity Press, 1992.

Hammonds, Evelynn. "Black (W)holes and the Geometry of Black Female Sexuality." *Differences: A Journal of Feminist Cultural Studies* 6, no. 2–3 (Summer–Fall 1994): 126–45.

Haney, Lynn. *Naked at the Feast: A Biography of Josephine Baker.* New York: Dodd, Mead, 1981.

Harding, Sandra, ed. *The Racial Economy of Science: Toward a Democratic Future.* Bloomington: Indiana University Press, 1993.

Hare, Nathan, and Julia Hare. *Crisis in Black Sexual Politics.* San Francisco: Black Think Tank, 1989.

Hart, Lynda. *Fatal Women: Lesbian Sexuality and the Mark of Aggression.* Princeton, N.J.: Princeton University Press, 1994.

Hartley, John. *Studies in Television.* London: Routledge, 1992.

Hartman, Jon. "The Trope of Blaxploitation in Critical Responses to *Sweetback.*" *Film History* 6, no. 3 (Autumn 1994): 382–404.

Hartman, Saidiya. *Scenes of Subjection: Terror, Slavery and Self-Making in Nineteenth-Century America.* New York: Oxford University Press, 1997.

Harvey, David. *The Condition of Postmodernity: An Enquiry into the Origins of Cultural Change.* Cambridge, Mass.: Blackwell, 1990.

Haskell, Molly. *From Reverence to Rape: The Treatment of Women in the Movies.* Chicago: University of Chicago Press, 1987.

Heaton, Jeanne Albronda, and Nona Leigh Wilson. *Tuning in Trouble: Talk TV's Destructive Impact on Mental Health.* San Francisco: Jossey-Bass, 1995.

Hegel, G. W. F. *Phenomenology of the Spirit.* Translated by A. V. Miller. New York: Oxford University Press, 1977.

Heidegger, Martin. *Being and Time.* Translated J. Macquarrie and E. Robinson. New York: Harper and Row, 1962.

Hendrickson, Hildi, ed. *Clothing and Difference: Embodied Identities in Colonial and Post-Colonial Africa.* Durham, N.C.: Duke University Press, 1996.

Hengen, Shannon, ed. *Performing Gender and Comedy: Theories, Texts and Contexts.* Amsterdam: Gordon and Breach, 1998.

Herdt, Gilbert, ed. *Third Sex, Third Gender: Beyond Sexual Dimorphism in Culture and History.* New York: Zone Books, 1993.

Hernton, Calvin C. *Sex and Racism in America.* New York: Grove Press, 1965.

Higginbotham, Evelyn Brooks. *Righteous Discontent: The Women's Movement in the Black Baptist Church, 1880–1920.* Cambridge, Mass.: Harvard University Press, 1994.

Hirshfeld, Magnus. *Transvestites: The Erotic Drive to Cross Dress.* Translated by Michael Lombardi-Nash. Buffalo, N.Y.: Prometheus Books, 1991.

Hobson, Janell. *Venus in the Dark: Blackness and Beauty in Popular Culture.* New York: Routledge Taylor and Francis Group, 2005.

Hodgen, Wendi Ann. "An Examination of the Unlikely Success of Whoopi Goldberg as a New Kind of Movie Icon." Master's thesis, San Jose State University, December, 2001.

Hollander, Anne. *Seeing through the Clothes.* Berkeley: University of California Press, 1993.

Holmlund, Chris. *Impossible Bodies: Femininity and Masculinity.* London: Routledge, 2002.

Holquist, Michael, ed. *The Dialogical Imagination.* Austin: University of Texas Press, 1981.

hooks, bell. *Ain't I a Woman: Black Women and Feminism.* Boston: South End Press, 1981.

———. *Black Looks: Race and Representation.* Boston: South End Press, 1992.

———. *Feminist Theory: From Margin to Center.* Boston: South End Press, 1984.

———. *Outlaw Culture.* New York: Routledge, 1994.

———. *Reel to Real: Race, Sex, and Class at the Movies.* New York: Routledge, 1996.

———. *Talking Back: Thinking Feminist, Thinking Black.* Boston, South End Press, 1989.

hooks, bell, and Cornel West. *Breaking Bread: Insurgent Black Intellectual Life.* Boston: South End Press, 1991.

Hoover, Stewart. *Mass Media Religion: The Social Sources of the Electronic Church.* Newbury Park, Calif.: Sage, 1988.

Hoover, Stewart, and Knut Lundby, eds. *Rethinking Media, Religion, and Culture.* Thousand Oaks, Calif.: Sage, 1997.

Horton, Andrew, ed. *Comedy/Cinema/Theory.* Berkeley: University of California Press, 1991.

Horton, Luci. "The Battle among the Beauties: New Black Actresses Vie for Top Film Roles." *Ebony* 29, no. 1 (November 1973): 144–50.

Hulsbus, Monica. "The Double/Double Bind of Postwar Race and Gender in *Duel in the Sun.*" *Spectator* 17, no. 1 (Fall/Winter 1996): 80–87.

Hunt, Jean. "What Audience Members Are Aware of When Listening to the Comedy of Whoopi Goldberg." *Humor: International Journal of Humor Research* 8, no. 2 (1995): 135–54.

Huyssen, Andreas. "Mass Culture as Woman." In *Studies in Entertainment* (189–207), edited by Tania Modleski. Bloomington: University of Indiana Press, 1986.

Hyam, Ronald. *Empire and Sexuality: The British Experience.* Manchester, UK: Manchester University Press, 1990.

Ignatiev, Noel. *How the Irish Became White.* New York: Routledge, 1995.

Illouz, Eva. *Oprah Winfrey and the Glamour of Misery.* Columbia University Press, 2003.

———. "That Shadowy Realm of the Interior: Oprah Winfrey and Hamlet's Glass." *International Journal of Cultural Studies* 2, no.1 (April 1999): 109–31.

Jaeger, C. Stephen. "Charismatic Body–Charismatic Text." *Exemplaria: A Journal of Theory in Medieval and Renaissance Studies* 9, no. 1 (Spring 1997): 117–37.

James, Darius. *That's Blaxploitation: Roots of the Baadasssss 'Tude (Rated X by an All-Whyte Jury).* New York: St. Martin's Griffin, 1995.

James, Joy. "Black *Femmes Fatales* and Sexual Abuse in Progressive White Cinema: Neil Jordan's *Mona Lisa* and *The Crying Game.*" *Camera Obscura: Feminism, Culture and Media Studies* 36 (1995): 33–48.

Jameson, Fredric. *The Geopolitical Aesthetic: Cinema and Space in the World System.* Bloomington: Indiana University Press, 1995.

———. *The Political Unconscious: Narrative as a Socially Symbolic Act.* Ithaca, N.Y.: Cornell University Press, 1981.

———. *Postmodernism, or the Logic of Late Capitalism.* Durham: Duke University Press, 1991.

Jewell, K. Sue. *From Mammy to Miss America and Beyond: Cultural Images and the Shaping of US Social Policy.* New York: Routledge, 1993.

Joseph, Gloria I., and Jill Lewis. *Common Differences: Conflict in Black and White Feminist Perspectives.* Boston: South End Press, 1981.

Kahn, Ashley, Holly George-Warren, and Shawn Dahl, eds. *Rolling Stone: The Seventies.* Boston: Little, Brown, 1998.

Kaplan, Ann. *Motherhood and Representation: The Mother in Popular Culture and Melodrama.* London: Routledge, 1992.

Kerr, Paul "Out of What Past? Notes on the B Film Noir." In *The Hollywood Film Industry,* edited by Paul Kerr. London: British Film Institute, 1986.

Keylin, Arlene, ed. *The Fabulous Fifties.* New York: Arno Press, 1978.

Keyser, Les. *Hollywood in the Seventies.* San Diego, Calif.: A.S. Barnes, 1981.

Kincaid, Jamaica. "Pam Grier: The Mocha Mogul of Hollywood." *Ms. Magazine* 4 (August 1975): 49–53.

Kitt, Eartha. *I'm Still Here: Confessions of a Sex Kitten.* New York: Barricade Books, 1989.

Knee, Adam. "The Weight of Race: Stardom and Transformations of Racialized Masculinity in Recent Film." *Quarterly Review of Film and Video* 19, no.1 (2002): 87–100.

Kristeva, Julia. *Powers of Horror: An Essay on Abjection.* Translated by Leon Roudiez. New York: Columbia University Press, 1982.

Lacan, Jacques. *The Four Fundamental Concepts of Psycho-Analysis.* Translated by Alan Sheridan. Edited by Jacques-Alain Miller. New York: Norton, 1977.

Ladner, Joyce A., ed. *The Death of White Sociology.* New York: Random House, 1973.

Landry, Bart. *The New Black Middle Class.* Berkeley: University of California Press, 1987.

Landy, Marcia. *The Historical Film: History and Memory in Media.* New Brunswick, N.J.: Rutgers University Press, 2001.

Lane, Christopher, ed. *The Psychoanalysis of Race.* New York: Columbia University Press, 1998.

Langer, Mark. "Exploitation Film." *Film History* 6 (1994): 147–48.

Latham, Rob. "Art, Trash and Sexploitation: The Aesthetics of '*Le Bad Cinema.*'" *Vanishing Point: Studies in Comparative Literature* 1 (1994): 89–99. Department of Comparative Literature, Stanford University.

Laqueur, Thomas. *Making Sex: Body and Gender from the Greeks to Freud.* Cambridge, Mass.: Harvard University Press, 1990.

Leavy, Walter. "Who Was the Real Dorothy Dandridge?" *Ebony* (August 1999): 102, 104, 106.

Lentz, Kirsten Marthe. "The Popular Pleasures of Female Revenge (Or Rage Bursting in a Blaze of Gunfire)." *Cultural Studies* 7, no. 3 (October 1993): 374–405.

Lerner, Gerda, ed. *Black Women in White America: A Documentary History.* New York: Vintage Books, 1972.

Levin, David Michael. *The Opening of Vision: Nihilism and the Postmodern Situation.* New York: Routledge, 1988.

Lichtenstein, Alex. *Twice the Work of Free Labor: The Political Economy of Convict Labour in the New South.* London: Verso, 1999.

Lightning, Robert K. "Dorothy Dandridge: Rumination on Black Stardom." *CineAction* (July 1997): 32–39.

Lindolm, Charles. *Charisma.* Cambridge, UK: Blackwell, 1990.

Lorde, Audre. *Sister Outsider: Essays and Speeches.* Trumansburg, N.Y.: Crossing Press, 1984.

Lott, Brett. "Celebrity Hollow: When Oprah Called, He Answered." *Utne Reader* (May–June 2000).

Lucas, Bob. "Pam Grier: A Sexy Body Is Not Enough!" *Black Stars* (May 1975): 38–42.

Luci, Horton. "The Battle among the Beauties: Black Actresses Vie for Top Movie Roles." *Ebony* (November 1973): 144–46.

Lyotard, Jean-François. *Libidinal Economy.* Translated by Iain Hamilton Grant. Bloomington: Indiana University Press, 1993.

———. *The Postmodern Condition: A Report on Knowledge.* Translated by Geoffrey Bennington and Brian Massumi. Minneapolis: University of Minnesota Press, 1979.

MacDonald, Fred J. *Blacks and White TV: African Americans in Television since 1948.* Chicago: Nelson-Hall, 1992.

Madsen, Douglas, and Peter G. Snow. *The Charismatic Bond: Political Behavior in Time of Crisis.* Cambridge, Mass.: Harvard University Press, 1991.

———. "The Dispersion of Charisma." *Comparative Political Studies* 16 (1983): 337–62.

Mair, George. *Oprah Winfrey: The Real Story.* Secaucus, N.J.: Carol, 1994.

Manatu, Norma. *African American Women and Sexuality in the Cinema.* Jefferson, N.C.: McFarland, 2003.

Marable, Manning. *How Capitalism Underdeveloped Black America.* Boston: South End Press, 1983.

———. *W. E. B. Du Bois: Black Radical Democrat.* Boston: Twayne, 1986.

Marcus, John T. "Transcendence and Charisma." *Western Political Quarterly* 14, no. 1 (March 1961): 236–41.

Marling, Karal Ann. *As Seen on TV: The Visual Culture of Everyday Life in the 1950s.* Cambridge. Mass.: Harvard University Press, 1994.

Marshall, David P. *Celebrity and Power: Fame in Contemporary Culture.* Minneapolis: University of Minnesota Press, 1997.

Martin, Luther H., Huck Gutman, and Patrick H. Hutton. *Technologies of the Self: A Seminar with Michel Foucault.* Amherst: University of Massachusetts Press, 1988.

Marwick, Arthur. *Beauty in History: Society, Politics and Personal Appearance, 1500 to the Present.* New York: Thames and Hudson, 1988.

Masciarotte, Gloria-Jean. "C'mon Girl: Oprah Winfrey and the Discourse of Feminine Talk." *Genders* 11 (Fall 1991): 81–110.

Mason, B. J. "New Film: Culture or Con Game?" *Ebony* (December 1972): 60–68.

Mast, Gerald. *The Comic Mind: Comedy and the Movies.* Chicago: University of Chicago Press, 1979.

Mauss, Marcel. "Techniques of the Body." *Techniques of the Body* 2, no. 1 (February 1973): 70–88.

McCaughey, Martha, and Neal King, eds. *Reel Knockouts: Violent Women in the Movies.* Austin: University of Texas Press, 2001.

McClintock, Anne. *Imperial Leather: Race, Gender, and Sexuality in the Colonial Contest.* New York: Routledge, 1995.

McDowell, Colin. *Dressed to Kill: Sex, Power and Clothes.* London: Hutchinson, 1992.

McGee, Mark Thomas. *Faster and Furiouser: The Revised Fattened Fable of American International Pictures.* Jefferson, N.C.: McFarland, 1996.

McGee, Sherri. "The Amazing Grace of Oprah Winfrey." *Upscale: The World's Finest African American Magazine* (August 1998).

McLean, Adrienne. *Being Rita Hayworth: Labor, Identity, and Hollywood Stardom.* New Brunswick, N.J.: Rutgers University Press, 2004.

Medovoi, Leerom. "Theorizing Historicity, or the Many Meanings of *Blacula.*" *Screen* 39, no. 1 (Spring 1998): 1–21.

———. "A Yippie-Panther Pipe Dream: Rethinking Sex, Race and the Sexual Revolution." In *Swinging Single,* edited by Hilary Radner and Moya Luckett. Minneapolis: University of Minnesota Press, 1999.

Mellen, Joan. *Women and Their Sexuality in the New Film.* New York: Dell, 1973.

Mercer, Kobena. *Welcome to the Jungle: New Positions in Black Cultural Studies.* London: Routledge, 1994.

Mérimée, Prosper. *Carmen and Colomba.* Translated from the French by Eric Sutton with an introduction by V.S. Pritchett. London: Hamish Hamilton, 1846.

Merleau-Ponty, Maurice. *Phenomenology of Perception.* Translation by Colin Smith. New York: Routledge, 1989. Originally published as *Phénoménologie de la Perception.*

Merrill, Lisa. "Feminist Humor: Rebellious and Self-Affirming." *Women's Studies* 15 (1988): 271–80.

Meter, Van. "Oprah's Moment." *Vogue* (October 1998): 322–30, 392–93.

Miller, Douglas, and Marion Nowak. *The Fifties: The Way We Really Were.* New York: Doubleday, 1977.

Mills, David. "Blaxploitation 101: A Brief Film History of Sticking It to the Man." *Washington Post,* November 4, 1990.

———. "Funk in the Age of Rap: The Return of Blaxploitation." *Black Film Review* 6, no. 3 (1991): 6–25.

Mills, Earl. *Dorothy Dandridge.* New York: Holloway House, 1991.

Morgan, Roberta. "Oprah Winfrey: The Highest-Paid Woman in Show-Biz Still Has a Heart." *The Hollywood Reporter* (Women in Entertainment Special Issue), December 9, 1997.

Morley, David. *Television, Audiences and Cultural Studies.* London: Routledge, 1992.

Morley, David, and Kuan-Hsing Chen. *Stuart Hall: Critical Dialogues in Cultural Studies.* London: Routledge, 1996.

Morrison, Toni. *Playing in the Dark: Whiteness in the Literary Imagination.* New York: Random House, 1992.

Morse, Margaret. "The Television News Personality and Credibility: Reflections on the News in Transition." In *Studies in Entertainment,* edited by Tania Modleski. Bloomington: University of Indiana Press, 1986.

Mulvey, Laura. *Visual and Other Pleasures.* Bloomington: Indiana University Press, 1989.

Munson, Wayne. *All Talk: The Talkshow in Media Culture.* Philadelphia: Temple University Press, 1990.

Neal, Mark Anthony. *Soul Babies: Black Popular Culture and the Post-Soul Aesthetic.* New York: Routledge, 2002.

Nelson, Cary, and Lawrence Grossberg. *Marxism and the Interpretation of Culture.* Chicago: University of Chicago Press, 1988.

Newton, Huey P. "A Revolutionary Analysis of *Sweet Sweetback's Baadasssss Song.*" *The Black Panther Inter-communal News Service* 6 (June 1971): A–L.

Nichols, Bill. *Ideology and the Image: Social Representation in the Cinema and Other Media.* Bloomington: Indiana University Press, 1981.

Nicholson, Linda. *Feminism/Postmodernism.* New York: Routledge, 1990.

Nyong'o, Tavia. "Racial Kitsch and Black Performance." *Yale Journal of Criticism: Interpretation in the Humanities* 15, no. 2 (Fall 2002): 371–91.

Oakley, J. Ronald. *God's Country: America in the Fifties.* New York: Dembner Books, 1986.

Outlaw, Lucius, Jr. *On Race and Philosophy.* New York: Routledge, 1996.

Palmer, Jerry. *The Logic of the Absurd: On Film and Television Comedy.* London: British Film Institute, 1987.

Parish, Robert James. *Whoopi Goldberg: Her Journey from Poverty to Mega-Stardom.* New Jersey: Carol, 1997.

Peck, Janice. *The Gods of Televangelism.* Cresskill, N.J.: Hampton Press, 1993.

———. "Talk about Racism: Framing a Popular Discourse of Race on *Oprah Winfrey.*" *Cultural Critique* (Spring 1994).

Pharr, Suzanne. *Homophobia: A Weapon of Sexism.* Inverness, Calif.: Chardon Press, 1988.

Pick, Daniel. *Faces of Degeneration: A European Disorder, c.1848–c. 1918.* New York: Cambridge University Press, 1989.

Pieterse, Jan Nederveen. *White on Black: Images of Africa and Blacks in Western Popular Culture.* New Haven, Conn.: Yale University Press, 1992.

Pinckney, Darryl. "Where the Guests Call the Host's Tunes." *The Financial Times,* July 11, 1998.

Porter, Greg, Darrell Midgette, and Dan Smith. *Macho Women with Guns.* Swindon, Wiltshire, UK: Blacksburg Tactical Research, 1994.

Poussaint, Alvin F. "Blaxploitation Movies: Cheap Thrills That Degrade Blacks" *Psychology Today* 7 (February 1974): 22–32.

Pratt, Mary Louise. *Imperial Eyes: Travel Writing and Transculturation.* New York: Routledge, 1992.

Price, Sally. *Primitive Art in Civilized Places.* Chicago: University of Chicago Press, 1989.

Priest, Patricia Joyner. *Public Intimacies: Talk Show Participants and Tell-All TV.* Cresskill, N.J.: Hampton Press, 1995.

Probyn, Elspeth. *Sexing the Self: Gendered Positions in Cultural Studies.* New York: Routledge, 1993.

Randolph, Laura. "Halle Berry: On How She Found Dorothy Dandridge's Spirit—and Finally Healed Her Own." *Ebony* (August 1999): 90–98.

Read, Alan. *The Fact of Blackness: Frantz Fanon and Visual Representation.* Seattle: Bay Press, 1996.

Rippy, Marguerite H. "Commodity, Tragedy, Desire: Female Sexuality and Blackness in the Iconography of Dorothy Dandridge." In *Classic Hollywood, Classic Whiteness,* edited by Daniel Bernardi. Minneapolis: University of Minnesota Press, 2001.

Robertson, Pamela. *Guilty Pleasures: Feminist Camp from Mae West to Madonna.* Durham, N.C.: Duke University Press, 1996.

Robinson, Cedric. *Black Marxism: The Making of the Black Radical Tradition.* London: Zed Press, 1983.

Robinson, Louie. "Have Black Actresses Really Made It in Hollywood? New Films Increase Job Prospects but Most Stars Still Have Problems." *Ebony* (April 1975): 33–40.

Roediger, David. *The Wages of Whiteness: Race and the Making of the American Working Class.* New York: Verso, 1991.

Rogin, Michael. *Blackface, White Noise: Jewish Immigrants in the Hollywood Melting Pot.* Berkeley: University of California Press, 1996.

Rose, Jacqueline. *Sexuality in the Field of Vision.* New York: Verso, 1986.

Ross, Andrew. *No Respect: Intellectuals and Popular Culture.* New York: Routledge, 1989.

Rowe, Kathleen. *The Unruly Woman: Gender and the Genres of Laughter.* Austin: University of Texas Press, 1995.

Rubin, Martin. "Make Love Make War: Cultural Confusion and the Biker Film Cycle." *Film History* 6 (1994): 355–81.

Russell, Kathy, Midge Wilson, and Ronald Hall. *The Color Complex: The Politics of Skin Color among African Americans.* New York: Doubleday, 1992.

Russo, Mary. *The Female Grotesque: Risk, Excess and Modernity.* New York: Routledge, 1994.

Ryan, Mary P. "Femininity and Capitalism in Antebellum America." In *Capitalist Patriarchy and the Case for Socialist Feminism,* edited by Zillah R. Eisenstein. New York: Monthly Review Press, 1979.

Samuels, Allison. "Angela's Fire." *Newsweek* (July 1, 2002). Accessed November 6, 2008, at http://www.newsweek.com/id/100553.

Sanello, Frank. *Halle Berry: A Stormy Life.* London: Virgin Books, 2003.

Sartre, Jean-Paul. *Being and Nothingness: A Phenomenological Essay on Ontology.* Translated by Hazel E. Barnes. New York: Washington Square Press, 1956.

Schaefer, Eric. *Bold! Daring! Shocking! True!: A History of Exploitation Films, 1919–1959.* Durham, N.C.: Duke University Press, 1999.

———. "Resisting Refinement: The Exploitation Film and Self-Censorship." *Film History* 6 (1994): 293–313.

Schickel, Richard. "Celebrity." *Film Comment* 21, no. 1 (January–February 1985): 11–19.

Schor, Naomi. "Female Fetishism: The Case of George Sand." In *The Female Body in Western Culture: Contemporary Perspectives,* edited by Susan Rubin Suleiman. Cambridge, Mass.: Harvard University Press, 1986.

Schulman, Bruce J. *The Seventies: The Great Shift in American Culture, Society, and Politics.* New York.: Free Press, 2001.

Schultze, Quentin J. *Televangelism and American Culture: The Business of Popular Religion.* Grand Rapids, Michigan: Baker Book House, 1991.

Schweitzer, Arthur. *The Age of Charisma.* Chicago: Nelson-Hall, 1984.

Scott, Gini Graham. *Can We Talk? The Power and Influence of Talk Shows.* New York: Insight Books/Plenum Press, 1996.

Shattuc, Jane. *The Talking Cure: Women and Daytime Talk Shows.* New York: Routledge, 1997.

Shohat, Ella, and Robert Stam, eds. *Talking Visions: Multicultural Feminism in a Transnational Age.* Cambridge, Mass.: MIT Press, 1998.

———. *Unthinking Eurocentrism: Multiculturalism and the Media.* New York: Routledge, 1994.

Sims, Yvonne D. *Women of Blaxploitation: How the Black Action Film Heroine Changed American Popular Culture.* Jefferson, N.C.: McFarland, 2006.

Smith, Christian. *American Evangelicalism: Embattled and Thriving.* Chicago: University of Chicago Press, 1998.

Smith, Valerie, ed. *Representing Blackness: Issues in Film and Video.* New Brunswick, N.J.: Rutgers University Press, 1997.

Smith-Shomade. *Shaded Lives: African-American Women and Television.* New Brunswick, N.J.: Rutgers University Press, 2002.

Sochen, June. *Women's Comic Visions.* Detroit: Wayne State University Press, 1991.

Sontag, Susan. "Notes on Camp." First published in *Partisan Review* 31, no. 4 (Fall 1964): 515–30.

Spiller, Hortense. "Interstices: A Small Drama of Words." In *Pleasure and Danger,* edited by Carole S. Vance. London: Pandora, 1989.

Spurr, David. *The Rhetoric of Empire: Colonial Discourse in Journalism, Travel Writing, and Imperial Administration.* Durham, N.C.: Duke University Press, 1993.

Stacey, Jackie. *Star Gazing: Hollywood Cinema and Female Spectatorship.* London: Routledge, 1994.

Stafford, Barbara Maria. *Body Criticism: Imaging the Unseen in Enlightenment Art and Medicine.* Cambridge, Mass.: MIT Press, 1994.

Stallybrass, Peter, and Allon White. *The Politics and Poetics of Transgression.* Ithaca, N.Y.: Cornell University Press, 1986.

Stam, Robert. *Reflexivity in Film and Literature: From Don Quixote to Jean-Luc Godard.* New York: Columbia University Press, 1992.

———. *Subversive Pleasures: Bakhtin, Cultural Criticism, and Film.* Baltimore, Md.: Johns Hopkins University Press, 1992.

———. *Tropical Multiculturalism: A Comparative History of Race in Brazilian Cinema and Culture.* Chapel Hill, N.C.: Duke University Press, 1997.

Stanley, Tarshia. "Icono-Clash: Whoopi Goldberg and the (Re) Presentation of Black Women in Hollywood Film." PhD dissertation, University of Florida, 1999.

Steele, Valerie. "Clothing and Sexuality." In *Men and Women Dressing the Part*, edited by Claudia Kidwell and Valerie Steele. Washington, D.C.: Smithsonian Institution Press, 1989.

——. *Fashion and Eroticism: Ideals of Feminine Beauty from the Victoria Era to the Jazz Age*. New York: Aperture, 1991.

——. *Fetish: Fashion, Sex, and Power*. New York: Oxford University Press, 1996.

Stember, Charles Herbert. *Sexual Racism: The Emotional Barrier to an Integrated Society*. New York: Elsevier Scientific, 1976.

Stodghill, Ron. "Daring to Go There." *Time* (October 5, 1998): 80–82.

Stoler, Ann Laura. *Race and the Education of Desire: Foucault's History of Sexuality and the Colonial Order of Things*. Durham, N.C.: Duke University Press, 1995.

Stoller, Robert. "Transvestism in Women." *Archives of Sexual Behavior* 11 (1982): 99–116.

Straayer, Chris. *Deviant Eyes, Deviant Bodies: Sexual Re-orientations in Film and Video*. New York: Columbia University Press, 1996.

Stuart, Andrea. *Showgirls*. London: Random House, 1996.

Studlar, Gaylyn. "Midnight S/excess: Cult Configurations of 'Femininity and the Perverse.'" *Journal of Popular Film and Television* 17, no. 1 (Spring 1989): 2–13.

Szakolczai, Arpad. *Max Weber and Michel Foucault: Parallel Life-Works*. New York: Routledge, 1998.

Tasker, Yvonne. *Spectacular Bodies: Gender, Genre, and Action Cinema*. New York: Routledge, 1993.

——. *Working Girls: Gender and Sexuality in Popular Cinema*. London: Routledge, 1998.

Terry, Jennifer, and Jacqueline Urla, eds. *Deviant Bodies: Critical Perspective on Difference in Science and Popular Culture*. Bloomington: Indiana University Press, 1995.

Thompson, Andrew O. "Fly Girl: L.A. Backdrops Add Streetwise Vibe to *Jackie Brown*." *American Cinematographer* 79, no. 1 (January 1998): 44–52.

Tibbetts, John C. "Oprah's Belabored *Beloved*." *Literature/Film Quarterly* 27, no. 1 (1999): 74–76.

Tobing-Rony, Fatimah. *The Third Eye: Race, Cinema, and Ethnographic Spectacle*. Durham, N.C.: Duke University Press, 1996.

——. "Those Who Squat and Those Who Sit: The Iconography of Race in the 1895 Films of Félix-Louis Regnault." *Camera Obscura* 28 (January 1992): 262–89.

Toll, Robert C. *Blackening Up: The Minstrel Show in Nineteenth-Century America*. New York: Quill, 1984.

Torgovnick, Marianna. *Gone Primitive: Savage Intellects, Modern Lives*. Chicago: University of Chicago Press, 1990.

Tucker, William H. *The Science and Politics of Racial Research*. Chicago: University of Chicago Press, 1994.

Turner, Bryan. *Regulating Bodies: Essays in Medical Sociology*. New York: Routledge, 1992.

Ukadike, Nwachukwu F. *Black African Cinema.* Berkeley: University of California Press, 1994.

Vale, V., and Andrea Juno, eds. *Modern Primitives.* San Francisco: Re/Search, 1989.

Vance, Carole S., ed. *Pleasure and Danger: Exploring Female Sexuality.* London: Pandora, 1989.

Van Deburg, William L. *Black Camelot: African American Culture Heroes in Their Times, 1960–1980.* Chicago: University of Chicago Press, 1997.

Van Peebles, Melvin. *The Making of Sweet Sweetback's Baadasssss Song.* Edinburgh: Payback Press, 1996.

Wald, Gayle. *Crossing the Line: Racial Passing in Twentieth-Century U.S. Literature and Culture.* Durham, N.C.: Duke University Press, 2000.

Wallace, Michele. *Black Macho and the Myth of Superwoman.* London: John Calder, 1978.

———. *Invisibility Blues: From Pop to Theory.* New York: Verso, New Left Books, 1990.

Wander, Brandon. "Black Dreams: The Fantasy and Ritual of Black Films." *Film Quarterly* 29, no. 1 (Fall 1975): 2–11.

Warner, William. "Spectacular Action: *Rambo* and the Popular Pleasures of Pain." In *Cultural Studies,* edited by Lawrence Grossberg, Cary Nelson, and Paula Treichler. New York: Routledge, 1991.

Weeks, Jeffrey. *Sexuality and Its Discontents: Meanings, Myths and Modern Sexualities.* London: Routledge and Kegan Paul, 1985.

Weinraub, Bernard. "Hollywood's First Black Goddess and Casualty." *New York Times.* Sunday, August 15, 1999.

White, Hayden. *Tropics of Discourse: Essays in Cultural Criticism.* Baltimore, Md.: Johns Hopkins University Press, 1985.

Wiegman, Robyn. *American Anatomies: Theorizing Race and Gender.* Durham, N.C.: Duke University Press, 1995.

Williams, Linda. *Hard Core: Power, Pleasure, and the "Frenzy of the Visible."* Berkeley: University of California Press. 1989.

Williams, Melanie. "Light on a Dark Lovely: Yvonne Mitchell and Stardom in British Cinema." *Quarterly Review of Film and Video* 19, no. 1 (2002): 31–41.

Wilson, Sheryl. *Oprah, Celebrity and Formations of Self.* Houndmills, Basingstoke, and New York: Palgrave Macmillan, 2003.

Wilson, Tony. "On Playfully Becoming the 'Other': Watching Oprah Winfrey on Malaysian Television." *International Journal of Cultural Studies* 4, no. 1 (March 2001): 89–110.

Wilson, William J. *The Declining Significance of Race: Blacks and Changing American Institutions.* Chicago: University of Chicago Press, 1978.

———. *The Truly Disadvantaged: The Inner City, the Underclass and Public Policy.* Chicago: University of Chicago. 1987.

Wiltz, Teresa. "RuPaul Is All Decked Out for a New Ad Campaign." *Chicago Tribune,* March 16, 1995.

Witt, Doris. "What (N)ever Happened to Aunt Jemima: Eating Disorders, Fetal Rights, and Black Female Appetite in Contemporary American Culture." *Discourse: Journal for Theoretical Studies in Media and Culture* 17, no. 2 (Winter 1994–95): 98–122.

Wolf, Ernest S. *Treating the Self: Elements of Clinical Self-Psychology.* New York: Guilford Press, 1988.

Wright, Richard. *White Man, Listen! Lectures in Europe, 1950–1956.* New York: HarperPerennial, 1955.

Young, John. "Toni Morrison, Oprah Winfrey, and Postmodern Popular Audiences." *African American Review* 35, no. 2 (Summer 2001): 181–204.

Young, Robert. *White Mythologies: Writing History and the West.* New York: Routledge, 1990.

Zahar, Renate. *Frantz Fanon: Colonialism and Alienation: Concerning Frantz Fanon's Political Theory.* Translated by Willfried F. Feuser. New York: Ethiopian Publishing, 1974. Originally Published as *Kolonialismus und Entfremdung* (Frankfurt: Europäische Verlagsanstalt, 1969).

Zalcock, Bev. *Renegade Sisters: Girl Gangs on Film.* London: Creation, 1998.

Zamora, Lois, and Wendy B. Faris, eds. *Magical Realism: Theory, History, Community.* Durham, N.C. and London: Duke University Press, 1995.

Zavotzoamps, George. "Homeovestism: Perverse Forms of Behavior Involving Wearing Clothes of the Same Sex." *International Journal of Psychoanalysis* 53 (1972): 471–77.

Zillax, Amy. "The Scorpion and the Frog: Agency and Identity in Neil Jordan's *The Crying Game.*" *Camera Obscura* 35 (1995): 24–51.

Index

Pages references in italics refer to illustrations

MIA MASK is an associate professor of film at Vassar College. She has been a contributing author to *Cineaste, The Village Voice, Film Quarterly,* and the *Poughkeepsie Journal.*

The University of Illinois Press
is a founding member of the
Association of American University Presses.

Composed in 10.5/13 Adobe Minion Pro
with Meta and Bodoni Poster display
at the University of Illinois Press
Designed by Kelly Gray
Manufactured by Sheridan Books, Inc.

University of Illinois Press
1325 South Oak Street
Champaign, IL 61820-6903
www.press.uillinois.edu